We as Architects in the Wheel of Life

Is this the Mathematics we should be learning?

Paul Stang, M.A.

Illustration credits are noted on the pictures, throughout the book.

We as Architects in the Wheel of Life @ 2007 by Paul Stang. All rights reserved. Third printing by Lulu. No part of this book may be reproduced without written permission of the author (except in the case of the lesson plans – for personal use in the classroom – which is encouraged).

First Published 2007
Second Edition 2008
Lulu published 2009

Printed by Lulu 2009

Printed on recycled paper

Stang, Paul

We as Architects in the Wheel of Life / by Paul Stang

ISBN 978-0-578-02907-8

Forward

What was so unique about the "Renaissance Man"? Such minds as Copernicus, Galileo and da Vinci were educated so that they could fill a multitude of roles as scientist-priest, doctor, lawyer, or astronomer. Predecessors like Bacon, Magnus, and Aquinas were theologians accomplished in alchemy. Their European system of education taught mathematics through number, music, measurement in the plane (geometry) and a study of the stars (trigonometry). With a thorough education, diversity was more readily possible.

Science in the 18th century wrested chemistry and astronomy from the "arcane", and about this time died the generalist; educated and skilled in many fields, replaced by the specialist. Two hundred years later, our knowledge has been greatly expanded by their deep explorations. Questionable is whether wisdom has been commensurate.

Great scientific minds of the past had their education tempered by theological, moral, and philosophical development; supplemented by language, literature and art. Great scientific minds of the present are discouraged from and even denied such considerations throughout their channeled educative processes. Standardization under IB, GCSE, NCLB, etal is killing thinking further.

This book is meant to return mathematics instruction to a more "holistic" approach; to interest a wider clientele, and broaden the gifted. Today, as perhaps then, we have primarily two types of students in the general math classroom: those who can grasp the material (about a third), and those who struggle and even fail. Those gifted in math are encouraged to go further with it and enroll in a technical field. Education in math, science and computers is funded and pushed. Parents are extolled to not let their child be left behind, to give them a head start, and to help them be prepared earlier.

This presents a challenge for a great deal of the child population. Many times I've talked with intelligent and successful adults who express feelings of stupidity, regret, failure, and negativity towards their youthful math careers; usually abruptly ended (as fast as was possible). Our math minds are pushed and even streamed early in life, while those who are unskilled are essentially jettisoned to other fields.

This book is meant to enliven high school and college level mathematics for the student, teacher, and student-teacher of this particular subject, explain concepts for parent and youth, bring in teachers of other subjects, give suggested direction to school administrators, and be more than just another reference for librarians. It is also for artists and hobbyists, trying to build knowledge and skill. It is hopefully a means of positively affecting education in our world, should it find its way into the hands of fellow idealists, and school directors interested in a course of child development supporting childhood and human growth in place of what we have too long practiced. It is a supplement to mathematics instruction, a packet of ideas for related subjects, and a guide for several subjects to be bridged; a process shown to be very promising in motivating students, with excellent results.

That is the initial focus of this book. Results; positive ones. The practices outlined here-in have given amazing assessment data. Students who are failing in math, as they walk into my high school classes, with grades between 30-60%, will almost always have a D, if not better, before the year ends. An encouraged student will try. An interested student will attend. The student who is rewarded and recognized for the intelligence that they have, even be it non-mathematical, will come further. They will smile to have finally *passed* a year in mathematics! They will often have a C by the end of the next year.

They may "top-off" there, they may not. There do seem to be some limits to ability, and moreso - desire. However, their peers are also seeing tremendous grade mobility with these techniques. Confidence encourages growth. Rewards of non-"traditional" methods see the bell-curve become obsolete, as 50-70% of the population *will* improve by at least one letter grade through use of techniques exposed in the text. Classes are more fun when people are engaged.

The teacher may at times feel they are reviewing primary topics too basic to repeat, though they will be surprised by the lack of skill as they do so. As a result, they will find that the students aren't stumbling through the more complex processes, as before. We don't have to spend so much time teaching and explaining if the students do it themselves, especially if they seek out their peers and seniors for answers. That's what the motivated student does.

One of the best results of these techniques is with that of the normally "A" student: usually quick to answer, proving themselves before others have had a chance to get their thought formed and delivered. Often first mathematically, they many times conversely lack in ability to write, visually represent, or orally present effectively. We can improve these skills, challenge them to work better within the class, and develop them more personally. This book offers challenges, while making the class more inclusive.

As schools compete for funding, and receive it based on results of specific testing, the obvious next step is that education has been tied up with teaching to the test, rather than educating. We see students going on to the better schools with their results and getting a better paying job as a result of better grades at a better school. Grades become the emphasis, rather than the nebulous concept of life-long education.

The author has fortunately avoided, in twelve years of teaching, the trap that faces most teachers in the "system". Curriculum guidelines are much more open to interpretation in private schools and universities, and parents are more willing to listen, reason and experiment, than a bureaucracy.

Diversion can be made, and time given from standard instruction can be recouped by more dynamic students. Many techniques in this book merely develop themes we must already instruct; like algebra, geometry, trigonometry, sciences, and specific topics there in. This book creatively covers standard curricula, repeatedly bringing these subject areas together, with the arts and sciences. Schools wishing to be more technical can have that, while also encouraging the arts, by marrying the two. Sure, students may complain that the art is too "geometrical", but some of our greatest forms of art and architecture are as well.

The more we make connections the clearer the reasons become for why we have to learn math: 1)as a means of being able to work ever harder problems, 2)in order to apply them in the Sciences, and 3)to develop creative thinking abilities. This third realm is partly why we need to hold on to as many non-mathematicians as we can, for as long as we can, so that people continue to be able to think for themselves, in a world where the media is cleverly crafted to mold opinions for them.

The second focus of this book, as presented more in the latter chapters, is to widen awareness; to see math in symbolism, to find math mysterious and fascinating, and see unique applications. A further goal is to encourage that education use this information age to develop a clearer understanding for youth of how the world operates and to turn out a new kind of mathematician; a humanist.

My experience shows that for many youth math mentality can blossom later, especially when given a second, alternative, chance. History shows that math owes much to persons educated, and educating, in the humanities. Allowing for this in the classroom enables a broader discussion and livelier class. It can further challenge the strictly mathematical types to consider things that they are currently ignoring. If we instead educate people to specialize, without rounding themselves out, we cannot be surprised that they create horrors of unconventional, biological, and nuclear warfare, or technology and chemistry that has no real assurance that it will not have harmful biological effects.

Robert Oppenheimer, upon detonating the first atomic bomb quoted Hindu text, "I am Vishnu, the destroyer of worlds." Stephen Hawkins, a genius of our time (handicapped and left to a wheelchair so advanced that it speaks for him), sees no problem in the idea of humans some day being born outside of a mother's body, with enlarged heads to accommodate greater brain capacity, and that it is very positive that we incorporate technology into the human body.

What can we do when scientists' eyes alight at prospects of that great next thing that they can create (with little or no regard for unforeseen/unlooked-for consequences)? Is this but technical adolescence; for the sake of ego? At present, there are few, beyond the Amish, who left it all long before now, that would have anything dilatory to say against the rush of technology. Most people enjoy the "power" at their fingertips in this push-button world, and how much a modern house or auto "thinks" for them. However, as this book will posit, from direct teaching and technical experience, ease is not equating into improvement in every case.

Mathematics and computer studies are increasingly emphasized. We now guide our children very early into technical and mathematical training, fearing that they be left behind, undervaluing genius that they may show in artistic fields, undervaluing that they have a childhood of play. Do we not need a modern Rembrandt, Rafael or Michelangelo? Do we ourselves no longer wish to develop multiple skills like da Vinci or Copernicus? Or do we simply need our youth to be computer literate so that they can be "plugged-in" somewhere?

While pushing students to learn more mathematics, we encourage them to use calculators, at ages where they not only don't need them, but it is counterproductive. By high school few students can (nor want to) do hand and mental calculation or understand/perform *operations*. The result is often a pitiful level of mental effort as the teacher spends a good portion of a lesson explaining to each student how their particular calculator functions or if answers are correct; which they may be (or certainly are not).

The computer is further degrading skills; as shown by sloppier handwriting, resistance to writing, drawing, and reading, and a mindset of "cut-and-paste" or minimal editing in place of real research. Hands that still aren't clear on how to hold a pencil, or write in cursive, are being shown how to push a mouse around and press on a keyboard. As much as we might think we are educating children this way, or helping them, it is ludicrous.

More technology and techno-toys are being pushed upon our youth, who are spending hours with video games (often violent and competitive), headsets (listening to music full of questionable lyrics) and internet (with excessive advertisement and easy access to porn). Every chance they get otherwise, they are pulling out their mobile phones, taking superfluous photos of each other, trading bland messages, or actively engaged with an equally noteworthy activity centered on one of their electronic gismos.

We can pity our youth, for they have such a fog of distraction around them now that they are seeing very little of their world, though admittedly they do have much more information available to them.

Fear, gimmickry, "compassionate" donation, and consumerism have pushed calculators, computers, mobile phones, music players and other appliances into high school, primary education, and childhood at large. There are becoming available reputable pieces of research and literature that reflect upon what is referred to as a "toxic childhood", where there is too much junk food, techno, and competition.

We are in a most strange time in our history. Advertising is being pushed not to the adult, as in times past, but to youth, who are more easily separated from cash (a situation made necessary to keep our heavily indebted countries from going bankrupt). Who cares that these rapidly obsolete items will in a very short time end up on a junk heap somewhere, definitely leaching toxic materials into someone's water supply, and that wars on the environment and against other humans are intensifying in pursuit of the component raw materials.

The dangerous result is that youth have become the newest growth industry in the global economy, particularly regarding technology. Youth (not adults) are taking us into our future. In almost every realm they are being plied to buy the product and listen to the advertiser, no matter the product or politics that is being sold. Youth know this and are wondering where is true leadership today.

As we awaken to inconvenient truths, and attempt to do something about it, those we need to reach most are running rapidly counter. We can deny, or we can look at this, and make changes that are encouraged in the home and school.

This book is taking the risk to bring discussion on all of this into the mathematics class (if no one else is going to address it), hoping to re-humanize the Sciences. Humanistic and Holistic. It is intended to get people normally going into those fields to be aware of and accept responsibility for the results of what they are creating. It also shows how those not normally choosing such paths can succeed and that they are desperately needed there.

Education must not keep up with the rapid changes occurring today as much as it should put itself in a position to harness them. Too, it must stand upon its foundation (not prostrate itself before corporate interest or political sanguinity), must stop assuming that technology is necessary (and risk-free, especially for younger minds), and must find ways to reach each student using modern (not necessarily computer) invention for that purpose.

We have a world where we have for generations had to fear atomic and now biological, neurological, and chemical weapons thanks to mathematicians, scientists, and engineers excited about the incredible things they can create or discover and shunning responsibility for the horrific ways these discoveries are then being used.

Our future desperately needs a new kind of scientist. A "reborn Renaissance" human, or perhaps with this information age – an omniscient one, inspired by the philosophers: Pythagoras and Plato the astronomers/astrologers: Kepler and Archimedes: and artists: Leonardo da Vinci and Dali: and finally, by unknown architects of history who have left us enigmatic constructions like Stonehenge and the Pyramids. These were the people who helped us develop.

The following pages show how to challenge the student who normally excels in mathematics and help them become a more rounded individual. It shows how to encourage, interest, reward and motivate students who have normally not done well with this subject. Once engaged they will then choose to be more involved and it is these musicians, artists, humanists, and thinkers that we desperately need to get into the Sciences along with morally developing those who mostly are there.

The reader will see too that "recreational" prospects exist in mathematics. There are phenomenal discoveries to be made, several of which are outlined in the pages to come, showing areas where more research could be done, and also the potential that others exist. Various aspects of this can be brought into math and science instruction. We can be doing much more with mathematics than just checking off a litany of what tasks students are to have accomplished.

This book is meant as a companion to other, very necessary, textbooks. It isn't given a title like "Making Math Fun", or "Math for Idiots" because I don't like teaching stupid people, or the idea that math isn't fun to begin with! It is titled, more quoted, directly from an adult student who returned to night school at university. My adult students, remembering less-than-successful attempts in high school math, and being more mature, were able to articulate their positive feelings towards these techniques.

Now, as I present to pedagogically trained teachers, the response is usually most favorable. There are occasional detractors, wondering where there is time for such "naïve" considerations. Too, in developing countries it is hard to redress the modern, when they feel the need, and admittedly the right, to share in what the West has enjoyed. But, the best feedback has been seeing students going into the Sciences who hadn't considered it before we met.

Original titles for the book began with "Teaching math to both sides of the Brain". In my earlier thinking I felt that we were only teaching math to people with the appropriately developed hemisphere, and force feeding it to the rest. When I relocated to another continent and married a child psychologist and educator I was exposed to a myriad of wider possibilities.

My title shifted to "Teaching math to eight intelligence types". I was learning that a person may be gifted in math to be sure. But just because they weren't, didn't mean they didn't have other intelligences. I realized that my techniques didn't just work on one or two wavelengths but were engaging people from a broader spectrum of interests and abilities. Though it could be argued that I lost time doing "non-traditional" things, I gained time and momentum because interested students came pretty far to meet me. Once they were interested, they were motivated. Results improved. Attitudes changed and results improved *more*.

And then, I was introduced to Jungian behavior analysis, which shows that not only is the variety of intelligence important, but the psychology of the person and their traits affect how they learn. Can they sit there all day and happily calculate? Do they need to do, feel, experiment? Do they need to be able to go off and think, processing the material?

Would they rather just be playing? How can we let them play here? I found that people who study enneagram think there are not four personality traits but nine. Briggs-Meyers has sixteen. Finally, teaching internationally has shown me that culture plays a role, as do gender and race. One might be amazed at all of the ways there are to do division.

We need to even consider the teacher and their charisma. We just never know how many different factors are involved.

The point is that there are many intelligences and personalities in the classroom. We should try harder to get them all engaged. Our textbooks, subject by subject, are pretty limited toward people who can decipher them. The rest have suffered through with whatever grade they get. To educate, we can consider that today we must be entertaining, and to a broader audience.

In a more impersonal world, we can also care.

We who are going to discourse on the nature of the universe, must invoke the aid of Gods and Goddesses and pray that our words may be acceptable to them and speak in such manner as will be most intelligible to you, and will most accord with my own intent. – Plato, Timaeus

I wish to thank for this endeavor Cyndy Bush-Luna. So many times she believed in my work before I myself did. Her enthusiasm for life in general and for my efforts has been unceasing and inspiring. I wish to remember the spirit of Joan Condon, who gave me the seeds. I want to honor and thank the many students and participants I have had, who have challenged and taught me, laughed at my jokes and even listened to my wilder ravings. I remember most of your names, faces and personalities, and I always will! Thank you to family and friends, for help, and for just being there, to Richard and David who reminded me as often as they could of how small and insignificant I am and to the people at RWCT who have opened doors of knowledge.

I also want to thank the many artists who have willingly donated their works to this project. I have tried to provide the best possible copies for the reader and I wish to encourage that we support the creativity of their human spirit.

I remember my aunt Dorothy, who was murdered in the Amazon Forest in 2005, after a lifetime caring for the poor and dispossessed of that region. She was a great woman with a wonderful sense of humor. She tried to help save the rain forest, which gives us a gift of breathable air. I hope that this book can make some small difference, as she has made a great one.

I appreciate my Dad, for his support, and that I can understand more, now that I too am a father. I remember too my grandfather, who always said, "Kids are what we called the goats. Why get upset at a child's behavior when you choose to always call them kids? They'll act like they've been called, like a bunch of mischievous goats!" Finally, thanks to Lucien, not just a great editor but the best darn pick-up music artist I know.

For Anna Marie, that she inherit a bright future for her children, in the Wheel of Life.

Nature is a vision of the science of the Elohim – Milton, by Robert Blake

Table of Contents

1 Basic Geometry – Mandala
Flower of life, 3- and 6-fold division, color wheel ... 1
Hexagon, fractals, artistry, mandala ... 4
12-fold division, 4- and 8-fold division ... 9
3-dimensional flat drawings, 3D constructions ... 11
Sound and geometry ... 14

2 Reacquainting ourselves with old friends
Fractions; x and ÷, algebra, conversions, percents ... 19
Negatives; scientific notation, roots ±, fractional exponents ... 24
Fractions; + and –, music, trigonometry ... 27
Graphing; lines, parabolas and cubics ... 29
Triangle; circumscribed, centroid, inscribed ... 31
Fun with bisectors ... 35

3 Towers Bridges and Forms in the Creative Atmosphere
Platonic forms, Kepler model ... 47
Stellations, Archimedean forms ... 51
Exploration with Astro-logix, Zometools and Cabri 3D ... 52
Building project ... 55

4 Using geometries to apply trigonometry
Pythagoras of Samos, his theorem, squares. ... 61
Measure of the cube, vesica piscis, octahedron, tetrahedron ... 63
Further trigonometric applications ... 68
Fun with radicals and more fun – Geo art ... 70

5 Φive rings
The intelligent student ... 77
The Golden Section, phi proportion, Fibonnaci sequence ... 79
The spiral; derived shapes, five-pointed star, phi proportions ... 81
Human proportions, planetary spacings ... 85
Dodecahedron, stellations ... 86
Phi in the 5- and 7-pointed stars, icosa- and dodecahedrons ... 88
Patterns with phi ... 90
Appendix – 8 intelligence types ... 99

6 The book of Numbers
Plato, his forms, and the myth and math of Atlantis ... 101
Base-20 counting systems, Base-12, and Base-16 ... 104
Gematria ... 108

7 The Magician
The use of 7 ... 113
Geometries of the Vitruvian Man, by da Vinci ... 114
Geometries of Stonehenge, the Great Pyramid ... 117
Geographic location and astronomical measurement ... 119
Freemasonry mathematical mysteries ... 125
Seven based mandala ... 127

8 The Alchemist
Neolithic chemistry, home-made pottery, early metals — 133
The birth of al-Khemie, spread to Europe, objective science — 136
The down-side of modern chemistry — 139
Health and economic education — 140
Technology in the classroom, media — 145

9 Rocketry and other applications
Altitude measuring device — 155
Rocketry, risks, construction, launch — 158
Calculation, reporting — 161
The mathematics of flight, navigation, building arches — 163
The Calendar! A dramatic presentation — 172

10 Astronomy of Algebra and Trigonometry
The parabola and its focus, the ellipse — 181
Radian measure, developing the sine wave — 185
Lunar applications, algebra of planetary alignments — 189
Further trigonometric graphing and AM/FM radio — 193
Polar graphing, cylindrical and spherical — 195
Fun with radians, radicals — 200

11 Astro Logos
The science of astrology, angular measure — 215
180, 120 and 90 degree relations of planets — 219
Water-ion relationships, engineering — 224

12 Light
Symbolism — 231
The physics of the aura, mathematics of Being — 232
Magic squares — 235
Lattices — 238
Psi and the 9-pointed star — 239
Appendix on assessment techniques — 245

Bibliography

1 Basic Geometry - Mandala

Each chapter of this book opens with questions (next paragraph) which the reader will hopefully think about and answer before proceeding. The chapters conclude with questions that seek reflection on the material and its place in a curriculum. We should encourage this questioning in the classroom.

Further, at the end are associated Lesson Plans, straight from classroom experience. Though they may look at times artistic, scientific, or non-traditional, it must be understood that they work.

Opening dialogue

Why do many students struggle in mathematics? What could be done to embrace, encourage and see improve the challenged student while challenging the gifted student in new realms? What purpose does the decimal system serve?

Introduction

We will begin in the same place that I start each school year, whether at high school, university or adult workshop: geometry and Mandala. The results are immediate. "This is math? I'll try this!" It greatly relaxes students and is a successful introduction to algebra, geometry and trigonometry classes.

This book contains techniques, written by an explorer trying to make the material interesting to students, colleagues, and myself.

  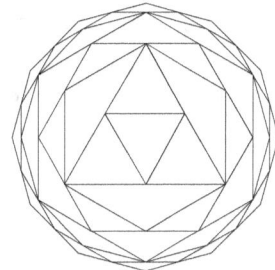

Figure 1 Geometric sketches.

The pictures in Figure 1 are ways we may introduce geometry and trigonometry to our audience. The students begin by making these, and others. Along the way, they revisit fractions, angles, the Pythagorean Theorem and various numerical manipulations.

At the end of summer, this is a great method for transitioning students from free time to the structure that is now expected of them. Its a good way too of introducing the teacher and subject to new students. They see right away that they are in for a different experience in math and science. For students, it is a chance for them to start fresh, should they have not been so productive in their math careers to date. Real or imagined, some students do hear from their teachers, in primary school, the message that they are stupid. This material has always been great at pulling in students, through arts and application, where they begin to push themselves and teachers need to do less.

This successful approach begins from an artistic and historical perspective. Students have a lot of fun with the following exercises, create and are rewarded in new ways, and learn a variety of things so unexpected from math class that they don't even realize it *is* math at sometimes. This can at times seem to conflict with pedagogical training, but should be seen to enhance it. Try these exercises and you will see eyes open in class, perhaps for the first time from some students. Compare that to the interest level from students working out of a textbook or other usual method.

Teachers, students, and adults find the material in this chapter to be easy, fun and interesting. It is new for them, and also very old, maybe from when the compass was invented.

First steps

Indeed, one of the easiest drawing instruments to make is a compass. Though the earliest such device is unknown to us, the fact is that any two sticks, somehow joined together, could make circles in the dirt. Or, two pegs joined by a rope could have the same effect. Simply drive one peg in the ground, stretch the string and use the other to draw as you proceed around the stake.

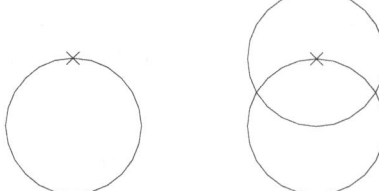

Figure 2 Getting started.

We will begin with some basic techniques from which we will build this chapter and much of this book. Be precise with every step. Draw a circle of about 2 inches (5 cm) radius in the center of a piece of paper. Mark a place on the circle as the top. Put the compass point here and draw a second circle, same size.

Turn the image sideways and we see a symbol often used in company logos. This figure, called the Vesica Piscis, is found in architectural and artistic usages. It will be revisited in detail soon.

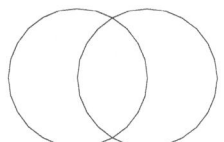

Figure 3 Vesica Piscis.

The Vesica Piscis is a good facsimile of a nebula discovered with the Hubble telescope. Some note should be made of this, for astronomy is an area many students are interested in, meaning it should be brought into class often as an application.

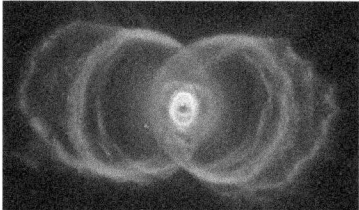

Figure 4 Hubble picture "Hourglass" nebula – (Courtesy of NASA and STScI).

Continue drawing, with the original alignment. Place the compass point at each of the marks and draw another circle.

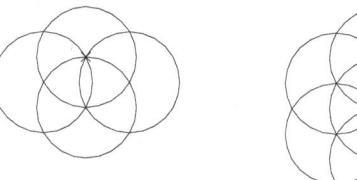

Figure 5 Finishing the initial drawing.

Done properly, with six circles around the central circle, the students will have created a daisy. Precision is most important. Check that all petals come to fine points at the edge of the circle, and at the center the petals also meet crisply, tangentially, with no overlap or gap. Also note the hexagonal shape. See Figure 6.

A further exercise in precision is to draw more outer circles. It is fun to see students attempt this without getting lost. Have them find and maintain the hexagonal form. Even those students who confidently drew the first step might begin to see mistakes start to appear. It is a great exercise in patience and diligence for teenagers, and will get more interest than normal in a math class.

For students, the range of possibilities here are endless. For the younger ones, say in primary school; let them color what they have created. Let them revisit the drawing, with a slightly larger size on the compass. They can now make a background to the petals, or erase carefully and have interweaving loops.

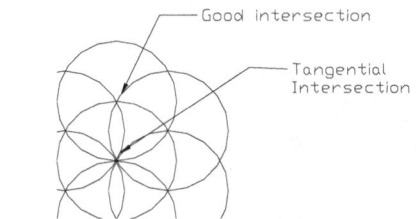

Figure 6 Checking for precision.   Figure 7 Precision exercise.

Expect more from advanced students. Assign drawing projects as homework. Grade work for creativity, detail, color usage, precision and contrast. It is difficult to grade art, but not hard to grade effort or how well they followed instructions. Be strict for those who want to free hand something. They are expected to do mathematical, symmetrical forms.

Figure 8 Some ideas.

Put the best pieces on the wall of the classroom. Artistic students, who never got noticed in math class before, are often first in line and will beam with pride at this recognition. Is it possible they will be willing to try something more mathematical? Most will work hard to get pictures posted. That kind of effort is a good way to start the year and complementing the better pieces will often reward students who have never received praise in math class. They're already off to a good start and open to the next task.

Figure 9 creative students in the creative classroom.

For art teachers (and mathematics teachers wishing to make bridges), the basic daisy can be used to present the color wheel. Students who are stumped for ideas in class can always draw geometric pictures and learn a great deal about color usage and contrast. They should learn how the primary colors; red, yellow and blue, mix to make the secondary colors of orange, green and purple; and that the opposite colors on the chart are actually very complementary, for example, green and red at Christmas time.

Figure 10 The color wheel.

With the color wheel, we learn that certain things go well together. Often, students will attempt to fill their creations by using every possible color. The result is almost always garish. But, we can teach them to use only a few colors - maybe just two, or even one. But which?

Figure 11 Stain Glass by Alphonse Mucha (Photo by William Stang).

The color wheel can be used as a guide (accordingly, opposite colors work really well together; for example blue and orange). They are said to contrast. Too, triangular colors go well together, like green, orange and/or purple. Or adjacent colors, like red, yellow and orange, with a little purple offsetting the yellow. Both of these are called complimentary. Really, any combination is possible but using these techniques works well. Also, to enliven a drawing, the use of dark areas next to lighter ones, as shown, gives contrast as well, alleviating the tendency to use too many colors.

Figure 11 is an example of a great study in color (see color plates). We can note the contrast between yellow in the center and blue to the outside, and green and red above and below the central figure. We can feel how the central colors of yellow, orange and red appear to be warming, while blue and purple are cooling. Colors can be used to express various emotions, thoughts and moods. They are used by color therapists to understand and work with the psyche. Let's get our mathematical minds to experiment!

Again, this is not free-hand art class. It is mathematics and therefore should retain structure. Insist that the students do work requiring geometric precision and studied use of color.

Linear progression

The next step is to start again, with another circle. It should be larger. Humor them by saying they can create a circle of any size and *shape* on their page. Again, they must make a top mark, and use the compass to get six marks around the circle but this time, they will only mark points. Make them small, so as not to detract from the figure.

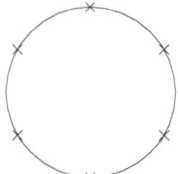 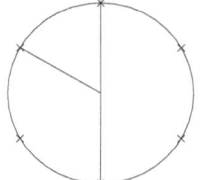

Figure 12a Equally spaced marks.   Figure 12b Division of the circle by six.

Draw straight lines to, or through the center, connecting with the outer points. Notice that the circle is now divided into pieces (Figure 12c). For younger students, this is a great way to express relationships between 1/6, 1/3 and 1/2. Addition of these fractions can also be worked with. This can be used then to explain things like different denominators and how to get common denominators. Have them cut out the pieces and play with them.

See in Figure 12b that 1/6 + 1/3 + 1/2 makes one whole unit. Showing how thirds and halves relate to sixths can be done visually and helps a lot of students.

One thing students *must* learn is that fractions are their friend; the calculator and decimals are not necessarily. They merely make mathematics and calculation easier, and trigonometry and logarithms practicable. Yes, use the technology as a tool. In algebra, trig and science it is vital to be able to work with numbers, as we will see throughout this book.

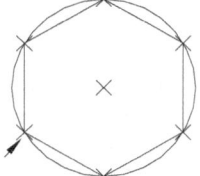

Figure 12c Division of the circle by six.   Figure 12d the hexagon.

Let students measure the internal angles in Figure 12c (60° on each). This technique perfectly divides the circle into six pieces. Measure the spokes and the sides of the outer hexagon, which can be made by connecting the points (Figure 12d). Only a hexagon has every side and radius equal. They will revisit this many times, in furthering their understanding of 30 and 60 degree angles.

Students can create various shapes like equilateral triangles, hexagons and the Star of David. The equilateral triangle will be the basis for later constructions.

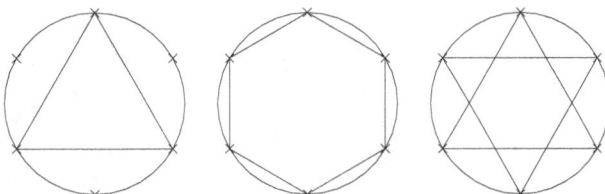

Figure 13 Basic linear shapes.

Note that here are figures drawn with hard, straight lines, where we first worked with curves, making a daisy. This is a simple representation of masculine and feminine properties found in art and architecture. Further, go look at flowers and note the variety with 3, 4, 5 and 6 petals. Have them compare a cathedral with other buildings in their area. When working with students, try to get them to use both straight *and* curved lines in later drawings, so that they give balance, often lacking Today.

One of the interesting things about these shapes is the ease with which fractals can be generated from them.

Figure 14a Fractal patterns.

How students color these can make great differences. The hexagonal fractal works well with just two colors. Painted carefully, a spiral swirl can be carried to the center. Or, it can seem like rays of arrows. The teacher will see the students relax into this work. They are beginning to paint mandalas and it is a very restful activity, especially for all these children diagnosed with A.D.D., or for grounding excessive hormonal activity!

Figure 14b Options for painting the fractal (right figure by Brianne Franke).

5

Notice that one of the images drawn in Figure 14a is the Star of David, also known as Solomon's Seal; a very old symbol represented by two triangles. The one pointing upward symbolizes masculine, fire energy while the downward triangle is said to represent feminine, watery energy. We can mention these in class, as concepts other cultures and times have acknowledged.

Artistic expression

These drawings are only the beginning of what students can create. More detailed pieces are shown in Figure 15a. The central drawing employed only two colors and lots of shading.

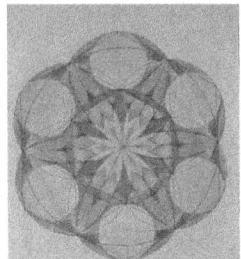 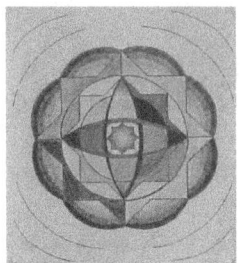 

Figure 15a, Student work (by Michelle Geiger, Olinga Gerhold and Mona Aiff).

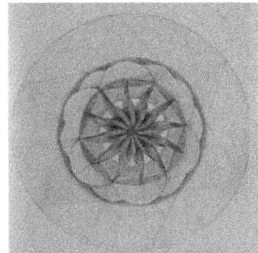 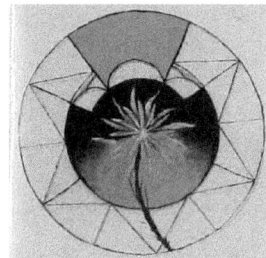 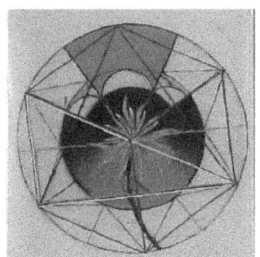

Figure 15b, Student creativity. Original and two plastic overlays (R. Sandoval).

In 15b, note that transparent materials can be laid on top of drawings to enhance them. Sometimes, it is just amazing to see what creativity we can inspire.

Our students can be encouraged to expand here, limited only by the requirements that the art be geometrical, symmetrical and interconnected. Ultimately, a fascinating project could be on a larger scale, where a team (class) of students creates their own window or wall design. Figure 15c shows the result of nearly two months work performed by second year students, in decorating a window. First, we held a design competition for entrants, starting with the central window, measuring about 2 x 3 feet.

Figure 15c Class window project in interior design.

The top four most interesting submissions were combined, and their authors put to work on the central piece. It helped the group decide on the cross pieces and corners. Twice more, a design competition was held and each time the best ideas were combined to make a plan. Finally, the students had to work as a whole, and at times in individual teams, to create the image shown. In total it measures approximately two by three yards and student feedback was extremely positive with regard to their sense of accomplishment and learning of a real-life application of art, measurement, design and mathematics.

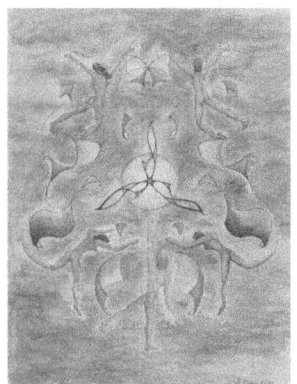 

Figure 15d Additional ideas of how to use the "daisy" pattern and hexagon

We can use the same type of geometry as a basis to make images as these shown in Figure 15d. Both come from six-fold division. We can help our students understand that many famous artists, like Michelangelo, Da Vinci and Dali, have used geometry and math in their work. The paintings they created may hide interesting forms beneath.

Mandala

Students can now be more free, so long as they use a geometrical basis; creating a type of drawing called Mandala, from the Sanksrit word meaning "circle" - "wheel". Mandalas are found all over the world, though given different names. They are in the roofs of Oriental pagodas, the domes of Islam, the rose windows of the cathedrals of Europe, the Aztec calendar and Native art.

Figure 16a Mandalas;, British Museum, Chartres, Beijing, Aztec, Tibetan

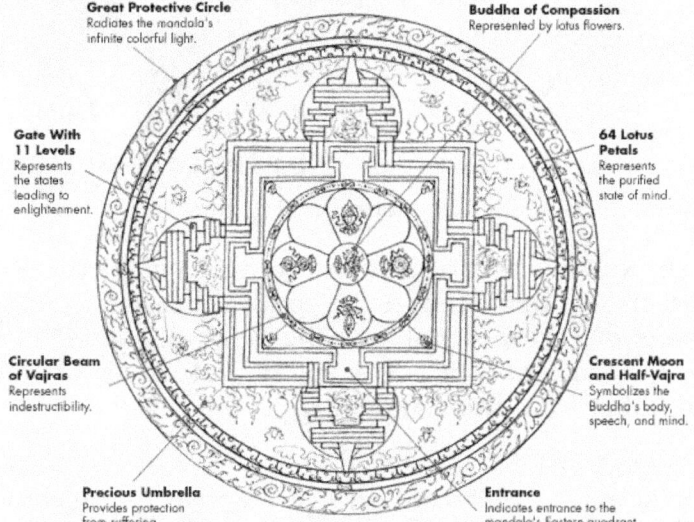

Figure 16b Mandalas and their meanings (© Hannah Bonner, illustrator. Permission for use granted by WGBH Educational Foundation)

Mandalas can be simple or complex designs. They can be used for meditation, where one can find a quiet space to focus on such an image and relax. They are not merely pictures but particularly in Asia each component can have deeper meanings, as shown in Figure 16b. The process of creating them is also very calming, as countless students, and their teachers, will attest.

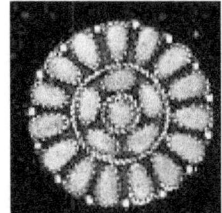   

Figure 16c More mandalas, Indian jewelry, lace, Persian rug, and African ceremonial mask – (Photo - William Stang).

We don't have to use these techniques only for drawings. We can make cutouts. Have students draw a circle or hexagon, with the three crossing lines, as shown in Figure 17. They should cut out the hexagon, and fold along the lines, to make a wedge shape. Let them then cut as they like, along the edges and folds. When opened, they will have snowflakes. (Not the 4- or 8- sided ones seen in many grade school windows, but those with real six-fold nature). Tape to windows, or make another, larger, from colored paper and underlay the darker color. Again, let them use their hands to learn about geometry.

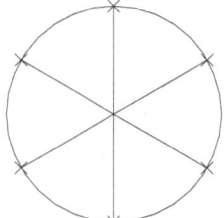 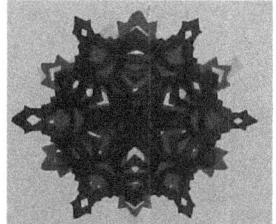

Figure 17 The snowflake, fold the hexagon along the three axes and trim.

The drawings can continue, inserted anywhere in the process the teacher desires. They are a great activity to have after a long holiday weekend, on a day when a lot of students are absent or away, or when teacher and students just seem to need a change in routine. Students will ask for this activity. Better than hearing them complain about the homework.

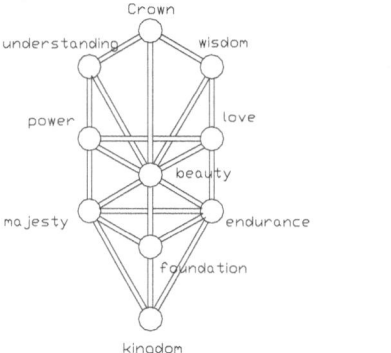 

Figure 18 The Kabbalah - Porta Lucis (Paulus Ricius, 1516).

Expanding these techniques, we can draw something called the Kabbalah, (Qabbalah) or tree of life. This is a very old Jewish mystical path, possibly associated with Tarot and divination. The left image of Figure 18 shows the Kabbalah as it is seen today. But, it has gone through many permutations. The right picture is of Joseph ben Abraham Gikatilla, a Spanish Kabbalist from the 13th century.

Major arcana of the Tarot:
```
   0 Fool          1 Magician    2 Priestess     3 Empress    4 Emperor   5 Heirophant
   6 Lovers        7 Chariot     8 Strength      9 Hermit    10 Wheel    11 Justice
  12 Hanged man   13 Death      14 Temperance   15 Devil    16 Tower    17 Star
  18 Moon         19 Sun        20 Judgement    21 World
```

Kabbalah is used to study self and creation. Each of the ten circles represents a facet of our route to enlightenment. If we notice the ten terms, translated from Hebrew, we can see that these are significant activities. There are 22 paths, as there are 22 major arcana in the Tarot deck. Interestingly, there are 56 minor arcana in the Tarot system. We will see this number again.

Figure 19 Other symbols which come from the hexagon.

Where does the word Arcana come from? Arcane? Magical? As we have our students go through mathematics, we can follow the path of the textbook, or we can go off from it, depending on what we value as knowledge. Our students will find this all interesting, and they will be more attentive, knowing that they are somehow studying things like astrology, and tarot. Why not let pop culture help us in positive ways? This book is not suggesting that we substitute astrology lessons for math time. It only serves to show how to make mathematics more interesting, creative and fun, with all of these little bits of detail. Doing this will get the students to come much further than typical math "instructions'" encourage, or discourage.

Expanding our work to 12

Now place a circle in the center of a piece of paper. The circle could be large enough to mostly fill the page. With the same technique used for six, we take the additional intercepts between each of the points (located outside of the circle). Some of these points may now be off the paper. So, students must reduce their compass size to obtain them, perhaps inside the circle. Lay a ruler across them and draw lines upon the circle.

Figure 20 Building the wheel.

Try to get the students to understand the idea of symmetry and that it is not actually necessary to draw all of the intercepts; only half, connected through the center. Things become very interesting now for the students who would rather study history than math. Now they can do both. Or, ask a question: "Who would like to know something about astrology?" Nearly every student's eyes will light up at the mere suggestion. Measure the angles now. Each of the twelve is 30°, strangely similar to our calendar of twelve months of nearly thirty days. It should be, for all of this material so far comes from the same place: Sumer and the Semitic cultures it spawned and later Greco-Roman culture it influenced.

Try a mathematical exercise now with your students. Have them work up all of the factors of 360 by hand. Sadly, for those so used to calculators, this can be an arduous task. Make them do it without their cherished calculators and mobile phones.

1	2	3	4	5	6	8	9	10	12	15	18
360	180	120	90	72	60	45	40	36	30	24	20

Table 1 Factors of 360.

How many numbers are there? How many pairs? Better to ask how many hours in the day, and how are they counted. Students interested in linguistics, can find how many languages use a similar word for hour. How many letters are in the Greek alphabet? Answer: 24. How many gods in many ancient pantheons? How many apostles and inches in the foot? Twelve. Why do many languages have a special word called "dozen"?

We use the decimal system for one reason, which every high school student can say, "It's easier." We have the French to thank for it. And how did they come by this genius? The scientists who accompanied Napoleon's expedition to Egypt rediscovered the Egyptian based decan system, and threw out their own (most of Europe followed), casting aside their twelve, sixteen and twenty based systems. Those earlier systems are a unique section covered later.

A lot of information can be gleaned from Table 1; the factors of 360. Notice certain numbers which are common in our daily lives, like twelve and twenty-four. What about sixty? It's not just used for seconds and minutes of time but of location in latitude and longitude. Something interesting is to have the students count the first numbers to twelve. How many numbers are there? Ten. What is their total? Sixty. Interestingly, the two great cultures of the ancient Middle East, Sumer and Egypt, counted in tens and twelves. The Egyptians used the decan to count time. And yet, at the end of the annual flood, when they must again measure and restake their fields, they used a rope with twelve knotted segments to obtain the 3-4-5 triangle to get their right angles.

One of the things interesting to this number system is how the ancients used it. They divided the sky into twelve equatorial constellations (clusters of stars that 'rotated' above the Earth's equator). Why did they measure the sky, and circles by 360, and not something easier, like 100? Perhaps because 100 cannot easily be divided into thirds, sixths and eighths. Each of these fractions is very useful to working with circles. When developing the metric system, they just couldn't find a way to make time work accordingly, so Base-12 counting is still necessary to learn but not strongly reinforced in a decimal world.

Figure 21 Horologes, Prague – Padua; rich in astrological symbols (B. Batoková).

We will come back to Table 1 as we deepen our study of these shapes. After all, this is meant to be a creative mathematics book and not just, "How to draw a Mandala!"

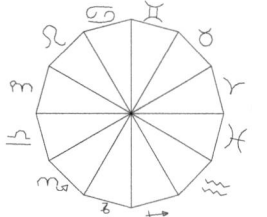 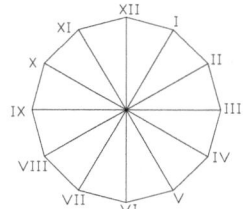 

Figure 22 Horoscopic chart, clock face and Latitude and Longitude.

Lastly, anyone familiar with astrology should recognize that Figure 20 is the basic shape of a horoscope or clock. There are, of course, 12 signs in the zodiac. Indian-Vedic astrology also uses the concept of twelve. The Chinese astrological system also has twelve signs (dog, pig, dragon, etc.), twelve double hours and a great cycle of 60 years.

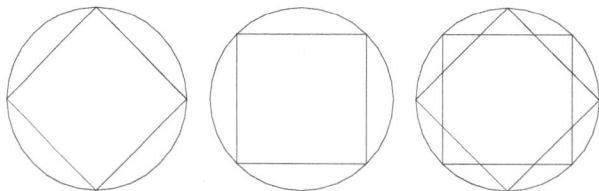

Figure 23a The Diamond, the Square and the Octagon.

We see in the dodecagon the four key directions. Using only these points, we obtain a diamond. Continuing with compass and ruler, we can bisect the sides of the diamond to make a square, and then use both to create an 8-sided figure.

There is something interesting about eight. Figure 23b shows the Bagua, consisting of eight trigrams (symbols), often used in Taoism, the I Ching, and other features of Chinese culture. For further connections we can recommend that students read about the Eight Immortals of Chinese-Taoist belief, the Ogdoad of eight paired gods in ancient Egypt, or the Eight-Fold Path of Buddhism.

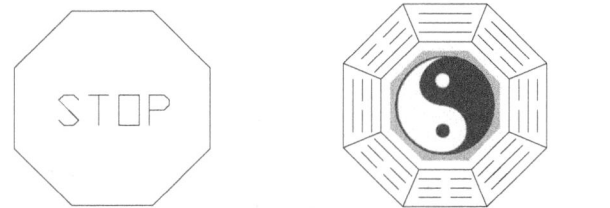

Figure 23b Familiar shapes, and not so familiar.

This concludes the introduction to use of the compass, where students can now confidently divide a circle by 3, 4, 6, 8 and 12. They are now no longer a novice with compass and ruler, have done a lot of mathematics along the way, and have seen relationships between math, art and their world.

Three dimensions

How now to have them create apparently three-dimensional forms from two? There are many more fascinating things that can be drawn using the easy divisibility of the circle by six, such as the cube, the octahedron, tetrahedron, icosahedron, cube-octahedron and star tetrahedron (Figure 24).

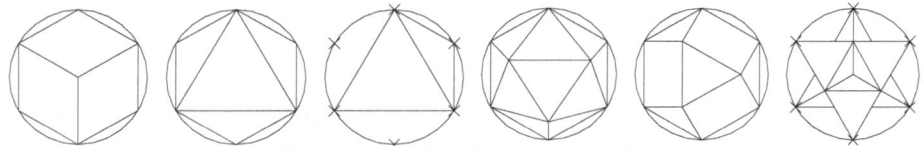

Figure 24 - 3D shapes from 2D.

The reader should imagine how to make lines fit to the six points, with some erasure, and drawing of some lines from crossings. We should acknowledge that the icosahedron is unique in that the lines require slight manipulation that the student artist needs to learn how to do for the desired effect.

Figure 25a Geometries by Dali and da Vinci.

These shapes are particularly fascinating, when we see that da Vinci and Dali used them in their works, and especially the remarkable images of a Renaissance artist named Wentzel Jamnitzer.

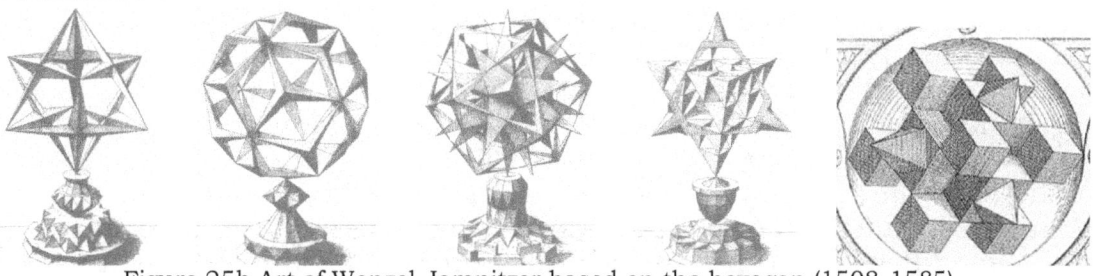

Figure 25b Art of Wenzel Jamnitzer based on the hexagon (1508-1585).

Finally, we can take these drawing techniques and really go three-dimensional. See Figure 26a. Draw a new hexagon. It is a good idea to have several students make theirs at exactly 2 inches and other students at exactly 4 inches (which will enable construction of the star tetrahedron...) Cut out the hexagon and fold as shown.

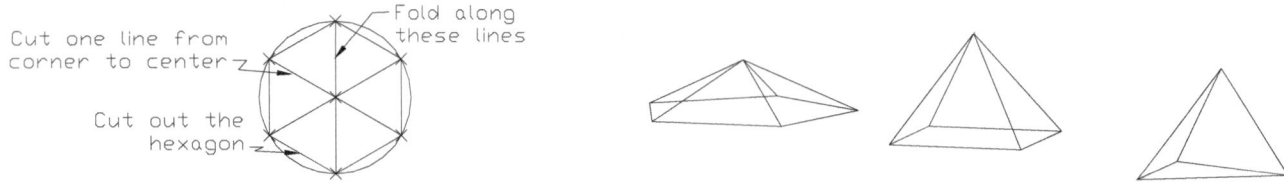

Figure 26a The cutout.   Figure 26b The foldup.

The students readily notice that they can progressively fold the cutout to get the shapes shown in Figure 26b. From these, three of the platonic solids can be built. We use the large and small tetrahedrons to stellate that particular form.

Provide a heavy weight paper or card stock, for student use in making one of the forms. Colors and designs can be put on the flat pattern. NOTE: students should leave tabs on the edges for gluing, plus it is a great idea to glue a string inside the model during construction so that it can be hung up in the classroom.

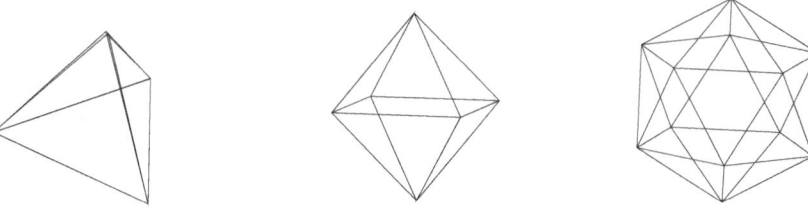

Figure 26c The final product.

Many possibilities can be created. A "basic" shape is the icosahedron. It can be further stellated by using tetrahedral pyramids whose flat-pattern radius was exactly half. The cube-octahedron is interesting in that it uses inverted 3- and 4-sided pyramids. Note the star tetrahedron. If we were to rotate it so that the centers lined up, we would essentially have the Star of David. Again, we can visualize the upward pointing tetrahedron as representing fire, with the downward representing water.

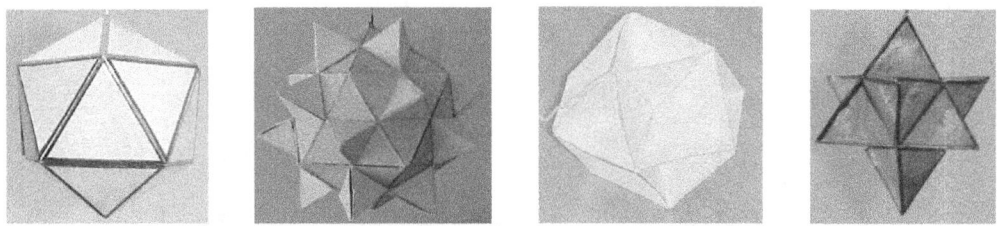

Figure 27 Icosahedron, stellated, cube-octahedron and star tetrahedron.

The last symbol in Figure 27 is called the Merkaba, with the upward pyramid said to symbolize Agni (fire-masculine), and the downward as Shahkti (water-feminine). There are meditational techniques where we imagine one of the tetrahedrons rotating in one direction, while the second rotates opposite. In a rigid form, this is a bit difficult to imagine. What is interesting here are the artistic and symbolic uses of geometry.

If we break down this word Merkaba and look at the ancient Egyptian language, we find that MR, their name for pyramid, is very similar in pronunciation and concept to the mythical Mt. Meru of Hinduism. (The Egyptians generally did not use vowels.) In India they also refer to the Staff of Meru, the central energy channel within the human body, through which Kundalini is channeled. Meru is not just a pyramid, or a mountain, but a sacred pathway, through which energy flows. There are cultures which use "mer" to represent the sea, "mir", to mean peace, and "vesmir", to mean cosmos. Further, the words Ka and Ba essentially meant "spirit" and "soul". What is the difference? A student of astrology should have the same question, for Sun and Moon are thought to represent these two qualities in a persons' horoscope. It is further interesting that the syllables "ka" and "ba" are found in the term Kabbalah, and in the Muslim holy of holies; the Ka'aba.

Let's talk about this in math class. Teenagers are curious of such things and this brief exposure to different ideas can inspire further reading, greater interest, and participation.

Figure 28a Merkaba meditation.

Figure 28b Stellated dodecahedron.

Notice what happens when we rotate the stellated dodecahedron. We get a virtual Star of David, now containing what appears to be an octahedron.

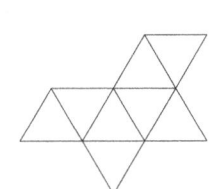
Figure 29 Making the octahedron.

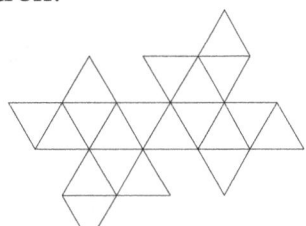
Figure 30 Making the icosahedron.

By modifying the techniques used at the beginning of the chapter, the flat patterns can be drawn on a single piece of paper. Carefully cutting and folding will allow for construction of the octahedron and icosahedron. Again, leave tabs on the edges. The flat pattern for the icosahedron looks a bit complicated but comes from the same techniques. It's not so hard, for these techniques should be pretty clear by now. Do the circles and marks lightly, so that the final coloring will cover them. Too much erasure messes up the paper.

Figure 31 The ceiling of the creative classroom.

As the students fold it and curl it into form, their hands are transmitting to their brains all of this work which you have performed together.

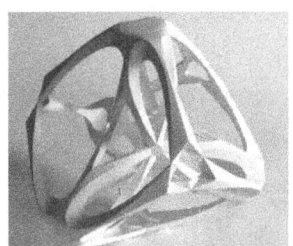

Figure 32a Tetrahedron, dodecahedron and icosahedron - (Richard Sweeney).

Figure 32b Ideas with the Tetrahedron (Gregory Epps and Rinus Roehlofs) and Stellated dodecahedron – (Ulrich Mikloweit)

  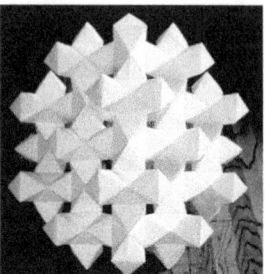 

Figure 32c, Spiked star – (David Springett). Open icosahedron, Benzene matrix, Variation on truncated dodecahedron – (Bradfrod Hansen-Smith)

We see in Figures 32a-c, sculptures created by modern art/math enthusiasts. Additional media to create the Platonic solids will be seen in later chapters.

Kymatics

We have looked at a variety of ways to approach mathematics here, artistically and practically. Let us look at one more subject to which we could open the door, if just a little.

There is a stream of study, apparently begun by Ernst Chladni in the 1780's regarding figures which can be created by sound. What is required are metal plates, called Chladni plates. These can be circular, square or have another shape. We must firmly hold one plate (a central screw works well), place fine sand, or rice, upon it and then stroke perpendicularly across an edge, with a violin bow, creating a tone, or vibration. The sand granules will start to dance, and form patterns, from the vibration. It is easy to create simple stars, often six pointed.

In 1967, Hans Jenny renamed this material Kymatics, from the Greek word "Kyma" (wave). As we can see from research, sound waves and vibrations can make material form images. Could we create physical material? Could we essentially dematerialize things also? Modern sonic weapons engineers think so.

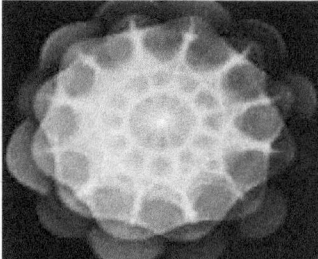

Figure 33 Cymatic image of water under the effects of audible vibration, by Dr. Hans Jenny.
©2001 MACROmedia Publishing. Used by permission.

If nothing else, we have another great topic to introduce into the classroom, if we are enterprising enough to get the tools together. There are so many realms that we could touch on in our classes. So, let's do that!

Concluding dialogue

Ask the students to write quietly into their notes, their thoughts on the following questions. You have learned a lot about angles, triangles and shapes in your previous mathematics classes. What mathematical skills have you further developed here? What items are clearer to you that you weren't quite sure of? What are some areas that you might wish to now learn more about? How can we make three dimensions from two? Write your biggest surprise from this material – the thing that made you say, "Wow, this is interesting!"

Figure 34 Ideas

Hopefully, teacher and student will have thoroughly enjoyed this material. Take the time from the full curriculum to somehow fit this in. It's worth it if for no other reason than to fill the math classroom with beauty! We will return to 4, 6, 8, and 12 – fold division in studying geometry and trigonometry. Our work so far has created a great base. For now, enjoy further ideas from Today and Yesterday, awaiting Tomorrow (see further images in the color section).

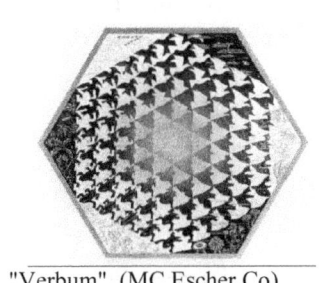  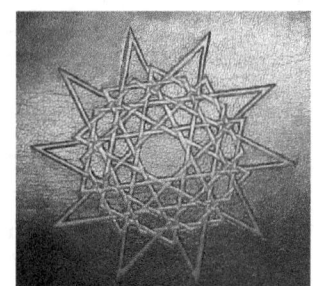

"Verbum" (MC Escher Co).   Knot – (Leonardo da Vinci)   Ten pointed design – (Paul Galiunas).

A common conception of mathematics is that it is the study of numbers. A more appropriate and complete definition would be that mathematics is the study of patterns. – Jim Lowdermilk

Further reading and sites of various artists mentioned in the text:

http://www.georgehart.com/ George Hart

http://www.polyedergarten.de/ Ulrich Mikloweit

http://www.intent.com/bruce/links.html Bruce Rawle's Sacred Geometry homepage

http://www.rinusroelofs.nl/ Rinus Roehlofs

http://www.richardsweeney.co.uk/ Richard Sweeney

http://www.cymaticsource.com/ Cymatics

http://www.charlesgilchrist.com/SGEO/ Charles Gilchrist geometry

http://www.cs.berkeley.edu/~sequin/ Carlo Sequin

http://www.sckans.edu/~bridges/ Bridges Math conferences

http://www.drunvalo.net/ Drunvalo Melchizedek sacred geometry and Flower of Life

http://www.francenehart.com Francene Hart - Visionary Artist

http://www.wholemovement.com/ Bradford Hansen-Smith Paper fold presenter.

Class Exercise 1   **Building Confidence with the Compass**

Objective:
Develop precision with compass and ruler. Work with hexagonal division of the circle, rather than decimal, as a prelude to understanding basic trigonometric angles. Widen number – arithmetic skills. Learn symbology of male/female in art and architecture.

Procedure:
a) Have students draw the daisy, using 2" radius and check for accuracy at the center and at the edges of the first circle. (figure 6)
b) Draw a hexagon using a larger radius of 2 to 4". Draw crossing lines from vertices, again checking accuracy at the center. (figure 12c)
c) Students draw a new daisy and color and shade the color wheel, with ideas on mixing, contrasting and balancing. (figure 10)

Homework:
Students draw personal "mandala", using 6-fold division of the circle with curved and straight lines. Color with various shades of only one color.

Evaluation:
Assess how well they followed instruction. Did they see their mistakes on the first drawing and make improvements on the second (Were they motivated enough to redraw the first)?

Evaluation of homework should be done one at a time, as the class looks on. Show what is strong in each, be sensitive, but comment on what is weak, to demonstrate what can be improved and share ideas and suggestions.

Things to encourage are quality, creativity and experimentation but not free-style sketching, loops thrown together with no mathematical correlation, or sloppiness. Take off points if it shows no growth or experimentation, or especially if they didn't draw a new picture but just colored or copied the one done in class.

Bridges:
We should think as teachers of promoting career ideas for our students. There are already foundations in this exercise for interior design, architecture, artistry and design. The emphasis on precision will carry over into what is expected in their regular mathematics class and home work so that they see that precise work, and not sloppy rushed material is more presentable and appropriate.

Class Exercise 2   **Division of the circle with only the compass**

Objective:
Learn further usages with the compass, like bisection. Divide the circle by 3, 6 and 12, and then 4 and 8 to become familiar with common angles used in trigonometry like 30°, 45°, 60° and 90° and what fraction of a circle they represent. Make left/right brain connections between images and numbers, fractions of a circle and easily calculated factors of 360. Pull in artistic students who aren't normally so engaged with math.

Procedure:
a)   Students draw a circle, radius 3 to 4 inches, and divide it into twelve sections. (figure 20)
Ask questions: "What does if look like?" (clock, horoscope)
"Where do we use the number 12?" (hours, dozen, apostles, etc.)
b)   Have students calculate and write the factors of 360. Ask, "How many pairs of numbers are there, and how many numbers in total?" (12, 24)
c)   "We have divided a circle by 6 and 12. How could we divide it by 3, or 4?" Let the students discover this on their own.
d)   Divide the circle by 4, using the cardinal points of the 12 sided figure. Have them bisect to get 8 fold division, and/or a square which is parallel to the page. Relate 8 to the concepts in the text. (figure 23b)

Homework:
Draw and color one of the fractal images, or a different 12- or 8-based design of their choice. Use the color wheel and shading.

Evaluation:
How hard did they try to get the factors of 360°? (The calculator is obviously banned from such an activity). Note: Don't let this be a one-time activity. Quiz them on these numbers.

How substantial does their art piece look? Well worked, rushed, or non-existent? Typically 90% of the work will be in the B+ to A+ range and should be put on the "Wall of Fame".

Bridges:
All non-mathematically oriented students get pulled in by this work, when we mention its historical relation to Sumerian counting, when we make it visual, and hand-work, and when we show everyday connections.

Class Exercise 3   **Going 3D with the Protractor**

Objective:
Further methods to pull in artistic- and sports/motoric- intelligent students. Additional practice with precision. Provide familiarity and understanding of regular solids and build models for use in trigonometry.

Procedure:
a) Have students draw three hexagons of the same size. Have them see how to make the image appear to be 3 dimensional. (figure 24)
b) Draw hexagons on a new page. For each student that uses a radius of 4", have three who do theirs to a size of 2". Draw the crossing lines. Cut out the hexagon, fold along the three crossing lines and then cut one of them in toward the center.
c) The shape wants to fold (figure 26b), and close inward, to start forming for the icosa-, octa- and tetrahedrons. Put halves together to make the octahedron. Continue, and make the tetrahedron. Tape one large tetrahedron together and then tape three of the smaller pyramids to it to stellate. Show how to put 3 and 4 sided pyramids together to get the "skeletal" cube-octahedron (figure 27).

Homework:
Provide card stock and flat patterns for the octahedron and icosahedron (figures 29 and 30). Have students design and color a pattern and then build any of the forms so far explored. They should glue a string inside, so that the piece can be hung in class. They will of course ask if they can work together. Allow pairs or individual work with high expectations.

Evaluation:
Grade pieces on quality, experimentation, complexity, aesthetics and effort. (Best pieces should be hung up. After a few years, the class room will have inspiring examples to pose challenges for ever-better work).

Bridges:
The tetrahedron is the strongest of structures, used in bridges and architecture. It is the shape of the CH_4 molecule. Salt is a typical crystal showing octahedral bonds between atoms. Lastly, we have tools to be used later in trigonometry.

2 Reacquainting ourselves with old friends

Opening dialogue

Of what value is an understanding of fractions in high school? Which processes relate to fractions? Where in advanced mathematics are fractions and negative numbers involved? How is graphical representation a useful tool in upper-level problems?

Fractions

No matter the depth of a given theme, very often the mistakes students make in their calculations are due to the lowly fraction, a missed negative sign, or that they did not read the graph which could have helped them understand the problem. This chapter will discuss ways to revisit these topics, within high school course material, showing the need to understand them. It is highly recommended that teachers avoid the calculator and encourage students to work the fractions, especially in grade school.

Fractions are your friend! In high school, I must say this at least once a day, in some algebra, geometry, trigonometry, calculus, or physics class. Students normally have two to three years of working with me so like it or not, they have to hear it a lot.

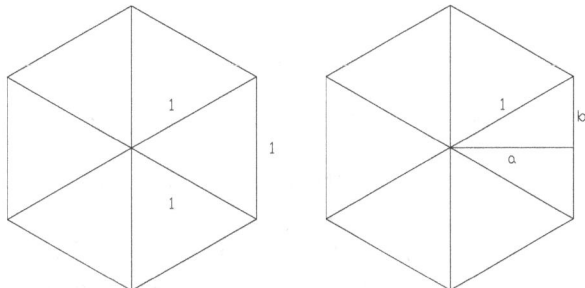

Figure 1 Getting ½, and something more.

Fractions are very valuable in a high school classroom, and yet typical textbooks revise them in only minor detail, if at all. Should the students have had most of this earlier? Yes. Did they understand it at that time, or choose to avoid it? Usually, the latter appears to be true. What is important is that they will be working with fractional operations throughout advanced math.

Here is an example of a quick exercise to do with geometry. Have the students draw the hexagon from the previous chapter.

Note that each length in the hexagon measures the same, which we will call unit '1'. Each angle within the triangles is 60°. Now, ask the students to bisect an angle, as shown in Figure 1. It stands to reason that they have made a 30-60-90 triangle. It is logical for them to deduce that "b" measures 1/2. What about "a"? By Pythagoras, it is √3/2, but make them work through the problem using the theorem to come by this answer. They *will* struggle with fractions, by hand. With the calculator, they obtain decimal numbers that don't show the pattern we will find.

Operations with fractions seem to be one of the more difficult number tasks students face, and this doesn't mean 1/2 + 1/4. Addition, subtraction and multiplication of whole numbers is fairly easy, though a surprising amount of students are reluctant to do this today, backing away from mathematic challenges, deferring to classmates willing to calculate and think, or who might press buttons on a calculator faster than themselves. Perhaps a lot of students struggle in mathematics because we don't provide them a relationship to numbers. It is interesting to note the value the ancients placed on teaching numbers in their mystery schools.

It is amazing how many students shy away from fractions, and teachers too, under the fallacy that someone earlier should have taught this material and was enough. Yet, there are those students who didn't get it when it was taught, who maybe tried to ignore it and were allowed to pass, and who quickly forgot about it. We check it off as having been taught, but can we assume that it was learned, to be picked up for later use as a tool?

We should stress that fractions, percents, proportions, ratios, and division, are essentially the same things; parts of a whole. There are students who do understand how to work with them, and can be resentful about having to revise. Their parents wonder too. Don't listen. There is not one student who couldn't use a lot of practice with fractions. For even the most gifted will not be able to clear an algebra equation by multiplying by the reciprocal:

$$\frac{2x}{3} = 6 \quad \rightarrow \quad \frac{3}{2} \cdot \frac{2x}{3} = \frac{6}{1} \cdot \frac{3}{2}$$

They will rather insist on multiplying by 3 and then dividing by 2, when only one step is needed, with a useful jump in understanding of fractions.

They may not easily find the negative reciprocal relationship of the slopes of two perpendicular lines, shown in Figure 2, where;

$$y = \frac{2x}{3} + 3, \text{ is intersected by one having slope } -\frac{3}{2}.$$

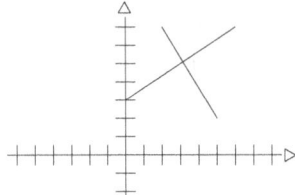

Figure 2 perpendicular lines, with slope m and $-1/m$

They will find challenge in the idea that radicals can be expressed in terms of fractional exponents: $\sqrt{x} = (x)^{½}$ They will stumble with physics equations which must be manipulated, not by dividing fractions or multiplying them but by clearing variables or radicals from the denominator. They may think that 1/0 is zero! They may not be aware of the fractional nature of slope = $\Delta y/\Delta x$, and its usage as the derivative in calculus. Then, there are the trigonometric ratios and reciprocal functions, trig identities, and operations with large fractional values, like we see when working with Newton's Law of Universal Gravitation or Coulomb's Law.

A surprising number of students in high school are weak with fractions, and even the best find revision useful. We can worry that here we are teaching the slowest person in the class, but really this helps them all. Advanced students may not struggle with fractions, but application will still give challenge. By revisiting it for slower students, they will do better with more fractional operations and hence hold back the class less often.

High school math depends a lot on algebra. For example; once we reduce $3x + 7 = 9$ to $3x = 2$, what is the next step? We should divide by 3: $\quad \frac{3x}{3} = \frac{2}{3}$

One of the interesting things about being an international mathematics teacher is seeing all of the ways students of different nationality do their division. Some like showing the steps to the side. It is strongly recommended that students, especially weaker ones, need to see what is going on inside the problem, and for better students, there are frequently mistakes, like sign changes that they don't see.

Algebraic division should be done within the problem, showing the student that they are clearing the coefficient from in front of the variable, and how it is to obtain a fractional answer. It's amazing that some students will struggle with 2 divided by 3, but in the end can more easily accept the idea of writing a 3 under the 2 and getting a fractional answer.

For a problem like, $-3x = 9$, show the value of reducing within the equation: $-\frac{3x}{-3} = \frac{9}{-3}$

By this technique, it is easier to see that the result is negative. But, those students who get in a hurry, will say that x = 3.

Start algebra with fractions, and work your revision very carefully. Early steps of high school math, physics, and chemistry, require a lot of work with formulas, conversions and manipulations. All of this will need the student to be very capable of multiplying and dividing by fractions and reciprocals.

Start easy

Let's begin with the basic rules of multiplication, that fractions multiply straight across. Perhaps the problem with fractions for a lot of students is that there are so many rules, of how to add, multiply or divide. Though addition is normally the easiest operation to teach, addition of fractions is not, because it requires a search for a common denominator, then multiplication, and finally addition. That gets so jumbled for some people. We will revise addition later, not first.

What this chapter hopes to do is show how to weave fraction revision in with application throughout a spectrum of high school applications, in a general sequence that flows also with teaching the sciences.

Get students to begin work with multiplying fractions, like:

$$\frac{1}{2} \times \frac{3}{4} \quad \text{or} \quad \frac{1}{2} \times \frac{2}{3}$$

Does it seem too easy? Well, it is. This is not an attempt to teach fractions. The students should have had that long ago. We are going to solidify how they work, and we may seem to be oversimplifying the revision, but we will be moving quickly with it. Let them remember how to multiply across. Encourage and then encourage them again to look for how to reduce fractions before they multiply. Then, give them problems like:

$$\frac{22}{55} \times \frac{5}{24} \quad \text{or} \quad \frac{7y}{9z} \times \frac{3z}{14}$$

Next, do basic algebra problems like 5x + 3 = 7, making sure that they can do this. Several can't. By going over this, we *are* arguably holding the class back for the slowest. But, if we don't, the slowest will definitely hold them all back *more* later.

Telling the students to see what math operation is going on and then doing the opposite function seems to help. For example: there is "+ 3" so they need to subtract 3. Do they realize that the 5 in front of the "x" means that this is multiplication? Seems basic but it isn't always.

Ensure that they understand

$$\frac{5}{5}, \frac{11}{11}, \frac{x}{x}, \text{ and even } \frac{1000 \text{ m}}{1 \text{ km}} \text{ all equal '1'},$$

that $1x = x = x^1 = x/1$ are all clear to them, and

that dividing by x, (or x/1) is the same as multiplying by 1/x.

Now, see that they can solve $\frac{x}{4} + 3 = 5.$

Here, the trick is that the fraction means division, and so the opposite step is multiplication, by 4, or 4/1.

Give Application

The revision of these things is important because even if the students got these concepts in earlier years, they probably never really put them all together, as is necessary in high school math and science.

About this time, our physics book is asking students to be able to solve for a given variable, for example, "a": $v = v_i + at$, $v_f^2 = v_i^2 + 2ad$, and so forth. Students with limited fractional ability not only can't, they won't, and for even the best it will be unfamiliar. Science colleagues often complain of poor math skills, but many times are more reluctant than the students to do a little revision of their own, particularly with fractions.

Revise the basics in math and science class; it will only make life easier later. When covering advanced topics, watch where students often stumble. It will be sign changes and fractional operations. Fractions are your friend. I once had a student tell me, "We sure have a lot of friends Mr. Stang," with regard to fractions, exponents, negative numbers, etc. Right!

It is not long before these students must learn conversions, usually associated with velocity equations:

$$V = \frac{d}{t}$$ where we are looking at miles/hr, feet/sec, km/hr or m/s.

Get them to take the steps: $\dfrac{40 \text{ feet}}{\text{second}} \times \dfrac{1 \text{ mile}}{5280 \text{ feet}} \times \dfrac{3600 \text{ seconds}}{1 \text{ hr}}$

There are a number of reasons why these steps are valuable to work in. One is that different numbers and quantities can be equivalent, making a strange fraction whose value is '1', so in multiplying by 1 changes nothing (1x = x). Another good point is that "like numbers", and "like terms" cancel each other out. This makes the teenager, who is always in a hurry, slow down and put the labels in, so they know what the label should be at the end.

Note, for those converting meters-per-second to kilometers-per-hour or vice-versa; a large number of students are taught to memorize that they should multiply or divide by 3.6. Test them with a problem like 20 mps and ask if they think they should divide by 3.6. You might be surprised by how many will say "yes." Memorizing whether to divide or multiply by 3.6 is questionable because when it comes time to use it, given the choice between two processes, don't we often as not mess it up and choose the wrong one? Conversion never fails, and is great practice with fractions.

In chemistry, students begin by converting between ounces and pounds, grams and kilograms, moles, density of mass/volume, percent errors, and percent concentrations, all involving fractions and conversions. Often, chemistry teachers either go right through this material, or just ignore it, happily, and leave it for the math people to somehow have time to do. Thanks for that!

If the teachers of these subjects concentrate efforts at the start of the high school education, the student would be encouraged by the necessity. It is a great way to link between subjects, which the science teachers should be doing more of anyway.

Percents with fractions

And hey, what about percents? Revise-quickly. Do the students know what the word "percent" means? Do any of them speak Spanish? Who knows why we have cents? This little question might just wake up a couple students from the back of the room who normally don't involve themselves in the daily activities (if English is a second language).

Now have them do division-by hand. Another thing that often is a surprise about being an international teacher is the number of ways people divide. Talk about a culture barrier! It is bad enough trying to use math terms in a class full of people who barely understand English. Imagine my surprise when I first did a problem in long division and the students looked at it as though I was from, well, the United States. I will humbly suggest that this is the one technique best for division. The reason being that one always sees where zeroes and the decimal go:

$$\frac{1}{16} = \begin{array}{r} 0.0625 \\ 16\overline{)1.0000} \\ \underline{0.96} \\ 0.040 \\ \underline{0.032} \\ 0.0080 \end{array}$$

After showing this technique, be sure that the students can go back and forth between decimals and percents. The calculator is not usually able to do this for them, so they must think and know how numbers work. Percent means per one hundred and the 6 above is in the hundreds column. So, this means 6.25%.

More fun is getting them to go the other way and making a percent, like 31.25% into a decimal of 0.3125, then into a fraction, which can be reduced: (note the following trick; if it ends in 00 or another number divisible by 25, reduce by counting how many thousands there are; times 40, how many hundreds there are; times 4 + how many 25's. They won't get it, so repeat it..)

$$\frac{3125}{10000} = \frac{125}{400} = \frac{5}{16}$$

Three thousands: 120, one hundred: 4 and one 25: 1 – total - 125

Oh, how they'll howl with delight on this problem. But, forget for a moment the standardized tests, the deadlines and all. The question is do we want these people to be able to think? If the answer is yes, revise fractions in every way possible

Another strength of the US and UK systems is the mighty inch. It is great to grow up in a system using inches, feet, miles, ounces, pints, quarts and such. After all, I love a good pint! I hope so much that they never adopt the metric system. Seriously though, the system makes the student think more, plus it's tied into our rhythm of time keeping and solar and lunar cycles, from which our time keeping comes.

But more, ask a student why they like the decimal system and they will say, "Because it is simple." Do we want to teach simpletons? Anyone can count on his fingers and toes, or push buttons on the calculator. But where is the thought, and even magic?

The great thing about the English system is all of those fractions and weird numbers, like 1/16 of an inch, 12 inches to a foot, 5280 (12 x 440, or 11 x 12 x 40, or 11 x 16 x 30) feet to a mile, 16 ounces to a pint, two pints to a quart. Ask "decimal" people how much a quarter is worth and they'll ask, "A quarter of what?" In international classes, students from the US and UK are often better with fractions and then applications like algebra, because they live with such varied fractions and numbers. Others see tenths or hundredths and immediately switch to decimals. Not that this is bad but we can miss seeing patterns develop, miss properties of numbers and even begin to introduce error by how and where we round off the decimal answer.

A good example is the magic we will find buried within the angles of 0, 30°, 45°, 60°, and 90° (all 12- and 16- based fractions of a circle). Sometimes, I wonder as I teach these materials if I am not presenting something that is about to go extinct.

Ancient Egypt and fractions

A note for less math oriented students; the ancient culture of Egypt had an interesting way of expressing and working with fractions. In their hieroglyphic style, they had the following figure, sometimes called the Eye of Horus. They used components of it in performing fractional addition.

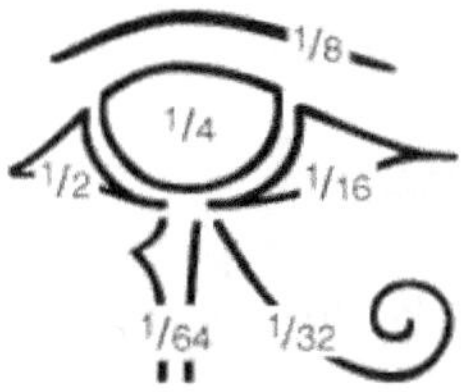

Figure 3 The eye of Horus - (courtesy of Scot Bruaw).

The individual pieces in Figure 3 add to...? 63/64 – a curious total. How were such fractions used? Was it hard to calculate with them?

Negative numbers

Negative numbers are also our friends. In the early days of high school, the student of physics and chemistry will have the chance to revise and work with scientific notation, though they probably learned this in late elementary math. Again, that doesn't mean they truly got it.

At some point, the student will have to work through complex problems, with large scale numbers. They will learn about pico, micro, mega, giga and kilo. But, many of them will become horribly lost, trying to work through problems on their calculator, ending up with an answer like 10^{35} when it should have been 10^8. We have a choice: revise and show why, or watch frustration and failure.

The reason to ban calculators until trigonometry (and then only sparingly), is to show students how to set up problems. Give them numbers that work well by hand. Can they determine if the final answer is reasonably correct? In a moment, we will see.

But first, let's see how negative numbers are also valuable in algebraic problems. Given the following, how many students know to simplify first by clearing either the fractions or the negatives?

$$\frac{3x}{4} + \frac{2}{3} = \frac{5}{6} \qquad\qquad -3x + 1 = -2x - 3$$

We can never assume that all the students know this, have even received it in primary school, or "got it". Sure, we should expect it. The revision is helpful for everyone. In our rush forward, we shouldn't deem these tasks too elementary and hence unnecessary. It is amazing the number of countries who have already streamed students at early ages into math and non-math fields. For some people, the lights turn on later, but they do turn on. Let's try to hold onto them until this occurs.

Review basic addition and subtraction with negatives. Most will be just fine here, but we are about to work with scientific notation, so let's make sure they know it.

Go over two particular concepts. The first examples something like: $-3 - 5$ or $6 + (-2)$. In the former, note that the 5 is positive. We are subtracting a positive. This is the same as adding a negative, $+(-5)$, and that negatives add like positives, only the answer is negative. They won't get this the first time, so repeat this step, and have them say it out loud. Get those brain synapses to start firing with this information. In the second problem, adding a negative is just like subtracting a positive, but we normally don't write the + sign: $6 - (+2) = 6 - 2$.

The second idea is an example like: $-3x + 2 = -2x - 3$. Many times, we get the students used to putting the variable on the left side and then they are "locked in". We need to get them to look for the lesser value of the coefficients and move *this* one. So, we add '3x' to each side and this means we will work with positive coefficients, and thus have less chance of error. Should the students be able to divide by a negative? Sure, but they often miss that little step. Not only does selecting the lowest value coefficient increase the chance of working with positive numbers, it gets the student to read the problem, and be comfortable working it from either side of the equation.

One last thought on the quick revision of negatives is that if students struggle still, and they may, the number line doesn't always help. But, a thermometer usually does. What does it mean that the temperature drops, or that it is getting colder? It means minus. What if it is really cold, say below zero? How do we express that? (With a negative number) What happens if it is cold, and it gets colder? Give questions like this to students who struggle with negatives and they may start to get it.

Negative exponents and scientific notation

When students are "warmed up" we can go into practical application (which comes early on in high school science). In math, an algebra problem may look like:

$$\frac{x^7 y^{-4} z^2}{x^{-1} y^3 z^5} \cdot \frac{x^{-3} y^2 z^{-3}}{x^{-5} y^4 z^2}$$

Obviously, there are a lot of things going on here, for example that we work with x, y and z separately, that exponents in multiplication add, and subtract in division (in this case, the fraction). Better to revise fractions *and* negatives first.

I teach calculus at high school for students who voluntarily take it. These are usually the best of the litter. The surprising thing is that as they learn how to take derivatives and integrals, they struggle most with fractional and negative exponents. They are also reluctant to take the extra time to draw the graph, which would confirm their results.

In science, we like using the speed of light: 3×10^8 m/s, Planck's constant of 6.626×10^{-34} J•s, and Avogadro's number; 6.02×10^{23}. When we talk about the mass of an electron, or of the Sun, distance to Pluto, or diameter of a blood cell, the scale is incredible. That is why we use scientific notation.

It is amazing the idea that if the nucleus of an atom were the size of a baseball, the nearest electron would be a few miles away. That everything is built upon this minute element, with so much intervening space means everything must be held apart, and together, by electromagnetics, nuclear forces, and gravity.

Molecular models are not any different say from our solar system, where our students will have to calculate gravitational and electrical forces, using $F = \dfrac{G m_1 m_2}{d^2}$ and $F = \dfrac{k q_1 q_2}{d^2}$

$G = 6.67 \times 10^{-11}$ Nm²/kg², for a problem involving gravity between the Earth and Sun, for example, will provide numbers like this:

$$F = \dfrac{6.67 \times 10^{-11} \text{ Nm}^2/\text{kg}^2 (1.991 \times 10^{30} \text{ kg})(5.979 \times 10^{24} \text{ kg})}{(1.4957 \times 10^{11} \text{m})^2}$$

The students can learn how to do this on a calculator, but if they don't first work them through by hand, they will lose the chance to advance their calculation ability and an understanding of what kind of answer they should be getting. Don't give them the calculator too early. It will not make the instruction any faster.

Honestly, I hate teaching students how to use their calculator to do this kind of problem. It is boring to learn the next newest model and have to show students how to use their machines. I thought them being techno "Wunderkind" meant they were supposed to be able to figure all of that out anyway.

But, I never tire of going through a problem with them by hand, to see what the expected result should be. Looking at just what is going on with the powers of ten, and labels, gives us this:

$$\dfrac{10^{-11} \text{ Nm}^2/\text{kg}^2 \times 10^{30} \text{ kg} \times 10^{24} \text{ kg}}{(10^{11} \text{m})^2} = 10^{21} \text{N}$$

Students need to be able to work with negatives, negative exponents, fractions with exponents, fractional exponents, and labels in fractional form. So first, have them write it out. Insist that they work the exponential portions in their head. That's one of the things their heads are useful for. The best calculator is the one on their shoulders.

In the end, finally, let them do the problem with their calculator. Don't let them come up to you, asking if the answer is correct. They work the exponents first, and that should get them pretty close. Good enough to confirm if their final answer is correct. Hey, if they did the work and the exponents match the expected result, then the answer is probably correct.

The square root and ±

With negative numbers we should consider the special case of the radical: $\sqrt{}$. In primary school, students learn to take the square root of something and get a positive answer. In high school it takes a surprising amount of fairly concentrated effort, along with all of these other things, to rewrite the programming of even the best math student to consider that there can be two possible answers; positive *and* negative. Often, the better students seem to take longer to come around. The fact is, a negative number, when squared gives a positive answer, just like its positive counterpart. For example, -2 and 2 both square to make 4, and so we need to realize that $\sqrt{4} = \pm 2$.

This becomes more obvious when working through graphing in high school. It's funny to see students who have been given trigonometry in grade school, (and graphing too). The system is trying to push things to lower grades and quicken the instruction. The mathematically oriented can handle it. For others it becomes a mess of ideas and in the end, they often can't do a basic line graph in high school. Yet, they are there, in agony.

To start, have them make a table of values for x and y for an equation like $y = x + 4$:

X	Y
0	4
1	5
2	6

We always make an X-Y table when facing a new type of graph and usually pick 0, 1 and 2 for the "x" value (for their ease of use in most cases). From the table, we make the graph in Figure 4a.

Next, look at the equation $y = x^2$. Again make the X-Y table, with the following results:

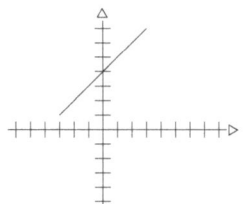
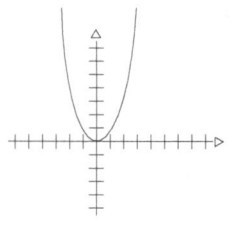

X	Y
0	0
1	1
2	4

Figure 4a graphing a straight line.   Figure 4b The graph of a parabola and its tabulation

In this case, the graph begins to form, and the students see that it curves, but they are not sure what to do. They need more values for x (negatives). In this case they can visually see that ±x will give equal results for y, creating symmetry about the y-axis.

In physics, the negative sign is associated with vectors, indicating magnitude *and* direction. Negative means falling, slowing, leaving, going backwards, or going to the left. (Sorry to you lefties out there – blame it on Descartes) As negative is a possible answer, we must consider it.

Radicals and their exponential powers – fractions

Radicals are another friend. And fractional radicals? Students need to be able to work out problems like these:

$$\frac{1}{\sqrt{2}} \qquad \frac{\sqrt{2}}{\sqrt{8}} \qquad \sqrt{x^2} \qquad (\sqrt{100})^2 \qquad \sqrt{(100^2)}$$

How do we get rid of the √2 from the denominator? By multiplying top and bottom by √2 (a fraction whose value is '1'). Can the students separate out √8 into √2 · √4 and then reduce? Do we write ± x as an answer? No, because the variable takes care of that. Do the students see that the two problems with 100 give first 100, and then ±100 as answers, and why the difference?

They will have to do this work throughout their school career, and that is why we spend a lot of time with the lowly fraction in the beginning of Algebra. In the second year, we revisit our friend, so that they learn that radicals can be expressed as fractional exponents. Man, does this ever get fun…

$$\sqrt{xyz} \cdot \sqrt[3]{x^2yz^2} = x^{1/2}y^{1/2}z^{1/2} \, x^{2/3}y^{1/3}z^{2/3} = x^{1/2+2/3}y^{1/2+1/3}z^{1/2+2/3}$$

When we go to take derivatives of radicals, we must first put them into an exponential form. Then, we take the derivative and put it back into a radical form. If this leaves a radical in the denominator, we must clear it, and the radicals and fractions are a great challenge for calculus students:

$$y = \sqrt[3]{x} = x^{1/3} \rightarrow y' = \tfrac{1}{3} x^{-2/3} = \frac{1}{3\sqrt[3]{x^2}} \cdot \frac{x^{1/3}}{x^{1/3}} = \frac{\sqrt[3]{x}}{3x}$$

Adding and subtracting fractions

From that calculus problem, it looks like we have come full circle, except that now our students must be able to add and subtract fractions. We want upper level algebra students to be able to solve problems like this. So, we better get them to work fractions.

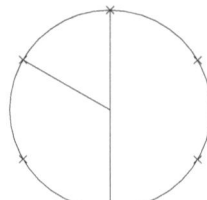

Figure 5a Fractions of a circle

At some point in our travels through the first year of high school, we should be preparing students for applications of fractional addition and subtraction, after reviewing multiplication of fractions and work with negatives as bases to understand fractions in order to manipulate and add them. Addition is just more complicated. Figure 5a can be very useful for explaining this. What is the sum of 1/2, 1/3 and 1/6? Draw it and see.

It looks like the answer should be 1. So what if we get a volunteer from the class to explain how the diagram works? Have them show the process of obtaining the least common denominator. Then, give the class some problems to try. Primary stuff to be sure, but always good practice and often successful with visual aids and encouragement. That is worth slowing down the rocket scientists so that they fill in the blanks. This picture helps a lot of people finally get fractions. Divide a circle by 12 and add 1/12 + 1/6 + 1/4 + 1/3. It looks strangely like the answer is 5/6. How is this possible?

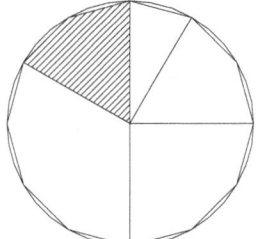

Figure 5b fractions of a circle

It should be clear that to add or subtract fractions, students need to know how to multiply them first. For people working under the decimal system, the ease with which they fall into decimal numbers lessens need and understanding for fractions. By reducing rote work, there are fewer practical applications to help understand fractional processes and decimal results. Are decimal numbers simpler? Of course. We strive constantly for ease, meaning our brains do less.

Music and fractions

Now, a chance to again put variety and interest into our work. Try walking into math class with a guitar some day. The students will be immediately alert. Pluck a string. Then, place a finger on that string, in the middle of its length, and pluck it again. How many students recognize that it's the same note, but an octave higher, just because it is half a string length? If we pluck both halves, we get the same tone. Now place a finger at 1/3rd the length and listen as we pluck both lengths. Note that they are the same tone, but differ by one octave; as one is twice the length of the other.

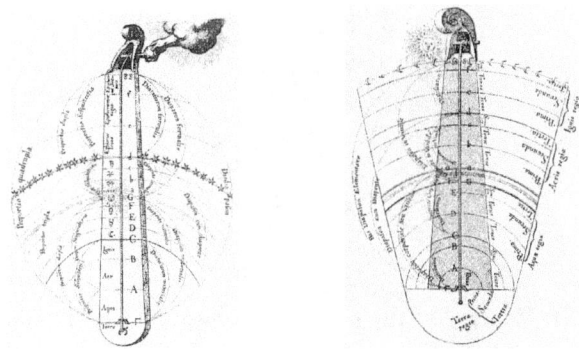

Figure 6 Fractions and Music (From Fludd's *De Musica Mundana*)

Robert Fludd, who lived in 16th-17th century England tried to demonstrate this further (Figure 6). He was a famous alchemist, Rosicrucian, astrologer and mystic.

Figure 7 Pythagoras working with music – numbers (Gaffurius: Theorica Musices)

Pythagoras was known to have looked into the ratios of string lengths, bell volume and other instrument characteristics to understand musical qualities. One experiment is easy to reproduce. Fill similar glasses with different volumes of water and "play" them.

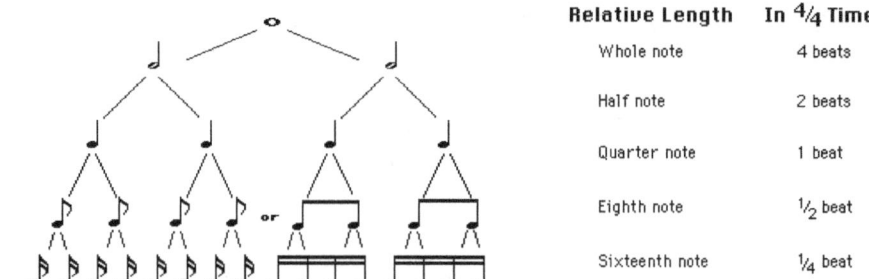

Figure 8 Timing determined by use of note symbols (courtesy Michael Furstner).

Music involves fractions. Notes ♪ describe a pitch or frequency of sound, by their placement. The length of time that a note is sounded is determined by the diagram in Figure 8. In music, there are rules about how many full notes make up what is called a bar. Give students a piece of sheet music and have them add up the length of musical time each line represents.

Figure 9 Excerpt, Das Wohltemperierte (by J. S. Bach).

We hear of intervals, like the fifth and fourth, which deal with special ratios thought to be pleasing or harmonious. Pythagoras advanced our knowledge of these. He also believed in something called the "music of the spheres"; essentially that there is "music" in the placement of the planets. Kepler took up this theme, trying to find a specific spacing of the planets in accordance with the platonic solids. He documented this work in his book Harmonice Mundi, "...as God the Creator Himself has expressed it in harmonizing the heavenly motions."

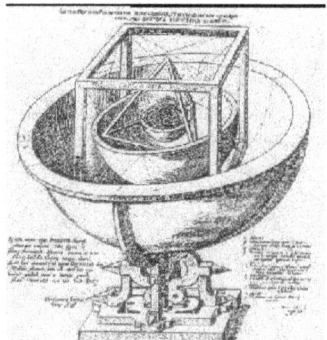

Figure 10 Mystery of the Cosmos (Johannes Kepler 1596).

Fractions and trigonometry

As students go into Trigonometry, they will see a lot of problems dealing with fractions. When talking about angular rotation, we might think about 1/3 revolution for example. Students will need to understand that −2/3 revolution is angularly equivalent but opposite in rotation, because it deposits us in the same place, just as 1⅓, and an infinite host of other measures do.

They will need to convert between revolutions and degrees and between radians and degrees. Fractions help with this, by understanding that one revolution is 360° and half a revolution is 180° = π radians.

So, it is easy to realize that a half revolution is 180°. But what about 1½ revolutions, or maybe 3/4 revolutions in the other direction? How do we multiply a fraction times a whole number? It might be a good idea to write the whole number as 360°/1. And here too, it shows a great reason why we reduce before we multiply.

It's funny how rigid our students can be. They learn that the square root of 16 is four. It can take months to get them to relearn that it can be ±4. They initially learn that to measure angles we use degrees. The concept of radians is very foreign. It's a fraction, a proportion of a circle. Instead of measuring an angular rotation, we are comparing two lengths; a hard-to-measure length of arc, divided by the radius of whatever circle it is on. As the circumference of a circle is 2π • radius, an arc length is some fraction of this. The entire circle measures 2π radians. Anything less is some fraction of *this*.

For example, if we have a 60° angle, we convert, with fractions:

$$60° \cdot \frac{2\pi \text{ radians}}{360°} = \frac{\pi \text{ radians}}{3}$$

In addition to radian conversion, students should understand how the trigonometric functions are expressed as ratios of two sides in a triangle. Don't let them go to the calculator. Instead, work out a lot with the 3-4-5, 6-8-10 and 5-12-13 triangles. Whole numbers let them trust the process. Decimals get them to trust the tool. Not one before the other. Provide triangles with two sides given, and solve for the missing side using Pythagoras. See how many people make mistakes if the hypotenuse is given along with one side. They can often become conditioned to just add the squares of the two given numbers and then take the square root of the sum. It is surprising how many cannot take the square root of 169, or even square the number 12.

This is pretty easy, and most students quickly remember how to do it. A further challenge is to give them Cos θ = 3/5 and have them figure out the other trig ratios. To begin, they make any triangle so long as the hypotenuse is a multiple of five, and the side adjacent to the angle θ is the same multiple of three. Then, using Pythagoras, they can solve for the last side and write the fractions for the other trig functions. We can further push by looking into different quadrants and thus negative possibilities...

To do secant, cosecant and cotangent, they must take the reciprocals of the appropriate functions. In other words, flip the fractions. This book doesn't show all of these processes. It's only reminding again and again of the need to work with fractions.

When we go to graphing, particularly the sine function, we must realize that the ratios are now in terms of x, y and r, and that x and y can be negative as well as positive (for now, r is only positive, but in polar graphing, the student must learn that it can also be negative).

Graphing is also your friend

Before we do sines and all, let's try easier problems. We have two interesting fellows to thank for graphing. The first was named Abu Ja'far Muhammad ibn Musa al-Khwarizmi, who studied and taught at the Bayt al-Hikmah, or House of Learning, in Baghdad in the 800s. This was the "Alexandria" of its time, since the West was in ruins as far as structured education was concerned, having long since done away with Plato's Academy, Aristotle's Lyceum and the School of Alexandria.

This school translated many surviving Greek texts from Alexandria, and was also connected with the cultures of India. Without these efforts, we wouldn't know about Euclid's Elements or Ptolemy's Tetrabiblos and Al Magest. Nor would we have stopped counting, and adding, with Roman numerals. Specifically, we have al-Khwarizmi to thank for his book Hisab al-jabr wál-muqabala. We get from this title Algebra. Various writers translate this term to mean "reduction", while others say "completion".

The second individual was Rene Descartes. This French Philosopher gave us the Cartesian coordinate system, which our students use when they draw their graphs. As we will see in this book, there are many philosophers and free thinkers who have advanced the subject of mathematics.

Let us begin with a basic graph. When we try to graph a straight line from an equation, for example y = ⅔x + 2, we graph the "y" intercept of (0,2) and then count up two places and over three. The slope of the line is the fractional number in front of the "x". If a whole number is in front of the "x", have the students put a 1 under it to make a fraction, which will help them for counting purposes.

In Figure 11 we see the graph y = ⅔x + 2. Read the other line. All should agree that it is y = 4x + 1. Have the students try to solve for the point of intersection, by setting them equal to each other:

$$\tfrac{2}{3}x + 2 = 4x + 1$$

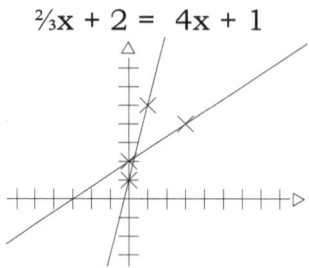

Figure 11 graphing lines and using the picture to confirm calculated results.

It is usual for students to be asked to solve equations with variables on both sides of the equations, but intercepts show one reason for doing this.

Students must be encouraged and expected to draw a graph, to see how to do visual analysis, which can easily verify their results. Students often get obviously wrong answers, e.g. (2,4), even if they did graph correctly. They just didn't look at the picture and grasp what it was telling them. The point of intersection looks to be around (½, 2). So, when they calculate and get x = 3/10 , y = 11/5, they should hopefully realize that this is right. Don't let them give only decimal answers; make them also give fractional.

Another worthwhile application is being able to find the graph of a perpendicular line, which intersects this one shown in Figure 12, at a given point, say (1,5). Can they get the slope (Δy/Δx) and y-intercept of the first line? Then, they need to learn about reciprocals, negative ones, and if they forget the negative (as many wish to do), insist that they graph their final results and that picture and numbers agree.

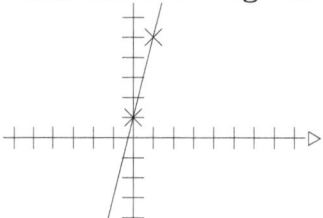

Figure 12, Finding slope, equation and perpendicular intercept, with fractions.

We can have students graph, work fractions, and calculate negatives, more than we are doing today – and all without a calculator. It is awesome for their understanding. It's just too bad to see them in the end, when given the choice, still with a calculator in hand. Well, you can lead a horse to water but you can't make him think!

One of the reasons why they must work with negatives, and with positive and negative results of square roots, is when it comes to solving the quadratic formula.

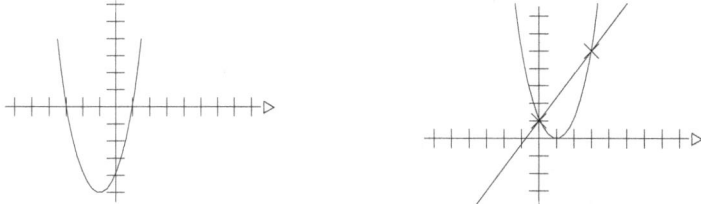

Figure 13 Using the quadratic formula to find intercepts

The two graphs in Figure 13 use the quadratic formula, to see where the parabola crosses the x-axis, or to find the points of intercept with other graphs. The steps needed to do this should go hand in hand with the drawing of graphs. Get the students to calculate, get them to draw. Several who don't like the former probably like the latter, and vice-versa. All of them, when it means extra work, will smile with delight at the thought.

Most importantly, when we math teachers rush through this work, we must realize that those students who seem very slow at it, might possibly be doing *exquisite* work. We should circulate and take a look. Those supposedly D or F students often do amazing graphs, with several colors. It looks neat, is fun, and easier to understand. But it takes time to make. The geniuses have the work done a long time earlier, but it is often sloppy, curt, and unreadable. We mustn't worry about holding them back. Tell them to improve the quality of their work.

We should give extra testing time also, to accommodate these slower, more diligent people. Remember, the tortoise won!

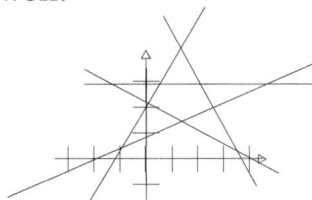
Figure 14 Picture created by five lines.

With graphing, we can get students to understand how to read a graph, and write an equation, or how to draw a picture from an equation. By drawing images like Figure 14, we are playing, making something other than just empty lines.

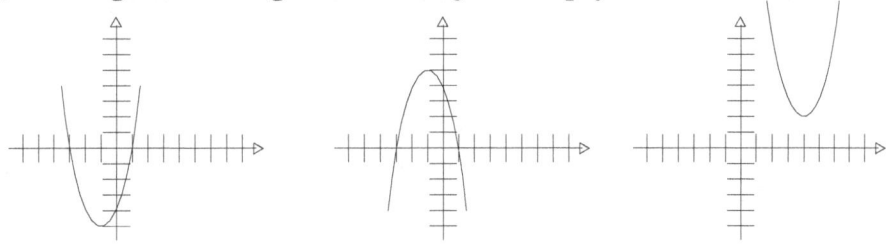
Figure 15 Positive/negative parabolas. The 3rd graph has a negative $b^2 - 4ac$.

Every figure has a formula and every formula generates a line, or curve. What about the parabola that curves downward? Or a line that does not rise from left to right but drops? How do negatives affect equations? What kind of parabola does not cross the x-axis? Students learn that the square root of a negative number doesn't exist, until they are introduced to complex numbers. When using the quadratic formula, if we get a negative inside the radical, it means there is no solution. In other words, the graph doesn't cross the axis. Does the picture agree, or should the student go back and recalculate? The ones who should probably won't, or still can't.

Graphing: another friend!

The difference between x^2 and x^3

An interesting problem in Calculus is to find the area defined by the graphs x^2 and x^3. To find an area, it must be known which curve lies above the other, and their points of intercept. The graphs have to be investigated, primarily in the fractional region between $x = 0$ and $x = 1$. This challenges the students to square and cube fractional values, and thus is yet another "helpful" example.

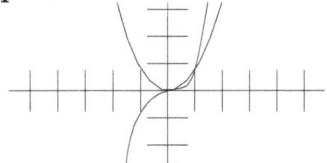
Figure 16 The graph of x^2 and x^3.

Circumscribed circle, centroid, and inscribed circle

Work with fractions, graphical analysis, and processes can be taken further, and should. Once students have learned all of these techniques, have them draw three lines on a graph, making a triangle, for which they must find the center of a circumscribed circle, the centroid, and the center of an inscribed circle. They were shown how to do this in grade school, with a compass, though it doesn't mean they learned it or remember it. Regardless, now we will find the points through calculation instead of drawing. This will be the culmination of working with fractions, negatives, and graphing, at least for now.

First find the corners. Again, this means setting equations equal to each other. We spend a lot of time in Algebra class working equations such as 5x + 2 = 3x + 4 (and ever harder versions), but not a lot of time showing that one big application is to find where lines meet. This is the part that students in later years can lack.

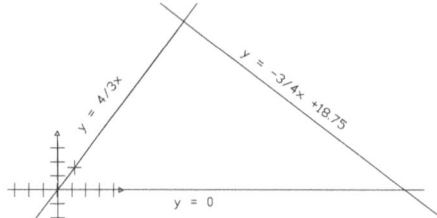

Figure 17 Three equations: 90° and horizontal line intended (Jan Greis – student).

This set of lines works really well, despite one y-intercept being 18¾. Blame the student who developed this problem. Our first step will be to find the points of the triangle, where each pair of lines meet. The first of these is extremely easy:

$$y = 0 \stackrel{set}{=} 4/3x.$$

Therefore, x = 0 and our first point is (0,0), as it looks on the graph. Have the students write the word "set" above their work, so that they show their understanding of what they are doing, and why.

By similar processes:

$$\frac{-3x}{4} + \frac{75}{4} \stackrel{set}{=} 0 \quad \text{gives } x = 25 \text{ and therefore } (25,0)$$

And finally, $\frac{4x}{3} \stackrel{set}{=} \frac{-3x}{4} + \frac{75}{4}$ gives x = 9 and y = 12: (9,12)

Having our three corners, we may proceed. In order to draw a circle which will encompass all three, the student should remember from elementary education that they must bisect each side of the triangle, draw perpendicular lines through these midpoints and calculate where these lines meet to find the center of the circle.

To begin, use the Midpoint formula: $M(x,y) = \left(\frac{x_1 + x_2}{2}, \frac{y_1 + y_2}{2}\right)$

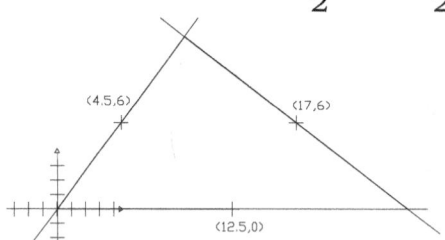

Figure 18 Midpoints of the three sides

We will obtain from our calculations that the leftmost midpoint is $M_1(4.5,6)$, the rightmost; $M_2(17,6)$ and the bottom; $M_3(12.5,0)$. (Figure 18) We next find the perpendicular lines through these points. Here is a valuable usage of fractions. The students must use the negative reciprocals of the slopes of each line, which always seems to be a challenge with regard to that horizontal line. What is the negative reciprocal of 0 slope? A vertical line is clearly the result, the slope of which is undefined, being infinitely positive and negative at the same time. This line's equation is x = 12.5. Though they may struggle here, the result is completely simple.

We then consider the line through M_1. It will have a slope of –3/4. We need to plug the M_1 coordinates, with this slope, into the equation y = mx + b. The result will be b = 9⅜. Repeating these steps for M_2 with a slope of 4/3 will result in b = –16⅔. So our three equations are:

$$y = \frac{-3x}{4} + \frac{75}{8} \qquad y = \frac{4x}{3} - \frac{50}{3} \qquad x = 12\frac{1}{2}$$

32

Now, we could use our calculator, except that 4/3 as a decimal, rounded off, will introduce some slight error, which retaining the fractions won't. We could also take the "shortcut" of plugging 12½ into one of the equations to solve for "y". Actually, let's do both:

$$y = \frac{-3x}{4} + \frac{75}{8} \stackrel{set}{=} \frac{4x}{3} - \frac{50}{3} \quad \text{or} \quad y = \frac{4(25)}{3(2)} - \frac{50}{3} \quad = \rightarrow 0$$

Both of these require a little thought, and a lot of experience with our friend, the fraction. Did they think to multiply the first equation through by 24? Or, did they add fractions, to then try to get common denominators, and finally multiply by the reciprocal in front of "x"? For the "simpler" case, were they able to work the fractions?

These exercises can reinforce the need to understand fractions. Try them with your students and you will see it.

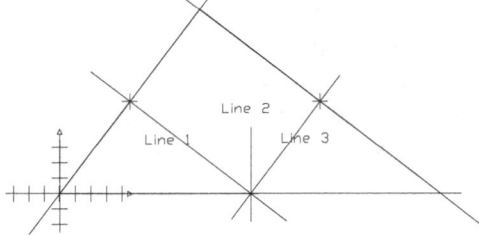

Figure 19 Perpendicular lines at Midpoints make the center of the circle.

We can now draw in our circle, and confirm that it touches each of the three endpoints. We need to find the radius now, which means using the distance formula, which is really just the Pythagorean Theorem:

$$r = \sqrt{(x_2 - x_1)^2 + (y_2 - y_1)^2}$$

We can easily calculate the radius here, as the center and two other points are on the x-axis. But, in most instances, this will not be the case and we will need to use the distance formula. Our result is r = 12.5.

Finally, the equation for the circle: $(x - 12.5)^2 + y^2 = 156.25$

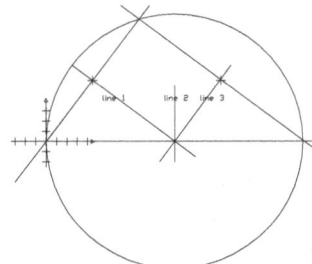

Figure 20 The circumscribed circle.

Centroid

While we have the midpoints fresh in our mind, we can then "quickly" obtain the center of gravity for our triangle. In this case, we must draw lines through the midpoints, to each corner. It should be seen that we need to obtain the slope of each line, then the y-intercept, and finally, set two equations equal to each other to find the center. Of course, we can set two other lines equal to confirm our results, or *at least* look at the graph to check if the numbers seem correct. Even this is often overlooked, and that is why we emphasize that they draw these things.

We find the slopes with our fraction friend: $m = \frac{(y_2 - y_1)}{(x_2 - x_1)}$

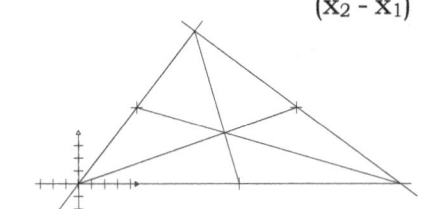

Figure 21 The centroid or center of gravity.

Eventually, in our case study we have these equations (the slopes and intercepts are painful but workable):

$$y = \frac{6x}{17} \qquad y = \frac{-12x}{41} + \frac{300}{41} \qquad y = \frac{-24x}{7} + \frac{300}{7}$$

And this for our center:

$$\frac{6x}{17} \stackrel{set}{=} \frac{-12x}{41} + \frac{300}{41} \quad \rightarrow \quad x = \frac{34}{3}$$

Thus, we get (11⅓, 4), which is the same as what we obtain from the easier route of:

$$\frac{(x_1 + x_2 + x_3)}{3}, \frac{(y_1 + y_2 + y_3)}{3}$$

Certainly, getting the average of the endpoints is much easier. But, if we want to show the need for working with fractions, this is a superb exercise. The students can only benefit from this work, and the last exercise will challenge them still. All of the work shown here is made simpler by the horizontal line and right angle in the triangle. Even greater challenge can be given when we use non-vertical/horizontal lines.

Inscribed circle

Now begins the biggest of challenges and a great learning exercise. We can easily bisect the angles with a compass. But how by calculation? By relating the slope of each line, via $\tan^{-1}$, to an angle. When we figure the angle of each line, we get an average of the two at each vertex, and retake the tangent to get the slope of their bisector. Easy!

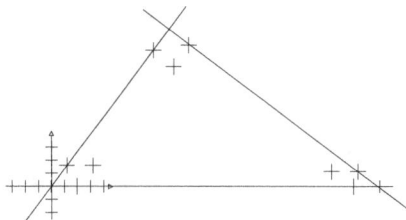

Figure 22 Bisecting the angles.

For this case study, the line $y = 0$ has an angle of 0°. The line of slope 4/3 has an angle of 53.1° and the last line has an angle of −36.9°. To get bisector 'a' (Figure 23), add 0° and −36.9° and divide by two to have −18.45°, which we take the tangent of to get m_a = - 0.333 (at this point its usually unavoidable to use decimal numbers, though here we have 1/3). We find that m_b = Tan (26.5°) = .5 or 1/2.

The last part is the trick. We add 53.1° and −36.9° to get 16.2° and divide by 2 to get 8.1° We need to recognize that this is not however the bisector that we seek. Graphically, it bears to the right and slightly upward from the point of intercept, disagreeing with the image. So, the students must use *logic* and subtract 90° to get an angle of −81.9° and hence slope m_c = −7 (In the text, we rounded off the angles. However, the numbers were kept intact in the calculator and gave results of 1/3, 1/2 and −7.)

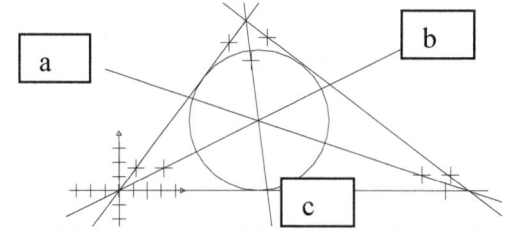

Figure 23 Intercepting bisectors and Inscribed circle.

Whew! Having the slopes, we use the equation $y = mx + b$, each individual slope and the coordinates of the point of intercept (the vertices). We obtain three line equations (we only need two). They all work but, let's use the fractions for the practice…

34

Bisector "a" will be y = – ⅓x + 8⅓ and "b" will have y = ½x. We set them equal, multiply through by 6 to clear the denominator and find the intercept at x = 10, y = 5. Having the midpoint of the horizontal line directly below this easily provides us the radius of the circle as being 5, and so we could finish and record the equation of the inscribed circle. But, what if the students don't have such an easy case study? They must find a line going from the center of the circle and intercepting one of the sides of the triangle perpendicularly at a point not yet determined. We must then do the distance formula from this point to the center.

For these processes, we see over and over the need to manipulate equations, work with fractions, confirm results or even make judgments based on analyzing the graph.

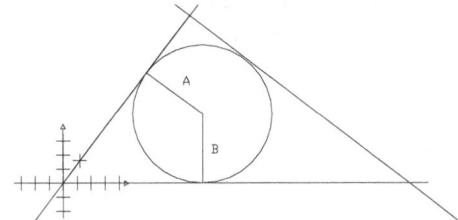

Figure 24 Perpendicular intercepting radial lines.

Figure 24 shows line "A". One coordinate of this radial is our center (10,5). Also, the radial line is perpendicular to the line y = 4x/3, so its slope is –3/4 (again the negative reciprocal). We can calculate its equation (5 = – ¾(10) + b) to get: y = –¾x + 12½. Next,

$$y = -¾x + 12½ \overset{set}{=} 4x/3 \quad \text{gives us x and y of (6,8)}$$

Now put (6,8) and the center (10,5) into the distance formula to confirm that the radius is 5. Finally, we have achieved:

$(x – 10)^2 + (y-5)^2 = 25$ Looks just like the graph.

Lastly, the case where no lines have parallel relations, nor are vertical or horizontal. The work is the same as above, but much (much) more detailed!

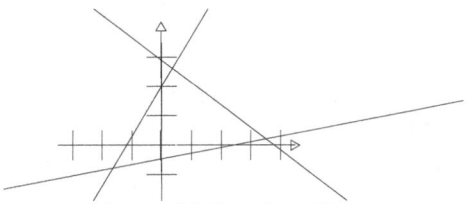

Figure 25 Random lines.

Fun with bisectors

Previously, we might have noted an interesting occurrence when bisecting the lines of slope -3/4 and 4/3. The bisectors were reasonable fractions of –1/3 and 1/2 (respectively). We see right off that the bisector does not have a slope exactly half of the original. The angle is half but slopes don't correspond, though in some cases we can guide the students through interesting discoveries.

Let's try a similar process, with the 5-12-13 Pythagorean triangle. When we bisect lines whose slopes are 5/12 or 12/5, we find that the bisectors have "nice" slopes of 1/5 and 2/3. Go thru the Pythagorean triangles; 3-4-5, 5-12-13, 7-24-25 and so forth to find amazing patterns, shown in Table1.

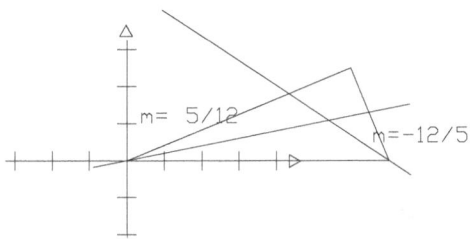

Figure 26 Bisectors of angles created by lines of slope 5/12 and –12/5.

Are there cases other than Pythagorean triangles that are interesting? If we bisect the 45° angle, whose slope is 1, to get 22.5° and take the tangent, we get approximately 0.414 This looks familiar. Did anyone recognize it as √2 −1?

What happens if the slope is 2? The bisector will have a slope of 0.618, the value of Φ − 1 (or 1/Φ). Can we guess at a slope of 3? Could it have something to do with √3? Almost. It is 99.35% of √3 − 1. Its even closer to e − 2, but neither is exact. What is?

We can investigate fractional slopes. What happens if we bisect an angle whose upper line has a slope of 1/2? The bisector has slope of 0.236 . Can anyone find this one? It is 1/Φ³ .

There are possibly, probably, other interesting slope/bisector relationships to discover. Where else might simple fractions, and functions of √2, √3 and Φ, lie lurking; waiting? For now, see the values in Table 1 and look for patterns in the triangle slopes and other unique places. Notice the prime numbers.

	Line slope	Bisector slope		Line slope	Bisector slope
Pytha-gorean Triangles	3/4	1/3	Patterns in √2, √3 and Φ	1	(√2−1)/1 = √2 − 1
	5/12	1/5		2	(√5−1)/2 = Φ − 1
	7/24	1/7		3	(√10 − 1)/3
	9/40	1/9		4	(√17 − 1)/4
				x	(√(x^2 + 1) − 1)/x
				2(1+√3/3)	√3 − 1
Reciprocals	4/3	1/2		√2/2	√3 − √2
	12/5	2/3		√3/3	2 − √3
	24/7	3/4		1/2	1/Φ³ or √5 − 2
	40/9	4/5		√2	(√3 − 1)/√2
			Radicals and primes	2√2	√2/2
				√3 or √3/1	√3/3
				√5/2	√5/5
				√7/3	√7/7
				√11/5	√11/11
				√13/6	√13/13
				√17/8	√17/17

Table 1 Interesting bisectors with "whole" values.

Concluding dialogue

These last have been exhaustive exercises which required that the student be able to think, calculate, and work with fractions, radicals, negatives, and graphing.

How are student understanding of fractions, negatives and graphing vital to their work in mathematics and the sciences? What types of things could we do to show their relevance? How could we create applications that are interesting and rewarding just for their challenge? Hopefully, the text here has given a great deal of justification and method on why and how to use fractions, negatives and graphing.

Additional reading and resources:
http://www.maxlearning.net/default.htm   Great source for materials on creative teaching of key math topics by a fellow enthusiast.

Class Exercise 1   **Fractional exposition**

Objective:
Review fractional multiplication as an introduction to direct application. Pull together a number of themes covered in primary education.

Procedure:
a) Give students a variety of fractions to multiply, like:
$$\frac{1}{2} \times \frac{1}{3} = \qquad \frac{2}{3} \times \frac{4}{5} = \qquad \frac{3}{4} \times 2 =$$

Ensure that they remember that fractions multiply straight across.
b) Continue with further problems like:
$$\frac{3}{8} \times \frac{4}{9} = \qquad \frac{55}{81} \times \frac{9}{22} = \qquad \frac{3y}{10} \times \frac{5}{6y} =$$

See that they properly reduce first, and then multiply across.
c) Explain reciprocals and find them for such fractions as:
$$\frac{1}{5y} \qquad \frac{3}{6} \qquad \frac{1}{5} \qquad \frac{x}{4} \qquad \frac{2}{x}$$

d) Clear fractional equations through multiplication by reciprocals:
$$\frac{3x}{5} = 6 \qquad \frac{2x}{7} = \frac{4}{5}$$

e) Work through division by y/x being the same as multiplication by x/y.

Homework:
Provide problems for reducing fractions to lowest terms, multiplication/division of fractions, and algebraic equations involving fractional coefficients. (Note: Never review addition/subtraction of fractions at the same time as multiplication/division. Those who can handle the varied rules already got it, the others still won't.)

Evaluation:
Most high school students will need review. Many will need only slight review before they can work independently. Make part of their grade based on how they help others. Take homework and have them trade, grading each other's work, seeing how someone else did it.

Bridges:
High school students in calculus struggle with derivatives of fractional exponents. Routine application and conversions (in chemistry and physics) involving fractional operations often seem intimidating.

Class Exercise 2   **Review with negatives**

Objective:
Revisit negative numbers, so exponents and application to scientific notation challenge students only as something new, not building upon an area in which they are often weak.

Procedure:
a) For students who don't understand negatives, instead of a number line, go through operations using a thermometer. For example, "The temperature is 5 degrees, what does a 15 degree drop result in?"
b) Do problems like: -5 + 3 = , -5 – 3 = , and -5 + (-3) = . The answers to these intentionally easy problems are –2 or –8. Consider:
- 5 + 3 and 5 – 3 result in only 8 and 2. All possible combinations, whether positive or negative, will not see some other result, say "–4".
- In the first two cases, it is a positive 3 that we are either adding or subtracting, and we don't put a + sign in front of such a number.
- Subtracting a positive gives the same result as adding a negative. Negative numbers "add" like positives, but with a negative answer.
c) Solve a problem like -3x – 1 = -2x + 3. We get conditioned to have "x" on the left side, even if we end up with a " –x" to deal with. Negatives are often lost in the process. We need to be able to work both sides of an equation, identifying the greater valued "x" term and proceeding.

Homework:
Assign various problems from the textbook requiring addition/subtraction of negatives. (Note: be careful when assigning addition/subtraction of negatives at the same time as multiplication/division. Some struggle a lot with the varied rules. Assign equations where the variable on the right side of the equation will be of greater numeric value (both variables can be negative).

Evaluation:
When they bring the problems to class, have them trade papers and grade them together. Let students be in the place to decide if a problem is answered correctly and what "grade" each person should get.

Bridges:
In physics and chemistry, students often struggle with numbers of large scale. A better working knowledge of negatives and fractions helps everyone. Non-mathematical students often don't connect to this in grade school and a second chance, at greater maturity, can help.

Class Exercise 3   **Negative exponents - Scientific Notation**

Objective:
Review exponential operations, including negatives, to improve problem-solving skills in the sciences, particularly scientific notation.

Procedure:
a) We begin by reviewing rules of multiplication, division and raising of exponents to higher orders. Provide textbook problems such as:
$$x^2 \cdot x^3 = \quad , \quad \frac{x^5}{x^2} = \quad , \quad \text{and } (x^4)^2$$
b) Once they have reviewed the "basics", have them work through more complex problems, and those with negative exponents, such as

$$\frac{x^7 y^{-4} z^2 \cdot x^{-3} y^2 z^{-3}}{x^{-1} y^3 z^5 \quad x^{-5} y^4 z^2} \qquad \frac{10^{-11} \text{ Nm}^2/\text{kg}^2 \cdot 10^{30} \text{ kg} \cdot 10^{24} \text{ kg}}{(10^{11} \text{m})^2}$$

Encourage them to first identify the greater value exponent. We don't want them locked into only working above the line. If the larger exponent is in the denominator, they need to see that they can reduce or increase it. E.g.: $\dfrac{x^2}{x^5} = \dfrac{1}{x^3}$ and $\dfrac{x^{-3}}{x^2} = \dfrac{1}{x^5}$

Everywhere we need to show how numbers, variables *and* labels cancel.

Homework:
Assign various problems from the textbook requiring addition/subtraction of negative exponents in increasing complexity. Assign equations where the variable in the denominator will be of greater numeric value.

Evaluation:
When they bring the problems to class, have them trade papers and ...

Bridges:
Exponents and related operations are the basis for understanding logarithms, manipulating derivatives and integrals, and work with large scale numbers in physics and chemistry. All students need their review.

Class Exercise 4   **Fractional and negative exponents**

Objective:
Work problems involving roots and their equivalent fractional exponents, to improve problem-solving skills via applications of fractions – thus a greater complexity.

Procedure:
a) Have students solve fractional exponential problems like:
$$x^{1/2} y^{1/2} z^{1/2} \cdot x^{2/3} y^{1/3} z^{2/3} = \qquad \frac{x^{2/3} y^{1/2} z^{1/3}}{x^{1/2} y^{1/3} z^{2/3}} =$$

b) Have them convert the radicals into fractional exponents, solve and return back into radical form: $\sqrt[4]{x^3 y^2 z^5} \cdot \sqrt[3]{x^2 y z^2}$

c) Review how to clear a radical from the denominator:
$$\frac{1}{\sqrt{2}} \cdot \frac{\sqrt{2}}{\sqrt{2}} = \frac{\sqrt{2}}{2}$$
Have them do it with complex radicals. Here, they need to see that we don't multiply the final denominator by the same quantity but one that will raise the exponential value to '1'.
$$\frac{\sqrt[6]{x^3 y^4 z^5} \cdot \sqrt[3]{x^4 y z^2}}{\sqrt[4]{x^{-1} y^2 z^{-4}}} \qquad \frac{\sqrt[5]{x^{-4} y^3 z^2} \cdot \sqrt[3]{x^2 y z^2}}{\sqrt[4]{x^3 y^{-2} z^3} \cdot \sqrt[4]{x^2 y^{-3} z^5}}$$

Homework:
Assign various problems from the textbook.

Evaluation:
When they bring the problems to class, have them trade papers and ...

Bridges:
These are "brain twisters" and give great challenge to all students, as long as they have had good preparation. Otherwise, they continue the frustration that mathematics can provide.

Class Exercise 5   **Fun with fractions**

Objective:
"Fractions are our friends". Let's play with them and prepare students for conversions and complex operations involving fractional exponents. Though this follows the lesson plans for fractional multiplication, it is strongly recommended that other material be placed in between, allowing a separation of concepts and rules.

Procedure:
a) Give students the Eye of Horus (figure 3). Have them total up the individual pieces for an answer (63/64). Where do they see fractions like these today? (inches and ounces) Why does the Eye not total '1'?
b) Have them divide a circle to express the sum of 1/2 + 1/3 + 1/6 (figure 5a). They see that the sum is '1'. Show how to obtain this answer.
c) Read a musical scale (figure 9) and calculate the total of fractional notes in the top line (use figure 8).
d) Review addition and subtraction and how it involves multiplication by fractions having a value of '1', such as 2/2, 4/4 and x/x. (Note: this is why we strengthen multiplication before we do addition.)
e) Review addition/subtraction with mixed numbers.

Homework:
Assign textbook problems involving addition/subtraction of fractions and mixed number. For extra credit have them do the following: Get a piece of sheet music and add the notes. Draw the following using polygons:

$$\frac{1}{12} + \frac{1}{8} + \frac{1}{6} + \frac{1}{4} + \frac{1}{3} + \frac{1}{2}$$

Evaluation:
In class, have them trade papers and grade them together. Let students be in the place to decide if a problem is answered correctly and what "grade" each person should get.
Reward extra credit efforts generously, and especially applaud any "weaker" students who choose to do it. This is a chance to pull in those who are gifted in other realms, and are trying harder than results sometimes show.

Bridges:
When multiplying such things as $\sqrt{xyz} \cdot \sqrt[3]{x^2yz^2}$, we solve with fractional exponents. To improve understanding of trigonometric ratios we will perform the Pythagorean Theorem with fractions.

Class Exercise 6   **Conversions**

Objective:
Use fractional techniques to convert various quantities to other "values".

Procedure:
a) Ask the students what the following have in common: (they technically equal '1')

$$\frac{2}{2} \qquad \frac{x}{x} \qquad \frac{\sqrt{3}}{\sqrt{3}} \qquad \frac{180°}{\pi \text{ radians}} \qquad \frac{5280 \text{ ft}}{1 \text{ mile}} \qquad \frac{16 \text{ oz.}}{1 \text{ pint}}$$

b) Review the steps needed to get common denominators for say, 1/5 + 1/6. or to convert 1/√3 to √3/3. When numerator and denominator are identical, we are multiplying by a factor of 1, changing nothing.

c) Discuss equivalent terms; set 5280 feet equal to 1 mile and divide through by one of them. We see that 5280 ft./1 mile is in fact '1'.

d) Multiply various fractions, looking to cancel before multiplying:

$$\frac{55}{81} \cdot \frac{9}{22} = \qquad \frac{5xy}{8z} \cdot \frac{16}{7x} = \qquad \frac{\sqrt{3}}{5} \cdot \frac{15}{\sqrt{6}} =$$

e) Proceed with conversions, showing the steps, as the following example demonstrates:
    40 fps (feet per second) to mph (miles per hour)

$$\frac{40 \text{ feet}}{\text{second}} \;\Big|\; \frac{1 \text{ mile}}{5280 \text{ feet}} \;\Big|\; \frac{3600 \text{ sec}}{1 \text{ hour}} = \frac{25 \text{ miles}}{\text{hour}}$$

Homework:
Assign conversion problems from a variety of math- science text books.

Evaluation:
When they bring the problems to class, have them trade papers and grade them together. Let students be in the place to decide if a problem is answered correctly and what "grade" each person should get. The teacher can assess completeness of work and effort.

Bridges:
To understand angular velocity and trigonometric graphing the student must be able to convert from degrees to radians. In science conversion is necessary between various units of measure. Further, monetary conversion is a real-life application. Conversions never miss, as they show terms that will cancel.

Class Exercise 7   **Graphing fractional slopes and intercepts**

Objective:
See how to graph a fractional slope. Learn how to determine perpendicular lines. See how to graph with fractions.

Procedure:
a) Graph $y = 2x + 1$. From the y-intercept, we count up two and over one. This is the "fractional" value of 2/1 in front of the x-term. Next, graph:

$$y = \frac{x}{2} + 2 \quad \text{and} \quad y = \frac{2x}{3} + 3 \quad \text{and} \quad y = \frac{-3x}{4} - \frac{1}{2}$$

The fraction in front of x still determines how to count the slope.

b) Review the reciprocals, for example, when dividing by a fraction, that we multiply by the reciprocal, or that in working an equation like:

$$\frac{4x}{3} + 4 = 7 \quad \text{we first subtract the 4 and then multiply by } \frac{3}{4}.$$

c) Instruct on the concept that in graphing equations, negative reciprocals of the slopes indicate perpendicularity. For example:

$$y = \frac{2x}{3} + 3 \quad \text{and} \quad y = \frac{-3x}{2} + 4 \quad \text{are perpendicular}$$

Set these equations equal to find the x value, and use this to get the y value of the coordinates of intersection. Ugh, (6/13, 43/13). Fractions!

d) Graph the equation $y = 2x + 1$. Find the line perpendicular whose y-intercept is -2. Graph to confirm. This is a fairly easy example. Others of more strenuous nature can also be given.

Homework:
Assign reciprocal problems and various perpendicular graphing problems from a math textbook.

Evaluation:
When they bring the problems to class, have them trade papers and grade them together. Assess the quality of their graphs and effort.

Bridges:
When trying to find centroids and to graph circumscribed circles, it is vital that students understand the methods contained here. In design and manufacture, perpendicular relations are important.

Class Exercise 8   **Graphing with negative numbers**

Objective:
See how the negative inverts a graph, and indicates opposite direction, or function such as accel/decel. See what a negative discriminant means.

Procedure:
a) Review/introduce that there are two solutions (±), to $\sqrt{\ }$, $\sqrt[4]{\ }$, $\sqrt[6]{\ }$ etc. :
   $\sqrt{25} = \pm 5$, $\sqrt[4]{16} = \pm 2$, $\sqrt[6]{64} = \pm 2$
b) Graph $y = x + 1$, $y = x^2$, $y = x^3$, $y = 1/x$, $y = \sin x$ etc.
c) Now, graph $y = -x + 1$, $y = -x^2$, $y = -x^3$, $y = -1/x$, $y = -\sin x$. The students should see that the negative sign simply inverts the graph.
d) Two typical physics formulae are $v_f^2 = v_i^2 + 2ad$ and $d = v_i t + \frac{1}{2}at^2$. Here, direction and deceleration can make negative quantities. For example; a car moving to the left at 10 m/s is decelerating by 2 m/s², over a distance of 20m. Here, $v_f^2 = (-10 \text{m/s})^2 + 2(-(-2 \text{ m/s}^2))(-10 \text{ m/s})$. Deceleration is negative, but in the negative direction makes it positive! Squaring the velocity; negative due to direction, gives a positive. In the end, $v_f^2 = 60 \text{ m}^2/\text{s}^2$. The square root is 7.75 m/s, and the student must *decide* that it is negative, due to its direction. In gravitational problems "a" (we use g), and y are also negative.
e) Graph $y = x^2 + 6x + 8$. The quadratic formula, gives –2 and –4 as the x intercepts. If we factor, we obtain $(x+2)(x+4)$. Who can explain the difference? Use the quadratic formula on $y = x^2 + 6x + 10$. What does it mean when $b^2 + 4ac$ is a negative quantity? It gives information that the parabola does not cross the x-axis.

Homework:
Assign a variety of negative problems, graphs and physics applications from math and physics textbooks.

Evaluation:
When they bring the problems to class, have them trade papers and grade them together. Assess quality, completeness and effort.

Bridges:
In solving equations, students often make mistakes with positive and negative. Drawing a graph could confirm results. Slow them down, and get them to do it. Further, the physics problems make the student put down the calculator and think about what the answer *should* be.

Class Exercise 9   **Circumscribing a circle**

Objective:
Fully apply the learning from this chapter, particularly on finding perpendicular lines.

Procedure:
a) Draw three lines on one graph. $y = 2x + 1$, $y = -x + 7$ and $y = \frac{1}{2}x - 2$. Find points of intersection by setting two equations at a time equal to each other, eg. $2x + 1 = -x + 7$. We obtain, (2,5),(6,1) and (-2,-3). Calculate midpoints: $M = (x_2+x_1)/2, (y_2+y_1)/2$. (0,1), (4,3) and (2,-1)
b) Using another color, draw perpendicular lines through these midpoints. Their intersection is the center of the circumbscribed circle. How to calculate it? Each of these new lines has a slope which is the negative reciprocal of the line it crosses. Put this, and the respective midpoint coordinate into y=mx+b to get equations for the three lines: $y = -\frac{1}{2}x + 1$, $y = x - 1$ and $y = -2x + 3$. Set two of these equal to each other. Confirm by plugging the numbers into each equation, set two other equations equal, and/or look at the graph. (4/3,1/3)
c) Calculate the distance to one of the vertexes of the original triangle, using the distance formula (Pythagorean theorem) $d = \sqrt{(x_2-x_1)^2 + (y_2+y_1)^2}$ We obtain from this $d = \sqrt{200/9}$. Not a problem as the final result gets squared anyway in the circle equation. Thus, we have as our final equation: $(x - 4/3)^2 + (y - 1/3)^2 = 200/9$

Homework:
Provide one problem with reasonable solutions. Have the students, as a major project, then create lines and equations for a second problem. Somewhere, they will have to deal with fractions and negatives.

Evaluation:
Grade their homework carefully, noting its correctness and also how well they came up with their own equations, solved them and finally presented the work. This will be a major effort.

Bridges:
A significant amount of learning goes into this problem, as students are applying just about everything they learned from algebra. Thus, it is a significant application assignment.

Class Exercise 10   **Finding the centroid**

Objective:
Work with line equations to find the center of a triangle.

Procedure:
a) Draw again $y = 2x + 1$, $y = -x + 7$ and $y = \frac{1}{2}x - 2$. Find their points of intersection by setting two equations at a time equal to each other,
eg. $2x + 1 = -x + 7$. We obtain, (2,5),(6,1) and (-2,-3).
Calculate midpoints using $M = ((x_2+x_1)/2, (y_2+y_1)/2)$. This gives (0,1), (4,3) and (2,-1)
b) Using another color, draw lines through these midpoints to opposite corners of the triangle. Their intersection is the center of gravity. How to calculate it? Each of these new lines has a slope which can be determined from $m = (y_2-y_1)/(x_2-x_1)$. Use corresponding vertex-midpoint values. Put this m, and one of the two coordinates into y=mx+b to get equations for the two lines: $y=1$ (m=0) and $y = x - 1$.

Note, x = 2 will be hard to obtain from the slope formula but not from the graph. Normally, we set two of these equal to each other. But, it can be readily seen that the centroid is (2,1)

Homework:
Combine this with the homework given in assignment 9: one problem from the teacher and one that the student creates.

Evaluation:
Grade their homework carefully, noting its correctness, but also how well they came up with their own equations, solved them and finally presented the work. This will be a major effort.

Bridges:
A significant amount of learning goes into this problem, as students are applying just about everything they learned from algebra. Thus, it is a significant application assignment. Note, the centroid could be obtained by M = (($x_3+x_2+x_1$)/3, ($y_3+y_2+y_1$)/3), which is much too easy.

Class Exercise 11   **Inscribing a circle**

Objective:
Key application of Algebra *and* Trigonometry. Bisectors and Angles.

Procedure:
a) Draw again y = 2x + 1, y = –x + 7 and y = ½x – 2. Find their points of intersection; (2,5),(6,1) and (-2,-3).
b) Now bisect the angle at each vertex. This step converts slope, $\tan^{-1}$, to an angle, providing angles of 63.435°, -45° and 26.565°. Average the angles at each intersection: (2,5); 9.217°, (6,1); -9.217°, and (-2,-3); 45°. Note, that at point (2,5), the bisector of the lines is outside of the triangle. So, we must subtract 90° to get -80.8°. Take the tangent of these angles to get slopes of -6.16, -0.16 and 1, respectively.
c) Put each slope and its intersecting point into y=mx+b to obtain angle bisector equations: y=x-1, y=-6.16x+17.34 and y=-0.162x+1.972.
d) To get the center of the inscribed circle, set any two equations equal to each other and then confirm. (2.56, 1.56). The hard part is to get the radius and equation for this circle, tangential to each side of the triangle.
e) Get a line perpendicular to at least one of the sides using the negative reciprocal for its slope. Put it, with the center point, into y=mx+b to get an equation, set equal to the line it crosses to get the intersection. eg: y = 2x + 1. The perpendicular slope is -1/2. Its line equation will then be y = -1/2x + 2.84, intersecting 2x+1 at (0.736, 2.472)
e) Now find the radius, with the distance formula: d = $\sqrt{(x_2-x_1)^2 +(y_2+y_1)^2}$ d = $\sqrt{4.16}$, so the equation of the circle is $(x-2.56)^2 + (y-1.56)^2 = 4.16$

Homework:
Combine this with the homework given in assignment 9: one problem from the teacher and one that the student creates.

Evaluation:
Grade their homework carefully, noting correctness, and how they made their own equations, solved them and presented the work. A major effort.

Bridges:
A significant amount of learning goes into this problem, as students are applying just about everything they learned from algebra and trigonometry.

Class Exercise 12   **Fun with bisectors**

Objective:
Find interesting patterns in bisectors and recurrence of $\sqrt{2}$ and $\sqrt{3}$.

Procedure:
a) Take a slope of 3/4, from the 3-4-5 Pythagorean triangle and calculate the $\tan^{-1}$. Divide this angle and take Tan of the result to get the fraction 1/3. Take the reciprocal; 4/3 and do the same process, resulting in a bisector of 1/2. Do the same with the 5-12-13 triangle, obtaining exact fractional bisectors of 1/5 and 3/4, for 5/12 and 12/5 respectively.
b) Now, let's explore other relations, like whole numbers of 1, 2 and 3. Do the $\tan^{-1}$, divide by 2 and take the Tan. See if the decimal answer, like 0.414, means anything.
c) As students proceed, digging, finding perhaps familiar terms, they find interesting relations with Φ, $\sqrt{2}$ and $\sqrt{3}$, as shown in Table 1.

Homework:
Repeat for the 7-24-25 and 9-40-41 slopes. The students should see that there are developing patterns.

Evaluation:
Grade their homework carefully, noting how well they came up with the patterns.

Bridges:
A significant amount of digging goes into this problem, as students are searching for patterns.

3 ToWers, bridges and fOrms in the Creative Atmosphere

Opening dialogue
How can we let students learn about math through their hands, as well as their heads? What special features are locked inside the Platonic solids?

Getting started
There are products today which can be very helpful for math teachers to explain concepts, and allow students to develop better understanding of things geometrical, while also having fun. Two of these are called Zometools and Astro-Logix. The variety of uses they provide to the classroom are extensive, from chemistry, mathematics, and physics to architecture, art, and computer design. More than that, they are fun.

In this section we will use them to demonstrate the process of building and designing structures, which can then be designed on an architectural drafting software like AutoCad. The exercises help students learn what geometric shapes give strength and how things are made in real life. In the end, they find it interesting competing against other designs and having to go back and redesign their own work when things fail.

Figure 1 Potentials with Zometools.

Picture a high school graduate with his senior project: a bridge built from Zometools, designed on architectural software and presented to a board of teachers (Figure 1). The student came to school with only a vague idea of graduating from high school but finished enrolled in a technical program at university. His parents were *very* happy.

More and more, students want to know why they learn the things schools provide. They want to know how the different concepts fit, and what makes each subject valid.

At the same time, schools and teachers are becoming more intelligent too. Isn't the information age great? Zometools/Astro-Logix are a great way of connecting themes between subjects. The motor-skills, social involvement, colorful nature, and potential are superb for attracting people not normally so gifted in the sciences but capable in realms of arts, athletics, and society. Engaging these students in the general classroom is a lift to the atmosphere.

Platonic forms and atomic modeling
When we first put these products on the table, students really go to them, experimenting freely. There will be time for that later. We will approach this the same as with chapter one. We are not here for freestyle work. First, we will learn how to make form, and then be creative with it. Let the students work in groups of 2-3 people, to discover the Platonic solids, shown in Figure 2a. What do they know about the platonic shapes? What is significant about them?

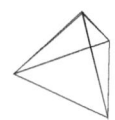    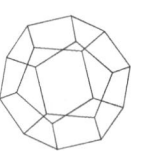

Tetrahedron   Hexahedron(cube)   Octahedron   Icosahedron   Dodecahedron
Figure 2a Plato related them to fire, earth, air, water and the cosmos.

What does it take to make a 3-dimensional shape? With Astro-Logix, we can use 3-, 4-, 5- and 6 - legged joints and begin to construct 3D forms, with no set goal in mind. If students maintain equal side lengths, and equal numbers of legs at each joint, they will see as they install tubes, that they can make triangles, squares, pentagons and hexagons. If they try to fold the structure into 3D only five regular forms can be constructed: the Platonics. No other polygons can be used to make a basic, regular shape (except the Archimedean forms, which are mixtures of polygons).

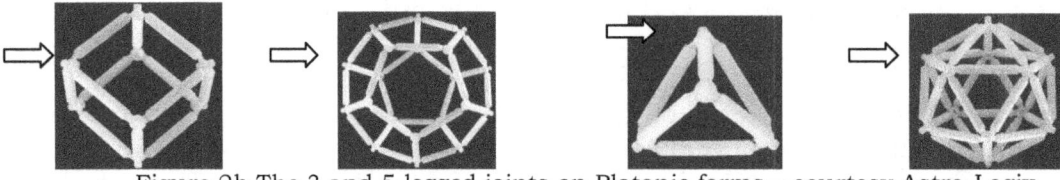

Figure 2b The 3 and 5 legged joints on Platonic forms – courtesy Astro-Logix

Interestingly, words like "atom" and "electron" come from Greek science, as do the names of these five forms, dating 2000 or more years ago. Hand sized stone balls (clearly in the form of Platonic solids) have been unearthed in Scotland, dating back 5000 years.

Figure 3 "Platonic" stones of antiquity (courtesy Graham Challifour and Keith Critchlow – Time Stands Still).

It was not until the last 100 years that atomic and molecular models could be understood. It is taught that certain electron orbitals form an octahedral shape and that the tetrahedron is a fundamental molecular model for chemistry instruction.

At the minutest level, electrons and elements "desire" that they bond. Yet, as they do this, it is a dynamic situation where every like charge tries to get as far away from others as possible. It is an interesting analogy to humans and how we seek partnership, yet struggle when we have it. Dynamic balance.

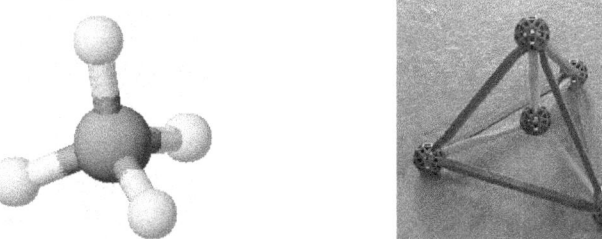

Figure 4 Methane and the Zometool model.

The tetrahedron is great for demonstrating basic molecular modeling. We will begin by using it to demonstrate CH_4: methane. Note the resemblance between the chemical model and the Zometool (Figure 4). To get the central carbon, insert yellow struts within the tetrahedron. Note that everything is equidistant in 3D. How does one calculate distances and angles? This will be answered in Chapter 4.

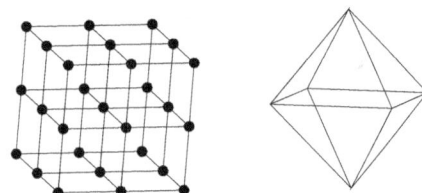

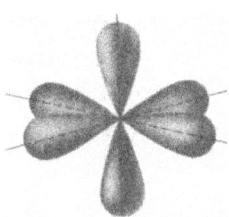

Figure 5 Crystalline structures. Figure 6 Fluorite in natural octahedral shape, electron orbitals.

Now, the cube will be considered. This is the easiest of all the forms to make with Zometools. Salt is represented in its minutest chemical form as NaCl. However, even the smallest visible grain of salt has perhaps millions, more or less, of these individual molecules. Due to the ionic nature of the bonds, each atom of sodium and chlorine interacts with six elements of its opposite. This can easily be demonstrated in cubic or octahedral form.

As this material is placed in water, the elements begin to separate into the solution which becomes an electrolyte. This can be demonstrated by merely pulling away the nodes and associated struts from the structure.

Finally, regarding the platonic solids, it can be noted that many gems and minerals naturally form in these and related shapes. Notably, diamond, in its natural state has the shape of the octahedron, as does fluorite. Maybe we could get the science teachers to study minerals, crystals and key molecular structures concurrent to these activities.

In regard to chemistry, many shapes have benefit. The equilateral triangle, square, and pentagon can be used for the basis of various modeling structures, also the structure of ice, from which students can understand why snowflakes have six points.

Kepler model and relation of 5 basic forms

We can use the five Platonic figures together. Johannes Kepler, in trying to model the solar system, produced a configuration to demonstrate the ever-increasing orbital distances of the planets. He tried to "nest" the Platonic forms where each lay inside the sphere that could contain it. This sphere then touched tangentially on the faces of the next form. The sequence of forms which he chose actually worked out to be fairly close to the correct planetary spacing.

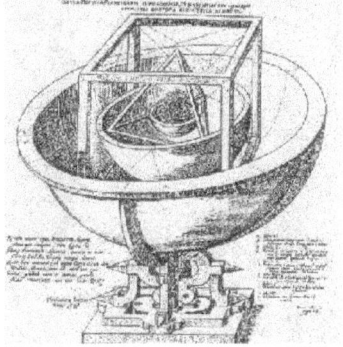

Figure 7a Kepler's model of the planetary spacing –(Mystery of the Cosmos 1596).

Wouldn't it be interesting or even fun if Zometools could do this? The great thing about this product is that so many times, the answer to that question is yes! What follows is a great discovery project for students.

Looking at the objects, where could one begin? When the objects are displayed next to each other, it is seen that the tetrahedron fits perfectly inside the cube. That alone is interesting. Notice too that a second tetrahedron could also be placed inside. (It is suggested that students make a cube with the smallest blues.)

It makes sense that the rather simplistic octahedron could relate somehow here. See if the students can find how. Notice that the cube has eight points, which is the number of sides that the octahedron has. So, a means must be found of connecting the two. Zome doesn't have a central point in the plain of each face, but it has a means to connect to them (using yellows). Let the students discover how to do this.

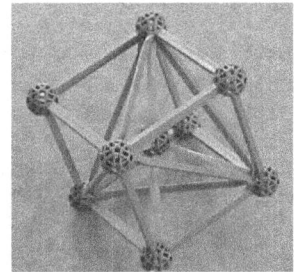 

Figure 7b Tetrahedron in the cube...inside the octahedron, inside an Icosahedron

As the construction process continues, notice that in rotating the octahedron, we could relate its six corners to corresponding corners of the icosahedron, which has 30 points, thus aligning within the icosahedron in many different ways. Considering the internal tetrahedron and its different rotations enables a multitude of possibilities. Presenting this in a picture is difficult, as the image is a mélange of lines.

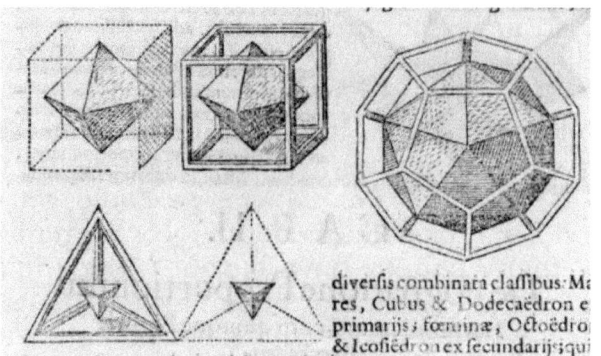

Figure 7c Diagrams showing interaction of Platonic forms (Mystery of the Cosmos).

The students should be encouraged to investigate further with these forms. Do they see that the icosahedron interacts with the dodecahedron? Could we put one inside of the other? (It doesn't matter which.) Perhaps they see that the tetrahedron fits in the dodecahedron. Actually, five of them do, as shown in Figure 7d. In the end, we achieve a nested form, which we can also produce with Astro-Logix (Figure 7e).

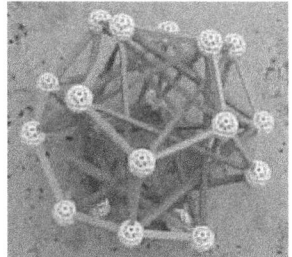 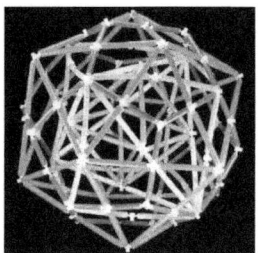

Figure 7d Five tetrahedrons in a dodecahedron.   7e Platonic nest – (Astro Logix).

A final note on the basic Platonics is to have fun shadow casting. Shine a light through a model and look at the shadow on a wall. The two dimensional shapes can all be made to appear hexagonal. We see in Figure 8b that both products can be bought in glow-in-the-dark, great for nighttime with children. The forms can be tied to a string, and twirled, which is fascinating for young children to see as they are falling to sleep.

Figure 8a Shadow-cast of an icosahedron   Figure 8b Astro-Logix icosahedron.

Stellations and transformations to Archimedean shapes.

We can create further from the Platonics, using Zometools/Astro-Logix, beginning with stellating the figures. This means to project the edges to make three dimensional stars. With Zome there are also internal projections which can be made, though they are too busy with lines to be able to present well. Going into the faces is pleasant because it often includes introducing a second color into the piece. There are so many possibilities.

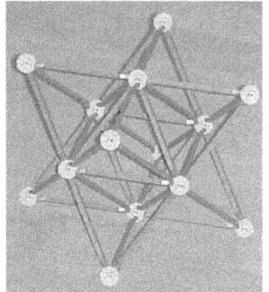 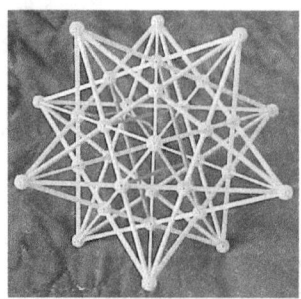 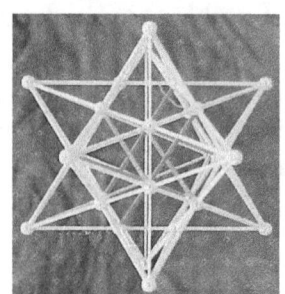

Figure 9a Star tetrahedron and stellated dodecahedron (two different rotations)

Stellations are star forms of the platonic solids, as we saw in Chapter 1. Notice that overlapping two tetrahedrons creates an octahedron inside the model.

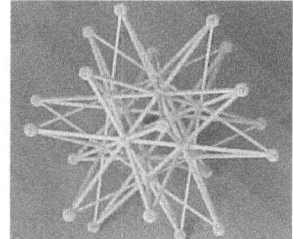 

Figure 9b Stellated Icosahedron. Two views

In Figure 9a are two views of the stellated dodecahedron. It is better to see in beautiful 3D. Notice how it can look like a flat 6- pointed star while actually, as we will see, it consists of three dimensional 5-pointed stars. Truly a fascinating piece and one of the more interesting for displaying the phi geometries, of which more will be introduced. Lastly, explore the complexity and beauty that comes from stellating the icosahedron. We can see it here in Figure 9b, noting exciting similarities to its twin; the dodecahedron.

The Archimedean forms

At the end of the Greek era - beginning of Roman times, a great scientist and mathematician named Archimedes graced the Mediterranean with his knowledge. He stands out as one of the giants of science and is always a good subject to include. Again, this helps pull in students who may have more interest in history than the mathematics and science at hand.

For our concern, Archimedes took the 5 Platonic forms and by cutting off their corners, was able to find 13 additional semi-regular solids. These are different from the Platonics by having at least two different types of face, and yet similar in that each edge has the exact same length, no matter its face.

Many, or all, can be made with Zometools and Astro-Logix. Letting students make these, in groups especially, is a great process, to discover which can be made and which can't, and why. Let them work in teams and make part of their grade for the exercise based on their teamwork.

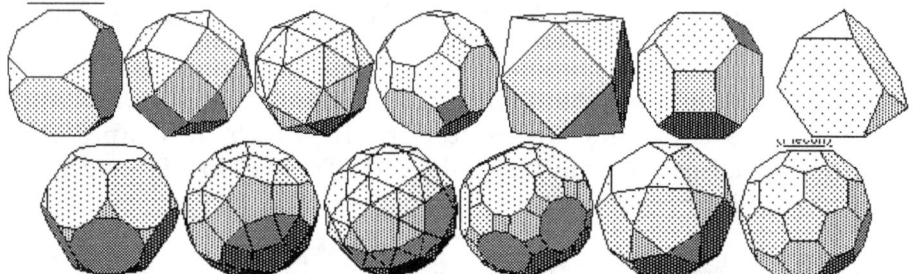

Figure 10 Thirteen Archimedean forms - with permission of Elysian Publishing

The Archimedean solids are interesting for a number of reasons. We can ask our students, "Where specifically should we cut the Platonic forms in order that all side lengths still remain equal?" Zome can help us with this. We can take the cube, and imagine cutting a little off of each end. In place of corners, we will have triangles. As we cut off more, and the triangle grows, at some point, all of the edges will be the same length. We will now have octagonal faces in place of the squares. At each corner will now be a triangular face whose edges are equal in length to those of the octagon. If we continue cutting, as that triangular face enlarges the octagon gets distorted, creating the cube-octahedron. Continuing will result in a diamond, the octahedron; whose square faces are rotated 45° from the original, with sides $\sqrt{2}/2$ in proportion. These steps are shown in Figure 11a.

We can do similar de-constructions. An interesting one is the icosahedron. If we cut each of the twelve vertices, we obtain pentagonal faces. These must grow until the edges on all faces are equal. With Zome, it is easy to see that the result will be an object with pentagonal and hexagonal faces. Looking carefully at Figure 11b, we see that each edge of the original icosahedron must be cut into thirds to get this new shape. Thus, Zome helps show mathematical relations. The diagram shows one of the triangular faces, with white struts indicating the pentagonal corners which must be removed.

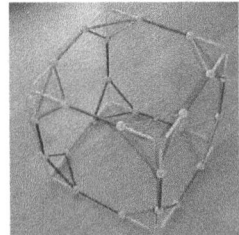 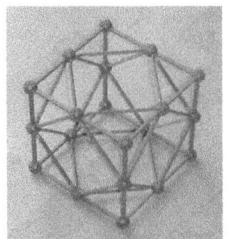 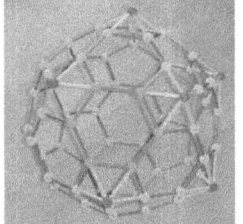

Figure 11a Faces change as corner triangles enlarge.   11b Icosahedron "trimmed".

Zometools/Astro-Logix are great for use at various times throughout the year, whether a teacher is facilitating math, science or art, or all three if lucky enough. Particularly, those steps shown so far are a good exercise at the start of the year, when students may not be "completely back" from summer. It can break the ice between new students and teacher. It's also good for Mondays, Fridays or other times when students and teachers just can't seem to focus. More importantly, they can seriously be part of any math, science or artistic curricula.

Further shapes with Astro-logix and Zome

There is an array of methods, tools, toys and software programs which can be utilized to make regular forms. While Zometools were designed with specific math ratios in mind, Astro-logix allows for its own unique means of exploration, particularly the ease with which the tubes can be cut to different sizes, allowing further possibilities. Just a few are shown in Figure 12a.

Figure 12a The versatility of Astro-logix.

By using various joints, we can obtain the Archimedean forms. One of the things that is best about Astro-logix is that they are softer in the hand and smaller, so are much more manageable and pleasing for smaller children. They enjoy falling to sleep with the glow-in-the-dark forms in their hands.

Figure 12b Various creative Astro-logix geometries – (Courtesy Astro-logix).

With Astro-Logix, we are much freer to explore different forms, and maybe even invent new ones.

 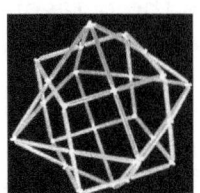  

Figure 12c Stellated tetrahedron, cube-octahedron, and more - (Astro-Logix).

With Zome, we can construct proportioned models and see mathematical relations. Zome can give unique possibilities as Figure 13 shows. In an integrated approach, we can link mathematics with art and science lectures, showing structure in symmetry and beauty in form.

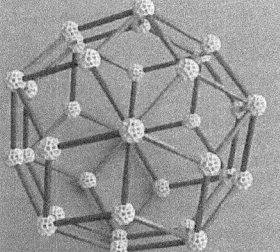 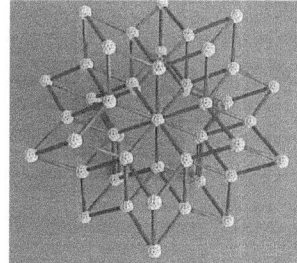

Figure 13 Forms and stars with Zome.

Constructing with intention - √2 and √3 using basic forms

The geometries of the cube, octahedron and tetrahedron can be explained with increasing complexity, simplified by some commonality.

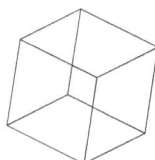 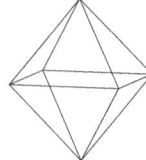 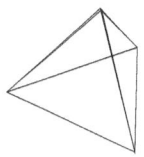

Figure 14 The more basic Platonic forms.

So far, we've constructed many forms. This is a great process, when coupled with geometry and trigonometry in high school, or college. We can never encourage the weaker math students enough. Zometools/Astro-logix are fun for talented students but more, are a great way to draw in those more gifted in artistic, physical, or social activities. Once the hook is in the fish's mouth the rest is much easier. Motivated students come part way, seeing how things form and having a sense of discovery.

Sooner or later, it becomes time to crunch numbers. How do we now work practically? We will show the math for this in the next chapter. But, the skeletal nature of Zometools is excellent for making visual aids. Zometools are a colorful way to help students enjoy learning with these angles and calculations, which will then help them understand trig functions, graphs and processes.

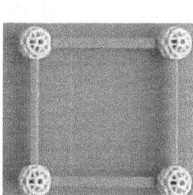  

Figure 15 Making the square and cube with their diagonals.

We will need to build various models, as shown in Figures 14 and 15, for use in calculations to be performed in Chapter 4.

The tree of life, and fractals

A fractal is a repeating structure (often thought to be two-dimensional) that we can lay out with Zometools/Astro-logix. The students should realize by now how to make equilateral triangles. We can then make basic fractals shown in Figures 16 and 17. Notice the fractals created with 3D forms (Figures 8, 9, 12 and 13).

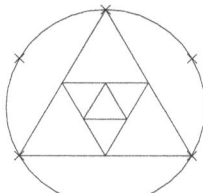 

Figure 16 Triangular fractal. Figure 17 Hexagonal fractal.

One example of fractals 2D and 3D is the 5-pointed star and its relations, as found in Figure 18. The dodecahedron is shown on top of a five pointed star, which could be drawn upon any of its twelve faces, stellating the form, and showing that there are twelve axes. What could we do with the icosahedron? We will see more on these.

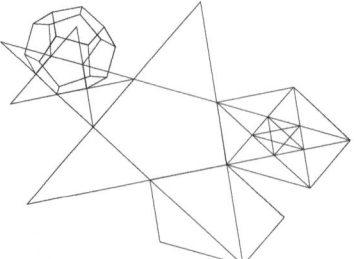

Figure 18 Fractal nature of the five pointed star, which we can expand to 3D.

In discussing phi, we can construct a set of three phi rectangles as shown in Figure 19 (with blue struts of varying length). What if we tried building an object using the external edges of the planes? In chapter 5, we will find out.

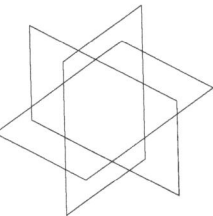

Figure 19 Perpendicular phi rectangles.

Software usage to construct regular forms

So far, we can make the 18 regular forms, plus stellations, in paper and with plastic strut construction. There are other regular polyhedra and a fascinating way to approach them is with a product called Cabri3D software.

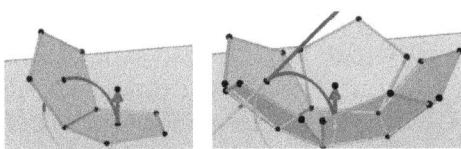 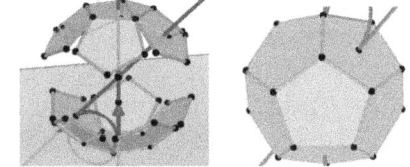

Figure 20a Starting the design. Figure 20b "Finishing"

This program can be used to create polygons quickly and easily; then copied, moved, attached or rotated (Figure 20a). Once we have the "cup", a mirror image can be created above it. With simple strokes, the two are "gathered" together (Figure 20b).

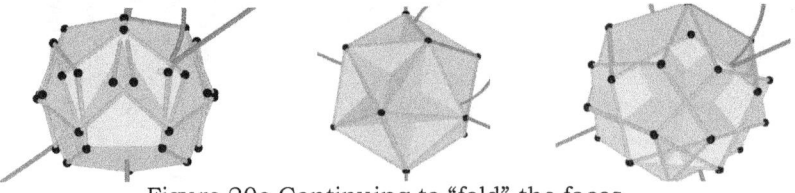

Figure 20c Continuing to "fold" the faces.

If we would continue to gather and "fold" the faces, we see the shape transform beautifully into an advanced polyhedron.

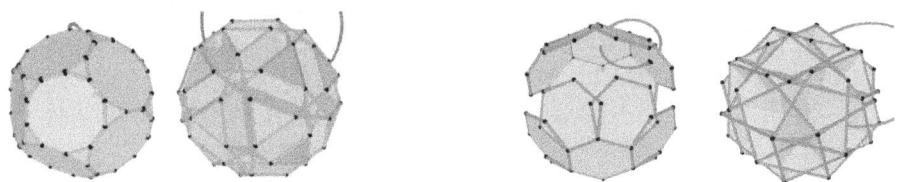

Figure 20d Archimedean form and an "impossible" polyhedron "gathered" together.

We can do this process with Archimedean forms as well. Further, non-regular polyhedra can be experimented with, all as shown in Figure 20d

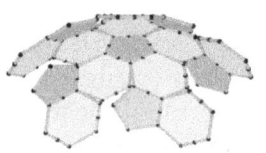 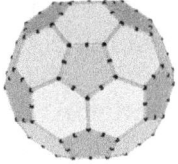 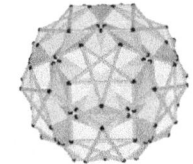

Figure 20e Another Archimedean form gathered.

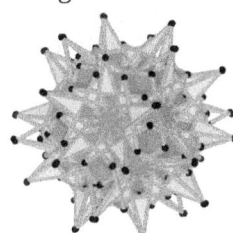 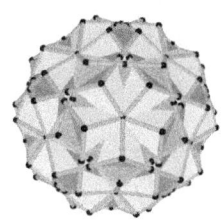

Figure 20f More possibilities (All images - Kate Mackrell, Cabri3d Artist).

With the Cabri3D software, it is possible to show what the ancients amazingly discovered without it; further forms and how they relate to each other. More, it is possible to see how one transforms into another. The author does not profit from recommending these products. It's only that they are exceptional.

Building with Zometools.

Now that we've had some directed activities to make rigid forms, and gain familiarity with the product, we can proceed further to give real-life examples of how structures around us are built. What gives buildings strength?

In this last section we will use Zometools to demonstrate the process of designing and building structures. This work can then be transferred to an architectural drafting software, like AutoCad. These exercises help students learn how geometric shapes give strength and how structures are made. They find it interesting competing against other designs and having to go back and redesign their own work when things fail.

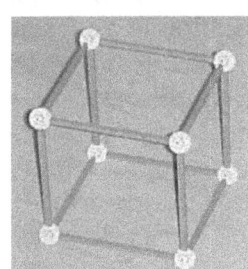 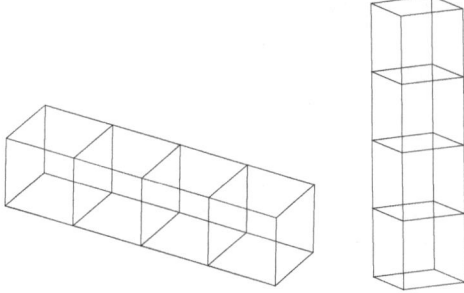

Figure 21a The cube.   Figure 21b The truss.

To begin, let's recognize that the buildings we live in are basically boxes. To demonstrate this, we use the cube. Best to build it with long blue struts (Figure 21a).

Let the students wiggle this structure. Put a large textbook on it. Press and twist lightly. See how the cube holds the weight and yet how it reacts to it. It's weak! How could we strengthen the design?

Next have them add on three more cubes. This creates a basic truss, like the structure of an airplane wing, a bridge, or a tower. Have the students wiggle this, to see that it is slightly stronger than just the cube, meaning each unit supports the other, and yet overall is still very weak.

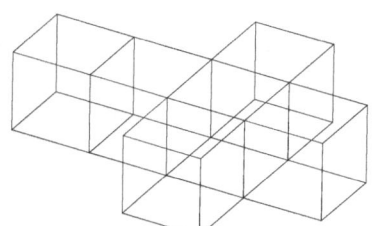 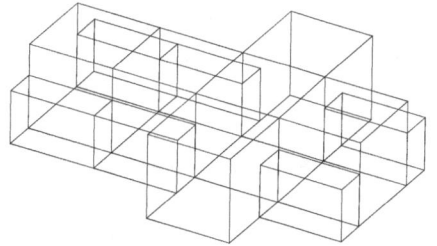

Figure 22a The cross truss.   Figure 22b Basic cathedral.

55

Next, we will add two cubes to either side of the figure. Notice how these add support to the basic structure. Does this shape resemble any buildings they have ever been in? If the cathedral is guessed, correct. We might assume that the building is shaped like a cross due to the nature of the Christian religion, and yet we also see that it adds a good bit of support. There are non-Christian buildings which also have a "t" shape.

Those who have been in a cathedral know that there are side areas that add to the beauty of the building. Let's put those in. Unfortunately, this means taking the sides apart to insert shorter blues, but it gets the students involved in real construction tasks, and lets them see how strength increases.

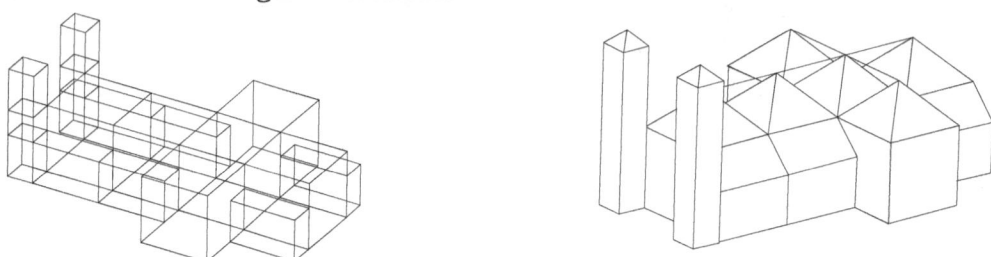

Figure 22c Finishing the cathedral.

Put in the towers; even more strength. Each beautiful element adds support. Using yellows, put little pyramids on the towers, and big ones on the cubes, connecting across the top with long blues. We have a cathedral (Figure 22c).

This structure, and most of the figures presented in this text were designed on AutoCAD software. This is a rather pricey architectural design program, but state-of-the-art. There are cheaper options put out by the same company and cheaper still put out by others. Integrating computer design is very interesting to students, and is appropriate use of the machine, as is the chemical modeling shown previously (Done with Chemsketch).

The students, with guidance have now constructed a building, have made basic rooms (boxes) and seen how to give support. Finally, after all of these Platonic forms, Archimedean shapes, fractals, and math, they can be turned loose to create their own architectural design. They must completely break down the cathedrals so they don't use them for shortcuts. Group sizes seem to work best with three members.

One of the two following options is possible. The first is to have a bridge building competition. While great in visuals, and practical problems, it unfortunately doesn't work so well with Zometools because downward weight on the bridge tends to push the pieces apart to the sides. Still, even though this happens, it is in itself very educational.

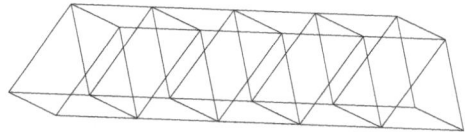

Figure 23 The Basic Bridge

What math is involved in a bridge? Why are triangles important? Where else is this form used? (Inside airplane wings and buildings) It should be possible to construct a holding mechanism to clamp the end nodes and provide some lateral rigidity, but short of gluing the pieces, the horizontal can't work as well as the vertical.

Tower building

This is the part which students thoroughly enjoy. Have them build a structure, minimum 2.5 feet tall. It must have a flat top, upon which text books can be stacked. They need to, and are encouraged to put yellows, reds and blues together to build a structure. No further diagrams are provided here as there are so many lines it is unreadable, and besides, students should start completely fresh.

The teacher or committee of judges, will grade the projects as entries in an architectural competition. Criteria are as follows:

1) Aesthetics. Does the structure look nice? Is it realistic/ functional? (has cubic/rectangular 'rooms') How creative is it?

2) Price. How much would it cost to create it in real life? For this, have the students use the following scale to add up the costs of their design.

Reds	$4000	$3000	$2000
Yellow	$3500	$2500	$1500
Blue	$3000	$2000	$1000
Balls	$5000		

Total value will show cost effectiveness of the design. Is it extremely beautiful, but very expensive? Can it bear weight?

3) Finally, the load test. Begin stacking books on the tower. Have someone strong crouch beside the tower, to help guide the books should they start to fall (use old books). By all means stop once the structure begins to fail or pieces will get destroyed. While teenagers love THAT part, it tends to eat up supplies, and also <u>RISKS EYE INJURY FROM FLYING PIECES</u>!

Successful towers often hold 50 books. That is a good place to stop as the danger from so much weight is too great. Divide the cost by the number of books to get a good comparison ratio. Have the students do internet research as part of their process, and have them take notes along the way, to be included in a final report.

Concluding reflection

In the end, the tedious job of putting all the parts back in their bags has begun. What educational value have the students been given? How could Architects and designers use or incorporate techniques given here?

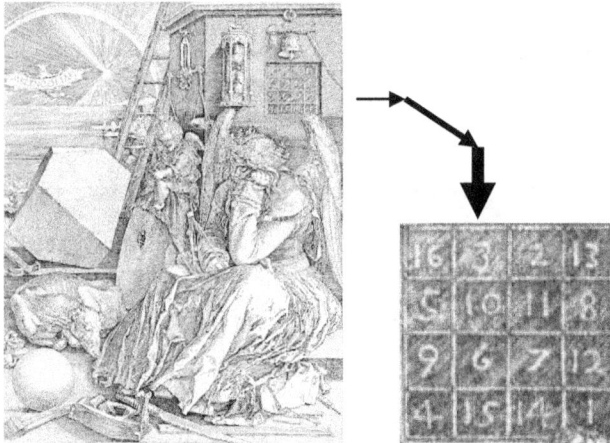

Figure 24 Form in art. Melancholia (by Albrecht Durer). Note the magic square.

Whom are we teaching to? We are not only instructing people who may someday use these tools at university or in some profession. We can try to *inspire* people to want to be architects, and interior designers, or at least recreational mathematicians. Wouldn't our world benefit from this?

Additional reading and resources:

http://www.Zometool.com/

http://www.astro-logix.com/

http://www.bfi.org/ Buckminster Fuller Institute. This was the-guy-in-the-know as far as tetrahedral constructions and such.

http://www.cabri.com/v2/pages/en/downloads_cabri3d.php Cabri software

http://www.acdlabs.com/download/ Chemsketch freeware for school

Class Exercise 1   **Introducing Zometools and Astro-Logix**

Objective:
Use Zome and Astro-Logix in the classroom for students to learn how to create three dimensional forms.

Procedure:
a) Take Astro-logix 3-, 4-, and 5- legged joints. Put tubes on them. Once each leg has a tube, put the same kind of joint in the end of each tube. Again put on tubes. Have students begin bending the forms, as they build. They will see that with the 3-s the tetrahedron, cube, and even the dodecahedron can be made. A great discovery process. With 4-s comes the octahedron and 5-s make the icosahedron. Figure 2b. Give 6- legged joints and see if they can make regular forms. (no) The question then is this: "Why can no other regular 3D form be made other than these five?
b) Have the students create a cube, with the shorter blue zome struts. Next, construct the dodeca- and icosahedrons, so they see how the product works and that they can make objects with triangular, square and pentagonal sides, all edges having the same length. Have them count the number of faces and tell them the names of these shapes.
c) Put greens in the cube, as the diagonal on each face, so they see how to make the tetrahedron, and that it fits inside the other form. Now, build the tetrahedron by hand, separate from the cube. Figure 4.
d) Stellate a tetrahedron. See the octahedron inside. Figure 9a. See if they can make an octahedron on their own. Greens are difficult.
e) Return to the cube. Have them install a green on the diagonal of one of the squares and two short yellow struts and a node as the diagonal in the cube. Figure 15. This will be used with chapter 4 lesson plans. Keep the star tetrahedron for exercise 3. Break down the rest.

Homework:
They should summarize their work and learning through this exercise. Their notes should include names and descriptions of the five forms.

Evaluation:
Read their notes, correct errors, and fill in omissions. Grade effort.

Bridges:
We will return to these shapes. Knowledge of them and the products is vital.

Class Exercise 2   **Archimedean forms**

Objective:
Learn further shapes and see relations between them.

Procedure:
a) Take a cube and imagine cutting off the corners. Each "corner" then looks like an equilateral triangular face. The original faces become oblong octagons. As the triangle grows, imagine that the edges of the octagons and triangles become equal length (called a truncated cube). What happens as the triangle grows further? Eventually, the points meet. Each original side is now a diamond – a rotated square (cube-octahedron). Figure 11a. Partner and build them both, with green Zomes.
b) Calculate relationships between the triangular –octagonal faces, and the triangular – diamond faces of the forms; compared to the original cube. At each square face, the section being removed is a 45-45-90 triangle. Its hypotenuse is $\sqrt{2}$ longer than the edge that is cut. For the octagon, each leg; $\sqrt{2}x + x + x$ = the original side. Given '1'

as the original length, $2x + \sqrt{2}x = 1$. Eventually we find the edges to be $\sqrt{2} - 1$. For the cube-octahedron, it is clear that each new edge should be $\sqrt{2}/2$ as long as the original edges of the cube.

c) Build the truncated icosahedron and figure out the form trimmed for it (icosahedron). What math relationship exists here? (The new lengths are exactly a third as long as original sides.) Figure 11b.

d) Build a cube-octahedron (Figure 12 Chapter 4) using colored Astro-logix tubes and glow-in-the-dark joints.

Homework:
Have them take this last item home and at night, they should rotate it around and describe the various geometric forms they see.

Evaluation:
Evaluate their in-class work and attempts at calculation. Give higher marks for those who try. Look at their homework descriptions. Did they see the Star of David, hexagon, cube and cross shapes? What else?

Bridges:
The Archimedean forms have further specific mathematical rules and applications to teach. Students understand that more regular bodies exist.

Class Exercise 3   **Stellations of the icosahedron and dodecahedron**

Objective:
See further relations between forms, understanding duals, and amazing geometries.

Procedure:
a) Take the stellated tetrahedrons from the first exercise. Notice how many corners it has. What other figure has this many corners? (cube) Make it by inserting blues.
b) Have students get into groups of 2 or 3. Have every other group make an icosahedron, and the rest make a dodecahedron, using the smallest blue Zome struts. Stellate each figure by extending each edge, using the next size larger strut. Figures 9a and 9b. Have them observe what they see here. In each case, there are five pointed stars as faces. Each star point meets with either two or four other star "planes". Depending on the viewpoint, they could also imagine the Star of David and ten-pointed star.
c) Finally, have them take the next size blue and connect across each point. What form will they have made? (the dual of the original) Essentially, three-dimensional fractals!
d) Break down everything to the point where the students just have plain tetrahedrons and dodecahedrons. See if they can figure out how the tetrahedron will also fit inside a dodecahedron. How many could go in there? Figure 7d. If the tetrahedron fits here, what does that mean about the octahedron and cube?

Homework:
They should summarize their work and learning through this exercise. Their notes should include names and descriptions.

Evaluation:
Read their notes, correct errors, and fill in errors of omission. Grade effort.

Bridges:
We will particularly return to the dodeca- and icosahedrons and their stellations in chapter five, so a good knowledge of them is valuable. Plus the forms are simply beautiful and it is good to encourage creative-artistry.

Class Exercise 4   **The cathedral/tower building project**

Objective:
As the students have seen how to use Zometools to make specific forms and learned how the pieces go together, they can now be given a real life process; Design and manufacture of an architectural structure.

Procedure:
a) Go through the steps in the text, beginning with the cube with long blue Zome struts. Encourage students to wiggle it to see that it is not such a strong form. Yet our homes and buildings are built from this? Extend one side to make the truss. Figure 21. Again, wiggle the form. They should see that it is a little more rigid, that each cube starts to support the others. Put in the crossing cubes and test. Even more strength. What buildings have this shape? (not just churches, but mosques, town halls and many forms of classic architecture)
b) Remove the sides and build the lower sections as shown in figure 22b. The form is looking very cathedral-ic, and is much stronger. Put in towers. They should notice that the towers don't just look neat. They also give support. Finally, put in the roof, using yellow struts. Not just practical, but also more rigidity.
c) Have them completely break down these models. They should now start their own. Form teams of 2-4 people, trying all the colors of materials, designing and building a scale model. The structure must stand at least two feet tall, and have an internal shape which would allow for realistic living - working quarters. All designs will be tested with textbooks. (BE VERY SAFETY CONSCIOUS HERE!)
e) In the end, the work area must be cleared and everything put away.

Homework:
Students should record their accomplishments - awards for aesthetics, performance and cost. They need to have a good accounting of the pieces used, their relative prices, and how many books they held, finally getting a weight vs. cost analysis. Encourage further architectural research.

Evaluation:
Students to be evaluated on teamwork, creativity and final report.

Bridges:
Real application. Usually one of the greatest tools in the classroom.

4 Using geometries to apply trigonometry

Opening dialogue

For what instructional purposes can the Platonic solids be used? How can the Pythagorean Theorem be put to use to figure out their geometries?

Pythagoras of Samos

Pythagoras was born on a Greek island, at the dawn of classical times, when Greek science, philosophy, drama, medicine, mathematics and politics were beginning. He was one of the greatest known mathematicians, and philosophers. Much of his mathematical work is perhaps in Euclid's Elements, written a few centuries later. Otherwise, not much remains.

Our man traveled to Egypt, and studied there, before Egypt's defeat by the Babylonians. He was taken to this city, perhaps as a captive, and was also to learn there. What ideas might he have picked up in Egypt, and then in Babylon, the heir of Sumer? Finally, he returned to Greece, later founding a school at Croton, a colony in the south of Italy.

People came there to study, and gave their possessions to his commune, becoming ascetic vegetarians. These students were called "Mathematikoi" (the Learned). There was a second group, who lived around the community but were not full members. They were allowed to come to the school and were called the "Akousmatics" the Listeners).

Pythagoras and his students philosophized on number; that each represented facets of the cosmos. They related number to space, to music. Pythagoras may have begun the idea of "the music of the spheres". They tried also to inspire political reform, which ended up being their downfall. Pythagoras lived to an old age, but his school and many of his students did not. His work was essentially squelched and so much was lost, and much that we have today is the basis of historical rumor.

Pythagoras is most remembered for the theorem that the sum of the squares of the two short sides of a right triangle equals the square of the longest side. Actually, this was known for millennia earlier, certainly by the Egyptians, who used the 3-4-5 right triangle to find 90° angles after each flooding of the Nile, in order to realign boundaries. In school, students learn quickly how to use the theorem. But do they ever simply demonstrate it?

Let's try, looking at the first basic Pythagorean triangle. To begin, draw two perpendicular lines, using just a compass and ruler. Mark off seven units, as shown in Figure 1. (Choose a scale which will fit on the page, leaving space to the upper right!)

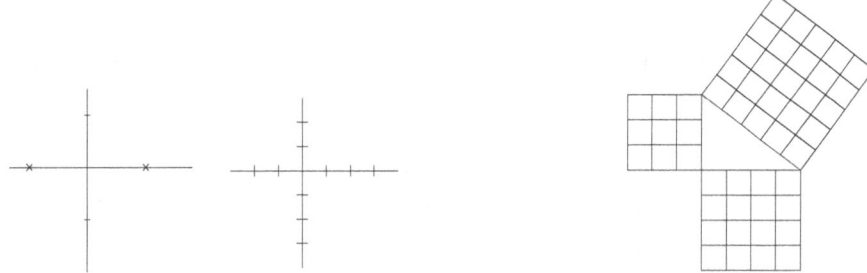

Figure 1a Making a 7 x 7 grid.   1b Pythagorean image using the 3-4-5 Triangle.

Continue now with the diagram, filling in the 3 x 3 and 4 x 4 squares as shown in Figure 1b. Have students count and label how many little squares are in each. Have them then measure the hypotenuse. Did they count five units? Can they draw the square from this line? It is a good exercise for them to try with a compass, because while they can usually do the perpendicular lines in Figure 1a, they often cannot get the perpendicular lines on the diagonal, in order to make the 5 x 5 square. Finally, have the students noticed that the sum of 3, 4 and 5 is 12? Did the teacher?

It is interesting that even today, carpenters and brick layers of Europe, who wish to obtain a right triangle, do so by measuring out two sides of an angle to 30cm x 40cm, from the point of intersection. They mark points here and swing the two legs until they are exactly 50 cm apart. They can be assured now of having their right angle.

A great speed exercise for high school students is to have them generate the square of the first twenty numbers. It is amazing how they may struggle, our modern youth. Worse is how poorly they can take the square root of numbers without a calculator.

1	2	3	4	5	6	7	8	9	10	11	12	13	14	15	16	17	18	19	20
1	4	9	16	25	36	49	64	81	100	121	144	169	196	225	256	289	324	361	400

Table 1 The squares of the first 20 numbers.

A logic exercise is to now have them look at, and see if they recognize any patterns in the table. There are several, but one very interesting one is the fact that given a square, like $10^2 = 100$, if we want to know 11^2, we don't have to multiply. We can just add 10 and 11 to 100 to make 121.

This is a sneaky way to work with squares and helps answer the next question. What is the next easiest Pythagorean triangle (one which gives whole numbered solutions)? We might notice that in the 3-4-5, the difference between the squares of 4 and 5 is 9 (sum of 4 and 5). Since this is the square of 3, we get whole number solutions. The next one (which the students may need help to find) is with the numbers 6, 8 and 10. Basically, these are all double the dimensions of the 3-4-5. Hopefully, the students now see how this works and can be turned loose to find the next Pythagorean triangle.

Note the difference between 12^2 and 13^2. It is 25. (12 + 13) This helps us find the 5-12-13 triangle. Note here the sum of the sides is 30. We might note that the position of the key station stones at Stonehenge is in the proportion of a 5 x 12 rectangle, which is tangentially touched by the outer circle of 30 upright stones mounted by 30 cross members. Are there any relations here? Well, it is fun enough just as a coincidence. It is also interesting that in the United States, 5 x 12 is a typical roof pitch. This kind of uniformity provides for harmony in building projects, and ease of construction

What would be the next Pythagorean triangle? Notice that so far the difference of squares has been 9, 36 and 25. So, we must look for numbers whose squares have a difference which is itself a square. Are there two squares whose difference is 16? (3 and 5) Are there two whose difference is 49? Students will have to continue their list of squares, or use the logic. In the 5-12-13 triangle, the two adjacent numbers 12 and 13 add to 25. Are there adjacent numbers that make 49? (Yes, 24 and 25) Therefore, we come by the 7-24-25 triangle. Another pattern, it seems. For odd values, like 9, 25 and 49, two adjacent numbers, whose sum is this value form two sides of the triangle. Let's confirm it with 81: 40 + 41 = 81. Squaring 40 is easy and gives 1600. Again, we don't need to square 41. Just follow the pattern and add 40 and 41 to 1600 to get 1681.

We can of course go the opposite way too. For example, how could we find the square root of 841? Assuming that it works out to a whole number, let's test our knowledge. We know the square of 20 is 400, and the square of 300 is 900. Our 841 is close to the latter. What happens if we subtract 30, and 29 from 900? We get 841. What this means is that 841 is 29 squared.

There are other patterns. Note from the table that squares always end in 1, 4, 9, 6, 5, 6, 9, 4, 1 and 0. We can use this to realize that numbers like 3<u>3</u> and 29<u>7</u> are not perfect squares of any number. But, 48<u>4</u> might be.

Creating the 3-4-5 triangle was a great exercise for the students in drawing perpendicular lines and visuallizing the Pythagorean Theorem. They will remember this.

Building the cube

We made three of the Platonic solids in the first chapter. Let's make another, using our techniques with perpendicular lines.

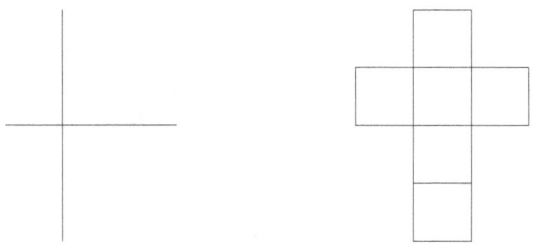

Figure 2 The cube pattern.

Have students draw a straight line, with the long axis of the paper, measuring either eight inches long, or perhaps twenty centimeters, depending on your unit of measure. Cross the line at its midpoint, with a perpendicular line that is six inches (15 cm). Note, however, that only two inches (five cm) of this second line should be to the left of the first. From this, have them continue, using proper construction techniques, until they get the cross as shown to the right in Figure 2. This cross can then be cut out (again, leave tabs) and folded along the solid lines to make a cube.

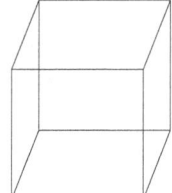

Figure 3 The Cube.

Interestingly, the flat figure that we used is in the form of a Masonic and Rosicrucian symbol. The roots of these secret societies could come from the Knights Templar of the Middle Ages, the Mithraists of the time of Christ, the temple of Jerusalem, or even ancient Egypt. The Masons were very visible during the rise of the British and Hapsburgh empires. They left symbols throughout the Christian world, in the holiest of holies of the great baroque churches and cathedrals of Europe. The founders of the United States were Masons, who wrote their tenets into their Constitution.

Figure 4 Symbol of the Golden Dawn Rosicrucian society.

This is yet another place where we can, if we choose, show that people have in fact used these forms, for practical or even mystical pursuits. We are not trying to convert (or subvert) any young minds. But we are wishing to draw their attention, interest, and curiosity while encouraging them to educate themselves. The Masons are yet another interesting course of study that students could look into. We will see more.

However students choose to receive this material, the interesting thing is that many human-created symbols surround us, and so many of them are made with surprisingly easy geometrical processes. This is what we are trying to encourage, that math is easy, unexpected, and magical.

Figure 5 Historic and modern symbolism.

Taking the measure of the cube

Starting with one face of the cube, we have a square. What can the students say about the angles? (90°) What do they notice about the sides? (they are all the same length) Where is the longest length they could make on the square? (the diagonal) Can they put a Zome piece in there? (yes, a green strut) What is the internal angle and the length of the green strut in relation to the blues? (The angle should be easy through logic – 45°. For lengths, let them imagine that each blue measures 1 unit.)

By Pythagoras, the diagonal will measure √2. Variations on this can be worked. If the diagonal measures 1 unit length, what will each side measure? (√2/2). Using the blue struts of 5, 8 and 13 inches, gives what measure of diagonal? (5√2, 8√2 and 13√2) Ah, so what is the diagonal if each side measures "x"? (x√2)

Let's go to the cube. What is the longest length within this object? (it is very easy for them to see the diagonal now between two opposite corners.) Can any Zometool be inserted in here? (yes, when using short blues, use two short yellows and a ball. Depending on the size blue, use the corresponding yellow.)

So, how do we come up with this length? (We must use the Pythagorean Theorem, and the √2 side, noticing that the one angle is 90°.) In their calculations, students see that this length is √3. Flat drawing - two dimensions; √2. Three dimensions; √3.

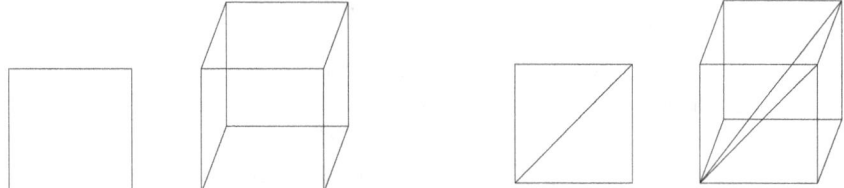

Figure 6a The Square and Cube.   Figure 6b The Diagonals.

Now, let's challenge the students. How can we work this problem if the diagonal of the square measures '1'? What about if the longest length in the cube measured '1'?

In the first case, we have to write the equation as: $x^2 + x^2 = 1^2$. This means that $x = 1/\sqrt{2}$, which gives √2/2 when we clear the denominator. Thus, the long internal leg would be √6/2.

When the cube diagonal measures 1, we use x for one side and √2x for the diagonal on the square. Use the equation $x^2 + (\sqrt{2}x)^2 = 1^2$, to find that $x = \sqrt{3}/3$. This eventually gives us the fraction of √6/3 for the diagonal of the square. This is a good use of the Pythagorean Theorem and of fractions, two of their best friends!

Though we rush through these steps here, in class they must be worked through as students are *always* weak with this process.

An exercise in radicals

Having tackled this, let us return to the vesica piscis. Let's have some fun working out the geometries of this figure. Assuming that the radius of each circle is 1, what does that make the following lengths a, b and c?

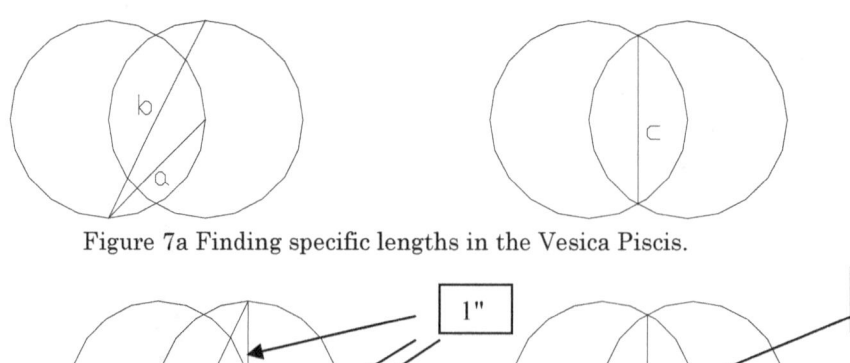

Figure 7a Finding specific lengths in the Vesica Piscis.

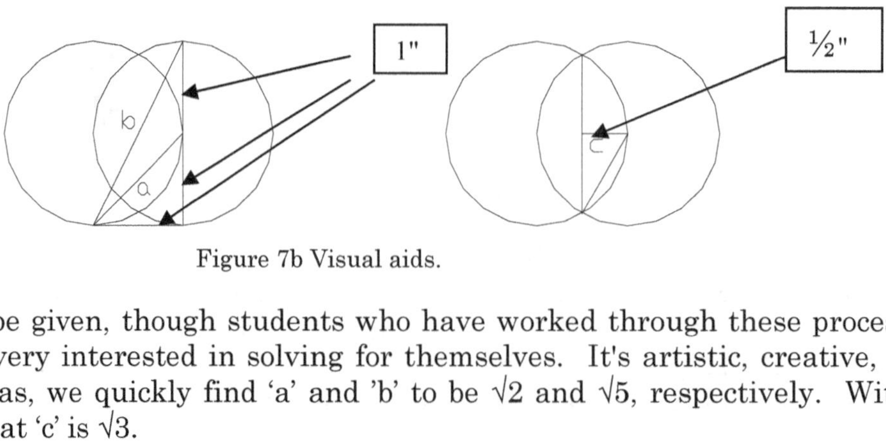

Figure 7b Visual aids.

Visual hints can be given, though students who have worked through these processes to this point will be very interested in solving for themselves. It's artistic, creative, and fun. Using Pythagoras, we quickly find 'a' and 'b' to be √2 and √5, respectively. With a little work, we find that 'c' is √3.

We will revisit in Chapter 5 obtaining √5, from a 1 x 2 triangle. Having gotten these techniques, let us proceed now to the triangle-faced Platonic solids.

Taking the measure of the octahedron

Moving to the octahedron, how can we calculate, and even predict its internal geometries? Again, the sides are the same lengths, each face has 60° angles, and between adjoining edges, each angle is 90°. Remember, this is the companion to the cube.

To figure things out in the octahedron, we have two choices. We can proceed via √2 or with √3. In both instances, we will assume that each edge measures '1'.

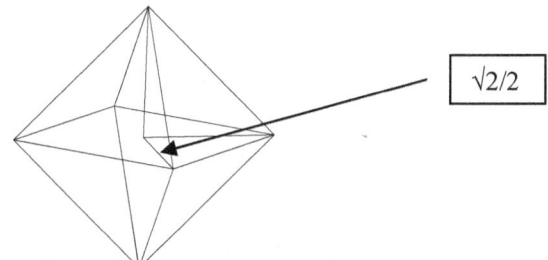

Figure 8a The Octahedron. Finding the center using √2.

In the first case, let's look at the octahedron (Figure 8a). We can work out, through calculation, experience, and logic that each of the three internal legs that are shown measure √2/2 (they are each part of a square). Therefore, in the Octahedron, when the edge measures '1', the longest length across the object will be '√2' units long. Ask the students what it will measure if each edge is 4 inches long (4√2).

Figure 8b The equilateral triangle.

The blue equilateral triangle can then be used for a similar set of steps. What do students notice now about this object? Equal sides and angles? What must the measure be of each angle? (since triangles measure 180°, each must be 60°). Note that with Zometools we can show how the difference between 3-, 4-, 5- and 6-sided figures is 180°, in accordance with the formula (N-2)•180°.

Take a long red piece and place it across the center of the triangle as shown in Figure 18b. By logic, what are the angle measures in each smaller triangle? (30-60-90) Can any assumptions be made about side lengths if we say the longest side measures 1 unit? (The shorter is 1/2, and by Pythagoras, the central one is √3/2).

These two processes, with the square and the equilateral triangle show the relationship between √2 and 45° angles and √3 with 30° and 60°.

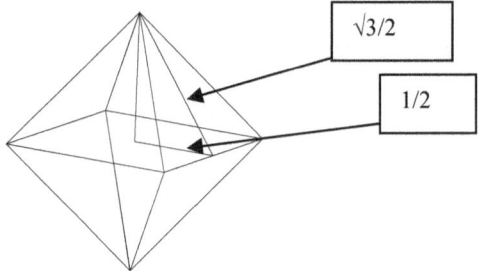

Figure 8c The Octahedron. Finding the center using √3/2.

Let's look at the object again, from the perspective of Figure 8c. Here, the bisector of the equilateral triangle we know measures √3/2. As it bisects the base leg of the triangle, it means each of the two short legs measures 1/2. This can easily be seen is the length of the short base leg of the internal triangle that is shown. Have students experience the joy of using the Pythagorean Theorem here:

$$\left(\frac{\sqrt{3}}{2}\right)^2 = \left(\frac{1}{2}\right)^2 + y^2 \quad \text{Thus, } y^2 = \frac{3}{4} - \frac{1}{4} = \frac{1}{2} \text{ and again, } y = \frac{\sqrt{2}}{2}$$

Of course, we get the same answer. Yet, this route is more challenging. The things we are figuring out will help students attempt the next step.

Taking the measure of the tetrahedron

We have been trying to find the longest lengths across the cube and octahedron. In the tetrahedron, which is the longest side?

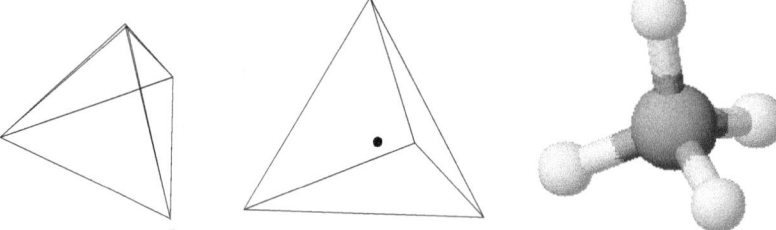

Figure 9 The Tetrahedron.

Does the student recognize now the *edge* is the longest side? Knowing this, let's look instead for the center, as we initially did for the octahedron. This is a great process to do parallel to atomic modeling in chemistry for we should notice immediately the configuration of the CH_4 molecule. (Teenagers like hearing that this being the methane molecule then a "fart" molecule has this form).

Where do we begin to try and figure out the geometries of the tetrahedron? Let us start by putting some lines inside. Again, this is possible to do with Zometools or similar construction kit. Figure 10b shows the view rotated and each internal line identified. Perhaps, this appears a daunting task. It is of interest to find a, b, c, d, e, and f, as we will see. So, let's embark on this voyage of discovery together.

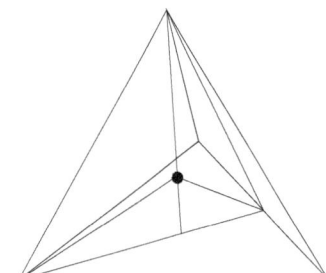 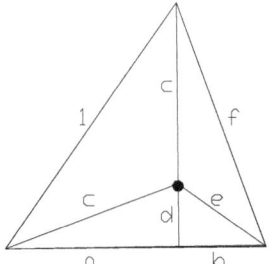

Figure 10a, Finding the center.   10b Identifying lengths to be solved.

Have the students write all of the equations they can think of:

a + b = f -> we know that since "f" is the bisector of one side of the equilateral triangle, it must measure $\sqrt{3}/2$.

1) $a^2 + (c + d)^2 = 1^2$ 2) $b^2 + d^2 = e^2$
3) $a^2 + d^2 = c^2$ 4) $b^2 + (c + d)^2 = f^2 = ¾$

from the first and fourth equations above, we derive $a^2 - b^2 = ¼$;

FOIL the first equation: $a^2 + c^2 + 2cd + d^2 = 1^2$; subtract the third: $2c^2 + 2cd = 1$.

A lot of formulas and unknowns. To solve this complexity we have one very big friend: the cube. We need to remember from our use with Zometools that the tetrahedron fits inside the cube and more importantly, that they share the same center.

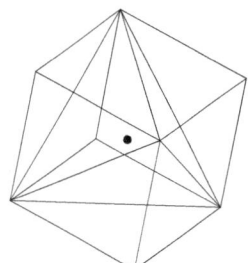 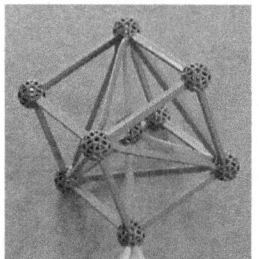

Figure 10c The Tetrahedron inside the cube, Zometools shown on the right

66

So, what was that relation again? When the cube measures '1', then the diagonal of the face is √2, which happens to be the leg of the tetrahedron. Also, the longest measure in the cube is √3. Therefore, to the center is ½ of this length, or √3/2. (this length corresponds to "c" of the tetrahedron figure) The problem is that now the leg of the tetrahedron is not √2 but is 1. So, we need comparison fractions.

Side "c" is to √3/2 as 1 is to √2. Nearly exhausted with fractions (with friends like these, who needs enemies?) we find that when the tetrahedron measures 1 on a side, the radius; "c", is √6/4.

$$\frac{c}{\sqrt{3}/2} = \frac{1}{\sqrt{2}} \quad \text{multiplying through gives:} \quad c = \frac{\sqrt{3}}{2} \cdot \frac{1}{\sqrt{2}} = \frac{\sqrt{6}}{4}$$

Returning to our equations from above now fills in the blanks, beginning at the end:

$$2c^2 + 2cd = 1 \quad \text{gives,} \quad \frac{3}{4} + \frac{\sqrt{6}d}{2} = 1 \quad d = \frac{2}{\sqrt{6}} \cdot \frac{1}{4} = \frac{1}{2\sqrt{6}} = \frac{\sqrt{6}}{12}$$

This has been a rather complicated process, but really a brain teaser for the best in the class. Try it with them. They will enjoy it. They may need a little help but not too much. This now shows that there is a 3:1 relationship between "c" and "d".

Continuing is easier, though still work.

$$a^2 + d^2 = c^2 \quad \text{gives } a^2 = \frac{6}{16} - \frac{6}{144} = \frac{48}{144} = \frac{1}{3} \quad \text{So, } a = \frac{\sqrt{3}}{3}$$

With $a + b = \frac{\sqrt{3}}{2}$, we see b must equal $\frac{\sqrt{3}}{6}$ (a 2:1 relationship)

And $b^2 + d^2 = e^2$ so $e^2 = \frac{3}{36} + \frac{6}{144} = \frac{18}{144} = \frac{1}{8}$ and $e = \frac{\sqrt{8}}{8} = \frac{\sqrt{2}}{4}$

The work has been worth it because the tetrahedron reveals to us a wealth of relations involving √2, √3, products of the two and fractions based on 12. Let's keep twelve based counting systems!

A final bit of fun with this object is to figure out where the points of the tetrahedron fit within a sphere. Why? Just wait.

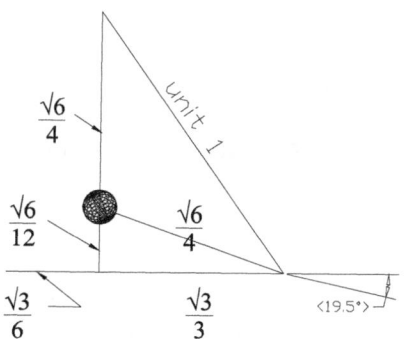

Figure 11 Solutions of the tetrahedron

By using "d" and "a" with the inverse tangent function, we see that the points are located 19.5° below the center of the tetrahedron. There are two things interesting about this. First, look at the globe and see that the Hawaiian Islands are at 19.5° north. The red spot on Jupiter, the Blue spot on Neptune and the largest of volcanoes, Olympus Mons, on Mars, are all near 19.5° above or below the equator of these planets. Tetrahedral planetary stress points?

The second point of interest about 19.5° is that it indicates the angle of separation between the hydrogen atoms in CH_4 of 109.5°. Perhaps the micro is a reflection of the macro after all.

Encore

Finally, we will look at an Archimedean form. The cube-octahedron lends itself well to the work we have accomplished. We can use models, variously rotated to see that two dimensionally, it is a hexagon. This means that if any given leg measures '1', then they all measure this, and logically, distances across the object measure '2'. By calculation, or remembering, distances across two directly opposing corners (two opposite square faces) measure? ($\sqrt{3}$)

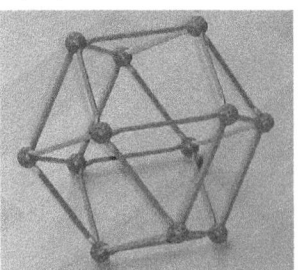  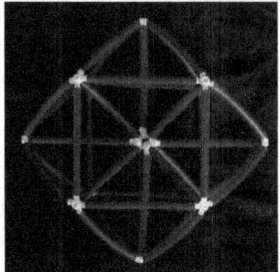

Figure 12 Cube octahedron. Note the hexagonal nature, and glow-in-the-dark.

Taking the measure of the icosahedron

Find the geometries of the icosahedron? The reader might think that the author has taken a total leave of his senses. But this is real calculation that shows how rich are use of the Pythagorean Theorem and Platonic solids, with faces of equilateral triangles.

We can make one "short cut" now by comparing the three drawings in Figure 13. Use "1" for all edge lengths. The height, h, is perpendicular to both x and y. Now x goes to a face midpoint and y goes to the vertex. Have students derive the following formulas, which will then apply for all figures:

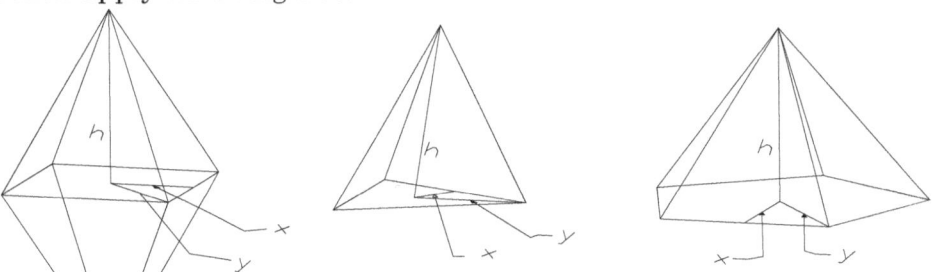

Figure 13 Common factors in Platonic forms having the equilateral triangle.

Using Pythagoras, we can see that the following work for all three, though x, y and h will be different in each case.

$$x^2 + h^2 = \tfrac{3}{4} \qquad y^2 + h^2 = 1 \qquad x^2 + \tfrac{1}{4} = y^2$$

We found x, y and h for the tetrahedron and octahedron, "fairly easily". For the icosahedron? All right, that will have to wait…

Trigonometry applications

Having gotten students to work with their heads and their hands with $\sqrt{2}$ and $\sqrt{3}$, let's put it to use. We will now develop hexagonal drawing techniques with further diagrams. Start again with the circle, whose radius is said to be '1', centered on an x-y graph. Make the hexagon with a top mark on the "y" axis. Draw a line from the origin to the upper right corner, as shown in Figure 14a.

Have the students go through a logic sequence to determine the angle of this small triangle. Do they comprehend it will be 30°, and that the vertical leg will measure '½'?

Have them do another, with the "top mark" on the "x" axis. Draw the triangle as shown in Figure 14b. Notice now that we should have a 60° angle at the origin, and that the horizontal leg of this triangle is now the "x" side whose measure is '½'. In both cases, our students should recognize that to find the missing side, they must use the Pythagorean Theorem, with fractions: $(½)^2 + a^2 = 1^2$. They must eventually take the square root to get $\sqrt{3}/2$.

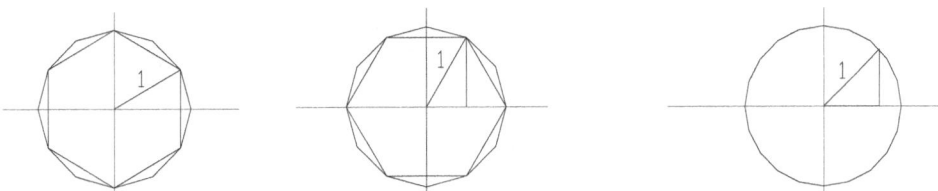

Figures 14a 30°, 14b 60°, and 14c 45°.   Trigonometric ratios via diagrams.

They need to then go through a different set of steps, bisecting the arc in the 1st quadrant as shown in Figure 14c. Again, can they logically come up with the angle at the origin being equal to 45°? Can they see that both horizontal and vertical sides are equal? Now turn them loose to see how well they can calculate the lengths of those sides. Students normally quite capable with math problems might surprisingly not do so well with application here.

$a^2 + a^2 = 1^2$ → $2a^2 = 1$ → $a^2 = ½$ Eventually, we see that "a" = √2/2.

How do sin, cos and tan of 30, 45 and 60 degree angles utilize the ubiquitous √2 and √3? As we work with angles and trig, we notice that easy triangles like 3-4-5 and 5-12-13 have decimal angles. With the calculator we see that sine and cosine of 30, 45 and 60 degrees give decimal readings like 0.5, 0.707 and 0.866. Why are there no "easy" relationships between angles and trig functions?

There are. For this, we must use fractions, and radicals. We can see that a pattern does develop for 1st quadrant angles. Begin by using x and y values for the trig functions, in place of the terms "adjacent" and "opposite". Thus, the "y" value of 0° is also 0. Therefore, Sin 0° is 0. By a similar measure the "x" value is same as the radius. So, Cos 0° is 1. We can obtain the other ratios from the material so far developed. Thinking logically, we can build Table 1.

$$\frac{\sqrt{0}}{2} \quad \frac{\sqrt{1}}{2} \quad \frac{\sqrt{2}}{2} \quad \frac{\sqrt{3}}{2} \quad \frac{\sqrt{4}}{2}$$

Table 1 First quadrant sine values.

This set of values corresponds to the sine of 0, 30, 45, 60, and 90 degrees. As we continue rotating, through the second quadrant, we will look at specific angles of 120, 135, 150 and finally 180 degrees.

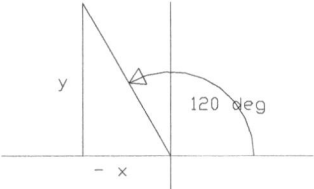

Figure 15a Beginning to calculate 2nd quadrant values.

Having completed the first quadrant table, demonstrate 120°, to see that as we continue rotating, we relate the angle back to the x axis, thus having now a negative value for x, and a decreasing positive value for y. This begins to show the need to consider ± when taking square roots. Otherwise, the sine, cosine and tangent values are values that we already saw with 60°, except some are now negative.

Next have them draw the figure for 135° and calculate trig values to see how well they understand. Then, they complete the second quadrant table as homework to see if they have gotten the concept. They can draw more graphs but hopefully it will become less and less necessary as their powers of reason grow, which is what we want!

$$\frac{\sqrt{4}}{2} \quad \frac{\sqrt{3}}{2} \quad \frac{\sqrt{2}}{2} \quad \frac{\sqrt{1}}{2} \quad \frac{\sqrt{0}}{2}$$

Table 2 Second quadrant Sine values.   Figure 15b 120 and 150 degree angles.

The sine values decrease in value as shown in table 2. We can see the angle of 120° and 150° demonstrated in Figure 15b. Note that the lines must always relate back to the x-axis.

A pattern! A similar pattern follows for greater angles, though now the sine value goes negative:

$$\frac{-\sqrt{0}}{2} \quad \frac{-\sqrt{1}}{2} \quad \frac{-\sqrt{2}}{2} \quad \frac{-\sqrt{3}}{2} \quad \frac{-\sqrt{4}}{2} \qquad \frac{-\sqrt{4}}{2} \quad \frac{-\sqrt{3}}{2} \quad \frac{-\sqrt{2}}{2} \quad \frac{-\sqrt{1}}{2} \quad \frac{-\sqrt{0}}{2}$$

Table 3 3rd and 4th quadrant sine values

We can look at a unit circle on a graph, and imagine how the x and y values change consistently (increasing and decreasing through positive and negative values) and what that means for the trig values. What happens for more than one revolution, greater than 360°, and also for negative revolution/angles (a negative radius)?

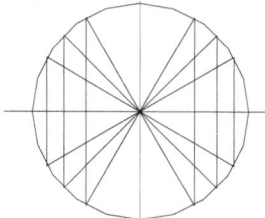

Figure 16 All of the 30, 45 and 60 degree angles in the quadrants

This material will prove useful when we later attempt to graph the sinusoidal function. We finish with a diagram containing these critical angles (Figure 16), fun to have students create and color.

Finally, note that adding √2 and √3 makes "π" (99.85% accurate). The fraction 22/7, which the ancient Egyptians used is 99.96%, and 6.25 for the megalithic builders makes 99.47% accuracy.

Fun exercises with radicals

We have done a lot of calculating in this chapter, not all of it easy. Let's do further drawing and calculating, giving students more practice with the Pythagorean Theorem, radicals and logic.

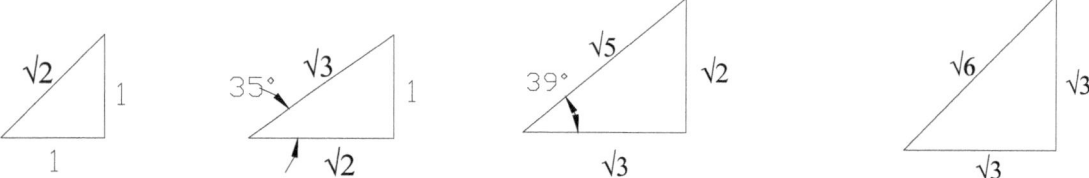

Figure 17 Building √2 and √3   Figure 18 Building √5   Figure 19 Building √6

How can we graphically show √2 and √3? By now the students know that in a square the diagonal measures √2. Next draw two perpendicular lines (again, legs measure '1'). Set a compass to the measure of √2 to help draw the length of the longer leg, in a new triangle. By Pythagoras we get the hypotenuse of √3. See Figure 17.

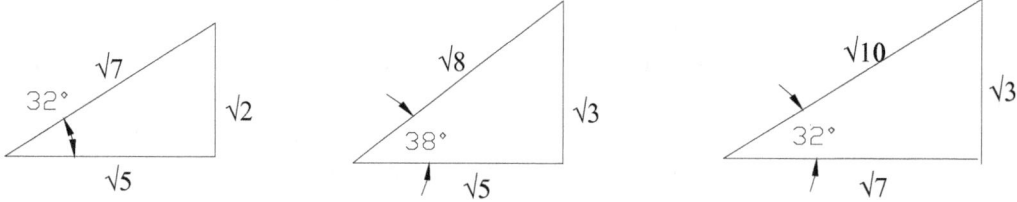

Figure 20a Making more radical lengths

How could students obtain √5? See if they relate that 2 and 3 add to 5 and that √2 and √3 do not sum to √5, but *do* build to √5 in a right triangle! Let them do the Pythagorean Theorem on a triangle having legs √2 and √3. Draw as shown in Figure 18, where they must set their compass to √2 and √3, from the previous work, to get each leg.

The next question is, how could we multiply, graphically by √2, to get √6? To multiply by 2 or 3 is easy. We just double or triple the length. Again, see if the students can figure this out. Essentially, we can pick any length we want, draw a perpendicular leg of the same length and the diagonal will be √2 units longer. By this technique, we can obtain √6 by using two-legs of measure √3.

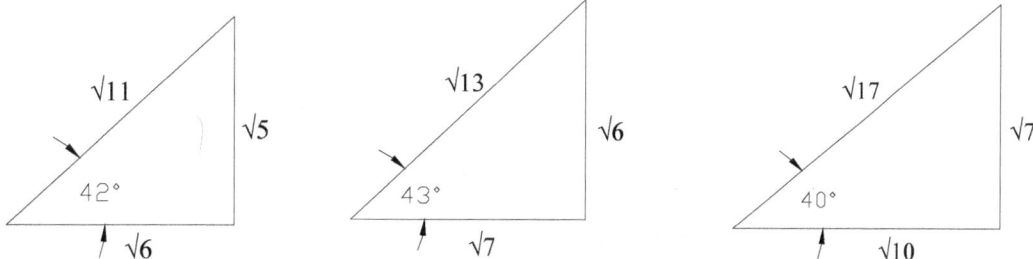

Figure 20b Making even more radicals

So now, how would one obtain √7, √8, √10, √11, and √13? Really, there is no end to the possibilities. Note the variety of angles that this provides. Have the students discover how to draw these figures only with a compass and straight edge. Have them do trigonometry to determine angle measures. Notice how √x and √y make √(x + y)

Further fun exercises

As we have worked extensively with the Platonic forms, a further application is to have the students build them with magnetic sticks and steel balls. These are rather expensive but fun, and uniquely interesting for this application.

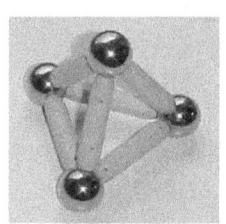

Figure 21 Platonic forms made with ball and stick magnets.

Have the students make the tetrahedron first, and then the octahedron. They should see that both are fairly strong elements. Next, have them build the icosahedron. In each case, they will see that the triangle is a very strong basic figure. When students go three-dimensional, they will see that the structure goes from being unstable to impregnable with the installation of the last strut.

When they build the cube, an interesting thing happens. The cube, upon which our homes and buildings are formed, is **weak**. This form easily moves all over. Let the students try to build the dodecahedron. It is not shown in the diagram because it cannot sustain itself. The weight is such that it flattens itself into a pile.

This further product is excellent for demonstrating the real electro-magnetic bonding which occurs in elements and why tetrahedral bonds are so strong.

It becomes clearer, perhaps, why Plato discussed his forms first with the tetra-, octa- and icosahedrons, and why Buckminster Fuller used the tetrahedron in his domes.

Figure 22 Icosahedron made from monkeys (the missing link?) – (Michael Green).

We can do a lot of things with geometric form, all meant to challenge the mind, but also link between artistic and mathematic. We can look to modern artistic mathematicians for further ideas. People of this caliber regularly give talks and presentations, particularly at the international "Bridges" conferences, where nearly anything can be used to make forms.

Concluding dialogue

How can we use models to help develop calculation skill requiring the use of radicals? How can we then feed in harder applications, coupled with art, to make it all seem more interesting? Why are many people today interested in recreational mathematics, mandalas and something called "sacred geometry"?

 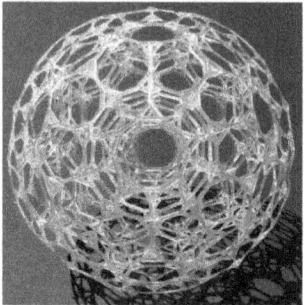

Figure 23 120 cell and truncated 120 cell. Courtesy George Hart

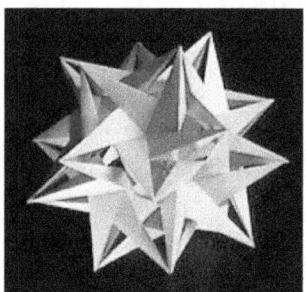 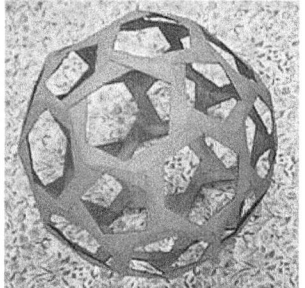

Figure 24 Paper models - Stellated & Truncated icosahedron – (George Hart).

 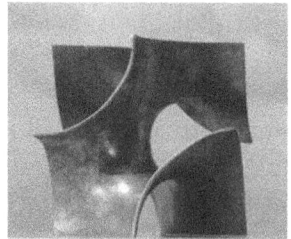 

Figure 25 Various Sculptures of 'regular' platonic forms – (Courtesy Carlo Sequin).

Further reading/research and Websites:
http://www.dartmouth.edu/~matc/math5.geometry/unit5/unit5.html
Dartmouth College's site:

http://www.bridgesmathart.org/
The Bridges international math meetings.

Class Exercise 1 **Geometry and the Pythagorean Theorem**

Objective:
Apply the Pythagorean Theorem to geometric problems. Strengthen exponential calculations and roots.

Procedure:
a) Have the students draw a horizontal line, 7 units long and marked at each '1' unit. Divide the line into 3 and 4 units and draw a perpendicular line, 3 units long, above the first line and 4 units below it. Make 3x3 and 4x4 boxes diagonal to each other. Draw in a grid of 9 and 16 small blocks. Use the compass to get all of these perpendicular lines. Draw a line, connecting a corner of the 3x3 square to the 4x4. What is its length? (5) Mark units, and now make a 5x5 box, exactly perpendicular to this line. See Figure 1a-1b.
b) Draw a vesica piscis, radius '1' unit. Mark top, bottom and center of both circles. Draw in lines a and b and ask the students to calculate their lengths. Hints: on the right circle, draw a line that connects top and bottom through the center. By logic, the students should realize this has length '2'. Draw a line connecting the two bottom marks. This should measure '1'. They have made a right triangle. Figure 7b.
c) Draw a second vesica piscis. Draw line c. Find its length. They can bisect c and draw a line to the center of one of the circles (length ½). From that center to an intersect is the radius, and thus 1. Easy.

Homework:
Do all the squares of the numbers from 1 to 20 without a calculator. Table 1. Show their work. Ask them to write down patterns they see.

Evaluation:
Quiz, without calculator, 7^2, 11^2, 17^2 and $\sqrt{361}$, $\sqrt{225}$, $\sqrt{169}$ etc. If they did their work these numbers should be easy. Check their notebooks. Did they show their work? Check their drawings and grade accordingly.

Bridges:
Squares and roots are basic numeric operations which need practice. Students can learn that the difference of squares between two adjacent numbers is their sum, eg. $19^2 = 361$ and 20^2 is 400, so subtracting 19 and 20 from 400 gives the same result. Add/subtract instead of multiplying. Pythagorean operations and these diagrams are very helpful.

Class Exercise 2 **$\sqrt{2}$ and $\sqrt{3}$ in the cube and octahedron**

Objective:
Within the Platonic solids are hidden $\sqrt{2}$, $\sqrt{3}$ and Φ. By application of the Pythagorean Theorem, we will begin to unlock their secrets.

Procedure:
a) Draw a square and a second square above and to the right of it. Connect, making a "cube". Draw a diagonal on one square face and also across the entire cube (use different colors). Figure 6b. Take the Zome cube previously constructed. Assume that each blue strut is '1'. Calculate the diagonals, the green and yellow struts. ($\sqrt{2}$ and $\sqrt{3}$)
b) Draw a hexagon, and three diagonal lines across it, to make equilateral triangles. Use the compass to measure that the radius and edges are the same. Bisect one of the triangles. If an edge is '1', then what is a bisected edge? (½) What about the bisector? ($\sqrt{3}/2$ by Pythagoras)
c) Take an octahedron, paper or Zome. If the edges measure '1', what is the height of this form? Have the students look at it two ways. See that from one perspective, the shape has a square plane. This means its diagonal is what? ($\sqrt{2}$) The second route is to take

the √3/2 bisector of one face, go inwards toward the center of the object, realize this leg is ½ and then solving the right triangle. This great application, with fractions and radicals gives √2/2, which needs to be doubled. Figure 8.

Homework:
If the longest leg inside the cube measures '1', what is the diagonal of the square and the edges on the cube? (This one is extra crispy. They need to use ratios.) Check the results they bring to class and partner them so each understands it.

Evaluation:
This is mostly formative and affective work. Evaluate their attitude, participation and attempt at understanding the mathematical relations.

Bridges:
In high school physics and chemistry, students often struggle with radicals. But, those with kinesthetic or artistic intelligence benefit from this work. For the mathematical student, they can tinker with the objects and discover further.

Class Exercise 3 √2 and √3 in the tetrahedron

Objective:
Apply logic, exponential operations, algebra, and fractions in working out the internal dimensions of the tetrahedron. A tricky algebraic task.

Procedure:
a) We will find the internal dimensions of the tetrahedron. Students should be in groups of 2-4 and have a Zome model on hand and reproduce Figure 10b in their notes. Given that each side measures '1', what kind of equations can they come up with regarding each denoted segment? Refer to the text and help the groups with hints along the way. This is pretty hard but they'll really dig in to it.
b) One equation can be solved, based on understanding the tetrahedron's relationship to the cube (Figure 10c). The center of the tetrahedron is the center of the cube, which involves √3. Provide the materials so they can build the cube around their tetrahedron. Again, let them solve this as they can, and give clues along the way.
c) Have them reproduce in their notes the diagrams from Figure 13 (without the lines, and letters denoting h, x and y). What do tetra-, octa-, and icosahedrons share mathematically? (equilateral triangles and their related geometries) What kind of equation could one use to describe the height of each? Now, encourage them to draw in h, x, and y and see if they can write Pythagorean equations to help solve for these variables. See if they can discover, surmise, and agree that the equations will be the same in each case, though the variables change.

Homework:
Summarize the activity and what they learned.

Evaluation:
Grade them for involvement and teamwork, creative thought and effort. Check their notebooks. Perhaps they didn't "get it", but at least did a great job of documenting the thoughts of others. Maybe they'll never be an engineer, but they might at least decide on a technical career.

Bridges:
The tetrahedron is a fundamental form in chemical bonds, and this fact should be bridged with the chemistry teacher to demonstrate why we learn some of these things and how the platonics (and other geometries) are actually found in nature.

Class Exercise 4 **The Hexagon and regular angles**

Objective:
"Fractions *and* hexagons are our friends." Whole-number relationships do not exist between easy Pythagorean triangles like the 3-4-5 and angles like 10°, 50° etc.. There is however *one* interesting pattern to discover.

Procedure:
a) Draw x and y axes and a hexagon in a circle, based at the origin, with a top mark on "y". Draw a line from the origin to the vertex above the +x axis, making a right triangle with the x-axis (Figure 14a). Given a radius of '1', what is the vertical leg? (½) Calculate the horizontal leg. (√3/2). Identify the angles in this triangle. (30-60-90)
b) Reintroduce sin, cos and tan functions, not just in terms of opposite, adjacent, and hypotenuse but now regarding x, y and r. Generate the three values for 30° as fractional values. (Sin 30° = 1/2, Cos 30° = √3/2 and Tan 30° = 1/√3 = √3/3)
c) Draw another graph, and hexagon, this time based on the "x" axis. Draw again a line from the origin to the vertex above the +x axis, draw another line perpendicular to the x axis to make another right triangle. Identify the angle at the origin (60°), and generate its three trigonometric values. (√3/2, 1/2 and √3/2, Figure 14b).
d) Draw a circle around an x-y graph. Bisect the +x and +y axes. Form a right triangle again with the x axis and identify the angles. (45-45-90) Generate the three trig values for 45°. (√2/2, √2/2 and 1)
e) Have the students begin to make a table for use in trigonometry. It should have columns for Angle: in degrees and radians – fractional and decimal, Sin – fractional and decimal, Cos – fractional and decimal and Tan – fractional and decimal.

Homework:
Students should put the values discovered so far into their personal trigonometric table. This should be very organized, as they will use it throughout the material as it develops.

Evaluation:
Check their trig tables, evaluate their participation and effort.

Bridges:
This work is extremely valuable as a basis to understanding a multitude of concepts in trigonometry.

Class Exercise 5 **Quadrant II**

Objective:
Further efforts at understanding trigonometric ratios and patterns.

Procedure:
a) Use x, y, and r in the trigonometric functions. Draw an x-y graph on the board. Take a large teacher's compass, and tie a string to one tip. Use the string to simulate a right triangle, formed with the other leg; the x-axis. As the compass opens the y-string gets longer, the x-leg shortens. What is "y" when the angle is 0°? (0) What is "x" when the angle is 90°? (0) What are the trig functions of 0° and 90°? Note: 0/1 is 0, and 1/0 is not!
b) Draw an x-y graph and a hexagon, based on x. Draw from the origin to the vertex above the –x axis, and from here to the –x axis. This right triangle is in quadrant II, but as with all angles, is rotated from the +x axis; 120°. Its three trig values, using + and – signs for x and y? (Figure 15a, √3/2, -1/2 and -√3). Fill in the trig table.
c) Draw a hexagon, pointing up, on an x-y graph. Draw from the origin to the vertex above the –x axis. This right triangle supplements 150°. Generate again the trigonometric proportions. The students should begin to wonder that the same values

keep appearing. Ask them to solve: $\sqrt{0}/2$, $\sqrt{1}/2$ and $\sqrt{4}/2$. (0, 1/2, and 1) Put these radicals into the trig table and students begin to fill in the blanks, seeing the "whole-radical" relationship to angles that are 1/3, 1/4, and 1/6 of a circle.

d) Go into Quadrant III, doing 210°. The rest of the table to 360° should be possible now without further diagrams or difficulty.

Homework:
Fill in the table, using their calculator to come up with the decimal values, which will make much more sense now.

Evaluation:
Evaluate how well they participate with this development. Create the same images on the chalkboard as they work, raising questions and see how they engage. With the hexagon, do they finally see the relations of 1/2 and $\sqrt{3}/2$ with 30° and 60°? How does their table look?

Bridges:
Laws of Sines and Cosines, Frequency modulation, rotation, and graphing will rely heavily on an understanding of the unit circle and related ratios.

Class Exercise 6 **Fun with Radicals**

Objective:
To provide a further learning experience with the Pythagorean theorem, with a visual application of radicals, using "the Power of 1".

Procedure:
a) Ask students to create a line of length $\sqrt{2}$, using only a compass and a straight edge. If they are unsure, have them make two perpendicular lines whose measure is '1'. By Pythagoras, the hypotenuse is? How could they now make a triangle to get $\sqrt{3}$? Let them work together as needed (Figure 17).
b) Having the lengths $\sqrt{2}$ and $\sqrt{3}$, draw perpendicular lines with those lengths and form a triangle. What will its hypotenuse measure? ($\sqrt{5}$)
c) Next, we want to obtain $\sqrt{6}$. 2 x 3 = 6. We can always draw a line of length 2 or 3 and make multiples of it. But $\sqrt{6}$ takes some thinking. How do we draw multiples of $\sqrt{2}$ or $\sqrt{3}$? If we remember that on the 45-45-90 triangle, the hypotenuse is $\sqrt{2}$ times the side, then this triangle must have side lengths of $\sqrt{3}$ (Figure 19)
d) Can they use triangles and the numbers given so far to find $\sqrt{7}$, $\sqrt{8}$, $\sqrt{10}$, $\sqrt{11}$, $\sqrt{13}$ and $\sqrt{17}$? They could go on and on but this will be creative enough and they should all get it, somewhere along the way.

Homework:
Have them look at their work through this chapter and summarize what they have learned about radicals and the Pythagorean theorem. Encourage them to draw Figure 16 and explain it, and why the lines all go to the x axis.

Evaluation:
Quiz them on radicals/exponents. What is the difference between $(\sqrt{100})^2$ and $\sqrt{(100)^2}$? (In the former, the answer is 100, and the latter is ±100).

Bridges:
Squares and square roots are important numerical concepts that are being overlooked as we seek decimal answers provided by the calculator. Too often in higher math, the calculator can give misleading or incomplete information when taking roots, or inverse trigonometric functions. The students will not only see that they need to be smarter than the machine, but that they keep finding $\sqrt{2}$ and $\sqrt{3}$. Just wait.

5 Five rings

Beginning dialogue

In a typical math classroom, with advanced students and failing students, how can we improve the learning of the "lesser-skilled" students, while also challenging those who are gifted?

Getting started

The techniques given in this book should already have been seen to provide many new avenues of learning and of making the materials interesting to a broader range of students so that they have motivation to try and engage themselves more. It requires effort from people gifted in math because they must think more, create, and work more with others. In the typical math class, how many students does the teacher normally have who "get it", who understand from the start, with very little input from the teacher? These few geniuses may even be ahead of the teacher at times.

Often, it is suggested having these students take the time to help other students, to help each other learn. This can certainly work, and allows students to be more involved with the teaching and learning process. However, there are varied and valuable things the normally gifted math student can further learn which are not so considered today and are vital to the health of our joint future.

In our classrooms, perhaps only a third of the students do well in mathematics. For an equal portion, there is the continual story of a failing, or barely passing grade, on test after test. The student may or may not have been called stupid, by classmates, or even a previous teacher, but certainly by high school, has formed this or some other low opinion about themselves.

There exist students who are difficult to teach. However, the vast majority of low scoring students are quite intelligent. There are students who function well in three languages, yet struggle with math (given in their non-native tongue). The thing is to tap into that intelligence, perhaps using it as a key to get these students to try again old themes, at higher maturity levels, where a renewed sense of motivation may just help them finally succeed. As this is a book centered in mathematics, we will use math as a model. However, the same ideas apply to all subjects and the challenge for teachers is how to find their own "tricks" to engage varied intelligences.

The intelligent student

First, let's look at what those intelligences are. Students may or may not be the best in a given subject. It doesn't mean only that they are or are not intelligent, talented, or capable with that material. They may be skilled, but with a different subject. Perhaps they have some or all of the following gifts: linguistic, mathematic, historic, spatial, kinesthetic, musical, social, and naturalistic. What these mean is that students who may not do well in math (which means more than half) aren't stupid. In so many cases, these same students may be extremely gifted in learning languages, building things with their hands, playing sport, performing music, carrying on social interaction, or of bringing history and natural sciences to life. We can see this when we have the same students for more than one subject.

Further, Jungian material shows that peoples' interests and abilities affect how and what they learn. Here there are four basic personality types: Epimethius, Prometheus, Apollo and Dyonisis. Maybe a student can sit and process numbers all day and not need too much from the teacher. Perhaps they are gifted and hungrily look for more complex problems. They may wish to quickly get on to other more urgent matters concerning social situations. Or they may just want to go play, and then play more. The challenge for math and science teachers is that the divisions are not equal. A good amount of the population is normally into society and play.

Those who study the enneagram see nine personality types; Briggs-Myers suggests sixteen. Some say there are nine intelligence types, others say seven. In India, the Ayurvedic system discusses three body energies that control the body; Pitta (fire), Vata (air), Kapha (water). Could this affect how a person learns? Could we just look at a person and make assumptions about them? The Waldorf system essentially does, by identifying students as Choleric, Sanguine, Phlegmatic and Melancholic. There are colour therapists who can assess personality based on what and how a person paints.

The point is, we should consider that our audience, in any subject is comprised of a variety of intelligence, personalities and needs, and to be more successful, we can try to tap into this deep well of possibility by whatever technique we choose. Does this detour from what we are asked to do in math classes? In many cases today, a detour *is* being sought.

Gone are the days of the traditional classroom, where a trained, respected teacher is able to lecture at will. Today's students are in a hurry and are less willing to sit through boring or confusing lectures. We know the potential and untrained talent of our youth. How do we hold on to them? Or more, get them to just want to stay in school, learn what we feel are important things, and get a valuable education - rather than be a mere stepping stone to further placement, fast cash, and material reward?

We can have surprising successes with students of mathematics, physics, arts, history, geography, chemistry etc., when we show how the subjects relate to each other, to the world around and to the individual. Youth want to know their world, and while the internet is so intoxicating, it lacks that which we can still provide: we can still be that guide.

In this chapter, we will use Φ (the Golden Mean - Divine Proportion) for engaging the varied intelligences and learning styles, but it should be seen that throughout the book this is what we are attempting to do.

Introductory quiz

The teacher should obtain some of the following items and place them on a table for students to look at. Ask them to write down and silently answer for themselves the associated question. Later, give them time to share their thoughts with each other. Sometimes it is good to test student knowledge at the start, rather than end, of a theme; to see what they already know and let them have the chance to display it to their peers.

Figure 1 Related imagery. Pentagram – (Heinrich Agrippa's *Libri tres de occulta philosophia*). Dodecahedron – (Da Vinci), Pyramid (courtesy David Furlong).

How do the pictures in Figure 1 relate? There will be many interesting answers and guesses given. Maybe a student in the class is already familiar with Φ (phi), the Golden Mean. Many books and internet resources are available on the golden mean and this is suggested. For now, we will look at the number as it can be used to assist the instruction of mathematics, with physics and art.

Figure 2 Ritratto di Frà Luca Pacioli (Museo e Gallerie di Capodimonte in Naples).

As is well known, the Fibonacci series relates to phi. What is this series? What is phi – Φ? Phi is a proportion whose value is approximately 1.618. It was called the Divine Proportion during the Renaissance, by a mathematician called Fra Pacioli. This monk was a contemporary of Leonardo da Vinci (who provided his illustrations). There was a great interest in this proportion during the middle ages, as found in art and architecture. A great many artists experimented with geometric form, in art we enjoy to this day.

There are many ways to determine the Divine Proportion. One we will use is to draw a 1 x 2 rectangle. From the upper right corner, swing an arc of unit '1' radius, and then draw a line across the rectangle, continuing to the arc, as shown in Figure 3. If we take the measure of this diagonal across the rectangle (by Pythagoras, √5) add the extending line (length of '1') and divide by 2 (from bisecting) we obtain phi: $1.618 = (1 + \sqrt{5})/2$

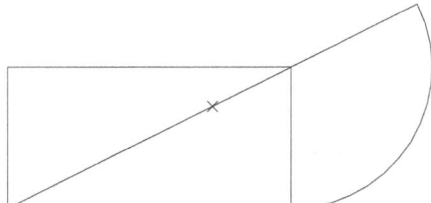

Figure 3 Creating the phi measure, from "x" to either end of the diagonal line.

The proportion may not seem like such a great thing, by this complicated technique. And yet, the builders of the United Nations building in New York, the Parthenon in Greece, and the Great Pyramid in Egypt used it within these constructions. We'll see much more in chapter 7.

Figure 4a Parthenon, believed to have been built to Phi proportions.

The proportion is just that, a comparison of two measures. For example, have students take a line and cut it (hence the alternative name "Divine Section"), such that the proportion of the longer piece to the shorter is the same as the whole to the longer. Students can use algebra *and* fractions to solve this one.

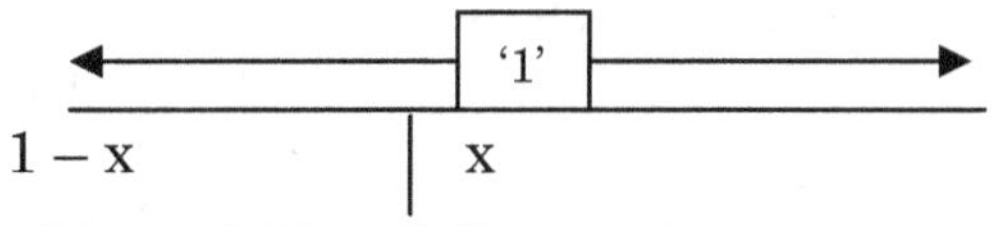

Figure 4b The "Golden" section.

$$\frac{1}{1-x} = \frac{1-x}{x}$$

The students will probably need help setting it up, and then how to solve? Did anyone guess that we need to cross multiply? Doing so gives: $x = 1 - 2x + x^2$

By working the equation into the form $x^2 - 3x + 1 = 0$, we see a real application of the quadratic formula for students. Have them memorize this formula. It will make their next years of mathematics easier if they do.

$$\frac{-b \pm \sqrt{b^2 - 4ac}}{2a}$$

Using this friend of ours gives two possible solutions: 2.618 and 0.382. The former, being greater than '1' is obviously not suitable, but the second is. (Interestingly, 2.618 is the square of phi.)

So, if "x" = 0.382, then 1 – x = 0.618 and their ratio is of course 1.618. This same process can be seen in the proportions of the human body, for which we will use da Vinci's Vitruvian man

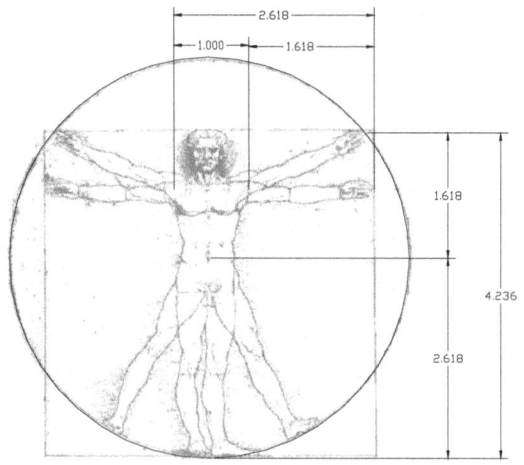

Figure 5 Demonstrating the phi proportions, roughly found in the human body.

Ask students where the center of their body is. Most will say their belly button. A great exercise to do in class is to have the students measure themselves. Have them stand up against a wall and measure their height from the floor. Then have them put their finger to their belly button and measure this height. (They will see that it is *not* half of their height, and hence *not* the middle.) Have them divide the larger number by the smaller. Then, take a class average. The answer should be pretty close to Phi. (The results will not be exact. Maybe they have their shoes on, and are also too nervous, being teenagers, to stand still and get the height to their belly buttons measured. But better than 99% accuracy *is* achievable (Figure 5).

Fun with numbers

Have the students pick any number that they like, and then partner with someone. Together, they should take the smaller number and add it to the larger. Take the result, and the larger of the two original numbers and add them. For example, say the numbers were 3 and 17. Add 3 + 17 to get 20. Add 17 + 20 to get 37, and then 20 + 37 to get 57 and so forth. Let them work independently, to check each others' addition skills. They should do at least 12 additions. Divide the 13th number by the 12th. They should all get the same result: 1.618. This is interesting that any two numbers can start a sequence which converges to the phi proportion. Note: all further additions merely continue this.

A Renaissance mathematician named Fibonacci discovered that many animals reproduce and some plants and trees branch according to a special sequence, named after him, which begins with 0 and 1 and then continues:

$$0, 1, 1, 2, 3, 5, 8, 13, 21, 34, 55, 89, 144, 233, \ldots$$

It was Fibonacci who journeyed east and upon his return introduced Arabic numerals to the West, in the 13th century. Otherwise, we'd be putting roman numerals into our calculators.

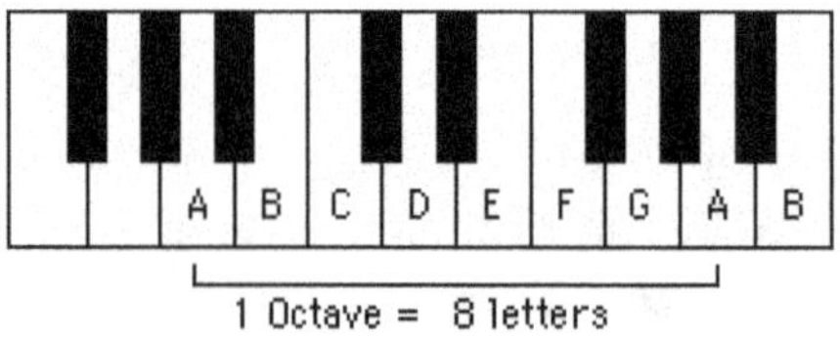

Figure 6 The keyboard, and its Fibonacci connection.

Where do you see the Fibonacci series on a piano? In every (1) octave, there are 2 and 3 black keys, making 5 altogether, intermixed with 8 white keys, and hence 13 in total.

The spiral

A great exercise to now have the students perform, with compass and protractor, is to draw a series of ever enlarging ¼ circles according to the sequence of numbers. A good place to start is in the lower right of the page. Then work clockwise. The teacher will have to practice this a bit before giving instruction. The trick is that after each ¼ circle is drawn, the compass must be enlarged and then the pencil (not the point.) must be placed back on the end of the previous arc. Each ¼ turn should begin and end parallel or perpendicular to the sides or top and bottom of the page.

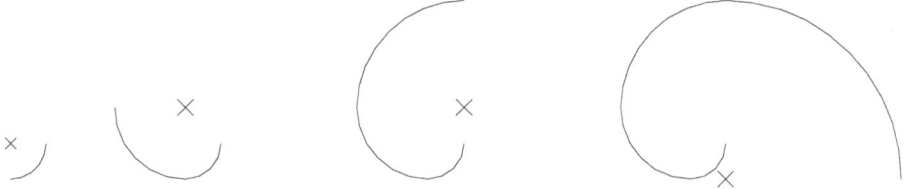

Figure 7 A spiral from the Fibonacci sequence. "X" marks the center of each radius.

The steps are shown in Figure 7. Begin with a downward ¼ turn, radius of '1'. Then, with the compass doubled in size, the center of the next arc will shift one unit above the starting point. Swing a ¼ turn. Then, enlarge the compass to '3'. Again, placing the pencil first means the center of this new arc must shift to the right, as shown in the third diagram of Figure 7. Continuing, enlarge the compass to '5', relocate the center (as shown) and draw the next ¼. By now, the students usually have the technique, though several will just not manage to swing their arcs enough and the resultant will not look very nice.

Centimeters work really well for this process, as they allow for better growth and drawing of a larger spiral on the page.

Once the students have drawn their spiral, ask them where they know spirals to exist, in Nature. Have them write down all the ideas they can come up with, working independently, and then have them share.

Sea shell	Galaxies	Tornado/hurricane	Fingerprints
Bighorn sheep	Pig's tails	Grape tendrils	Fern shoots
Pine cones	Sunflowers	Leaves/petals	Storms
Ears	Sea horse tails	Human/animal fetuses	Hair

Parts of the body (trace a spiral around the nose, eye and down the jaw)
An apple cut along its axis

Note. Most of these figures do **not** come in the proportion of an exact Phi spiral. The point is that the spiral is a natural form, and that we can obtain a few specific forms using phi.

The mirrored spiral

What happens if we take the spiral and reflect it back along its axis? (We create a leaf or petal) Depending upon how we then reproduce this image, while rotating (and how many times) we make images of flowers, like the rose or sunflower. The side view is like fruit, a pine cone, or an egg. We can also see that the pinecone has a three dimensional spiral shape, if we track the individual scales.

  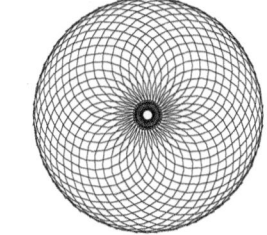

Figure 8a The Spiral   8b A spiral "reflected' about its axis, and rotated.   Figure 8c The sunflower

For what other purpose could we use this spiral, we humans? Let's start by having the students put one in a circle. For this, they can do the spiral roughly, by hand (as shown in Figure 9a – use the compass only for the circle). They should reproduce it in this form, three times on their page.

Beginning with the left one, try to draw another spiral across from it, or clocked around 180°. For the middle picture, have them place two additional spirals in the drawing, clocked now by 120° (the students can draw radial lines on the figure to help see how to mirror or rotate the additional spirals). Lastly, for the third diagram, have them rotate by 90°, placing three additional spirals in the drawing. Their work should look like Figure 9b.

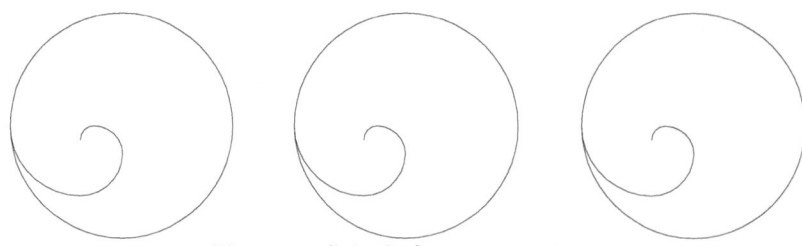

Figure 9a Spirals for constructions.

Do students recognize any of these forms? Usually, they quickly pick out the Yin and Yang symbol. What do they know about this? It can be thought to represent polarity: male - female, positive-negative, up-down, left-right, and other duality. Why is it a key symbol within Oriental culture, and is there anything we in the West could learn from it?

Figure 9b Spirals completed constructions.

The middle figure may be recognized as the triskellon; a Celtic symbol. This is often found in churches and cathedrals, particularly gothic and neo-gothic designs. Notice in Figure 10 how the image seems to reflect spirits in flight.

Figure 10 Typical Church carving, often found in gothic window frames as well.

Catholics have long used the symbolism of three to represent different facets of God; the Trinity.

Figure 11 Historic svastikas, in a cathedral, Basque Lauburu.

And the third image? It's interesting teaching this material to German students, for the sorry reaction they at first have when it is revealed that this is the swastika. This is a very ancient symbol, long predating its misuse and defamation. It can still be found throughout the Indian subcontinent, usually painted red, white or yellow. It has been used all over the planet, usually to represent the Sun, or as a sign of peace. Misuse has taken away such beautiful connotations. That is one of the points of this chapter. Symbols (of power) have many mathematical processes involved with their geometries, and Phi is a surprising unit within them.

The word originates from Sanskrit (svastika), and means a symbol of good luck or well-being, which might explain why it is so often found on buses in the Indian subcontinent. The Greeks called it tetraskellon, the Norse named it Thor's hammer. And Native

Americans also used the symbol as a sign for the Sun. It would be very positive if we could reintroduce the swastika into its rightful place as a positive emblem, and remove the negativity which it now reflects. We must be aware that any symbol can be put to evil representation, even as Neo-Nazis today are skirting prohibitions against the swastika and now are creating a three-legged form, which will *not* be reprinted here. Could this corrupt the historic use of the triskellon?

Finally, if we do five rotated spirals, mirrored, we obtain the images in Figure 12. Notice the five-pointed stars buried within.

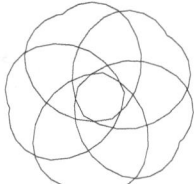 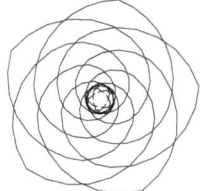

Figure 12 Five rotated-double spirals.

The interesting thing about the rose (the natural variety) is that many forms of edible fruit have this blossom in common (and hence are members of the rose family). For example; apples, pears, peaches, plums, cherries, raspberries, and blackberries. If we look at the back of the flower, the greenery that has opened to provide the flower is in the shape of a five pointed star, with which we will soon make further discovery.

Drawing the 5-pointed star

When we drew hexagons, equilateral triangles, squares, dodecagons, and even octagons, it was possible to do so with only a compass and ruler. To draw things like the five-pointed star, it is valuable to use this as an exercise in precision with a protractor.

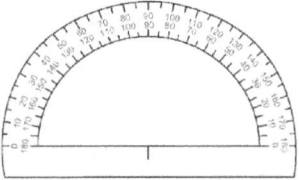

Figure 13 Common protractor showing the double counting scale.

This is yet another place where the high school, and college, teacher can be surprised. Many times, students don't really know how to use this item. With two sets of numbers, they may or may not know the difference between 60° or 120°. While the teacher may not wish to concern himself with that fact, what is important is how to distinguish between 68° and 72°, and again, many in the class will be surprisingly unsure.

Draw a large radius circle of 4 inches. Do NOT let students trace their protractor to pre-determine the size of the circle. Let them figure out how to transfer points. Make a top mark as before. Now figure out how to draw a five-pointed star. This is done by dividing 360 by 5, giving 72.

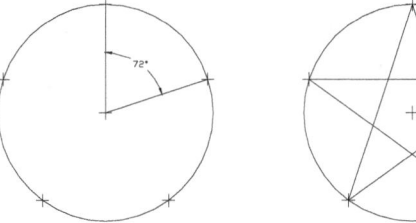

Figure 14 Creating the five-pointed star, with a protractor.

Carefully the students must align with the center of the circle and the top, and then measure every 72 degrees. Many mistakes are made as the students become aware of symmetry in only one axis. (They must begin one side at the top, flip the protractor, and do the other side, also from the top.) The pictures they create will show the teacher how much they know.

Why is the star such an important figure? How does it relate to the human body? How does it relate to flowers and plants? How about astronomy and weather?

Let's again draw a star using a radius of 2.25 for the circle (actually, 2.227 would be more exact but for those students using the inch, it will work well enough to get the idea.)

Have them measure across the inner pentagon of the star. Do they see that each side of the pentagon equals '1'? Now measure to the star tip, from the pentagon. Do they get about 1.6 to 1.625? This is what is interesting about the star. When the pentagon measures '1', the length of the point is phi, exactly 1.618.

Notice that each point has an internal angle of 36°. If we take the cosine of 36° and multiply the result by 2, we also get phi.

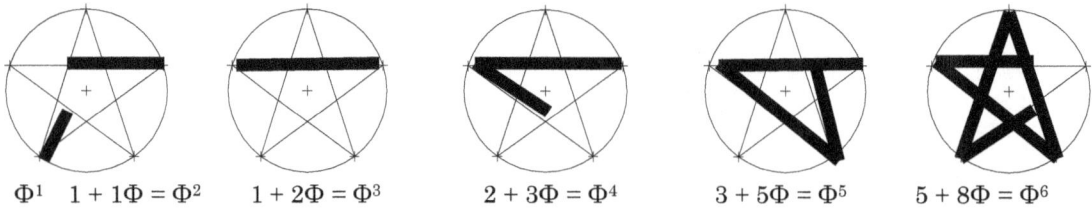

Φ^1 $1 + 1\Phi = \Phi^2$ $1 + 2\Phi = \Phi^3$ $2 + 3\Phi = \Phi^4$ $3 + 5\Phi = \Phi^5$ $5 + 8\Phi = \Phi^6$

Figure 15 Φollowing Φ around the star to Φind Φ^1 Φ^2 Φ^3 Φ^4 Φ^5 Φ^6....

Let's trace around the star, taking individual segments. Add one side of the pentagon to a line extending from it: $1 + \Phi$. This value, 2.618, is equal to Φ^2, as shown in the first drawing of Figure 15. Phi is the only number whose square equals the original number plus '1'. If we draw the whole line across the top of the star, we get $1 + 2\Phi$, a value equal to Φ^3. We can see how this further progresses as we trace around the star, as the pictures show.

Have the students go through the process of building the table shown in Figure 16. What is fascinating is that the Fibonacci sequence, (or any sequence) builds up to the phi ratio. But then, by taking exponent values of phi we find the Fibonacci ratio as multiples of phi added together. So, the sequence builds the number, and exponents of the number build the sequence!

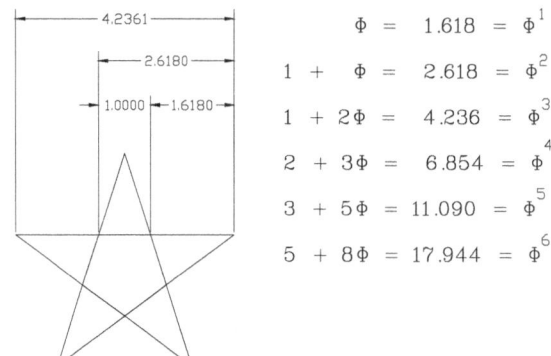

$\Phi = 1.618 = \Phi^1$
$1 + \Phi = 2.618 = \Phi^2$
$1 + 2\Phi = 4.236 = \Phi^3$
$2 + 3\Phi = 6.854 = \Phi^4$
$3 + 5\Phi = 11.090 = \Phi^5$
$5 + 8\Phi = 17.944 = \Phi^6$

Figure 16 Building the Fibonacci sequence from the Φ proportion - sequence.

Why do generals have stars on their shoulders and countries on their flag? (Note that flags, and credit cards, are in the phi proportion.) Where else is the star put to use? The five-pointed star has long been associated with pagan belief and magic, and hence today many people wish to then associate it with devilry and Satanism. Again, we should ask ourselves, "Why do humans use these symbols?" Why do the Chinese use the five-pointed star in their medical system?

Figure 17 Five Element Theory – (Mother Nature). Fractals – (courtesy Bruce Rawles), Eliphas Levi

Phi you later!

We will look at more measurements in the human body. For some reason, the middle finger seems to give the best results, and get the best response from students. Measure it. But first, we will make a pair of phi calipers. This is a good creative exercise.

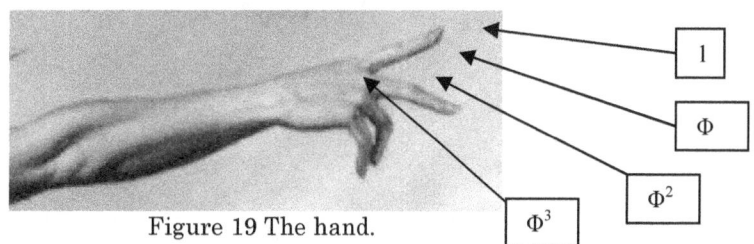

Figure 18 Making a simple "Φ" caliper.   Figure 19 The hand.

Have students take the large star that they made. They should cut two strips of hard paper, to the length of a cross member and then pin them together where they cross over, as shown in Figure 18. This is a phi caliper. Students can use it to measure between each knuckle in a given finger, to the wrist and out to the elbow; with a long enough caliper. Use the shorter legs to measure one digit. Flip the caliper, without opening or closing it, to measure the next digit, seeing that the caliper often agrees. Let them measure each other, *within reason*. They should notice things about height vs. width of the eye, the ear and other parts of the face. This is a neat discovery exercise.

If they measure the spacing between knuckles, particularly the finger of salutation, they will notice that the spacing is 'Φ' proportional. (Not exact yet close, depending on the hand.) This means that if from the finger tip to the first knuckle measures '1', then the next distance is Φ and the next Φ^2, Φ^3 etc.

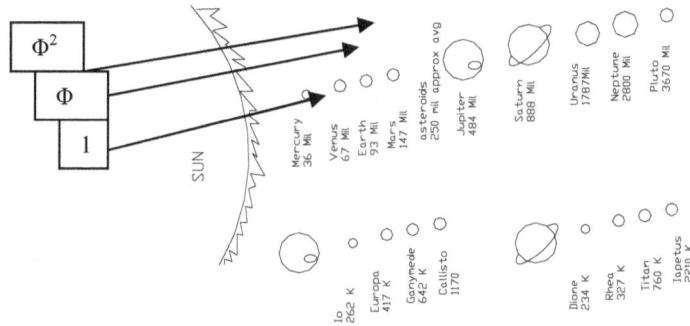

Figure 20 Planets around the Sun - moons around planets Φ^1 Φ^2 Φ^3 Φ^4 Φ^5 Φ^6...

It gets more interesting if we compare distances between the orbits of planets in our solar system. The proportions come about as close to phi as those we got from measuring our students. If we call the average diameter of Mercury's orbit '1', from Venus to the Sun is roughly Φ and the next are Φ^2, Φ^3 etc. The asteroid belt falls within this spacing, as do the large moons around Jupiter and Saturn. (In Saturn's case, we might have to consider Φ^2 for one of the moons.) It's not exact, though nothing in nature ever *is*, but it is a close approximation, and the only number which comes near.

Was the Creator a Mathematician?

Figure 21 Creator as Geometer (Bible Moralisée 1250)   Ancient of Days (God as Architect 1794 W. Blake)

Nature is a vision of the science of the Elohim – Milton, by William Blake

3-D application

As we have done with four of the other Platonic forms, let us now build the fifth. It's relatively easy, as shown in Figure 22a, so long as the students are precise. Be sure to leave tabs for gluing.

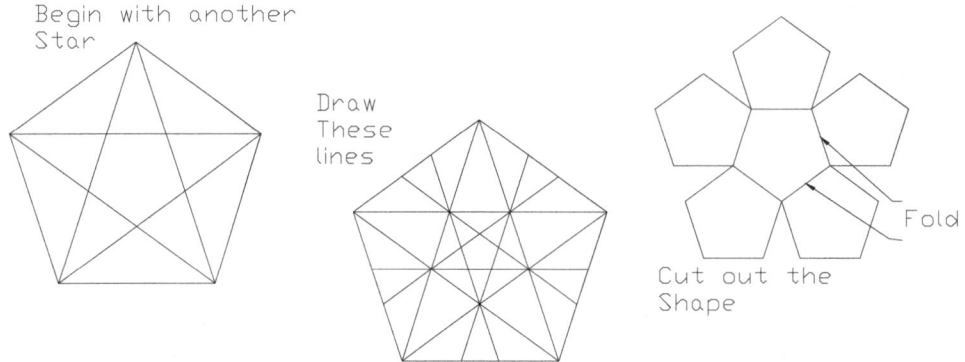

Figure 22a Making the dodecahedron from card stock.

We can make two halves and put them together to build the dodecahedron. If careful, we can make it all from one sheet of paper and fold. Leave tabs for gluing, and glue a piece of string to the inside before closing, so that we can hang it from the ceiling.

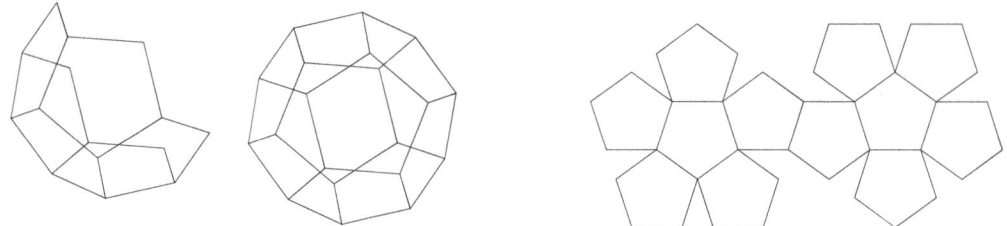

Figure 22b The dodecahedron, and the flat pattern for creating it from one paper.

We can perform a second technique, to create little pyramids by folding upward to join at a peak. By doing this, we create the five-sided pyramids that can be glued to a dodecahedron in order to stellate it. See Figures 23 - 24.

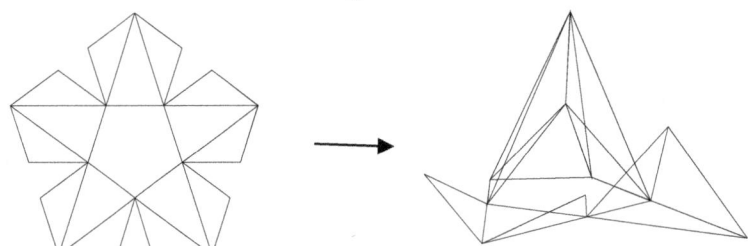

Figure 23 Flat pattern and folding to make a star pyramid.

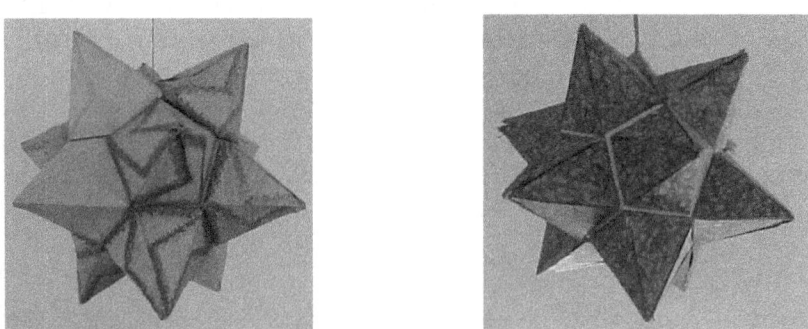

Figure 24a Encourage students to create exciting designs, before folding/gluing.

We can use zometools to explore these shapes further. If we stellate the icosahedron, we can see that five points of the star are in a plane, defining a pentagon. Connecting these will make a dodecahedron. As this can *also* be stellated, we can continue, seeing that a stellated dodecahedron defines an icosahedron. We can build outward in recurring cycles, thus making a fractal in 3D. We have come full circle, all with the phi proportion. As this is the approximate spacing of the planets, perhaps Kepler's diagram was not so inaccurate a model of the solar system.

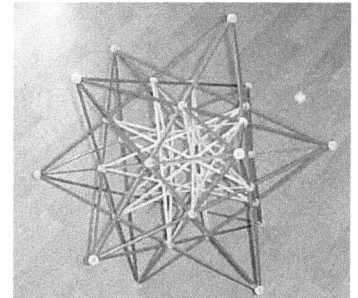

Figure 24b Stellated icosahedron inside a dodecahedron, which is then stellated.

Something more

The stellations were discovered by or at least attributed to Kepler, with two additional forms named after Louis Poinset, a French mathematician of the early 19th century.

There is an interesting study of words and numbers called gematria. This is somewhat related to numerology and particularly associated to the Hebraic alphabet but also used with Greek and Latin letters whereby each letter is given a numeric value, for example A, or Aleph representing '1'. Followers and students of gematria believe in mystical associations between words in the Bible, Quran, and other sacred texts; they also believed in the numerical quantities summed up in their letters.

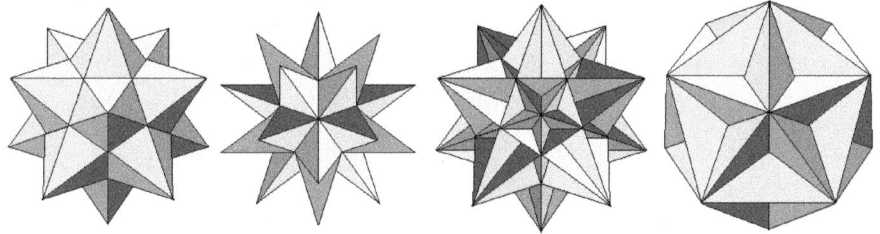

Figure 24c Kepler-Poinset forms (Steven Dutch, University of Wisconsin).

Certain numbers are thought to have special meaning, beyond lucky 7, or unlucky 13. Many think the number 666 represents something evil, while others see it and all numbers involving 6 as indicative of the Sun. (WWW in Hebraic appears to be "Vav, Vav, Vav".) Vav is the 6th letter of the alphabet.

Figure 24d Phi related art. Piercing the Veil – (F. Hart). Then – (P. Stang)

The word gematria may reflect that there are 22 letters in the Hebrew alphabet and a like number of regular bodies (five Platonic, thirteen Archimedean and four Kepler-Poinsot) and just as numbers are thought to hold certain mysticism, so too geometric forms.

Whatever we wish to believe for ourselves, allowing students to know about the existence of these other ideas and symbolic use of shapes and mathematics makes the subject a lot more intriguing.

Beginning our mystery studies

We have looked at creating the five pointed star by dividing a circle and using a protractor. It was more complicated than what we did for the hexagon. It could be easier to make the star, if there existed a technique by which we could again use only a compass and ruler. However, we cannot just make five marks around the circle, as we did for the hexagon, for we need to know the spacing between each mark.

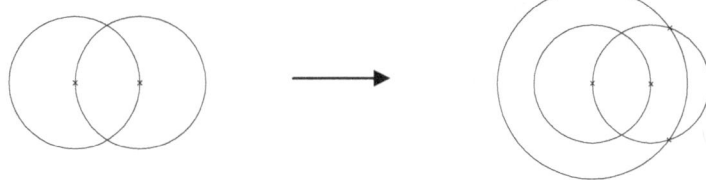

Figure 25a Vesica Piscis with radii of '1'.   25b Draw 3rd circle of radius Φ.

There is a technique we can follow, and it is of course related to phi. We will revisit our diagram in which we made the phi proportion (Figure 3). Let us set our compass to a measure of '1', by setting it to the short vertical length on the rectangle. Now, make a vesica piscis as shown in Figure 25a.

Next, reset the compass to the length created for phi. Note: It doesn't matter what lengths are in the rectangle, so long as they are exactly in 1:2 proportion. Precision is *very* important now. Draw another circle, as shown, with the same center as that original on the left but with the phi measurement.

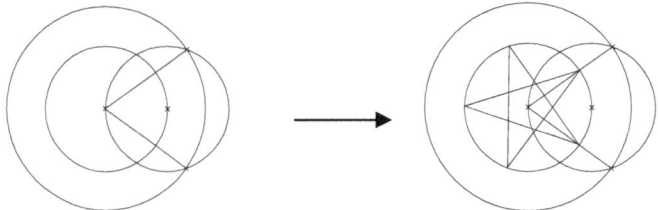

Figure 25c Φinishing the Φive pointed star.

Use a ruler to line up with the center of the first circle and the crossing points on the second, and make marks on the first circle. These points are exactly 72 degrees apart, if done correctly. Adjust the compass to this arc length and make three more marks around the circle. This one will really test precision. Done correctly, it is 100% accurate. Have students confirm by swinging an arc from both directions to see that they come together in the same place.

We can spend a lot of time in math lectures exposing students to phi and they will always come away with the same question: "Why do we hear so much about pi, but not about phi?" Why is this not considered important to teach, that their bodies have a mathematical relationship to the construction of the universe? Why also are a lot of mathematicians reluctant to admit to the "magic" and awe of Phi?

Further, why don't we hear anything about seven? In Chapter 7 of this book, we will. For now, let us see if there isn't something in this new technique, by which we could divide the circle. Later we will see why we would want to.

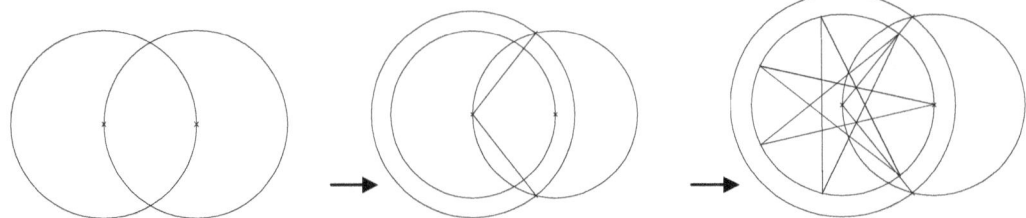

Figure 26a Vesica Piscis - radii Φ (3rd circle has radius of '2')   26b Φinishing.

Use a technique similar to that shown for making the five pointed star. Let's begin by drawing another vesica piscis, this time using phi as our radius (Figure 26a). Be careful of the layout so that there is enough room on the paper. Next, have the students set the radius to '2' on their compasses, now using that horizontal part of the rectangle from Figure 3. In this way they will have put everything in proper proportion. Again, draw from the original center and get two crossing points. Connect these points to that center.

Figure 27 Interaction of seven and five (Athanasius Kircher:*Oedipus Aegyptiacus*).

The two intercepts, and the center of the rightmost circle, provide three points of the seven-pointed star (to within an accuracy of 99.779% - a minor error that cannot be detected using a hand compass.) Set the compass to this size (just a bit less) and make four more marks around the circle. Have the students check to ensure that it worked. This is the ultimate test of their abilities (and very difficult to obtain).

Phi 3-D

We were able to solve the geometries of the cube and octahedron, with √2 and √3. The tetrahedron's make-up involves fractions and combinations of √2 and √3. But how to solve out the icosa- and dodecahedrons?

As previously mentioned, in the icosahedron are complex relationships, but at least each face relates to that of the tetra- and octahedrons. We could conceivably attempt to find the center of this volume, through a series of calculations. Or we can try logic and observation as a start.

 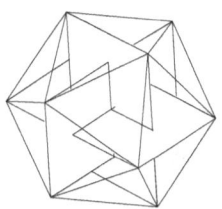

Figure 28a Φ rectangles on 3 axes.   28b All points and 6 edges of the icosahedron.

If we look carefully, we will notice that there are rectangular relationships between far edges in the icosahedron, perpendicular to one another; following x-, y-, and z- axes.

What is the nature of these rectangles? If we measure them, we find them to be exactly 1 x Φ. This makes finding the center easier, though it's radius is not so attractive: ½√(Φ² + 1) – by Pythagoras. Still, it is at least solvable, with a recognizable number. Figure 28a shows these rectangles within the icosahedron. Zometools are great for displaying this.

Each edge of the icosahedron is either a short side of a rectangle, or reaches to their end points. If we call the center point the origin, each corner of the icosahedron will have coordinates along x, y and z of ± 0, ½, and Φ/2.

And the dodecahedron? Do students notice that where it has 12 faces, the icosahedron had 12 points? For the Icosahedron's 20 faces, there are 20 points on the dodecahedron. This is why they stellate together. There are similar relations between the cube and octahedron, where we see relationships between √2 and √3. Too, we have seen that the tetrahedron interacts very well with the cube, *and* the dodecahedron. What does this then mean?

Perhaps, there is a phi relationship which could help us figure out the dodecahedral geometry. There is. First, we must notice that again, there are rectangles which cross over inside the dodecahedron, also at right angles to each other.

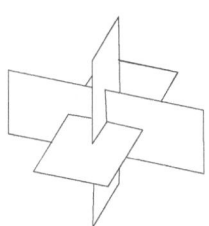 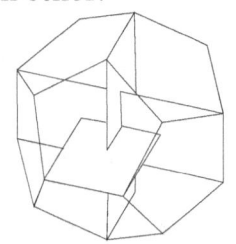

Figure 29a Φ² rectangles on 3 axes.   29b 12 points, 6 edges of the Dodecahedron.

Again, we can see that these help us to obtain the geometry of the dodecahedron, though this time not every vertex is picked up. However, enough points are captured to lock down the geometry (size) of each face. We can measure each rectangle, and here, if the short side measures unit '1', we will find the long edge to be Φ^2. Through calculation the radius of the dodecahedron is $\frac{1}{2}\sqrt{(\Phi^4 + 1)}$.

With the edge as '1', and our understanding of the star and pentagon, we find that Φ is the distance from the endpoint of one of the rectangular edges to the peak of a pentagonal face. Thus, if we denote the intersection of the three rectangles as the origin, every corner of those rectangles will have coordinates along x-, y-, and z- of ± 0, 1/2 and $\Phi^2/2$ (similar to those of the icosahedron). Of course, finding the last eight points will be a bit more work, but they can be seen to be symmetrical.

And the thing about Φ is...

In the cube, we found that the longest length measured $\sqrt{3}$. When the cube is made from the shortest blue Zometools, it takes two short yellow pieces to create the diagonal. Interestingly, when the dodecahedron is made from medium blues, it takes two long yellows to cross its center. While the blue increased by a scale of Φ, the yellow lengthened by a factor of Φ^2. It makes one wonder if there is some relationship between Φ and $\sqrt{3}$. There is...

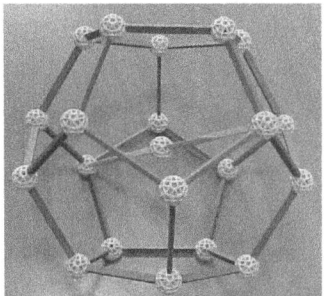  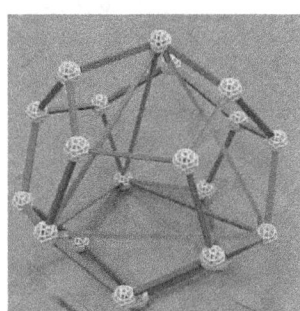

Figure 30 Models for calculating possible Φ-, $\sqrt{2}$ and $\sqrt{3}$ relationships.

If the edges of the cube measure '1', then those of the dodecahedron measure Φ. The long side of the rectangle, connecting opposite edges, is Φ^3 units long, so we note that the diagonal across the dodecahedron is $\sqrt{(\Phi^6 + \Phi^2)}$. Using Zome gives us a clue because in each color, the sizes increase by the Φ proportion. In this scheme, two long yellows would correspond to $\sqrt{3} \cdot \Phi^2$, which would be equivalent to $\sqrt{(\Phi^6 + \Phi^2)}$. We can factor out of the radical, reducing to $\Phi\sqrt{(\Phi^4 + 1)}$ and further manipulate the equation until we achieve $\sqrt{3} = \sqrt{(\Phi^4 + 1)}/\Phi$. It's not the neatest equation to work with, but there is a relationship between $\sqrt{3}$ and Φ.

Root	Φ relation	Number	Φ relation
		1	$\Phi^1 - 1/\Phi$
$\sqrt{2}$	$\sqrt{(\Phi^3 + 1)}/\Phi$	3	$\Phi^2 + 1/\Phi^2$
$\sqrt{3}$	$\sqrt{(\Phi^4 + 1)}/\Phi$	4	$\Phi^3 - 1/\Phi^3$
$\sqrt{5}$	$\sqrt{(\Phi^5 + 2)}/\Phi$	7	$\Phi^4 + 1/\Phi^4$
$\sqrt{6}$	$\sqrt{(\Phi^6 - \sqrt{5})}/\Phi$	11	$\Phi^5 - 1/\Phi^5$
$\sqrt{7}$	$\sqrt{(\Phi^8 + 1)}/\Phi^2$	18	$\Phi^6 + 1/\Phi^6$
		29	$\Phi^7 - 1/\Phi^7$
Radii		47	$\Phi^8 + 1/\Phi^8$
dodecahedron	$\sqrt{(\Phi^4 + 1)}/2$		
icosahedron	$\sqrt{(\Phi^2 + 1)}/2$	$\sqrt{5}$	$\Phi^1 + 1/\Phi$
		2	$\Phi^1 + 1/\Phi^2$

Table 1 Φ relations in various numbers.

Could some relationship exist also between $\sqrt{2}$ and Φ? When we see that the tetrahedron fits inside the dodecahedron, we know that this must in fact be the case, remembering that the green struts of the tetrahedron correspond to a $\sqrt{2}$ value in the cube. By quite a bit of work we come up with an interesting relation; $\sqrt{2} = \sqrt{(\Phi^3 + 1)}/\Phi$ Not only is there also a numeric link between $\sqrt{2}$ and Φ, but it forms a pattern with the root of 3.

If we manipulate radical numbers, by squaring and summing, and then taking the root, in combination with all of the "tricks" of Φ, we can find roots of further numbers. We need not restrict ourselves to roots. Numbers themselves can have interesting relationships to Φ, all as Table 1 shows.

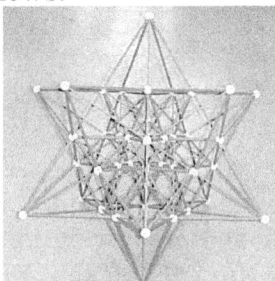

Figure 31 Star of David, or stellated icosahedron, inside a stellated dodecahedron.

This table also reveals a new pattern: 1, 3, 4, 7, 11, 18, 29, ... the second most known Φ sequence after that of Fibonacci. Seeing particularly that Φ is built into the makeup of √2 and √3, and perhaps all roots and whole numbers in some form, has brought all of our work in a circle. Each of the Platonic shapes interacts with the others, and all can ultimately be put into the dodecahedron, which Plato assigned to the universe, and which would most fill the encircling sphere. As Φ truly defines the geometry of this form, it *must* also define then all those others, which we have seen to be true.

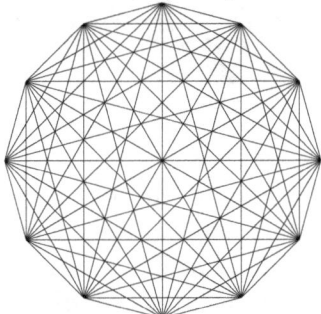 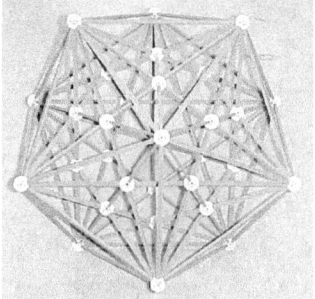

Figure 32. Typical student experimentation with a dodecagon. Similar result from stellating a dodecahedron, enclosed in an icosahedron.

Students struggle with operations involving fractions. The same is true of radicals. An interesting journey of discovery is to take the fraction/radical value of phi: $(1 + \sqrt{5})/2$ and "square" it. Afterall, do we learn $(a+b)^2 = a^2 + 2ab + b^2$ just to apply it to the equally abstract $(3x +2)^2$?

$$\text{Note: } \frac{(1+ \sqrt{5})^2}{2^2} = \frac{1^2 + 2(1)(\sqrt{5}) + (\sqrt{5})^2}{4} = \frac{1 + 5 + 2\sqrt{5}}{4} = \frac{3 + \sqrt{5}}{2}$$

This $(3 + \sqrt{5})/2$ is the value of Φ^2. Let's continue, using Pascal's triangle on Φ^3, again, so that we see real application.

Triangle: 1
     1 1
   1 2 1
1 3 3 1

applied: $\dfrac{(1+ \sqrt{5})^3}{2^3} =$

$$\frac{1^3 + 3(1)^2(\sqrt{5}) + 3(1)(\sqrt{5})^2 + (\sqrt{5})^3}{8} = \frac{1 + 3\sqrt{5} + 15 + 5\sqrt{5}}{8} = 2 + \sqrt{5}$$

When we continue, with one technique or other, we find that $\Phi^4 = (7 + 3\sqrt{5})/2$. Doesn't seem to tell us much unless we understand fractions and manipulate the value for Φ^3. With such efforts, we find patterns throughout the process, as shown in Table 2.

Radical value	Equivalent	Radical value	Equivalent
$(1 + \sqrt{5})/2$	Φ^1	$(1 - \sqrt{5})/2$	$1/\Phi$
$(3 + \sqrt{5})/2$	Φ^2	$(3 - \sqrt{5})/2$	$1/\Phi^2$
$(4 + 2\sqrt{5})/2$	Φ^3	$(4 - 2\sqrt{5})/2$	$1/\Phi^3$
$(7 + 3\sqrt{5})/2$	Φ^4	$(7 - 3\sqrt{5})/2$	$1/\Phi^4$
$(11 + 5\sqrt{5})/2$	Φ^5	$(11 - 5\sqrt{5})/2$	$1/\Phi^5$

Table 2 Fractional/radical values showing phi's dependence upon both of its sequences.

We now see both sets of numbers forming: (1, 1, 2, 3, 5...) and (1, 3, 4, 7...). And ± √5 presents very solid regularity, as we've come to expect from this amazing "number". This is an excellent means of getting students to perform these operations, while growing in awe of mathematics.

Phi you later

With phi we found perhaps that there is some mathematical property to creation. What of destruction? An atomic mushroom cloud is like two spirals reversed. Could it be according to phi, or some other mathematical relation? Notice a piece of wood burning in a fireplace. See the uniformity of the coals, each apparently of the same thickness. We have logarithmic formulas to describe decay. Just how involved is the destruction process?

Figure 33 Destruction (Trinity test photo courtesy of National Nuclear Security Administration/Nevada Site Office).

Concluding dialogue

So the reader should hopefully have hours of fun and really interesting drawing and discussion topics for the math classes to come. In what ways can we capture the attention of those students who normally do not like being in this class? Having their attention, how can we get them to use the math involved, and have them later be able to refer back to it?

 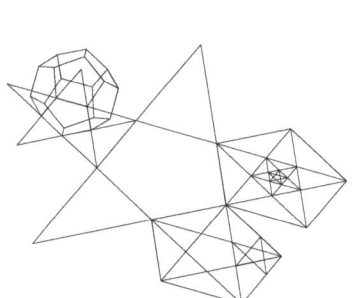 

Figure 34 Leda Atomica – (Dali)   Figure 35 possibilities   Figure 36 Starry Dream F. Hart).

What further discoveries await the adventurer/discoverer in mathematics? What numerics can be unlocked in the Archimedean forms? Our trigonometry is heavily based on √2 and √3, and they are based on Φ. Finish this statement: "The thing that really gets me about Phi is..."

Areas of further reading on Phi, the golden mean:

http://www.mcs.surrey.ac.uk/Personal/R.Knott/Fibonacci/phi.html   Lots of Phi info

http://www.crystalinks.com/sg.html Interesting site on Phi and Sacred Geometry

http://www.charlesgilchrist.com/SGEO/Gal1102.html   Great modern artist

http://www.heartbeat2000.com/phi.htm   The phi rhythm of the human heart.

http://www.floweroflife.org/ Informative site about the work of Drunvalo Melchizedek

Class Exercise 1   1.618

Objective:
Introduce sequences converging on a ratio more significant than π and yet little studied in standard education. Find interesting places where it exists.

Procedure:
a) Make available as many images from Figure 1 as possible. Include a pinecone, heart shaped leaves and dodecahedron. Ask the students how these objects relate to each other. This is a silent exercise where they first write thoughts into their notes. Then, they can share with a partner and finally the entire group.
b) Have students pick any number and write it on their papers. Pair them with another student and have each add their numbers, by hand. Then, take the larger of the two numbers and add it to the first sum. Continue. For example, 12 & 352 → 12 + 352 = 364. 352 + 364 = 716, 364 + 716 = 1080 and so forth. Insist that they each do this, separately by hand and check their results at the end to compare accuracy. Those who thought they'd be funny and choose a million will find that they have some work. After they have done 12 additions, take the final sum and divide it by the previous, with a calculator of course. They will all have 1.618, if they added correctly.
c) Any sequence of 2 numbers, added such that $a_n = a_{n-1} + a_{n-2}$ will reach this ratio by about a_{13}/a_{12}. The key sequence that Fibonacci discovered and that relates to natural growth is 0,1,1,2,3,5,8,13... Look at the piano keyboard. Notice how many black keys there are in 1 octave. There are 5, but they are split into groupings of 2 and 3. In this set of notes are 8 white keys. The sum of the notes is 13. All of these numbers are Fibonacci terms.
d) Ask students where the center of their body is. They usually say their belly button. Have them stand with their hands to their sides. The hard bone where their wrists are hitting is the true dividing line. Have them stand against a wall and measure their height and with their finger on their belly button, measure its distance to the floor. They need to divide the larger number by the smaller and take an average of the results. A typical teenage class will be surprisingly close to 1.618, which we will now identify with the Greek letter Φ.
e) What is Φ? It is often called the golden section because it is a special proportion occurring when a line is cut such that the ratio of the longer piece to the shorter is the same as the whole to the longer. Figure 4b. Have the students draw a line and make a mark on it that is not in the middle. If the short length is "x" and the whole is '1', then the other piece is? (1-x) Make the following ratio:

$$\frac{1}{1-x} = \frac{1-x}{x}$$

See if they can solve this, by cross multiplication, to get $x = x^2 - 2x + 1$ and so $x^2 - 3x + 1 = 0$. This can be solved with the quadratic formula to obtain x = 0.382 or 2.618. Using 0.382 gives 1.618 as the resulting ratio. This is essentially where the belly button resides.

Homework:
Students should review their notes and fill in any further thoughts on what they have so far learned. They should wonder where this ratio might exist around them.

Evaluation:
Evaluate them on how much they are pushing themselves through these exercises, or waiting on someone else to do the work first.

Bridges:
We are beginning to explore mathematical relations in our bodies that we will see have even greater significance, applying mathematical processes to do so. The bridge is that more than anywhere else in the mathematics curriculum, this material will be the most relevant to each of their lives.

Class Exercise 2 **The spiral**

Objective:
Learn about spirallic growth, the mathematics of the spiral, and Φ's relation to spirallic forms found in nature and Human creations.

Procedure:
a) Students should mark their paper in the upper left of their paper, about 3-1/2 inches from the left edge, and about 3-1/2 inches down from the top. From here, with a compass set at 1", draw ¼ of a circle. We must imagine a string connecting the point and lead of the compass. We need to start the turn when the line is parallel to the top of the page, and end when it is perpendicular. Enlarge the compass to 2". Now, have the compass positioned perpendicular, but this time put the lead at the place where the last one finished. Do another ¼ turn. Enlarge the compass to 3", and repeat. Continue, doing ¼ turns with radius 5", and finally 8". They should have a smooth spiral. Figure 7.
b) Ask students to list all the places where spirals naturally occur in nature. Share their ideas with the class. Compare it to the list in the text. This does not mean that all of these examples are in the proportion of the phi spiral. It is only that spirals are a naturally occurring object and we have learned how to make one.
c) Try to draw a spiral by hand. Then, mirror it about its axis. Notice that the heart shape is a very common form, found in leaves, eggs as well as affection. But, why is it used for the latter?
d) Next, draw three circles, so that they each fit on one page. Draw in each a spiral. In each, draw a radial axis through the spiral, lightly. In the first, then try to mirror and rotate and draw a second spiral. What has been created? If the students did this well, they will see the Yin and Yang figure. That always interests them. On the second circle, try to draw two other axes, each a third of the circle. Try to draw two new spirals here. This is tricky, but done well, it is a Celtic symbol. Finally, make an x- and y- axis here. Draw three more spirals. This will really get their attention when they are able to see that they have made a swastika. Figures 9a and b.
e) Finally, they should draw the heart shape, and rotate this four more times to get five petals (heart pointing inwards – Figure 8b). They may not realize it, but this flower form is the shape of all blossoms of the wild rose family, which they should appreciate, because this includes peach, pear, apple, plum, raspberry, blackberry and cherry.

Homework:
Students should review their notes and fill in any further thoughts on what they have so far learned. Ask them what other shapes might we get from five petals. (five-pointed stars) They should think what might be created by even more revolutions of the spirals. (six-petalled flowers, sunflowers and even pinecones) This should be checked in class to see if they gave it any thought.

Evaluation:
Evaluate them on how much they are pushing themselves through these exercises, or waiting on someone else to do the work first.

Bridges:
We are further exploring this mathematical ratio. This particular lesson was better suited for an art class. We can devote one entire week in the curriculum to this material, feeding appropriate lectures in for math, art, and physics, as will be seen. Again, this material will be most relevant to each of their lives.

Class Exercise 3 **The Star**

Objective:
Make a thorough study of the five-pointed star in order to see how the Φ proportion and higher orders of it make up the star.

Procedure:
a) Students should draw a circle, of 2¼ inches. Make a top mark and a center mark. Take a protractor and align with the top mark. Make additional marks each 72° around the edge of the circle. The protractor may or may not fit exactly to this circle, so the marks will have to be drawn in where possible, a ruler lined up between them and the center, and then transferred to the circle. Care must be taken to get these in the right place, particularly now that symmetry is on only 1 axis.
b) Connect the marks to create a five-pointed star. Figure 14. Measure one edge of the inner pentagon. (1") Measure one leg from that pentagon to the tip. (1.618", though students will think it is 1-5/8 or so, which is as close as they can get.) So, when the inner pentagon measures 1, the legs measure Φ. Have the students use their calculator now. They should take Cos 36° and multiply by 2. This is the exact value of Φ. 36° is the measure of each angle at the tips. Store Φ in the calculator. Add it to 1 to get approximately 2.618. Take the square root. (Φ) This is the only number which added to 1 makes its square.
c) Count across the top line, from tip to tip. Add this in the calculator; Φ + 1 + Φ to get 4.236. Take the cube root. (Φ) So, using different colored pencils, mark the portion of the line that is Φ, the portion that is $Φ^2$, and the entire length as $Φ^3$. Make a table listing sums, and decimal and exponential values of Φ. So far, it should look like this:

Sum	Decimal value	Exponent on Φ
1	1	$Φ^0$
Φ	1.618	$Φ^1$
1 + Φ	2.618	$Φ^2$
1 + 2Φ	4.236	$Φ^3$

d) Trace another line around the star, beginning at one tip, going across to another; then follow the star, adding the edge of one more leg and one more edge in the pentagon. This makes 2 + 3Φ. Put this in the table, with its decimal value. (6.854 - $Φ^4$) Take this last sketch and continue tracing, out to one tip, and back inward until meeting the first line. This sum; 3 + 5Φ is $Φ^5$. Record this in the table and see if the students notice anything. (The fibonacci sequence of whole numbered values and also the coefficients of Φ.) Have them continue tracing around, seeing if they can find $Φ^6$. The star is a map of Φ and its exponents. Figure 15.

Homework:
Students should review their notes and fill in any further thoughts on what they have so far learned. Ask them where we see five-pointed stars in use, and why. (Flags, generals ranks, black magic) Cut an apple perpendicular to its axis and report your findings (inside the circle is a five-pointed star). Work should be checked in class to see if they gave it any thought.

Evaluation:
Evaluate them on how much they are pushing themselves through these exercises. By now, interest is usually high, as they are discovering something so foreign and almost magical.

Bridges:
We are further exploring this mathematical ratio, finding that it relates spirals to stars: nature crafted, and human made.

Class Exercise 4 **The Extension**

Objective:
See fractals within the form and go on to build the dodecahedron.

Procedure:
a) Make a five-pointed star. Make an external pentagon. Draw across the internal pentagon, extending to this larger pentagon. A second, inverted star has now appeared inside the smaller pentagon. A third can be created within this, a fourth, and so on. Figure 22a, central figure. At each of the tips, there are pentagons now, of the same size as the middle. Further stars can be drawn, or we could extend each edge of the largest, outermost pentagon, noticing that this will create a further star. Figure 35, including 3-D.
b) Using a radius of 4", re-create Figure 22a, middle diagram. Cut out this shape, and fold along the edges of the inner pentagon. The shape wants to make a "cup". See that the cups can be joined to make a dodecahedron. Figure 22b. Further, have them fold some pieces along the lines leading out to the star tips. This figure will close to make a five-sided pyramid that can be attached to the cup, making a stellation. Figure 23. We saw this already from the Zometool work.
c) Get them into groups, provide card stock, string, glue, and colors, so they make quality pieces. Leave tabs on all the ends, to allow for gluing. Glue a string inside to allow for the object to be hung from the ceiling. Draw designs, color them and make either the dodecahedron or its stellation. Figure 24a.

Homework:
Allow a few days to complete the constructions. Hang the best efforts from the ceiling of the classroom. Point out that the stellations show five-pointed stars in three-dimensional space. How many stars are there?

Evaluation:
Grade their class effort and the final products. Did they incorporate what they've learned about colors and patterns? Is it creative, and well constructed, or hastily/sloppily done?

Bridges:
Fractals in 2- and 3-D are a fascinating facet of the star. We can learn many things from the dodecahedron.

Class Exercise 5 The Human and the Human who calculates

Objective:
See the Φ proportion in the human body and in the cosmos.

Procedure:
a) Have students create a circle of radius 4" and draw a five-pointed star. Cut out strips of cardstock, about ½" wide. Lay two on the star and pin them together at a corner of the inner pentagon. Trim their ends to points, ending at the circle. We now have Φ calipers. Figure 18
b) Open the calipers so that the small legs are as wide as the tip-to-the-first-knuckle in the index finger. Keep them open to this size, flip the caliper over and check from the first knuckle to the second knuckle. A fit. Open the short legs to this size and check the next segment in the finger. Another fit. Open now to this size and then check this last joint to the wrist. Check how each segment is the same as the sum of the previous two. The Φ proportion. Let them check each other, within reason. If they stand back from each other, they can see the shoulder width to arm width is this proportion. Figure 5.
c) Obtain the distances of the planets from our sun. Take Venus' distance and divide it by Mercury's. Take Earth's distance and divide by Venus'. Repeat this, always with adjacent planets, including the asteroids. Take an average of all these pairs of numbers. Surprisingly close to the Φ ratio. Do the same with the major moons of Jupiter and Saturn: not the oblong rocks but the properly formed satellites. They will again come close to this ratio. Essentially, if we lay out the solar system, according to scale we could use our Φ caliper to approximate the spacing. Figure 20, distances in miles.
d) And some math! Obtain the decimal exponential values of Phi, and their reciprocals. Do various additions and subtractions which provide whole numbers. These non-random numbers generated form the pattern found in Table1. Have students construct this table.
e) Calculate the exponential values of Phi by hand, using $\sqrt{5}$, normal algebraic rules like $(a + b)^2$ and Pascal's triangle. Develop with them Table 2. Do they notice any patterns here?

Homework:
Students should review their notes and reflect on what they are finding interesting. Check it in class to see if they gave it any thought.

Evaluation:
Evaluate them on how much they are involving themselves in these exercises. By now, interest is usually high, as they find things out about themselves.

Bridges:
They are learning that their bodies are reflections of the cosmos. The first section of material (parts a-c) are best covered during a physics lecture.

Class Exercise 6 Φ, 5 and 7

Objective:
See the Φ proportion in familiar and unique geometric shapes.

Procedure:
a) Start with a 1" by 2" rectangle. Swing an arc of 1" radius centered at the upper right corner and connect a diagonal across the rectangle, continuing to this arc. Bisect this diagonal line to get Φ, which is exactly half of the line. Figure 3.
b) Draw a circle-1" radius. Draw a second, to create a vesica piscis. Set the compass to Φ, and place its point in the center of the left circle to make another circle. (We only need its intercepts on the right circle.) Figure 25a and b. Draw lines from the original center out to those intercepts. Note where they cross the first circle. Reset the compass to the distance between *these* points. Make three more marks on the circle with this length. A perfect star can be created. Figure 25c.
c) Create a new vesica piscis using Φ as the radii. Enlarge the compass to 2" to get the intercepts on the right circle, draw lines to find the marks on the left circle and now set the compass to fit between one of those intercepts and the center of the right circle. Swinging this around the circle is 99.8% perfect in creating a 7-pointed star. Figures 26a and b.
d) See in the icosa- and dodecahedrons that pairs of edges are parallel and part of a rectangle. (Zomes of a given colour are in Φ proportions. Icosahedrons, using short blues, measure Φ here; dodecahedrons, $Φ^2$.) Figures 28-29. "Use" Pythagoras to find ratios of edge length to radius of a sphere containing each form. Stellate to develop the double and find the radius of this new sphere.

Homework:
Students should do a final summary of their work through this material, pointing out what they found most interesting and why.

Evaluation:
When all of the work is finished, include an essay question on the next test, evaluating what they have learned and can retain.

Bridges:
Students will often ask, "We hear about π all the time, but why not Φ?" Indeed. Ask them why education chooses not to!

Appendix on eight intelligences

Here are some final comments on how better to understand and involve each intelligence, and perhaps broaden each student's abilities.

Students of <u>Linguistic intelligence</u> write well, and have good memory for names. They often remember math rules and formulas which others will forget. Call on them for this area of their special ability. It encourages them to participate. Have students develop portfolios of their work, and grade them on it. Linguistic students will surprise with how well-organized their work is. By rewarding them for this work, greater participation is often achieved. Other students will tend to improve their organization skills. Another idea is to have students write a report on a math-oriented subject of their choice, for example: pyramids, fractals, chaos theory... Insist on one rule, that they relate it to mathematics.

<u>Mathematics intelligence</u> often test well, and are first to have answers, but may have incredibly sloppy work. Give them the projects outlined here. Grading them on quality of work and other areas really challenges them and makes them work much harder. The art drawings can be a rewarding challenge for them.

<u>Spatial intelligence</u> likes diagrams, maps, art, drawing and 3-D construction. These students respond very well to the geometric art included here. Get them drawing and even encourage them to doodle on their notes. Interest leads to greater participation and effort. Find ways to reward their work. Take students on a trip to cathedrals to see geometry in architecture and all of the artistry.

For those who like to move their body, particularly teenagers or those of <u>Kinesthetic intelligence</u>, do 3D constructions and Zometools. Also, find a group of 20 to 30 bricks and have them build their own arch. This really pushes them to understand geometry and trigonometry. Construct viewing telescopes to calculate heights of things. Work with levers to lift things. Explain mathematically how tools work.

<u>Musically</u> gifted students are said to have some natural math ability due to the mathematics of tone, scale, rhythm, timing and intervals. Engage this in the class. Show how music waves can create geometric images in sand or salt. Give examples of how notes work with fractions. Come to class with flutes and drums. How does size (geometry) make a different sound?

Children and teenagers generally like to socialize. Some are particularly high in <u>Interpersonal intelligence</u>. This skill can be drawn in through group activities. These students could be called upon to tutor others outside of class.

Others work better independently, <u>Intrapersonally</u>. It is a good skill for a mathematical mind to have. The ability to work in a quiet, focused manner is another skill that should be fostered, and one that is vital to those who cannot learn in a confused class setting.

Finally, there is <u>Naturalist intelligence</u>. Such a student should be given the material on the Golden Mean. This one number, or proportion, can be found in a myriad of places in nature and the cosmos. A good presentation of the golden mean will draw in this person.

Assuming that people have different intelligences, learning types, or preferred dominant halves of their brain; the following are some things we could do using mathematics as our guide, to enable them to work more productively in a given class.

Metaphor. When we need to introduce new topics, perhaps we could draw on non-mathematic topics for analogous themes. For example, when introducing trigonometric ratios, we could pick two students from the class and have them stand next to each other, comparing their heights (get students of noticeably different height). Students can relate their heights; by dividing one by the other. Perhaps person X is 1.2 times taller than person Y. This number 1.2 is called a proportion, a comparison of the two heights. Have person X lay down and person Y stands at their feet. This forms a right angle. They are still in the same proportion, but now they are two sides of a right triangle. Relating these two specific sides has a name, we call tangent. If we tied a rope to the top of each of their heads, this length is the hypotenuse of the triangle. Show that it is a different length entirely, and thus, when we compare it with either of the other two lengths, we get a different proportion, which we call either sine or cosine. Use different students to show that different results can be achieved because of different proportions.

Get students to come up with metaphors of their own: "A triangle and its proportions are like one person going up a flight of stairs, while another walked forward, and then went up a ladder."

The example under metaphor also included visualization. One thing to stress throughout math class is that students draw. Insist that the faster students do this too, because for them especially it is a great deal of work, and it allows the other students to catch up (they are the ones usually doing good diagrams). Make the problems fun, by drawing caricatures of students from your class and putting those students in interesting fictions. One of my biggest surprises came with a group of students who struggled throughout trigonometry, but excelled with the often-complicated system of graphing of trig functions. Drawing, graphing, and play enable other parts of the mind to open, and that is why so much art is included in this book.

Teach to various senses. Practical and hands-on work brings in kinesthetic learning. Let the eyes, and hands work through problems before the analytical mind has to. In physics, don't just talk about the Doppler Effect, have them close their eyes and produce sounds that mimic it (or drive around the school with your hand on the horn). Another idea is to throw rocks into water to create waves, observing wave fronts and concentric circles.

Make-believe. Get the class to relax, close their eyes and open their imaginations as you quietly tell or read them a story. For example, "Imagine that you are standing. (pause) You extend one hand straight in front of you, holding a seed in the palm. (pause) You raise your other hand, and arm) at an angle, as though you are trying to catch a cab. (pause) Imagine that upper arm is made of rubber and can extend until the hand is directly above the other. (pause) Finally, the seed begins to grow into a beautiful rose, straight up, until it touches your other hand. What does this form?"

From this example, we can see that the arms basically touch our heart, and are adjacent. One arm had to "grow", meaning it is longer – the hypotenuse. The rose is out in front of us. It is the opposite side. Depending on how high our arm was, the rose could be shorter or taller, in relation to the angle formed by the two arms.

This process is good to relax students, get them to slow down, and try other parts of their mind.

Student-learning. In our work, let's also find ways to get students to learn for themselves. Lab work is great for this, allowing them to read, decipher, and follow instructions and then record their results. Another is the field trip. Often times this seems to be a chance for students to get as far away from the teacher as fast as possible, hit the snack bar, hangout and generally be a nuisance for the other patrons. Give the students clear work sheets and a process, so that they seek out answers. It can be more academic, or worded like a "treasure hunt". Another method is to get the students to act out items, by plain demonstration, or through use of drama.

6 The book of Numbers

Opening dialogue

When did time begin? At what point in the iron, bronze, or even stone ages did Humans begin to count, and then to measure time and distance? What are the true origins of these concepts?

Bones and stones have been found from tens of thousands of years ago with lines etched on them, with the marks possibly indicating duration of a month: by their quantity, and phases of the moon, by their different lengths. This series of events would have been fairly easy to track, even by non-civilized people, as the phases of the moon are very distinct. It takes about seven days from the new moon to the first quarter, and about seven more to full. This seems to last for about a day and then seven to the last quarter and seven to the next new moon. It would be noticed that there are about two or three nights that are totally dark, without any moon at all. In total, the lunar cycle lasts approximately 29.53 days, meaning that 12 of them take more than 354 days (length of the Muslim year), leaving about 11 days remaining in our calendar year.

Figure 1 The Ishango Bone, ca. 20,000 BC (Science Museum of Brussels).

This counting rhythm of seven is reflected by the Western calendar using seven days per week (As the Egyptians had ten days to their week, it is no wonder the Israelites wanted to leave and start their own system, should each week have only one day of rest). The twelve moons in a year certainly could relate to the twelve-based counting systems which are known to exist.

This chapter will touch upon counting systems, to attempt to bring to the reader, and to classrooms, a curiosity about numbers.

Philosopher or prophet?

Who was Plato? As with Pythagoras, we are given the story in short bios but it is part of a much greater picture. Plato was among the three great philosophers of Greece, with Socrates and Aristotle. He was student to the former and teacher to the latter.

Plato founded a school known as the Academy, in Athens. Aristotle studied there and stayed on for a time until leaving to found his own school called the Lyceum. Both of these names live on in our modern world as common names for schools.

Aristotle also tutored a young man named Alexander of Macedonia; later conqueror of vast territories stretching from Greece and Egypt to Afghanistan and India. Importantly, this would open trade routes from farthest Asia to Europe and Africa, enabling transfer of each culture's wisdom; fused in Alexandria and found within the creed of Christianity; sharing common threads with other beliefs of that era.

Notably, this faith, in struggles for clarity within itself, slowly and inexorably closed and destroyed the old schools and libraries of Plato, Aristotle, Archimedes, and Euclid; and in a process of millennia, has continued to squelch disparate views and sciences, as witnessed by the closing of the oracle of Dephi, the burning of the library of Alexandria, destruction of the Irminsul in Germany, the Albigensian crusade, the Inquisition, the wars of the reformation, and the conquest of the Americas. If ancient and native wisdoms may be considered "simpler", why were they viewed as threatening?

Interestingly, through most of this time, the Church held to certain dogma of Aristotle, one feature of which was the geocentric theory, where the Earth, and with it Man, was the center of the universe and about which all else rotated. Though the Church has recently forgiven Galileo, and itself, it is obvious from human activity that we still often consider ourselves, and our modern world, as the Center, given how we hold "dominion" over other life forms on Our planet.

What of those ancient knowings, so lost to us through upheaval and time? We have an interesting source in Plato. He wrote many books; perhaps best known is the one entitled

"The Republic". As with many thinkers of his time, he set about discussing the ideas of societal and political reform.

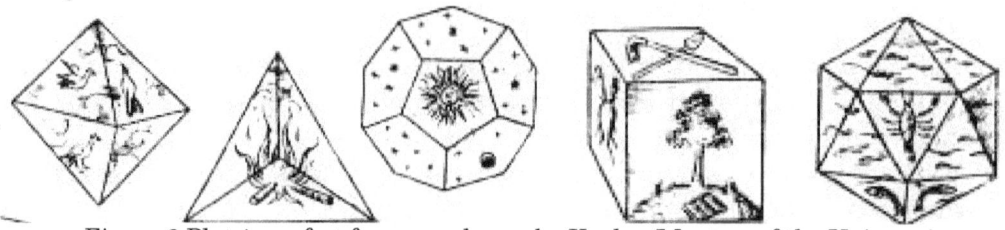

Figure 2 Plato's perfect forms, as drawn by Kepler (Mystery of the Universe).

In two particular texts of Plato, called Timaeus and Critias, we meet for the first time these five regular solids; called tetra-, hexa-, octa-, dodeka-, and icosahedron. Each was given by him to represent one of the five elements of Fire, Earth, Air, Water and Spirit (or cosmos). It is probable from these references that these shapes were accredited to him.

Within this same text has come to us perhaps the sole source on the fabled Atlantis. The story of Atlantis is an enduring one, of a great land, destroyed in a single day by volcanic eruptions and tidal waves. Few people, if any were thought to have survived. This idea, that a great city, an entire culture could be wiped out so readily has long been scoffed at. And yet, in our own recent memory, we have seen earthquakes, tsunamis, and hurricanes do just this. Some struck without warning, while in other cases warning was given or the results could have been significantly more catastrophic.

In these writings are tales of Atlantis, and a war which occurred some 9000 years earlier between this island land and that of his native Athens. A great deal of space will now be devoted to this story, for buried within are many interesting facets, whether or not we choose to believe in Atlantis itself.

The story is said to have been passed down from the Egyptians, who say they were once related to the very ancient Greeks, sharing the same goddess - Athena:

"In those days, the Atlantic was navigable, and there was an island situated in front of those straights which you call the pillars of Heracles ... this island was larger than Libya and Asia put together, and was the way to other islands and from these you might pass to the whole of the opposite continent which surrounded the true ocean, for this sea which is within the Straights of Heracles is only a harbor, but that other is a real sea, and the surrounding land .. a boundless continent."

This statement that the land was as big as Libya and Asia combined makes it often disputed, though the Libya and Asia of the Greeks were much smaller than we know them today. Yet Plato says it is still just an island and will proceed to state very clearly, "The whole country was said to be lofty and precipitous... but the land immediately about and surrounding the city (of Atlantis) was a level plain, itself surrounded by mountains which descended towards the sea, it was smooth and even and of an oblong shape, extending in one direction three thousand stadia but across the center inland it was two thousand stadia. This part of the island looked towards the south, and was sheltered from the north."

If we realize that our own word "Stadium" comes from the Greek, we will realize that the Stadia is their old unit of measure of approximately 600 feet. This means that the great land-mass of Atlantis, according to Plato, measured around 1,200,000 by 1,800,000 feet. In other words: approximately 240 miles by 360. About the size of Ohio, and capable of fielding "an army of 10,000 chariots". Perhaps, as many scholars have alluded, the first reference to size might have meant instead stature, or "reach" — as in lands controlled, rather than physical feature as later described in much more detail.

These stories are the very type of roadmap that Schlieman used to discover Troy, Mycenae and the truth of the Iliad, previously thought to be a mere poet's folly, just as many consider Atlantis.

Poseidon, lord of the island, mated with a human woman and to them were born five pairs of twin male children, and they divided the land into ten portions. "The eldest, who was the first king, he named Atlas and after him the whole island, and the ocean was called Atlantic. To his twin brother, who was born after him, and obtained as his lot the extremity of the island towards the Pillars of Heracles, facing the country which is now called the region of Gades ...he gave the name ...Gadeirus ... and as has been said, they held sway in our direction.. as far as Egypt." The region of Gades is thought to reference the ancient Phoenician city (hence known in Plato's time) now named Cadiz.

As the story continues we see that Poseidon's temple was about the size of a modern stadium and that there, "in the center was a holy temple to ... Poseidon ... surrounded by an enclosure of gold; this was the spot where the family of the ten princes first saw the light, and thither the people annually brought the fruits of the earth ... Here was a statue of Himself in a chariot ...pulled by six winged horses (all in gold)....and around the temple were placed statues of gold of all the descendants of the kings and their wives.."

Winged horses pulling a chariot sounds like Apollo (the Sun) going across the sky in his chariot. First seeing the light, at an annual celebration? Is this in reference to sunrise, on a specific day each year? Why are there six horses? (At the solar temple of Konarak in India, there are 24 wheels on the chariot of the sun.) The numbers 6 and 24 have often been used to relate to the sun symbolically. Why would a temple to the God of the Sea be aligned to a specific solar date? Indeed. Yet at Sounio, south of Athens, its "modern" (500BC) temple to Poseidon appears to align with Winter Solstice Sunrise.

Further reading shows the size of the army depended on each farming lot of about ten square stadia (there being 60,000 of these), needed to, "furnish for the war one sixth of a war chariot, so as to make ten thousand chariots," also, "two horses, two riders, a horseman, a charioteer, two armed soldiers, two slingers, three stone shooters and three javelin men ... and four sailors to make the complement of twelve hundred ships."

It is interesting that most of the numbers here-in are factors of five and six, or ten and twelve. The Sumerian counting system was sexigesimal, meaning sixty-based. Our measurement and time keeping of 360 and 3600 come from this (as does 12-based counting). And yet, if we look closely at how the Sumerians counted, we see that they counted from 1 to 10 by single marks, as did the Egyptians. And then, they counted up six-tens to get sixty. This is a unique system that we see repeated in Plato's text of 10,000 and 60,000. There is one further oddity in that the number of men and horses to be supplied by each holding was very specific and totaled 20.

Continuing: "You remember a single deluge only, but there were many ... you do not know that there formerly dwelt in your land the fairest and noblest race of men which ever lived, and that you and your whole city are descended from a small seed or remnant of them which survived. And this is unknown to you because for many generations, the survivors of that destruction died, leaving no written word. For there was a time, before the great deluge of all... when the goddess, common patron to both our cities, founded your city a thousand years before ours... of which is recorded in our sacred registers to be eight thousand years old."

"Many great deeds are recorded by us of your city but one exceeds all others... she defeated and triumphed over the invaders (from Atlantis) ... but afterwards there occurred violent earthquakes and floods and in a single day and night of misfortune, all your warlike men sank into the earth, and the island of Atlantis in like manner disappeared in the depths of the sea ... when there were any survivors, they were men who dwelt in mountains and they were ignorant of the art of writing and had heard only the names of the chiefs of the lands.

Even the remnant of Attica (the region around Athens) which now exists may compare with any region in the world for the variety of its fruits ... but in those days the country yielded far more abundant produce. Many great deluges have occurred in the 9000 years and through so many ages, there has never been any considerable accumulation of the soil coming down from the mountains, as in other places, as the earth has fallen all round and sunk out of sight. The consequences is that in comparison of what then was, there are remaining only the bones of the wasted body, all the richer parts of the soil having fallen away, and the mere skeleton of the land being left. But, in the primitive state of the country, its mountains were high hills covered with soil, and the plains, as they are termed by us, were full of rich earth."

The myth "realized"

If we wish to discount the story of Atlantis, we can fairly easily do so, for all of its meanderings through the lives of Gods and of civilizations so long distant as to not be considered realistic in our current historical sense. Yet comparing the wording to the biblical story of Noah doesn't seem to build up or discredit either. Both are flood narratives of a time too far distant to prove in accuracy. Yet there are perhaps those who would more readily accept one over the other.

In only the past few years are coming amazing discoveries. There is compelling evidence that the Noah story is true. We must first realize that the story of Noah is probably older, originating with the Sumerian culture which predates it.

There are many flood myths from around the world, from various ages. It is clear that the Indo-European cultures are thought to have spread out from the Black sea area some 7- or 8000 years ago. Recent corroboration of this migration, and many flood stories, comes from the discovery that the Black Sea was once a giant fresh water lake. Evidence shows that it flooded around 5500 BC, as waters from the Mediterranean broke through a great wall near modern Istanbul. What would have caused this?

In the time of Plato's story, 9500 BC (and earlier), the Earth was in the last great ice age. We cannot so easily grasp what this meant. Almost all of continental Europe, north of the Alps, North America above St. Louis, and elsewhere on the globe, were covered in a great layer of ice, probably similar to that still on Greenland and on Antartica, perhaps several thousand feet thick! As a result of all of this water being trapped on the planet's surface, the oceans were much lower as a result; by several hundred feet.

In other words, the continental shelf around most landmasses was above water at this time. This is what enabled the migrations of people from Asia across the Bering land bridge and into the Americas (if not by boat).

The ice did not recede immediately, nor was it probably gradual. As we see from nature, it occurs in dramatic steps, often accompanied by cataclysmic events. But it did recede, and as it did so the ocean levels rose.

As the Ice left the British Isles, but before the water enclosed them, the first people migrated there. Recent discoveries have found structures and even circles submerged in the English Channel. Elsewhere, as land became free of ice, migrations occurred as people moved into newly freed lands. These people may have brought science, of a sort.

Further, circular structures have been found, possibly observatories, and signs of an advanced culture spreading throughout Austria, Germany and Slovakia dating from 6000 BC. In northern Africa it has long been known that the Sahara was green during the Ice Age and recently have been found evidence of a circle of stones, and other alignments indicating a knowledge and study of the Sun's movements dating from about 5000 BC.

Figure 3 Reconstruction of the German "Stonehenge" (Courtesy AP).

Prior to these finds, most of the oldest previously known sites where humans have endeavored to erect stone "temples" aligning to the sun had been in Ireland and Malta. They date to approximately 4000 BC. At Malta in particular are grooves, cut in the stone of the land, which lead into the sea. They are called "cart ruts" though there is no clear evidence of how they were used. What is obvious is that they are from a time when the coast of Malta was further to sea than it is today.

And that is the important fact from all of this, which Plato's "sources" somehow were aware of. As the ice receded, the land around the coasts submerged. If we discount Plato's story, how then do we account for the fact that he knew of the land sinking, which had to have occurred several thousands of years earlier? Looking at an underwater map of Greece, we can in fact see that a one to two hundred-meter change in sea level would have presented a much different picture.

This means that in 9500 BC the land around modern Athens was above water, and was in fact a flat area, suitable for farming. Disparagers of the story have perhaps never read that portion of it.

More importantly, an underwater map of the area in front of the Pillars of Heracles (straits of Gibraltar) pretty accurately shows what he was describing.

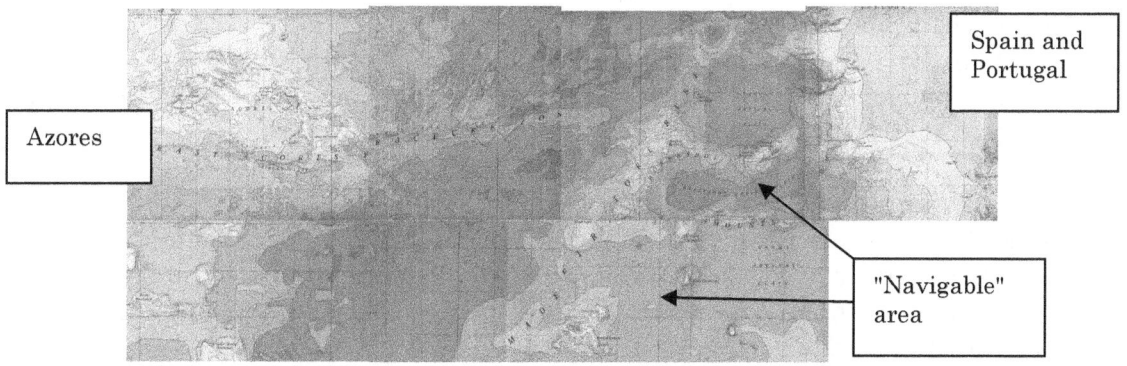

Figure 4 Underwater features, from the straights of Gibraltar to the Azores (Golden Age Project).

Note in Figure 4 that the lighter areas were above water, as islands, during the Ice Age, making the area "navigable". See in Figure 5 the underwater area around the Azore Islands. There is an oblong plain, facing south to the sea, with mountains to the north, as Plato described (these mountains are the current islands) and pretty near to the dimensions given by Plato. This plain is tilted and sunken more than the waters would have risen with the melt off. And yet this is the area of the mid-Atlantic ridge where seismic activity is quite common, and where subsidence of this nature is possible. Further, the area beyond the Azores could easily have been the *real* ocean which Plato wrote about, surrounded by a land mass easily being the north and south American plates. When looking at the Atlantic ocean of the time described by Plato, it matches.

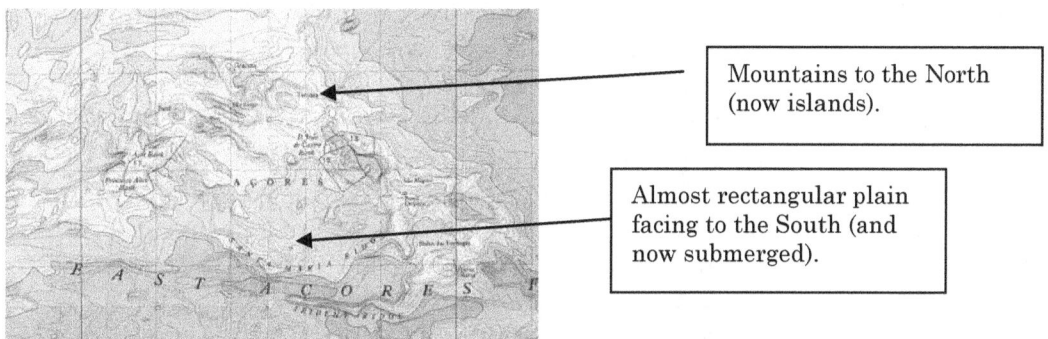

Figure 5 Above and underwater map of the Azores (Courtesy Golden Age Project).

During the ice age, much of the areas around the Azores would have been above water. We will see in the next chapter more of interest about these Azores.

It is clear that the seas rose, and in only the last few years, amazing underwater discoveries have been made, giving us a picture of what humans might have been doing in coastal areas during the ice age. In the Gulf of Kambat, India, and off Okinawa at Yonaguni, vast underwater structures have been found, indicating advanced civilization when these areas were above sea level, also ca. 9500 BC.

Serious researchers of today are in fact looking for Atlantis. Some seek it near Cyprus, or the smaller submerged islands in the straights of Gibraltar. As with the long known structures under the sea near the Bahama islands, there will probably be things found. But, will they be *the* Atlantis? Most every major culture near the sea has a story of a sunken land and lost kingdoms. There is the fabled Lyonesse off of Cornwall, England and the Isle of Ys, off of France. The Aztecs describe having come from Atlatl, to the East. There is the story from Turkey of Tartassos. The Indian stories tell of Atala and Patala. All stories of a once great kingdom, washed away by the seas. What this all points to is not one Atlantis, but several!

Why include this in a book about alternative Mathematics? Because, there is coming to light the very real possibility that our history of civilization, and mathematics, does not begin with the Sumerian and Egyptian cultures but much earlier, with cultures lost to us. Did civilization actually begin in coastal regions during a time when the climate was much different from our own? Did certain science develop with them? The professional archaeological community is remaining fairly mum on this issue. But amateurs are approaching it from many angles, several of which bring exciting, and plausible new theories forward.

This chapter will present the results of recreational mathematical studies, something that might idly interest the reader, and show that it's possible to investigate things mathematically. For that, let us look at how people count, or at least how they did it before they adopted metrics.

World counting systems

We do indeed have the metric system today, with which so many are comfortable. But there are still lands that have not adopted it, and two hundred years ago, many cultures who now measure and count in tens did not. Still buried in their language of today are clues as to how they did count.

Looking at languages from around the world seems to show four hidden, main methods of counting (with further unique aberrations found worldwide – eg. the Dogon of Africa count by eighties). Around the world, there are many cultures which count by ten, and this is easy to understand why. We have ten fingers. Island cultures of the Pacific, the Egyptians, Sumerians and others counted with individual numbers to ten (one, two, three, etc.). Symbolically, many cultures have used a single scratch upon clay, a line drawn on papyrus, or just a dot to represent "one", as found in Egyptian, Sumerian, Chinese, Mayan, early Greek and Roman styles. It is likewise understandable why some cultures had unique symbols for five, as did the early Greeks, Romans and Mayans.

Twenty-based systems

The Mayan culture counted in fives *and* twenties. Why twenty? Does this relate to something; other than all of the fingers, and toes? The Mayan calendar was very unique in that it ran two counting systems. The year was essentially 18 months of twenty days, making 360. They had a further cycle of 13 x 20 and these two calendars interacted, realigning in 52 years; the number of weeks in our year. While theirs was the most evolved 20-based system on the planet, we find remnants elsewhere. Vigesimal (relating to the French word for twenty) counting exists in the Basque country and in Wales, as shown in Table 1. This is a good diagram to allow students to investigate for themselves to see what patterns they might find. This is great for those with linguistic intelligence.

Number	Basque	Welsh	French	Mayan
One	Bat	Un	Un	Hun
Two	Bi	Dau	Deux	Kaa
Three	Hiru	Tri	Trois	Ox
Four	Lau	Pedwar	Quatre	Kan
Five	Bost	Pump	Cinq	Hu
Six	Sei	Chwech	Six	Wak
Seven	Zazpi	Saith	Sept	Wuc
Eight	Zortzi	Wyth	Huit	Waxac
Nine	Bederatzi	Naw	Neuf	Bolon
Ten	Hamar	Deg	Dix	Lahun
Eleven	Hamaika	Un ar ddeg	Onze	Buluk
Twelve	Hamabi	Deuddeg	Douze	Lahka
Thirteen	Hamahiru	Tri ar ddeg	Treize	Oxlahun
Fourteen	Hamalau	Pedwar ar ddeg	Quatorze	Kanlahun
Fifteen	Hamabost	Pymtheg	Quinze	Hulahun
Sixteen	Hamasei	Un ar bymtheg	Seize	Waklahun
Seventeen	Hamazazpi	Dau ar bymtheg	dix-sept	Wuklahun
Eighteen	Hemezortzi	Deunaw	dix-huit	Waxaklahun
Nineteen	Hemeretzi	Pedwar ar bymtheg	dix-neuf	Bolonlahun
Twenty	Hogei	Ugain	Vingt	Hun kal
Twenty one	Hogeitabat	Un ar hugain	Vingt et un	??
Thirty	Hogeitahamar	Deg ar hugain	Trente	??
Forty	Berrogei	Deugain	Quarante	Ka kal
Fifty	Berrogeitahamar	Hanner cant	Cinquante	??
Sixty	Hirurogei	Trigain	Soixante	Ox kal
Seventy	Hirurogeitahamar	Deg a thrigain	Soixante-dix	??
Eighty	Laurogei	Pedwar ugain	Quatre-vingts	Kan kal
Ninety	Laurogeitahamar	Deg a pedwar ugain	Quatre-vingt-dix	??
Hundred	Ehun	Cant	Cent	Hu kal

Table 1 Various vigesimal counting systems.

Where to begin? Let's look for patterns (as always!). We see similarities between the Welsh and French systems, and with our own because these are said to be Indo-European language systems. Yet, in the Welsh, we see in some cases, something very unique. Like the language itself, the pronunciation is Indo-European, but the "grammar", is sometimes related to the Basque. The Basque language, called Euskara, is important because it is thought to be an unaffiliated language, predating and somehow surviving the Indo-European, and other, invasions of the past 5-8000 years.

In the Basque system, counting seems to start fairly clearly from one to ten. This is followed by a fairly regular pattern of teens, beginning at twelve, until twenty is reached. This is something very similar in a great number of languages and counting systems in the world; the first ten and then the second ten numbers are often grouped differently than the other numbers, to one hundred. As stated, ten is a natural number due to the digits of our hands which are ever present in our vision. Maybe ten fingers and ten toes is reflected here, and after twenty is reached, we can count "normally". However, twenty is often not the real beginning of regularized counting either.

Let's dig further. If we look at the Welsh, we see 11 as perhaps, "one and ten". Twelve is written as two-ten, 13 as "three and ten", followed by "four and ten". Fifteen is unique, followed by "one and fifteen", "two and fifteen", "two nine", and then "four and fifteen". It is interesting that two-ten basically means "two and ten", but "two nine" means two-nines. We see that twelve, fifteen, and eighteen are somehow unique numbers.

Various old-British counting systems reflect this. Bretonic counts to twenty, as in the Basque system, with only one deviation. At eighteen, they say basically "three six".

In the French system, as in other romance languages (except Romanian), the numbers eleven to sixteen all have their own name, until becoming regular, and related to ten, after 16. This is interesting, for modern Italian follows this and Spanish is similar but makes the change at 15-16 instead of 16-17. What is further unique is that the Latin language from which they come counts differently; regular to 17 and then "two-from-twenty", followed by "one-from-twenty". We can see how language follows mathematics rooted in the culture rather than the import: The Etruscans numbers 17 to 19 can be translated as: three-from-twenty, two-from-twenty and one-from-twenty.

Some have special emphasis on 11 and 12. In English, and other Germanic languages, we also have unique names for the first twelve numbers. In many languages of Europe, there are interesting numbers, buried in the first twenty.

Twenty itself is an oddity. Why is it not "twoty"? Is there a relation to our use of the words twain, and twin? The same is found in German: zwanzig, dreizig, vierzig, etc. Note the uniqueness of twenty. Why not "zweizig"? For us, the pattern normalizes at thirty as with many other languages; thirty, forty, fifty, sixty and so seem fairly regularized. Thirty is a number we can recognize as essentially the days in a month. But, why did our forebears insert so many special numbers in between? There is a uniqueness of twenty from the other "tens" which come after, as is also reflected in how Semitic cultures (Hebraic and Arabic), and even the Hindi and Chinese count.

But more things happen at 20. The Basque count in twenties. Note that their numbers reflect "twenty", "twenty and ten", "two-twenty", "two-Twenty and ten", "Three twenty", etc. We see that the Welsh do something similar, "twenty", "ten and twenty", "two-twenty", "half hundred", "Three twenty", etc. And the French? Not to be outdone, they begin something at sixty, followed by 70 as "sixty-ten", 80 is "four-twenty", and 90 is "four-twenty-ten".

We find twenty in the old English monetary system of 20 shillings to the pound (with twelve pence to the shilling), and a special term for twenty, called a score. The name icosahedron comes from the unique word for twenty found in the Greek language.

Further afield in Europe we see that in Denmark they count twenty as a special number, and also thirty. Then, forty is perhaps "forry". At fifty, we see "half three-ds". This is assumed to be ten short of three twenties. Sixty is seen as "three-ds", seventy as "half four-ds", eighty is "four-ds", (four twenties presumably) and while ninety looks like half of five twenties, 100 is not five twenties. We see further evidence in the Bretonic. So, while Europe has many interesting numbers buried in their systems in the first twenty numbers, languages at the extremities still have great usage of twenty.

Twenty based systems are found in Albania ("njëzet" is 20, and "dyzet": two twenties), in Georgia ("otsi" is 20, "twenty and ten"; 30, and "three twenty"; 60), and the Caucasian Ainu of Japan. Each of these are somewhat geographically isolated cultures.

Number	Danish	Bretonic	Irish	Ainu
Twenty	Tyve	Ugent	A fiche	Hotnep
Thirty	Tredive	Tregont	A fiche ig deag	Wanpe etu hotnep
Forty	Fyrre	Daou-ugent	A dha	Tu hotnep
Fifty	Halvtreds	Hanter kant	A fhichid	??
Sixty	Treds	Tri-ugent	A trichid	??
Seventy	Halvfjerds	Dek ha tri-ugent	??	??
Eighty	Firs	Pevar-ugent	A ceithre fishid	??
Ninety	Halvfems	Deka pevar-ugent	??	??
Hundred	Hundred	Kant	??	Ashike hotnep

Table 2 Further vigesimal counting systems.

What made ten and twenty unique to ancient peoples whose counting is so removed from us? Was there a rhythm that they knew, but we do not? Lastly, though spread throughout Eurasia, the greatest concentration of twenty-based counting systems is in the Atlantic seaboard of Europe. Here, one of the oldest cultures seems to be the Basque, part of the Ibero-Berber language group, thus including the tribes of Morocco. Within this group are the extinct Guanche, from the Canary Islands (where there are pyramid structures). Across and very distant from them were the Maya, and in between; the Azores. Does the prevalence of twenty represent a long-lost common number? Does its density or existence on both sides of the Atlantic suggest contact, or even a common origin, centered in the region?

It is interesting to note that not only are there pyramid structures on the Canary Islands, but also throughout regions of Central and South America, and the Polynesian islands. This common architectural feature and many other archaeological finds, coincide with the fact that these regions are linked by the best, and only, ocean current, going from East to West. Not only have sculptures of men with very Phoenician features been found in these areas as well, but the Phoenicians had remnants of 20-based counting in their system, which they either transported, or acquired, in their long voyages. They counted 'tens' by sums of twenty, where 70 was for example written with symbols representing 20 + 20 + 20 + 10. The Olmecs probably counted in twenties.

Though most tend to insist that the Egyptians had a decimal system, it is interesting to note that in their hieratic (script rather than pictographs), as old as the culture itself, the number 60 consists of a line under three dots, while 80 is a line under four. Further, 90 consists of three horizontal lines, and the unique thing here is that other than symbols for 1's, 10's, 100's and such, the Egyptians apparently had specific hieroglyphic characters for one, two and thirty.

Egyptian symbols may be decimal but numeral names are not. They counted tens where 20 looks like ten-two, 30 and 40 are unique words and starting at 50 numbers look like "fivu, sixu, sevenu...", suggesting that the probably older language doesn't really follow the symbols. Again we see that 10 is very reasonable as a developmental base for counting, and thirty too, considering its relation to the lunar cycle. But, what is, or was, in twenty? Questions without answers, but which hopefully create curiosity.

Base-twelve

As we have so far noted, there are clear groupings in many languages of numbers by tens. Yet, there are patterns that repeat with the first ten numbers, immediately after ten, or more often after twenty or even thirty. Ten is understandable for the digits in our hands, and thirty for the days in a month. Twenty is open for debate, as is the number 12. We noted that in a few languages, 6, 9, 15 and 18, seem significant (all factors of 360).

What culture does not use twelve? We keep time in twelves and sixties. Many cultures have counted their year in terms of twelve months of 30 days each, with five or six holidays at the end. Many have kept a pantheon of twelve gods (sometimes twelve major and twelve minor – as hours in the day). We can see in the number systems shown above, and others, that they count individual numbers up to twelve, before counting further in the "tens". Even the Maya counted uniquely to the number twelve.

Astrologers in the West, India and China keep a zodiac of twelve, and other aspects of their systems also count in twelve, when not concerning the moon. The ancient and modern Greek alphabet has 24 letters. Ancient Egyptian Hieroglyphs used 24 symbols, and the Eldar Futhark of the Norse consisted of 24 runes. Many Polynesian languages have only 12 syllables or alphabets with 12 letters. There are twelve inches in the English foot, but this is not the only unit of measure to ever be divided in this manner.

Figure 6 Twelve division in medieval art – (A. Kircher; Turris Babel, 1676).

When we look at the divisibility of 360, we see that there are twelve pairs of factors. Looking at those angles with which we made our trigonometric table, we see that all of the radian fractions have as a common denominator: 12. We see 12 also in the Greek language with the unique number dodeka.

Base-sixteen

We saw in the Romance languages that sixteen was a number where transitions occurred. Other systems have more pronounced use of this number. There are 16 ounces in a pint in the English system, 16 cups in a gallon, and 8 lbs. is the weight of a gallon of water. In the measuring systems of the Sumerians, Persians, Greeks and Arabs, it was common to divide a "foot" by four palms, and a palm by four digits (finger). Interestingly, the Egyptian unit of length, the Royal Cubit (of 20⅔ English inches) was divided to give seven palms of four digits each. We will visit seven soon.

Today, we use sixteen directions; North, South, East and West, plus such things as Northeast and North by Northwest. We play chess on an 8x8 board, with 16 players for each team. So, we have two teams, two "colors", 32 pieces and 64 squares.

Fractions of sixteen work just as well as fractions of twelve (used with the English inch). Here, it is also common to make finer measure in 32^{nds} and 64^{ths} of an inch. The Egyptians used such division, with their "Eye of Horus", discussed in Chapter 2.

That counting systems may have something about ten, twelve or thirty buried within them is in keeping with our bodies, and celestial mechanics. But why did the ancients choose to count in sixteens (and talk of eight winds)?

It has been found in the stone-age sites of the British Isles that the megalith builders kept a calendar of sixteen months, numbering 22 or 23 days each. Hundreds of sites were variously aligned to key sunrise dates of the solstices and equinoxes, and dates close to May 1st, October 31st, February 2nd, and August 2nd. These latter were held by the Celts, of a more modern era. The much earlier denizens of this land kept eight more dates, in between. They particularly built Stonehenge, and much earlier sites, to the maximum sunrise position at the solstices. Many others are aligned to different positions, suggesting the 16 month calendar. Stonehenge was not only somewhat of a culmination of these efforts but its uniqueness clearly reflects outside influence, with building techniques which could be said to be Mediterranean.

The history of civilization that we learn in school focuses on Egypt and Sumer, for we have from them writing, great structures, and art. Yet the megalithic culture is found throughout the British Isles and coastal Europe. Such rough structures are found in the Mediterranean, in Morocco, Corsica, Malta and Israel, stretching into the Caucuses and beyond. Was this all from one geographically massive culture? How did they count?

Figure 8 Xaghra stone circle and Gigantja on Malta (courtesy Daniel Cilia).

These people left no writing per se, though we have what are called "cup and ring" marks that are still not definitively deciphered. (It can be noted that something called the "Azillian" script was discovered in France, similar to Grecian writing but predating it by thousands of years.) They also did not leave behind large organized urban areas. Still, they *did* leave a multitude of rock formations, erected in perfect circles, ellipses and egg shapes, requiring a high level of mathematics, and astronomy. Many were built on what are termed energy lines. These could be likened to the so-called twelve meridians in the Chinese acupuncture system.

Why did ancient Humans erect these rings on places where these energy lines have been found to cross? What knowledge did they perhaps have, which we do not hold nor appreciate, as we dig up these sites for housing or highways, or erect mobile phone towers upon them for their command of the surrounding terrain?

There is one called Rujm el Hiri in Jordan, thought to be about 5000 years old and circular in nature. There is the site at Nabta Playa, or the recently unearthed German Stonehenge (within 6 miles of the same latitude of Stonehenge and 3000 years older). Each of these has clear solsticial alignments.

In this last decade alone have been found 4-5000 year old cities in Peru at Caral, Greece at Helike and Central Asia's Bactria Margiana Archaeological Complex, from previously unknown bronze age peoples. In Miami Florida has been found beside the sea a calendar wheel 2000 years old. Many cultures have, and still do celebrate their key holidays or new-year around either a Solstice, or Equinox. How did ancient peoples count? What seeds did they give us?

Gematria

This subject was mentioned briefly in the last chapter. The term gematria is thought to be a derivation of the word geometry. Not only does it come from the Greek, but to understand it, we must understand Greek.

Though originally having a counting system predating, and essentially inspiring Etruscan and then Roman numerals, the Greek chose to change from this "simple" routine of 1's, 5's, 10's, etc. and instead associated number symbols to their alphabet. For example, α = 1, and β = 2. To count 1-9, 10-90 and 100-900 requires then 27 symbols, though their alphabet had, and still has, 24 letters. So they "resurrected" three archaic letters and used them to fill in.

By doing this, their numbers probably started to looked like words, perhaps like αρε, τοε, and such. Noting that numbers could seemingly form words, the opposite is also true, that each word would essentially be a combination, or sum of numbers.

And so, a mystical process developed, where certain words and numeric values were associated. Much has been made of the Greek spelling of Christ being equivalent to 1080 (3 x 360). Numbers come up often in mystical texts. For example 19 repeats a lot in the Koran, in the number of times certain terms are used throughout the entire text and in other instances. Gematria is a sacred science, where the languages and cultures that used letters for numbers, also developed a hidden subculture where specific words were formed to have specific meanings.

Hebrew is famous for having gematric associations, particularly through Kabbalah. There are twenty-two paths around the ten circles in their tree of life, seen in Chapter 1. We can remember too that there are 22 major arcana in Tarot. If we look at another arrangement, called the Sepher Yetzirah, or "The Book of Creation", we see that the Hebrew letters can be arranged in a series of important combinations of 3 "mother letters", 7 representing the planets and 12 for the signs of the zodiac, each represented by one letter from the alphabet (Figure 9).

These symbols have deeper meaning: for example the seven-pointed star representing directions of left, right, front, back, above, below, and that which is within. Hebraic gematria is complex. With only 22 symbols, some are used twice: 20-500, 40-600, 50-700, and finally 80-800, 90-900. What mystery then did the letters and numbers contain and why were these particular units paired? Too, numbers normally put together decimally, like 14 or 24, use the symbol for four coupled with that of ten or twenty. But 15 and 16 do not, for this would entail using the symbols that spell Yahweh. So, these two are actually counted 9 & 6 and 9 & 7. Numbers and counting systems aren't so "simple" after all.

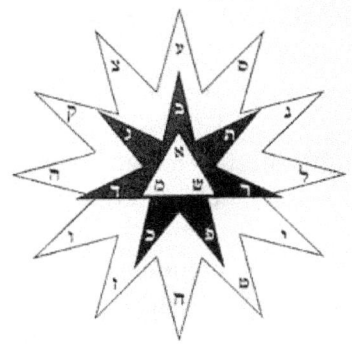

Figure 9 The three stars of the Sepher Yetzirah (Manly Hall, Secret Teachings of all Ages).

When was our dawn of Time, and what did it look like? For a clue, let us look to the Aboriginal people of Australia. These primitive people had a calendar, not connected to astronomical events, but to the cyclical return of rains, migrations of animals and the fruiting of plants. In other words, their calendar was tuned to their hunting-gathering way of life.

Perhaps elsewhere developed calendars that filled similar purposes. In southern Egypt at Nabta Playa the stone formations point to solsticial dates, and most importantly the onset of a rainy season, in which the surrounding area became a shallow lake.

Observation leads to counting. Using a different perspective to note the development of a calendar, what way of life for early peoples could have determined their methods of counting?

Body	Faces	Vertexes	Edges
Tetrahedron	4	4	6
Hexahedron	6	8	12
Octahedron	8	6	12
Icosahedron	20	12	30
Dodecahedron	12	20	30

Table 3 Numbers of faces, vertexes and edges in the Platonic forms

One final thought on archaic counting systems, buried in our languages and psyche, comes from a review of the Platonic solids. Here we see 4, 6, 8, 12, 20, and 30. Knowledge of these forms may not go back to the roots of our language though there is clear evidence of great antiquity, as we saw (Figure 3 – Chapter 3). Could here be a relation to our 12, 16, 20, and 30 – based counting systems? Note too the only shapes which work in these forms: Triangle – 3 sides; Square – 4; and Pentagon – 5.

Concluding dialogue

We have seen that ten is a counting system found worldwide. Easily understood by a mathematics teacher who has repeatedly seen even high school students count on their fingers. Twelve-, sixteen-, and twenty-based systems also occur. From where did these originate? When we go to Mars and more distant worlds, will we no longer need 12-based counting systems?

<u>Further reading/research and Websites:</u>
http://www.grahamhancock.com/news/index.php   Latest archaeological discoveries.

http://www.goldenageproject.org.uk/   Modern Atlantis research

http://www.zompist.com/numbers.shtml   Numbers in over 5,000 languages.

Class Exercise 1 **Learning about numbers**

Objective:
Get students to look at the origins of counting, pulling in those who are particularly interested in history, but providing for all a unique exercise.

Procedure:
a) Have students write the names of the numbers zero to forty, and then fifty to one hundred (by tens). Look over the list and write down anything that seems strange or interesting. (uniqueness of eleven and twelve, the teens and "twen"-ties) What do they think is important about zero? A number that represents nothing. (holds a place; tens, exponents.)
b) If you have Spanish speaking students (or other nationality) use their background. Count out the same numbers, so the class looks for clues (uniqueness of numbers above ten, the teens and higher).
c) Provide copies of Table 1 to pairs of students to try to find patterns and questions about how these people counted. Why did people 'regularize' their counting systems at 30? (days in a month) Why by tens? (fingers, perhaps why the Romans and early Greeks had a symbol for 5 *and* 10) Finally, why by twenty? If anyone has a good answer, other than their toes, please contact the author.
d) What other interesting features does our English counting system have? 12 inches to the foot, 12x440 feet to the mile, 2x12 hours in a day. The term dozen. 12 signs in the zodiac. What are common fractions of an inch? 1/16, 1/8, 1/4 and 1/2 are well known, but also 1/64 and 1/32 are used. How many cups are in a pint, in a quart and gallon? (2,4,16) Why was the Stonehenge calendar 16 months? How many nautical directions are there and what are they? (16; NE, NNE, NW, NNW, ENE, ESE, WNW, WSW, SE, SW, SSW, SSE, NSEW)

Homework:
Students should research a topic on counting systems of any other culture of interest and record a paragraph or two in their notes.

Evaluation:
Review participation and notes to see the effort made.

Bridges:
It is intended that this material raise a lot of questions from the students, particularly related to history and world cultures.

Creative students in the creative classroom.

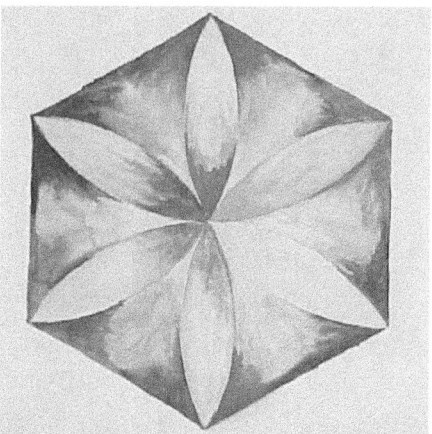
The color wheel.

Stain glass by Alphonse Mucha.

Student created "stain glass".

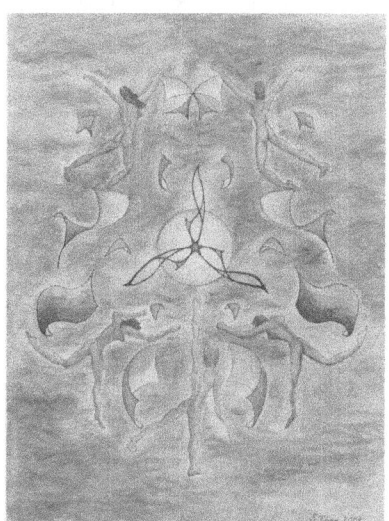
Additional ideas of how to use the "daisy" pattern (left) and hexagon (right).

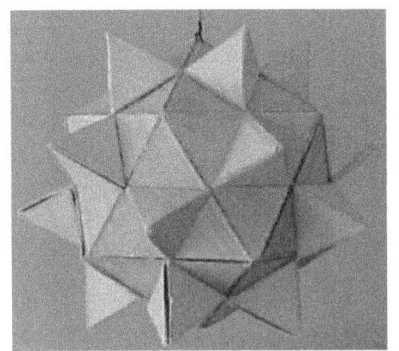 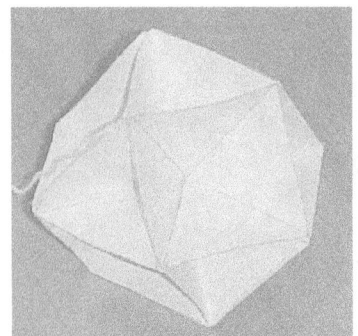 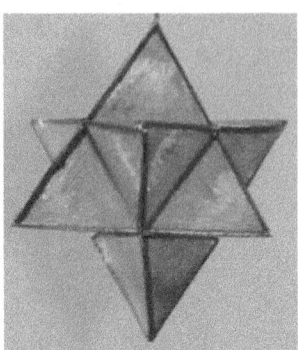

Stellated Icosahedron, "skeletal" Cube Octahedron and Star Tetrahedron.

  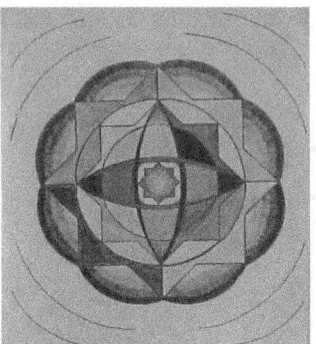 

Student work, created by Brianne Franke, Michelle Geiger, Olinga Gerhold, and Mona Aiff.

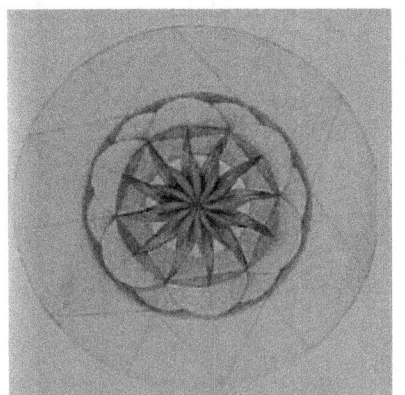  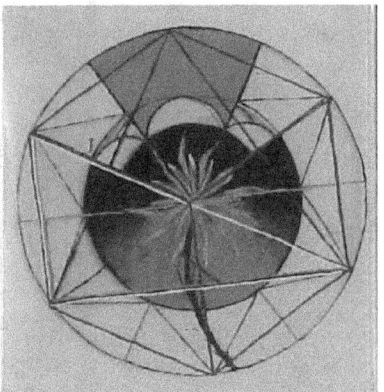

Student creativity. Original, with one and then two plastic overlays (R. Sandoval).

The ceiling of the creative classroom.

Starry Dream   Expanded Sri Yantra – (Francene Hart)   Invitation

Stellated truncated dodecahed. – (U. Mikloweit),   Spiked star in a sphere – (D. Springett).

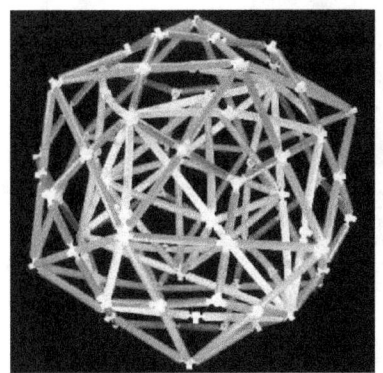

Platonic nest and other forms – (Astro Logix)

Magic Square of 12.   Some colored lattices

Metatron's cube – (Charles Gilchrist).

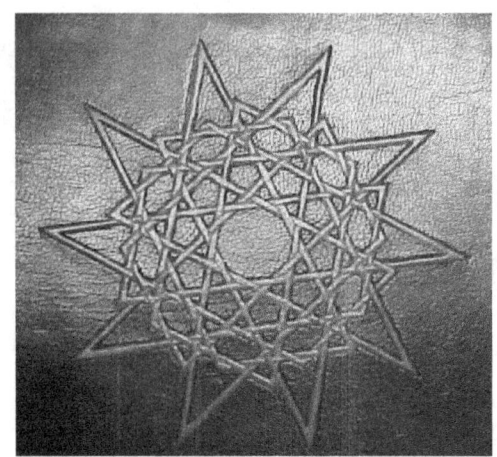
Ten pointed design – (Paul Galiunas).

Potentials with Zometools (center). Methane and the Zometool model.

Paper models - Stellated Icosahedron and Truncated icosahedron – (George Hart).

Ideas.

7 The Magician

Opening dialogue

How is 7 used in our world? What is 360° divided by 7? Have students work this out, by hand – just for practice. They will see that the number has an interesting repetition: 51.4287514287...

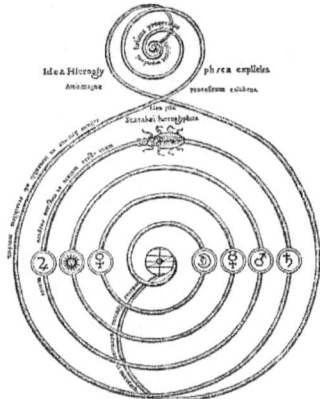

Figure 1 Oedipus Aegyptiacus (A. Kircher 1652-4).

Many of the ancient cultures which birthed our own had advanced studies of the motions of the planets. The idea of a heliocentric, Sun-centered solar system, far predated Copernicus, throughout the Egypto-Greco, Indic and Arabic lands. However, the geocentric won out, and from Ptolemy of Alexandria until the Renaissance, it was generally accepted that the Earth was the center, and seven "planets" rotated around it: Sun, Moon, Mercury, Venus, Mars, Jupiter and Saturn. Interestingly, mythologies show Saturn further out than Jupiter, reflected in Jupiter displacing his father Saturn. Also, their elder, Uranus, was pushed even more to the heavens. This may be metaphoric, though modern scholars are wondering that the Sumerians somehow knew of planets beyond Saturn, for which we needed the telescope to discover…

The geocentrists made a system which astrologers still follow today. Alchemists related the planets and seven known metals, partnering them; associating the Sun with Gold and Moon with Silver, Mercury with the metal bearing its name, Venus with copper, Mars with iron, Jupiter with tin, and Saturn with lead.

Interesting too is the fact that the symbols that astrologers still use for these seven "planets" are alchemical in origin: ♀ ♂. The alchemists of the 17th century were at their peak, at the dawn of modern science. Where did they and their knowledge then go?

Figure 2 L'Azoth des Philosophes (Basil Valentine, Paris, 1659).

After thousands of years of developing the arcane arts, the alchemists may have given way to the science of Chemistry. But, the science of alchemy had very deep roots, and there were many gifted alchemists like Francis Bacon, Thomas Aquinas, Albertus Magnus, and Cosimo de Medici, who helped this art transform and remain alive. One form it took was the Rosicrucian metaphysical science. As can be assumed from the name, the rose is present in their symbolism (Figure 3).

Notice the seven-fold nature of the petals of the rose. It would appear that from the Renaissance, we have some usage of the number seven, associated with the magical craft of alchemy.

Figure 3 Seven-petalled rose (Robert Fludd Summum Bonum, 1629).

In fact, the use is much older, and incredibly varied. Many of a Catholic background will realize that there are seven holy sacraments; baptism, communion, confirmation, confession, marriage, holy orders and last rites. From the East comes the idea of seven chakras. These are thought to be essentially energy centers of the body, as shown in Figure 4, including the root, sex, solar plexus, heart, throat, third eye and crown chakras.

   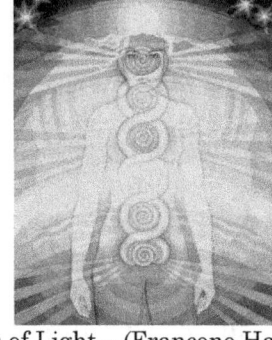

Figure 4 The Chakras.   Wheels of Light – (Francene Hart).

From a land in-between, Persia (where the three Magi and Zoroastrianism are thought to have originated), also came the religion of Mithra, a faith that predated the birth of Jesus by only a few hundred years. It revered Mithras as its son of God, Sol Invictus (Sun victorious), who was born of a virgin, on December 25th.

In Mithraism there were seven rites of initiation. First was Corax, or the Raven, associated with Mercury. Second was the Bride, represented by Venus; then came Soldier (Mars – whose astrological symbol was the spear), Lion (Jupiter), Persian (Moon - the scythe), Sun-runner (Sun) and finally the Father (Saturn). Is it possible that their symbols were the precursors of those eventually used in alchemy and astrology? Further, did undercurrents of Mithraism become imbued in the Christian faith? (Mithraism once replaced Christianity, as they both vied, with the respective emperors that consecutively hosted them, to dominate Rome.)

Figure 5, Statue of Liberty and Sol - Mithraic sun god (Mysteries of Mithra – Francis Cumont).

Did Mithraism affect Christianity, Freemasonry, and the Rosicrucians? A Freemason, Gustave Eiffel, built the Statue of Liberty. As seen in Figure 5, not only does it have seven rays on its head, it looks amazingly like the Mithraic Sun god.

Da Vinci

The biographies of famous personages are always interesting. We hold these people in high esteem, but in the end, despite their greatness, they were not so different from us.

Like us, Leonardo da Vinci had to eat, and so he had to make money. He made quite a lot while in the employ of an Italian duke as a military inventor. His sketches show a keen mind, skilled hand, and the viciousness of the dark side of humanity.

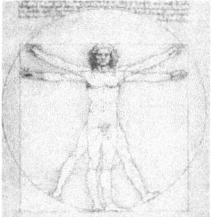

Figure 6 Vitruvius was a Roman architect who studied human proportions (da Vinci).

Da Vinci has always been of interest to art students, and has been made more famous in pop culture by modern novelty. However, as we will see in this picture of the Vitruvian Man, there truly is a da Vinci code. Da Vinci's drawing is acclaimed for its proportions, movement and exactness. But, how did he draw it? If we want, we may follow perhaps in his footsteps, and have our students join us.

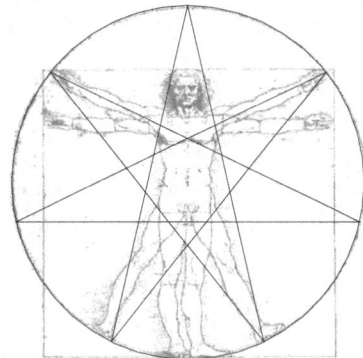

Figure 7a The seven pointed star overlay of the Vitruvian Man.

We begin with large copies of the diagram, and move our compass around to find the center of the circle, at about the navel. Then, draw a line straight up through the nose to make the top mark. Measure around the circle each 51.5° and make a mark. See if they notice the faint marks that are already there. Connect the points to make the star shown in Figure 7a.

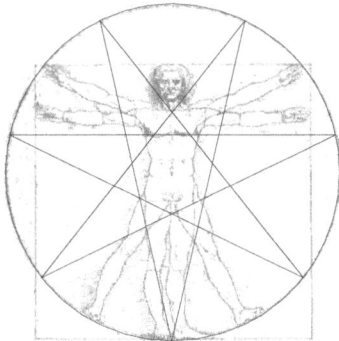

Figure 7b The inverted seven-pointed star overlay.

Did da Vinci use the seven pointed star to create this figure? Notice the placement of the upper arms, the chest area, the outstretched legs and feet. Many people will expect that 5- or 6- pointed stars can be used to similar effect. The teacher and student are free to look into this. It will be found that there are some possibilities which appear, but we will see others that are more likely, with even more complex geometries.

One thing we can also do is change from a "top-point" mindset. Notice what happens as we ask the students to draw an inverted 7-pointed star, and how it outlines the straight legs and chest area (Figure 7b).

Continuing, we will draw an 8-pointed star (Figure 8). Let the students discover how this star coincides with the straightened arms and shoulders. See how the head, elbows, knees, and feet are highlighted.

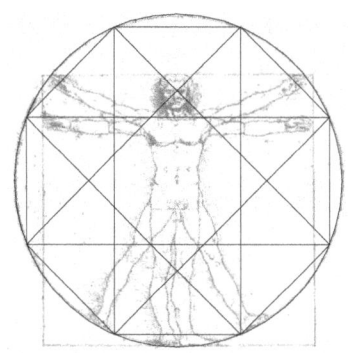

Figure 8 The eight-pointed geometry.

Finally, if we overlay a geometry which we have not yet talked about in this book, further interesting features appear. In Figure 9a, we see two overlaying 9-pointed stars.

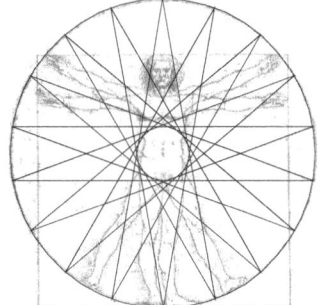 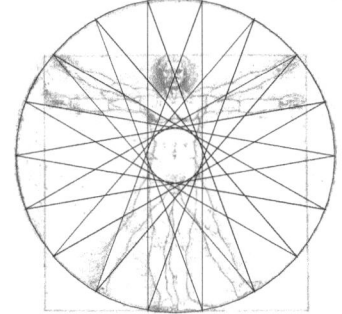

Figure 9a double nine-pointed stars.   9b Rotated double nine-pointed stars.

Notice the groin, where the actual midpoint of the body and this square exists. Otherwise, there is not much going on with this geometry that wasn't already covered. Let's rotate it by 90°.

In Figure 9b look at the arms (both sets), nose, torso and legs. Notice the places where the straight 7-pointed and rotated 9- pointed stars coincide. In Figure 10a, we see that the body is further defined by the eleven-pointed star, particularly one that is rotated 90° (here we see two stars – overlaid). We have progressed deeply in these diagrams, as we've shifted our axis from top to bottom, and also when we rotated it.

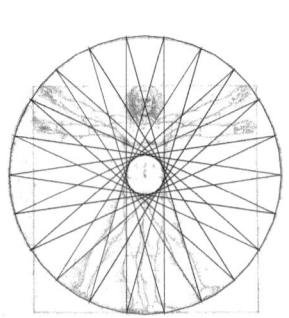 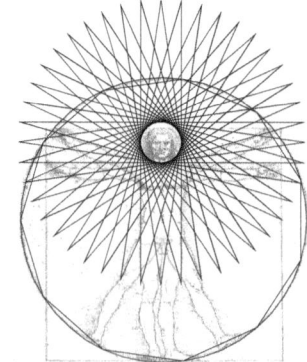

Figure 10 Double 11-pointed stars, rotated by 90°.   Figure 10b "Sol Invicti"?

Finally, we conclude our study (though this doesn't mean that further study is unnecessary) and shift the entire center. It is interesting what happens when we move the center to the heart chakra, or even to the third eye. Figure 10b shows four 11-pointed stars, each star aligned with a cardinal direction. The reduced figure is very busy with lines. And yet, it can clearly be seen the sense that the arms and legs are flying! An angelic figure?

Have we gone too far in looking for 11-based geometry? Not if we use the standard measurement system. It is another of those numbers hidden in plain sight. A mile after all is 11 x 12 x 40 feet. A furlong is 11 x 60 feet. An acre is 11 x 18 feet by 11 x 20 feet.

The question is whether da Vinci use these divisions of the circle to get his proportions. Did he understand ideas of the third eye, heart, and root chakras? Or perhaps unknown to da Vinci, are these geometries in fact buried within our own make-up?

Figure 11 Three-dimensional representation of mirrored stars.

Does there exist two *and* three dimensional meaning in the drawing, and human form? Notice the icosahedron in Figure 11 (a 2D picture of a 3D object).

The Architect of Stonehenge

Stonehenge is a well-known site situated in the plains of southern England. While the standing stones are famous, they are thought to be only the last of at least three main building phases which took place here. These stones are perhaps several hundred years younger than the rest, and also much smaller in floor plan.

The original "Stonehenge", was a circle of – holes. This was surrounded by a ditch and embankment. Actually, at this time, humans were making much more interesting sites, all over the British Isles, Europe, and the Mediterranean.

What is important to us is that many of these sites, of 3000-2000 BC show keen awareness of Pythagorean triangles, the heavens, pi, and the circle. Also, as at the early Stonehenge and other sites, the sheer size of the circle impresses.

How did they do it? Forget a compass. Did they drive a stake in the ground, and stretch a rope to a length of 144 feet? Did they have the ability to make a rope of this length, in 2000 BC? Did they instead have a way to triangulate? Such a technique would be of interest today.

At Stonehenge, there is a unique feature, named after the discoverer, John Aubrey: 56 holes, evenly spaced around the circle. This number is determined to be the amount of years in a repetitive eclipse cycle. An interesting thing for students to know is that solar and lunar eclipses are regular, meaning they are totally predictable. At some time, the Sun and Moon line up above a certain place to provide an eclipse. About 18⅔ years later, they do so again, as part of the mechanics of their movements, with that of Earth. This occurs at a point on Earth about 120° from the previous place. Thus, the region which experienced the original eclipse will again see one 56 years layer.

Now, there are eclipses happening all the time. Each year, there may be a couple of solar and a couple of lunar eclipses, each part of what is said to be a given, numbered, "saros cycle". A saros cycle can last hundreds of years, or more, until the alignment slowly changes and stops.

The etymology of this word is interesting. The word saros is thought to come from shar, or sar, a period of measure from Sumer, lasting 3600 years. It was said that certain kings' reigns lasted *several* of these saroi.

Interesting too is that at Stonehenge, the large stones are called Sarsens. Many writers have tried to relate this name to such ideas as "Saracens", but have any tried to relate them to a distant culture on the Euphrates, and the thought that the two could have had contact? It is hard to say just how extensive contact and trade were in those times. But we will see interesting things about mathematical knowledge.

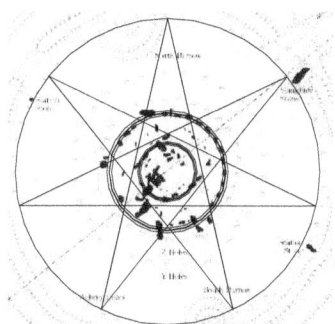

Figure 12 The seven-pointed star overlay of Stonehenge.

Let's begin by factoring this number 56. We see that 7 and 8 multiply to give this result. Let's again make enlarged copies for the students, this time of Stonehenge. Have them use the four so-called station stones numbered 91-94 to make an "x" to help find the center. Next, they should overlay a circle on the holes, and make a mark on the hole aligned with Stonehenge's axis toward the Summer solstice. Measure every 51.5° around and make a mark. Draw a 7-pointed star and see that the intercepts meet on the *inner* edge of the outer-ring of upright stones (Figure 12).

If we use the other factor, 8, we develop Figure 13. Here, the inner lines of the octagon appear to touch tangentially on the *outer* diameter of this circle of stones. And the star again lines up with holes around the circle. This again raises the question, worthy of further research as to whether these "circular" sites were made by triangulation.

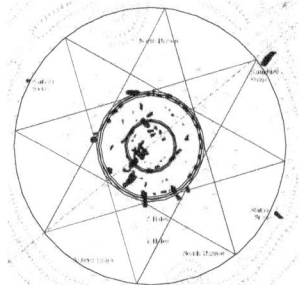 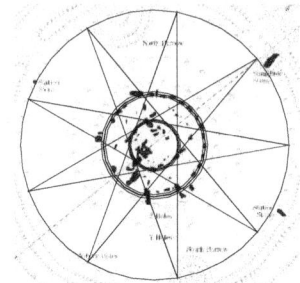

Figure 13 The eight-pointed overlay.   Figure 14 The nine-pointed overlay.

Finally, though the number nine has no obvious mathematical relationship to 56, let's put this star in the circle, just to see what it does, as with the da Vinci figure. We can see that it appears to determine the inner horseshoe of 10 standing stones and their five cross members. Does any of this mean that the builders used this knowledge and these techniques? By the way, 56/9 = 6.222; nearly 2π (99%).

The Architect of the Great Pyramid

The Egyptians used for their measurement of π an interesting fraction of 22/7. This is very accurate actually, to within 0.04%. This fraction has been found to exist within the great pyramid, whose dimensions, in Egyptian cubits (a unit of measure of about 20.7 inches), was 440 cubits wide at the base and 280 tall. In other words, a ratio of 11 x 7 (double the base to get 22). There is an interesting thing about this geometry. If we take half this base, 5.5, and were to call it '1', the sloping length of the pyramid is almost Φ. Here, we have an error of 0.03%. So, not only do Φ and π wrap themselves nicely around 11 x 7, but they do so with almost the exact same error.

We should note at some point that of all the factors of 360, from 1 to 12, only 7 and 11 are missing. We can also remember that the Egyptians measured 7 palms of 4 digits in their "foot". Doubling this makes a count of 56. Of these factors, seven was of great importance to the Egyptians, and eight was the number of gods in their Ogdoad.

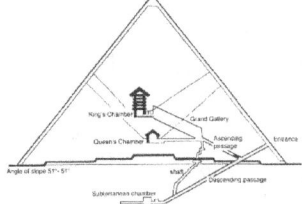

Figure 15 The Great Pyramid at Giza (Courtesy David Furlong).

Continuing with the arc-tangent of 7/5.5, we arrive at 51.84°: 100.8% of our 1/7th of a circle (51.43°). Not bad, considering that no other fraction of a circle comes close. The pyramid's overall dimensions fall close to these three very different proportions.

This is an exercise which the students can be taken through, that they will find fascinating after working through the material on Φ and seven.

One last interesting exercise is for them to add the royal cubit to the English foot. Not only does this equal the megalithic yard, the unit of measure used throughout the British Isles for Stonehenge and a myriad of other sites, but it works out to a value of 2.72 feet. (2.72 is the approximate value of "e") How is it that such disparate measurements relate?

Researchers have been giving exhaustive effort to the mathematics of the Great Pyramid, and many of their hypotheses have obtained for them the moniker "pyramidiot". Hopefully, the reader will not be too quick to discount this material.

Location, location, location

The builders of the Pyramids and Stonehenge obviously had technical and mathematical ability. Whether they used or cared about the seven-pointed star will probably never be known. This is the same for da Vinci.

These architects did have knowledge of geometry, and perhaps trigonometry. (The great pyramid was built very nearly true to the four directions). They also knew the skies above them, in order to tell time by the Sun and stars. (Time in terms of years, days, and hours.) This is no easy feat, for the stars shift in the sky each night, by about one degree. (They also shift by about one degree very 72 years, due to precession.) Thus, a star the Egyptians used to mark midnight in one month would be 2 am the next month, or 2 am in 2000 years, noticeable in their long history. The same is true for the Sun, against its backdrop of stars.

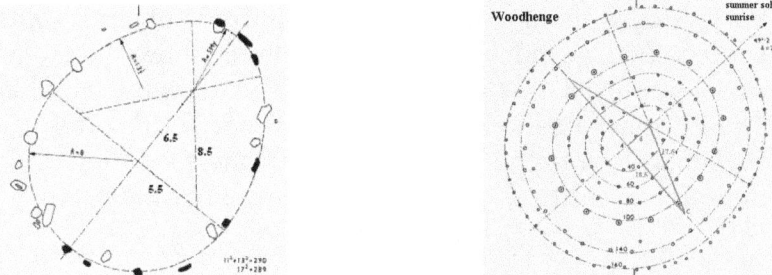

Figure 16 Megalithic sites in England – Pythagorean ellipses – (A. Thom).

Equinoctial sunrise at Egypt, like elsewhere, would have been, and still is, at about 6 in the morning, with sunset at around 6 p.m. This allows a fairly easy counting of the day. (For example, noon being when the sun points due south, and 9 a.m. and 3 p.m. being when it was at about a 45° angle.) But, as spring lengthens into summer, the mornings begin earlier and evenings last longer. How then to divide the sky to keep time? A Sun dial? This is really only accurate for hours closer to noon. Imagine, 7 p.m. in spring is already night, but in summer is only early evening.

It seems plausible that people able to build these sites would have been pretty developed in their astronomy, if they were this advanced in their architecture and mathematics. At Stonehenge, we have ample evidence of this. One is the fact that it is aligned to the solstice sunrise. Each year, the Sun rises in its extreme northern or southern horizon position at solstices. This is not a one-day event but actually occurs for approximately ten days before and then again after the solstice. An alignment is roughly accurate for nearly three weeks.

For a person observing toward the eastern horizon, the sunrise at each equinox will be in front of them. To the left, at some angle, they will see each spring sunrise occur ever-more to the left as we near summer, furthest left on and near June 21st. To the right, at about the same angle, are the winter sun rises, furthest being on and near December 21st.

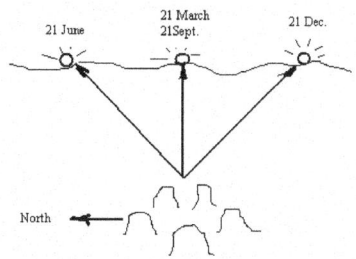

Figure 17 Horizon sighting lines for key sunrises.

The angle of that summer sunrise was at the time of Stonehenge's construction (2000 BC) in the neighborhood of 51.5° from north. The angle from north is referred to as its azimuth. Strangely, Stonehenge's latitude, *and* the azimuth of the sunrise are very nearly the same angle. And not just any angle. We will see a parallel to this...

Is there any relationship in that the pyramid at Giza has approximately the same angle on its sloping side? Do we wish to consider that humans built Stonehenge in *this* location to accommodate *this* specific angle, and that they were scientists working in cooperation with the Egyptians? There is more reason to wonder.

Let us consider the case of Karnak, in Egypt. The temple here, to Ra, the Sun god, points to the south-east/north-west, toward the winter solstice sunrise. It was built about the same time as Stonehenge. Its latitude is approximately 25.75° N, and the solstice angle to the sun was about this same angle, but from the east (in place of azimuth, this is called amplitude). This is a similar alignment as at Stonehenge, though measured from east instead of north. It should be noted that due to solar-earth mechanics, these are the only two latitudes where the solstice sunrise angle, from north or east, and latitude are congruent. Is there a connection that 25.75 is half of 51.5?

In either case, this is extraordinary work, but even more is the idea that the builders of Stonehenge, and Karnak, might have been able to calculate their latitude (if we take the solstice angles and site latitude being nearly equal as non-accidental) and *select* location accordingly. We may note that Stonehenge's latitude is not exactly 1/7th of a circle, but the complex of Avebury, just to the north is. Of the hundreds of circles and other sites around the British Isles, these two, with Newgrange in Ireland, show the most concentrated effort, so perhaps latitude mattered to the builders and they were capable of determining it. Back in Egypt, the Pyramid itself is at virtually 30° north (it's off by about a mile). Pretty accurate, and maybe as close to the appropriate latitude that they could find a site capable of handling the massive weight. Did the builders care about 30°, too?

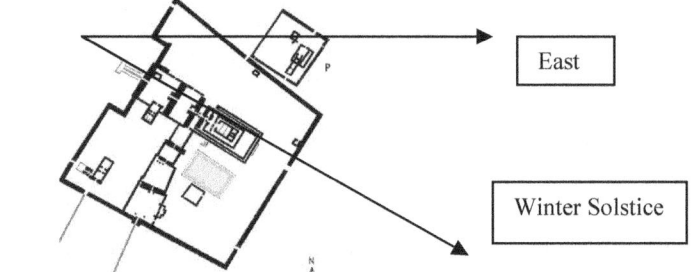

Figure 18 Karnak, showing the main axis.

We have already seen that the angle 51.5° relates to the slope of the Great Pyramid, and these various latitudes and solstice angles. We need to realize that the angle at the top of this pyramid is approximately 77°, the angle of separation between solstice sunrises at Stonehenge. If we halve this to get 38.5°, we get the angle between the solstice and due east. Here, we will have another interesting angle to work with.

Something else about Stonehenge

It has been found that at Stonehenge, there are four station stones, erected possibly before most anything else was done here. They form a large rectangle, approximately within the circle of 56 holes, with the short axis pointing toward the solstice sunrise. The long axis points toward a rarer event.

The Moon also has extreme positions but due to its mechanics they are much more complicated to study and explain. The Moon appears to travel between northern and southern extremes each month. These are not constant, as the plane upon which the moon travels is in motion relative to the plane the Earth lies upon as it goes around Sun.

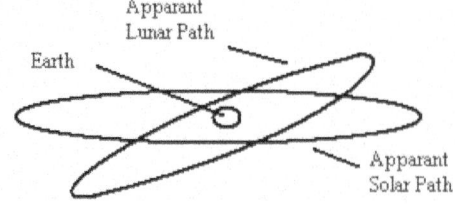

Figure 19 Mechanics - reflecting Geo-Centric perspective.

Think of the moon's plane as tilted to that of the Earth, and that the angle of tilt changes each day, slowly going from northern to southern extremes. Extremes sometimes coincide with a full moon, making the moon look very high or very low in the sky. It takes about 9.5 years between extreme high and low, or 19 years for a full cycle. There are many things which happen in our sky in 19 years, but they are beyond the scope of this text, other than to say that 19 is another of all of these rare, mystical numbers. (In this case, Muslim and Eastern mysticism.)

For our observer, facing east, the full moon can rise anywhere on the horizon that the sun is seen to rise. The moon's movements mean that it can be seen to rise even further north or south than the Sun's extreme points. Depending on site latitude, or distance from the equator, lunar rise can be 4° to 20° further along the horizon than the solstice sunrises.

At Stonehenge, the long axis of these station stones points to that once in 19 year event, the southern maxima of the Lunar rise (which occurs only in Summer, notably in 2006, for about two consecutive full moons). It is only at or near this latitude that these two events are at angles of 90° to each other (See Figure 21). It is always hard to be exact about these figures, as hills on the horizon can shift azimuth by as much as a few degrees, and then there is the question of were the sites designed to see the first point of light of the object, or the full circle, which again can add a few degrees of error.

Was there significance in the angle 90° between solar and lunar maxima? Did it help with eclipse prediction – which seems to have been one objective of Stonehenge? Notice that if the solstice sunrise was 38.5° north of east, then the lunar rise was 51.5° south of east. Was there a significance to *these* angles?

Are there other angular relationships between sun and moon that could be important? Say, 60° or 45°? For a temple to satisfy the needs of these other angular relationships, it must be at a different latitude. Further north and the angle of separation increases; further south and it decreases.

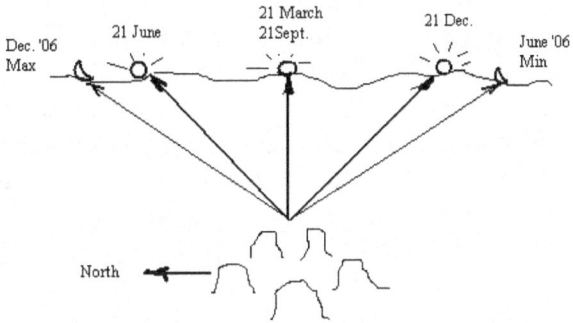

Figure 20 Horizon sighting lines for key sunrises and moonrise maxima.

Is it possible that 60 especially could have had significance, since it is a number so key to our time keeping and measurement, and as we have seen, is readily divisible and applicable?

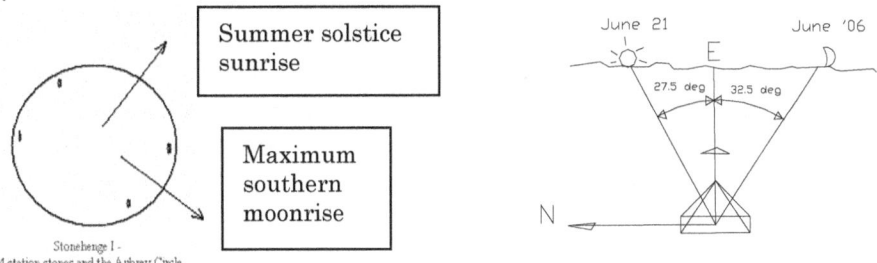

Figure 21 The 90° relationship at Stonehenge and the 60° at Giza.

If we look carefully, we see that the square relationship between Sun and Moon at Stonehenge is essentially hexagonal at Giza. Here, 60° separates both the northern lunar extreme and Winter solstice, or southern lunar extreme and Summer solstice. It is not yet proven if in fact either situation might have been tracked. (It would be interesting to check the alignment of Heliopolis to the pyramid as it might be in that general direction.) Further, 60° could have been perhaps possible at Sumer, just a few degrees latitude to the north, had the mountains to the east affected the sight lines at all. Certainly, the great Ziggurat at Ur appears to be aligned to the Summer Solstice.

More locations and mathematical anomalies

Were the scientist-priests of Egypt, Britain, Sumer, and perhaps beyond, working together, somehow trying to understand measurement of the Earth and cosmos? It is often taught to geometry students the story from Egypt of the water well, which once per year showed the noon Sun at its bottom. This perhaps would have been at the exact tropical latitude. At a site some distance to the North, on the same day and time, the side of the well cast a shadow. By measuring the shadow, and the distance between the two sites, an accurate calculation could be made for the distance to the sun, so long as the Earth's curvature were included.

At the Great Pyramid, there are interesting things about the noon sun. At summer solstice, it will be seen at very near 60° elevation above the southern compass bearing. At this time, and for only a few weeks before and after, the entire pyramid would have been bathed in light. At winter solstice, the sun's elevation is at about 36.5° elevation. This is the short angle in their 3-4-5 right triangle. Could any of this be reason for the site location? Could it be part of a giant research project?

Of further note, at a place up-river called Khmunu was the temple to Thoth, god of the Moon (and of math and writing), where the full Moon at its 19-year maximum is nearly 90° overhead in the middle night. Here, its path is described by a serpentine pattern across the sky. It rises well to the north of east and arcs high across the sky, though keeping to the southern half during most of its transit. As it nears its zenith, it appears to curve back northward for a brief time, just slightly more than 90° from south, until veering back to the south, to complete its arc.

Were sites built in specific latitudes just to see such rare events? Were they all part of a grand computational program? Are there things to learn from the thousands of large stones erected at Carnac, in Brittany, in extreme Western France, where nearly 90° separates extreme northern and southern Moon rise maxima, 9.5 years apart? Let us repeat that. Here, we are not talking about the difference between sun- and moon-rises, but between two specific *lunar* positions.

There is another curious array of stones, smaller in number and in size, far to the north (almost exactly due north of Carnac. Note that Carnac is as far west as it could be placed, and this other about as far to the east, both due to being beside and limited by the sea. Coincidence or intentional alignment? (If intentional – pretty skillful.) Here, at the "hill of many stanes", in Eastern Scotland, is a fan shaped array of stones, whose purpose has been only guessed at. At virtually the exact same latitude, to the Western extreme of Scotland, is the site of Callanish, one of the more unique sites of the British Isles (behind Stonehenge and Newgrange, to be sure, but not many others). For some reason, these two sites were built parallel to each other and what is also unique about them, at least with regards to this chapter, is that here, during summer solstice, the Sun will rise at 51.5° north of east.

Also at Callanais the solstice will see almost exactly 18 hours of sun. In winter, 6. Is there a connection between this and the fact that at Stonehenge, the solstice day is virtually 16 hours in summer and 8 in winter, or that at the site of the Great Pyramid, it is 14 hours in summer and 10 in winter? There are so many ways to research these stones. On one hand, we could be tempted to say that by this reckoning, something could be found in this for nearly every site. What if this is in fact the case?

More locations, more math anomalies

So far, we have considered major sites of the British Isles, and Egypt. In Mexico, it can be noted that the pyramid of Kulkukan at Chichen Itza, has corners aligned toward the solsticial sun rises and sets. This shows that the main staircases are not aligned to solsticial or equinoctal dates. Therefore, it must either be random, or aligned to some other event. It will be noted that the Lunar minima (where the moon is at its lowest northern travel or highest southern travel) once in 19 years would be seen along this line.

A similar thing occurs at the nearby Uxmal where the uniquely shaped pyramid of the magician, with its curved lines also aligns in this way. This pyramid is one of the most unique in our World due to its asymmetry on certain axes. One side slopes at exactly 60°. The other is steeper. Also, the pyramid is rounded and "sculpted". Could this be reminiscent of the phases of the moon? Further calculation is needed.

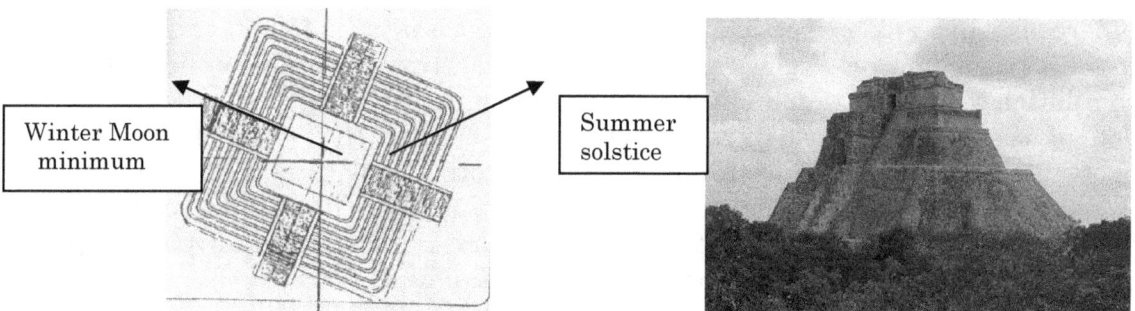

Figure 22 Yucatan pyramids: Kulkukan (left – courtesy Lain Sewell), Advino – Uxmal (right –John Coate).

Central America is on the best ocean-crossing current from Morocco, which then loops up toward the British Isles before tracing the Iberian Peninsula southward again. There are more comparisons between cultures along this East-West "highway" running from Morocco to Yucatan than just outward similarities of their pyramids in Egypt, the Canary Islands and Central America, and monumental architecture of Polynesia.

Geo – Logic

Pyramids require a great deal of mathematics in their construction. Perhaps there was an even greater effort involved in their location. Are there other mathematical relationships we could be looking at with regard to ancient cultures? Perhaps astronomical?

Site	Latitude	Feature	Angle	Notes
Callanais, Hillo'stanes	58°N	Solstice sunrise/set	38.5° azimuth from north/south	Solstice sunrises are +/- 51.5° from East.
Stonehenge	51.5° N 1/7 circle	Solstice sunrise/set	51.5° azimuth from north/south	Solstice sunrises are +/- 38.5° from East. 77° between them.
Stonehenge	51.5° N	Lunar max rise	38.5° azimuth from north/south	Moonrise maxima +/- 51.5° from East
Stonehenge	51.5° N	Sun-Moon rise angles	90° relation in sun/moon rise	90° sun/moon extrema.
Stonehenge	51.5° N	Moon rise angle	Lunar minimum rise along hypotenuse	Station stones built as a, (5x12) rectangle
Carnac	47.5°N	Lunar max rise	45° azimuth from north/south	90° between moon rise extrema
Crucuno	47.6°N	Lunar max rise	Sunrise at 36.9°, along hypotenuse	Site built as a 30x40, (3x4) rectangle
Newark Chillicothe	40°N 39°N	Lunar max rise	51.5° azimuth from north/south	77° between moon rise extrema. Possible 60° between Sun extrema
Delphi, Serpent Mound, Cahokia	38.5°N (90-51.5)	Solstice Sunrise/set	60° azimuth north-south Washington Azores, Sacramento	60° between sun rise extrema, +/- 30° from East
Giza, Lhasa Persepolis	30°N	Sun-Moon rise angles	60° between rise sun/moon extrema.	Pyramids and sphinx face due East.
Giza	30°N	Equinox sun	60° elevation noon	
Giza	30°N	Winter sun	36.9° elevation noon	3-4-5 triangulation
Giza	30°N	Great pyramid	51.5° sloped sides	Top angle is 77°
Giza	30°N	Second pyramid	53.1°sloped sides	3-4-5 triangulation
Hermopolis	28°N	Lunar maxima	90° moon elevation	Temple to Moon God.
Karnak	25.75°N	Solstice sunrise	51.5° between sun rise extrema	+/- 25.75° from East
Uxmal, Chi chen Itza	20.5°N	Lunar maxima	60° between moon rise extrema	+/-30° from East
Uxmal	20.5°N	Sun/Moon rise max	45° between sun-moon extrema	60° slope on front of pyramid of magician.
Konarak, Teotihuaca	20°N	Lunar maxima	60° between moon rise extrema	+/-30° from East

Table 1 Ancient sites, their solar/lunar features, and geometric relationships.

As many of the sites are on the Atlantic current, and not repeated, as though unnecessary, is it possible that they were all part of a great "international" process of discovery of the mechanics of Earth and Sun? There are many ancient structures and temples. Research so far on some of the more significant sites suggests many have been built where specific angles between sun and moon rises are 45, 60, and 90 degrees: fundamental trigonometric angles. And none apparently have been duplicated! We see them in relation to site location and solar/lunar mechanics in Table 1.

Much of the ancient world is still a mystery, despite the work of archaeologists, anthropologists and even geneticists, botanists, and others involved with trying to figure out how much, if at all, ancient cultures interacted. Linguists have found common words in early Egyptian and Mayan, as between early Chinese and Sumerian pictographs and words, in addition to all the other strange possibilities of links.

The math we should be learning and *researching*?

Our last thoughts on this subject will look at specific angles made by solar (annual solstice) and lunar (once in 19 years), maxima.

At Stonehenge and Giza there are 90° and 60° relationships between sun and moon positions. At Kulkukan there is 45°. Planned by the builders or not, they are there. Since the ancients gave us the 12, 60 and 360 system, would it not be reasonable to think that perhaps 60° could be an important angle? The numbers 6, 60 and 666 were often associated to the sun.

Whether or not 60° was important, the fact is that the latitude on the Earth where 60° separates solsticial maxima occurs at a latitude of about 38.5°. Our old friend. Here, at a temple to the Sun, an observer would see summer solstice rise 30° to the left of east, on the horizon, and winter solstice rise 30° to the right.

If we look at the globe, we find that Dephi occurs at this latitude, location of the ancient oracle of Greece, and a great temple to Apollo – the Sun god. Interestingly, the great earthen pyramid of Cahokia (largest pyramid structure north of Mexico), near St. Louis in the U.S. occurs here, as does the site known as Serpent Mound, near Cincinnati.

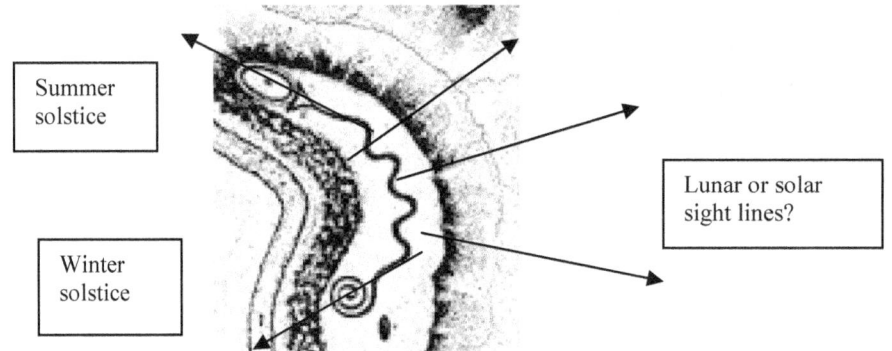

Figure 23 Serpent Mound (Squier-Davis 1848) 60° between solstice sunsets.

The Native Americans built many so-called effigy mounds. But this is the most famous. That it has astronomical alignments is clear, and it is interesting how they were sculpted in accordance with the solstices. Too, the loops of the snake reflect not only the true sinusoidal motion of the moon, but many researchers believe that they point to key sun and moon maxima.

Whatever latitude we find ourselves, the sun and moon rise each day at some angle which we can measure from either North (azimuth) or from East. In the United States, not far from Serpent Mound, this culture erected many very interesting sites. Like Stonehenge, several consisted of a tall circular embankment. And like Stonehenge, at least two aligned to an angle of 51.5°. But, the similarities end there.

At Newark and Chillicothe (Ohio) are the remains of three circles and two octagons. The size is amazing, as the walls of the embankments reach some ten feet. If one were to stop for a moment and wonder how humans made a circle as large as at Stonehenge, how then at Newark, where the diameter is over 1000 ft.? (The dots in the aerial photograph are full-sized trees.)

Here at Newark, the Moon, once in 19 years, will rise over distant hills and its energy and light will flow down the channel between the circle and octagon, at an azimuth that is about 1/7th of a circle – 51.5° (Winter 2006/7). Is this what the ancient Americans hoped for, about 1500 – 2000 years ago? Did they too see that this angle of 51.5° was important? (Note that here the latitude is not our 38.5° but just a bit over 40°. No relationship to 1/7th of a circle, but 7 miles from being 1/9th.) At the southern site of Chilicothe, it can be noted that the summer solstice noon-time Sun is at 51.5° above the southern horizon.

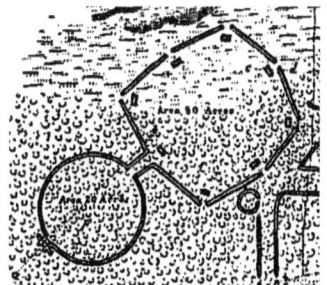 

Figure 24 Newark (Squier & Davis).   Aerial photo (Richard Pirko YSU).

There is a lot of mathematics to be investigated in these sites around the world. Various researchers have studied the geometric layouts. As shown earlier, the complexity of the British sites is amazing. And yet, prehistoric humans around the world erected gigantic stones and moved massive quantities of earth, in amazing constructions. Certainly some might have been aligned to key directions. And some very notable sites accommodate apparently *very* key directions. The angles 51.5° and its complement 38.5° repeat in many of these significant sites.

Freemasonry and 51.5°
The reader may roll their eyes at all of this math, and constant mention of Atlantis, Chakras, Swastikas, and Freemasonry. Yet, it is documented that many of the signers of the Declaration of Independence were freemasons, as have been many of the presidents of the U.S. Their symbolism is sprinkled throughout the USA and its lore.

Figure 25a Pyramid above pulpit, Worms Cathedral, US $1, Czech 50 crowns.

The Masons set the corner stone of each state capitol building, in ritual ceremonies. They designed the capitol city of the country, and located it in a *swamp*, at 38.5° north, 77° west. They placed the western capital of Sacramento also at 38.5° north, and though Denver (Colorado) won out, a town called Salida (38.5° north) was very nearly named the central capitol (In Salida there is a very clear Masonic presence).

 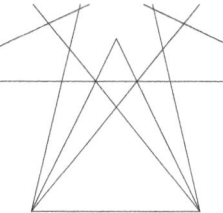

Figure 25b 7-pointed star: Giza/Masonic pyramid, the pyramid on the US $1 bill, and "A" on the Czech banknote. Where else might such geometry be found?

Masons had a great deal to do with the United States, perhaps still do, and one of their emblem is still on the $1 bill. A corresponding motif is found throughout the Baroque cathedrals of Europe, even though freemasonry was banned by the popes (Freemasonry was at its peak at the time of their construction). In both cases, the pyramids reflect the dimensions of a 7-pointed star (Figure 25b).

Latitude 51.5°

This chapter has shown that the number seven is very unique with regard to Human psyche. Medieval alchemists, cabbalists and mystics certainly had interest in it and the ancient builders too, worldwide. When we look at ancient sites, certainly we can find relationships to Pythagorean triangles, Φ, 5, 6, 7, 8 and 9 pointed stars; in a give latitude, solar/lunar site line, or even solar/lunar altitude at their peak.

Yet, we have found a coincidence in that many of the more significant sites have some relationship to 51.5° and its complement 38.5°. For peoples who believed in the sixty based counting system, the placement of a temple at 38.5° North, or South, latitude would correspond to sixty degrees, or one sixth of a circle. Maybe this was important to the people who built Cahokia, Serpent Mound, Washington D.C., and Delphi.

Archaeological study is continually needing to rewrite its books, particularly thanks to the fall of the Iron Curtain and underwater archaeology. Very close to this same latitude are the sites of Çatal Hüyük in Turkey dating back to 6000 BC, Karahundj Armenia –site of astronomical observatories from arguably 7000 BC, with holes of about 2" drilled in the standing stones for horizontal and sky observations, and the Bactria-Margiana Archaeological Complex (a newly discovered civilization from 2000 BC on the silk route).

New discoveries

As mentioned in Chapter 6, archaeologists are finding evidence that the Black Sea was once a fresh water lake, which flooded around 5500 BC, probably giving rise to the migration of the Indo-European peoples. They are finding too, at a place called Yonaguni in the Okinawan islands, amazing works suggesting human activity, in a place which would have last been above water ten thousand years ago.

A very large site has also been found in the Gulf of Cambay, India, thought to date from before 9500 BC. Evidence points to two cities having been along the banks of a river, all now submerged but above sea-level during the ice age. Pottery remains found here dramatically redate the start of this industry.

The ancient Indian stories talk of humans having *flying* vehicles and great metal spears that exploded like the sun. These myths, as with other mythic stories from around the world, talk of great wars between Gods and giants, humans, and each other. Is it possible? Is it possible that such technologies were available to these people, and that they did, as Plato suggests, destroy themselves? Were our culture to unleash our own "metal spears'", what would our world look like after nuclear winter had possibly started a new ice age, a time through which people would scavenge the remains of the old for raw materials, while trying to survive, clinging to remnant weapons and technologies as the knowledge of how to make them quickly waned?

Modern researchers, not taken so seriously by standard science, have been accumulating theories and suggestions that the ancients had significant technology, and usages of the Great Pyramid. Again, we could discount these as "pyramidiots". What technology existed at the time of Plato's Atlantis is hard to know from the scant materials still available to us. Other mysteries remain. Why do most megalithic sites use hardened stones containing a vein of crystal? Why were they placed on so-called ley lines and intersections of these leys? Did they understand, as we learned in the last hundred years, that crystals transmit energy? Were they aware of some vast natural energy, just as Tesla himself discovered? Could they harness it with their stones?

Figure 26 "Spherical" temple – Newgrange Ireland, encased in quartz!

What of this ley line, passing through England, from East to Cornwall in the west, along which so many mounds, and old churches, mostly named to St. Michael (and hence the name – St. Michael ley line)? If we continue to follow this, far out into the Atlantic, we come to the Azores, whose capital island is named Sao Miguel. And if we were to suggest that this is the remnant of Atlantis, would it be of interest to note that it is at 38.5° north?

Making a 7-based mandala

We have really gone exploring in these last two chapters. Let's return to a more mathematical-artistic approach. One interesting thing about seven is to give students seven equal-length sticks and see if they can make the image shown on the left in Figure 27.

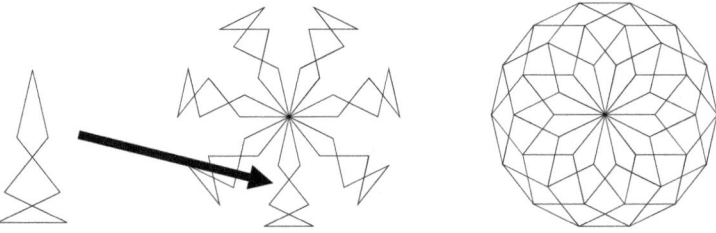

Figure 27 Seven equal-length sticks connected to make an image, and then more.

If we then rotate this "needle" around the tip, six more times, we will make a flower with seven petals. If we connect them we would make a seven-pointed star. Fourteen segments together make an attractive mandala.

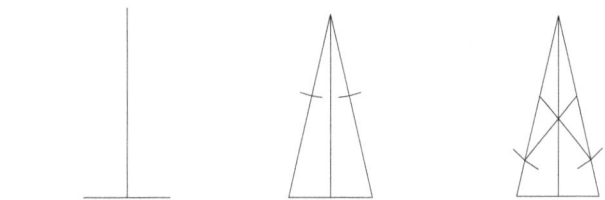

Figure 28 Steps involved in making the piece: one 14th of a circle.

To draw this figure, begin with a line '2' units long. Return to the diagram used to generate the Φ proportion (Figure 3 in Chapter 5). Bisect the line and from there draw a perpendicular line that is '6 – Φ' units long. A strange length (99.985% accurate). Lightly sketch lines from this peak to either end of the original horizontal line. Mark them '2' units from the top. Draw diagonals from them '2' units long to the opposite side of each slant line. Draw the final lines and erase the unneeded portions (left image of Figure 29).

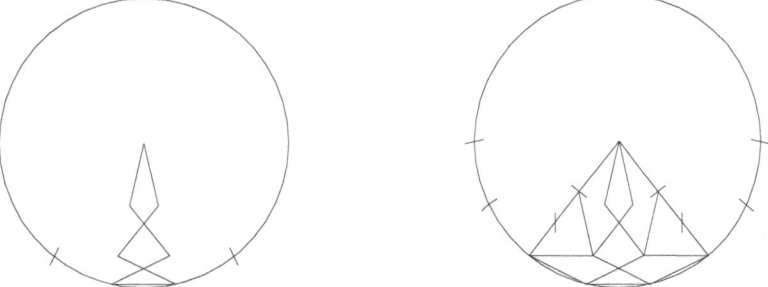

Figure 29 Steps involved in making a mandala.

A great exercise in precision is to then have the students try to make the mandala. Here, instead of the work coming from the center of the circle, as we learned in Chapter 1, we now must work throughout the image, creating a circle at the tip, whose radius is '6 – Φ' units. Mark around the edge of the circle every '2' units and continue (Figure 29). The second diagram in Figure 29 shows further construction lines and segments.

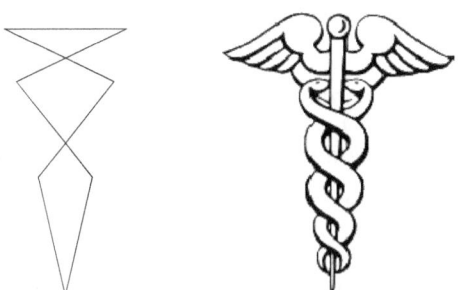

Figure 30 Seven and the Caduceus.

Notice in Figure 30 that the original image, when inverted looks reminiscent of the caduceus.

One last artistic item

We will conclude this section on seven, and Φ with yet more beautiful Eastern geometric art. The Sri Yantra is a form which we can show to our students, and ask them to draw. What is it? What are the symbols? What can the circles, the lotus petals, and squares mean? What do upward and downward pointing triangles represent? How many are there, and why?

Figure 31 Old and new Sri Yantras, center - Expanded Sri Yantra – (Francene Hart)

What proportion do the largest triangles have? Do they look familiar? They should, for they are those of the great pyramid.

Concluding dialogue

The material in this chapter is extensive and very complicated for introducing to a typical high school class, though not their teachers. Fascinating to think that there are these usages of phi and of seven.

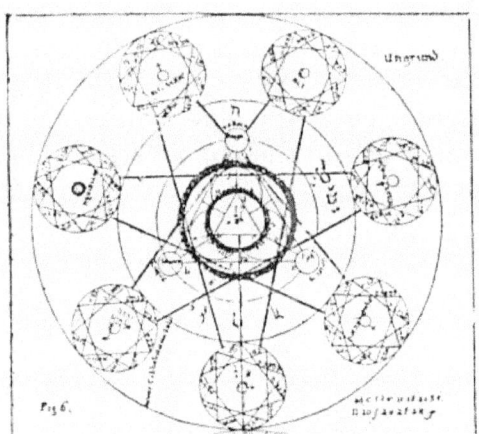 

Figure 32 Gregorius von Welling   33 Sigillum Lutheri (van der Heyden) seven-fold symmetry.

How could we bring mystery into math classes, and use this to enthrall our students and interest them in further independent study?

What mathematical knowledge would someone need to harness in order to create a calendar, and keep time? How was the relationship of Sun and Moon perhaps critical to the pyramid builders? Did ancient winds and currents of the oceans provide the pathway for language, number and architectural similarities to be transmitted among the different cultures and times?

Philosophy is written in this immense book that stands ever open before our eyes (I speak of the universe), but it cannot be read if one does not first learn the language and recognize the characters in which it is written. It is written in mathematical language and the characters are triangles, circles and other geometrical figures, without the means of which it is humanly impossible to understand a word; without these, philosophy is confused – wandering in a dark labyrinth. – Galileo, Il Saggiatore.

The tragedy of modern man is not that he knows less and less about the meaning of his own life, but that it bothers him less and less." Vaclav Havel

Further reading/research and Websites:

http://www.sacred-texts.com/ane/index.htm   Classic books now becoming available due to copyright expiration

http://www.levity.com/alchemy/index.html   Alchemy info.

http://www.knowth.com/index.htm   and http://www.carrowkeel.com/files/main.html   Irish megalithic sites.

http://web.genie.it/utenti/m/malta_mega_temples/index.html Maltese sites.

http://www.mysteriousworld.com/Journal/2003/Spring/Fragments/   Great source of alternative thought on ancient sites

http://www.megalithicsites.co.uk/home.html   Interesting pages on Megalithic Math, Calendar and much more

http://www.ga.gov.au/geodesy/astro/smpos.jsp *The* page for finding Sun and Moon azimuth and elevation for any time and location. Make your own discoveries.

http://sunearth.gsfc.nasa.gov/eclipse/eclipse.html   Eclipses.

http://www.morien-institute.org/index.htm   Ocean archaeology

http://www.grahamhancock.com/news/index.php
Great website listing the latest archaeo-astronomy news

http://sivasakti.com/articles/intro-yantra.html   Sri Yantra

http://www.megaliths.net/   Proposes that megalithic site locations around the world mirror constellations in the sky.

http://www.megalithic.co.uk/   Information on UK megaliths

Class Exercise 1 **Magnificent 7**

Objective:
Discover that 7 is important to various religions, philosophies and antique sciences. See 7-fold geometries in Human form and more.

Procedure:
a) Where do we use 7? (days of the week, "lucky 7", 7 sacraments, 7 chakras) See Figure 4. Count the petals on the first five chakras. We see 4,6,8,10 and 12. Could the symbols represent 3D forms?
b) Divide 360° by hand to get 51.4287514.. and particularly the repeating pattern of 514287. Notice that it counts 14, 28 and 7.
c) Provide copies of the Vitruvian man, from the internet. Mark the bellybutton as center of the circle. Verify with a compass. Draw a line to the top of the circle. Mark the circle, using a protractor, at each 51.5°. Draw a 7-pointed star on the figure. See the arms and legs. Use another color to draw a second star, inverted. Note the legs, chest and throat. See the faint marks on the circle, beside their own. Figures 7a and b.
d) On a new copy, lightly draw x-y axes at the belly button. Bisect to get the diagonals and bisect again to get 22.5°. Use these to draw an 8-pointed star on the figure. Note the straight arms, throat, "third eye", and where the legs separate. Figure 8.
e) On a new diagram, make the "top" mark to the side. Now do a 9-pointed star, each point 40° around the circle. Do a second star from the opposite side. Note the nose, both sets of arms, features of the legs and feet, groin and the lines of the torso. Figure 9.

Homework:
The drawing is one of the best proportion studies ever created. What else is significant? (It is hoped students will notice that we all have these geometries.) How many arm-leg position are there? (16) Which star was used to model the woman on this book's cover? (11 – depending upon the version purchased)

Evaluation:
Check their work and participation. Encourage precision.

Bridges:
Da Vinci was an amazing inventor and artist. We can show that he used mathematics within his works, and that geometry perhaps underlies biology. This material can very well be connected with arts instruction.

Class Exercise 2 **The Architect**

Objective:
See the 'da Vinci' geometries in ancient architecture to raise further curiosity and discover specific so called 'transcendental' numbers.

Procedure:
a) Provide copies of the Stonehenge ground plan. Note the 56 "Aubrey holes" (http://www.odessahistory.com/s_h_plan.htm). Use a compass to find the approximate center and draw a circle that passes through as many of the holes as possible. Draw smaller circles that touch upon the outer and inner edges of the ring stones. The stones to the Northwest are best for this.
b) Use the divider as the "top" and map out a 7-point star. See each two legs meet on the inner edge of the ring of stones. Use this "top" mark, different color, and generate an 8-point star. Note the tangential relationship to the outer edge. Many of the tips of both stars land on holes. Last, with a third color, create a 9-pointed star. See how it relates to the horseshoe of upright stones.
c) Provide copies of the Great Pyramid, measuring 440 x 280 cubits. (http://www.kch42.dial.pipex.com/keys_intro2.htm) Reduce this ratio (11:7) and multiply by two. (100.04% of π) Half the pyramid; make a right triangle, and solve the sides. Find the ratio of the hypotenuse to the 5.5 leg. (100.03% of Φ) Finally, take the Tan^{-1} of 7/5.5 (99.2% of 1/7 of a circle, 51.4°).
d) On a dollar bill measure the apex angle of the pyramid; 38.5°. Double it to 77°. Check the latitude and longitude of Washington DC. Note latitudes of Delphi oracle, Cahokia pyramid, Serpent Mound, Sacramento and the Azores. If a Masonic temple is in town find the pyramid that is often on the building. Measure the angles.

Homework:
Answer: "What is significant about the base to height, slope to half base and slope angle of the Great Pyramid?" (Φ, π, 1/7 of a circle)

Evaluation:
Grade effort, precision, and interest; particularly their questions.

Bridges:
There is math here to be sure, plus history, culture, and classic architectures.

Class Exercise 3 The Sri Yantra

Objective:
Draw the Sri Yantra, a meditational device from the East, using Φ. Follow precise instructions.

Procedure:
a) Give copies of this sheet to pairs of students, to decipher. Review Figure 3, Chapter 5, concerning the Φ ratio. Lightly draw a line across the center of a page, exactly "2 units" long. From either end, swing an arc of measure Φ. Top and bottom intercepts denote the apex of two large triangles, proportional to the Great Pyramid. (a)

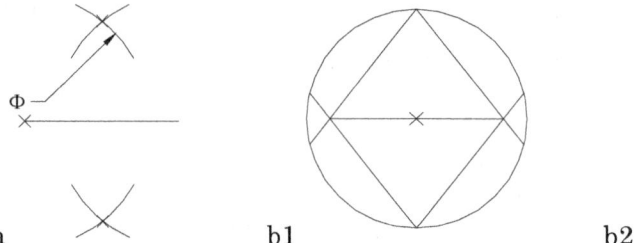

b) Bisect the line and draw a circle that touches the two intersects. Draw lines from these vertices through the ends of the line, to the circle. We have the start. (b1) Close out the triangles. Crossing points A, B, C and D are defined. (b2)

c) Draw a light line between the vertices. Take length EF and mark off equally above and below it to get points G and H. (c1) Draw lines from G thru D and beyond (a vague distance for now), and also its mirror. Do the same from H through C and its mirror. This defines I and J. (c2)

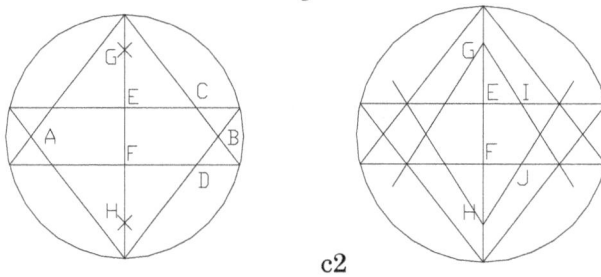

(At this point, we are departing from the traditional design, but only for the means of brevity and simplicity. Much more accurate, and complicated instructions are available on the net.)

d) Draw EJ and continue until level with H. Mirror. Close out this new triangle. Do the same with FI. This helps define more triangles. Lightly bisect the points shown. (d)

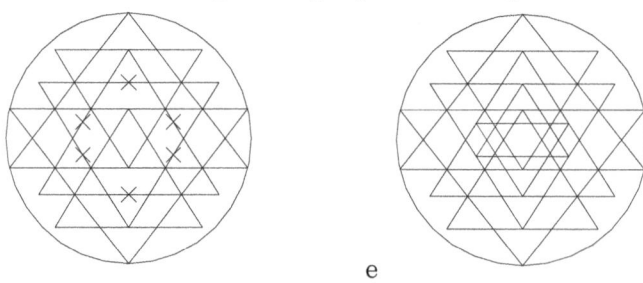

e) Close out the two inner triangles. (e) We have made a rough Sri Yantra. Of course, the outer circles, 8 and then 16 petals, and contour (meant to retain the energy of the form), are left for the student to create.

Homework:
Give students examples of Yantras. Have them take their pieces home and add detail and color.

Evaluation:
See how well they followed the instructions. It is challenging. Grade them also for quality. Their petals (mandatory) should show geometric knowledge which we will expect by this point.

Bridges:
This is geometric art. Art students and teachers may not like performing this, due to the technical instructions, but the link should also be made with world cultures instruction. Enjoy!

8 The Alchemist

Beginning dialogue

What is the meaning of the word Chemistry? What are the origins of this science? We have been seeing in this book undercurrents to our culture and history, where mathematical understanding and even symbolism have enriched our Human creativity. We have often alluded to Rosicrucianism, Kabbalah, and other mystery schools. Let us here look at another stream to which they may relate. Along the way, we will see a few more classroom applications.

Neolithic chemistry

Chemistry began with the first of human activities. The rocks they used for chopping, digging, and cutting required different chemical makeup. They might have noticed that one stone was very hard. Other stones were rough and easily worn, like sandstone. Archaeologists and anthropologists help us understand how humans began to use this "chemistry". Studies of finds, and of indigenous people to the present, show stones that were especially used. One example is ochre, a reddish iron ore. It can be ground, mixed with water and painted on the body for rituals or in cave paintings. Another stone, flint, is useful for tools and in chipping it gives off sparks, allowing for the creation of fire.

Fire hardened the mud and clay in their hearths. This "technology" went into plastering the walls of their first homes. Some of their work required crushing and heating materials to temperatures higher than available in an open fire. So, they developed the kiln.

We can show students the chemistry behind these "simple" process of plastering walls and floors. It's how concrete is made. A modern contractor mixing cement is probably no more interested in the chemical breakdown of this similar process. He merely counts how many shovels of sand should be mixed with how many of cement, and then adds water until the consistency is right. In the end, the material dries and becomes very hard.

Early humans found that another material, clay, became like stone in the fire. How did they discover this? Perhaps they noticed how mud and clay dried in the sun and tried to see what happened when even more heat was applied. From the earliest civilizations, we have examples of what they did with clay. The discoveries at Khambat have the potential to push back the horizon of this industry by thousands of years.

This is interesting to recreate. It is dirty and fun. Get some clay. If you can, get some that is dried out and add water, to see how the material bubbles and breaks apart. It will then need to settle. By this method, or using moist clay, they now have a nice plastic material. Let them "play" and make various shapes but try to get them to make thin and thick pieces, long and short. In other words, a variety. When they are finished, accurately weigh each piece, and measure one or two key dimensions and record them.

Material condition	Weight	Measurement 1	Measurement 2
Wet			
Air dried			
After firing			

Table 1 Recording chemistry pottery information.

Let this dry for a week, even three. In this time, have them build, and maybe even research how to make a kiln. This is a great high school project. What are needed are some basic bricks, stacked on a level place, having the shape of a tapering cylinder. There should be a low opening through which wood and charcoal can be fed to the fire. There should be a few small side holes through which air can be fed into the base of the fire. It's a good idea to have copper metal tubes, to blow into the coals, but *note* that if left in there, they will get very HOT! At our school, we made a bellows to force more air through the tube, and had small diameter tubes for students to blow through. (ONLY blow. Don't breathe in the hot vapors!)

As the kiln is built, it can have a diameter of about a foot-and-a-half (half-meter) and a height almost that tall. Some bricks should be placed pointing to the center as shelves upon which the pottery pieces can be placed.

Figure 1 The Kiln: Beginning, top view and final construction.

Leave the kiln in this state until ready, but have the rest of the bricks on hand. Next, go to the forest, or a park, and collect all the downed wood you can find. Put the wood under cover so that it can be dry for game day. Buy a bag or two of charcoal, needed to get even higher temperatures.

Wait until the clay pieces, the collected wood, and weather are agreeable. When it looks as though you are ready, have the students again weigh their piece and measure the same dimensions. They should see some differences. Why?

Go to the kiln, put in paper, and teepee of thin and then thicker sticks. When that's ready, place your pottery pieces around so that the heat should be able to circulate in there. Try to make it so the pieces won't be in the direct flame. Build up the sides of the kiln a bit higher, but still not all the way. It will be necessary to still add wood and charcoal, hopefully without damaging the pieces, or burning anyone's arm hair. It's a good idea to have fireplace tongs handy, and maybe a bucket or two of water. Safety goggles too!

Light the fire from the lower opening. You might need to supply some air to help it get going. Once the heat begins to rise, it will draw air in just fine. The flames might get high, and note too that as the heat comes on, there is always a chance that expanding internal gases can explode the pieces, so lab glasses are a good idea and nobody should put their head over the opening!

The teacher or someone mature can keep an eye on when to add more wood. Care must be taken to drop it into the middle, or try to feed it in from the lower hole, so pieces aren't damaged.

Get some good coals going and try to add charcoal now, using tongs or a fireplace shovel to feed it in from below. Again, its a bit rough but you can toss it in from above, but you risk damage to your pieces. Keep adding wood.

The thing here is that the pottery must be slowly brought above the boiling point of water. About the time the outside of the bricks are getting warm, this should be accomplished (about an hour). Now its time to put on the heat and do some other things while you are at it. Get those coals really going and build the chimney the rest of the way up, to about 5 feet (1½ meters).

Figure 2 A few pieces from the kiln. Crude, to be sure, but educational.

Continuing, with metallurgy

As the fire burns, the students can experiment with metals. They will need aluminum foil. Crinkle some up, to see what the material is like. Then, put it in the hot coals. Put in your copper tubes and stoke the fire. Let them hear the distinctive sound that the oxygen blast provides. Let students get down low by the opening so they can see the change in color of the coals. You can get metallurgical charts that will show the temperatures obtained. By this method it is very possible locally to exceed 1000° C, enough to begin smelting copper.

Put some aluminum foil in this heat and remove it after it seems to have been in long enough. Let them see how fast aluminum loses its heat. What has happened to the material? They should notice it has changed (thinned).

Next move to copper. If you have access to copper alloy sheets, they work the best. See how strong the sheet is. (This should be fairly thin material, about 1 mm thick). They can also put in the lid from a tin can.

Put this in the coals. Heap coals around it but don't bury it. Again stoke the fire. Let the students see the green and yellow gasses that are given off. What does this mean? (there is a chemical reaction taking place) Notice the metal will turn red, and then orange, and even white. These are all indicating how high of a temperature is being reached. With time, take out the metal, which will appear as a partially blackened, reddish piece of material. (USE TONGS AND BE CAREFUL OF THE HEAT!) The black is slag that can fall off easily. Let it cool. Then try to play with it. The students will see that it is much softer to work with. Before and after weights will reveal also a slight loss of material. (The scale must be very sensitive). Notice that the tin hasn't seemed to change at all.

This has provided a lot of heat in our kiln, which we wanted. Add more charcoal into a pile on top of the now substantial coals. Plug the holes and mostly close the chimney, so that the whole thing will slowly burn. Go off to the rest of your day and some hours later, or in the morning, come back.

The fire and coals should be gone, though the ash can be still very hot. Certainly, any pieces which have fallen could be too hot to handle.

Carefully dismantle the kiln about halfway and remove the pieces. They will probably be blackened in places, reddish in others and maybe orange or tan in others. The colors indicate how well the piece fired. They can still be quite warm.

Finally, have the students again weigh and measure them. They will see that there has been further material loss, which means that something transformed in the evaporation and then heating process. The thing that is most interesting is that even after the worked clay material appears to be "dry", there is "water" still locked inside as OH.

The age of metals

Having learned how to make pottery, the ancients then tried to decorate it. They used the same materials that were already familiar: ochre and bluish ores of copper, ground up and painted on as a paste. Many of these experiments failed and ended up in the trash heaps, for archaeologists to find, showing that the blue had turned black and other materials had balled up on the surface. They had smelted copper and discovered lead.

Fire and wood fed this work. These cultures decimated their forests, making the landscape susceptible to erosion and desertification. This ecological destruction undermined several early cultures. This is worthwhile to mention to students, as our regard hasn't improved so much in our combustion processes and their affect on our local and global environment.

The first metal to be fashioned was copper. Fine for ornaments, but too weak as a weapon, the copper age actually didn't last long, as bronze was fairly quickly reached, by mixing copper with tin or arsenic. A lot of this metallurgy took place in Sumeria and Egypt where tin was not so readily available (though it was found in southern England). So, most bronze was made with arsenic. The early metallurgists using arsenic were simultaneously giving themselves nerve damage. No wonder that it was discovered to be a good poison for assassination.

We are rushing through the material here but we must imagine the process of discovery over millennia.

The Bronze-Age was one where great works of beauty were created. In the West, swords were forged and small decorations produced. In China, incredibly large bronze castings were made, another great chemical and technical advancement.

It was not long before gold and silver were also smelted, hammered, and formed into nice shapes and ornaments. Before long the entire system of trade changed from barter to cash – precious metals exchange, a system that continued until the invention of paper money in only the last few hundred years.

As with star-gazers and other specialists of this time, some mystery must have developed around these people, who could essentially transform rocks into lustrous, malleable, and beautiful materials, as well as weaponry.

The next big step was the smelting of iron, which needed much higher temperatures and thus more advanced kilns. Further, iron isn't workable like other metals, since it never really forms a liquid. Another interesting thing is that as the smith hammers at the red-hot iron, beating out impurities, the charcoal dust that is ever present combines to harden the surface, resulting in steel. Dipping the metal in water then made it even stronger, and added OH back in. What discoveries this entailed.

This effectively ended the bronze-age, as new armies, with the new "weapon of mass destruction" crushed those bearing the old. Many cultures of the Middle-East ended at this time, as new ones like the Hittites arose. The Iron Age mainly began with those same cultures and areas with long histories of smelting. Of these, only one survived long enough to have its knowledge passed on to succeeding cultures and times; the Egyptians.

Wider efforts

Metal work required a lot of steps and the people performing them must have been quite inventive. The cultures capable of this were certainly continuing to experiment with other stones and ores. In the Orient and the Middle East, they weren't just looking to make metal. They made dyes for their clothing, and pigments for their art. They made cosmetics. In some cases, they were looking at the biological effects of these materials.

Today, we know that minerals are part of our body, and necessary in our diet. The ancients certainly experimented with them and to this day mineral supplements in the West and the elements in their native form in the East are still prescribed for ailments.

As many cultures died away, others arose. Knowledge might have been passed on, as well as lost. We are fortunate in that Egyptian culture survived fairly intact for three millennia, or more, and was able to mingle with Hellenic culture after the conquests of Alexander brought the two – and also India – into contact.

This was an early information age. While the Greeks were able to document much of the ancient wisdom, it was not long before the ancient Egyptian writings were to be nearly lost under Christian and Byzantine onslaughts. Fortunately, however, much information somehow survived long enough for the Arabs to translate and bring forward in time. They preserved and expanded world knowledge at a time when Europe chose to be bereft.

The birth of Al-Khemie

The Arab armies swept over Egypt and continued across northern Africa until stopped in France. Around 820AD, the Caliph of Bagdhad, al-Mamun, went to Egypt. With his gangs, he began to break into the Great Pyramid. To this time, the pyramid still was encased in an outer layer of smoothly cut white stones. It must have been an amazing sight, shimmering for thousands of years in the sunrises, occurring 300 or more days a year. At night, under a full moon, perhaps like ivory. One can imagine this by how the Taj Mahal of India may appear rose-colored at dawn and pure white at other times. Due to the motions of the heavens, at midday, in mid-summer (or at full-moon midnight – a few times in 19 years), all four sides of the pyramid would have been lit.

Al-Mamun's men broke into the main passage. Somehow, they knew to dig on the North side, and were fairly close to the right spot. They reported that they found nothing and went back to Baghdad. This is the story that all historical references provide.

Back in Baghdad, al-Mamun went on to do something very interesting. He founded the "House of Wisdom", or Bayt al-Hikmah. This was a great school, with observatories for studying the stars. It would be something to know from where the inspiration, and money, came from for this endeavor. We owe much then to the Arabs of this school, who translated Ptolemy's Μεγαλη Συνταξεο under the name "Al Magest" (the great work). Others of his books were likewise brought forward to us and the critical thing is that Ptolemy was our link to the ancient Egyptians' star science.

The Arab scholars expanded this astronomical knowledge. They collected the Indian form of numerical writing and also passed this on to us, or we'd still be trying to do numeric operations with letters of the alphabet (Roman numerals were used in math operations into the time of the Renaissance). We can also thank another product of this school named al-Kwarizmi who gave us his work; Al Gebiru, or "algebra".

There are many interesting innuendoes associated with these events. An Egyptian geographer and historian, al-Masoudi, wrote that there was a great emerald within the pyramid. This was recorded prior to al-Mamun's expedition. Another Arab historian, Edrissi, said that there were hieroglyphs on the roof of the Queen's chamber. Further rumors state that a star map was on the roof of one of the chambers.

Al-Mamun, and history, records that nothing was found. Yet, there was soon after a book published by the scholars of Baghdad called the Emerald Tablet of Thoth, who had been the Egyptian God of Science. This book was also known as the Book of the Secret of Creation. An appropriate name for the sciences and black arts they were practicing.

The final point is that the Egyptians themselves called their land Khem, usually translated as "the black land". The Arab scholars and scientists of this time were taking Egyptian knowledge of the stars, math, medicine, cosmetics, dyes, metallurgy and anything else and trying to make new discoveries. Those chemical works, developed from knowledge coming out of Egypt, the land of Khem became known as Al-Khemia.

Other cultures were also experimenting with these mysterious processes of breaking down materials into constituent elements, particularly China and India. Today, Chinese medicine and Indian – Ayurvedic medicine rely greatly on mineral compounds and processes discovered maybe millennia in the past. Modern Chinese medicine is very alchemical in nature. Along with the Ayurvedic system, it looks at "energies", elements, the entire body system, meridians, and astrology in diagnosing and treating.

The Chinese also discovered gunpowder and rocketry, but didn't exploit them, saving their hegemony perhaps for a later age.

Alkhemie comes to Europe

Alchemy made its way into Europe by a variety of routes. One was through Spain, whence it spread slowly into Europe, thanks to Jewish mystics and Qabbalists, who were able to live at relative peace under Muslim reign. Later, the Crusades opened up additional routes of contact with the East and more knowledge and wealth came in. This was the era of the Romanesque and then Gothic architectural masterpieces – much copied from Islamic.

Early scientists of this era like Roger Bacon and Albertus Magnus surely included alchemical experimentation in their work. Magnus' student was Thomas Aquinas. Where the former two might have been questionable to the Church (despite being members of religious orders) for their work in the "Black Art", Aquinas was a very respected intellectual and theologian, who may have also been an alchemist.

Part of the reason for the epithet "dark" ages was the lack of knowledge in Europe at this time. Metallurgy, and chemical processes required knowledge, which under feudalism, was not widespread. There had always been a mystique to these processes, and as the experimentation and knowledge began to grow, so did the mystery.

A goal of the European alchemists, as elsewhere, was to make gold. As the chemical elements were not broken down yet into the table we now know, it was thought that through heating and various other processes, a base metal could be transformed into gold. As more knowledge developed, so too did symbolism and dogma. Alchemists developed their own written and symbolic languages. We still use some of it today in astrology. The symbol representing iron also represented Mars, and still does. Each glyph we use to this day for the Sun, Moon, and the five inner planets were used by the alchemists to represent the planetary body *and* a specific metal.

As time progressed, more famous personalities experimented with the "Art". Cosimo de Medici was also known as an alchemist. Whatever his scientific success with making gold, economically he established one of the more famous and notorious dynasties of Europe, which would make Florence the jewel that it is today; their patronage of various artists color still our museum walls.

Alchemists were not only trying to make gold. They were looking for the "fountain of youth". Along the way, they discovered the mineral acids, allowing for further breakdown of materials, and the manufacture of gunpowder (an art imported from China). This particular compound, combined with knowledge of bronze casting for bells, allowed them to develop the cannon, which would lead to these next centuries of global domination by European and American armies.

Around 1600, when the Hapsburgs fled Vienna for fear of the Turkish invasion, their emperors moved to Prague, where they attracted to their court the leading alchemists and astrologers/astronomers of the time. This was in some ways the peak of the black science, as understanding was pushing back the shadows. Yet, even to the time of Newton, who also believed it should be possible, learned men were still trying to make gold.

The birth of objective science

Alchemists were also seeking in their long history the "Philosopher's Stone", a metaphor for gaining wisdom. This latter became their goal as knowledge developed what came to be known as Chemistry in the 18th century. As the black arts of astrology and alchemy gave way to "concrete science", the former were forced underground, and mystery and ignorance have enshrouded them ever since. With the rise of modern science, and its technologies, the learning of thousands of years have been minimalized, maligned, and refuted, just as when the ancient schools were closed long ago.

One of the last great alchemists was named Paracelsus. He worked quite a lot with minerals and helped developed what came to be known as pharmacy and even homeopathy owes its roots to him. To this day, the Pharmacist in England is called a Chemist.

Figure 3 Modern medical symbology which looks like the Eye of Horus.

Paracelsus pursued the medicinal effects of certain compounds, at a time when herbalists such as Culpepper were trying to codify knowledge of plants. There were incredible sums of knowledge at this time, as age-old remedies were documented. Influence of the planets on plants and humans was a given. To our modern world, with its Farmer's Almanac, we see some trace of this. That subjective knowledge of centuries and millennia has since been thrown aside by the rush of modern science has put the West behind the East in this regard.

Before the alchemical sciences died away, its adherents began to form societies like the Rosicrucians. This secret group, with others like Qabbalists and Freemasons, continued to keep mystery alive. They have hidden for very clear reasons, and yet, as the centuries have turned, and further groups have arisen, like the Illuminati and the occult groups of which Hitler and his henchmen were students, there has been much innuendo about interactions and hidden subcultures. Along the way, there has been ignorance and disinformation which have discredited much mysticism. This is fascinating reading to give to our students in a joint chemistry-history session.

The Egyptian science

Alchemists are often imagined as black magicians, making sinister spells, cooking potions, performing Satanism, and trying to make false claims. The perpetuation of these images and belittling of metaphysics by modern science does not take into account its own "dark" side.

Alchemists of the Middle Ages and before were among the greatest scientific minds trained and educated in a number of fields. The ancient Egyptians looked at it as their great science, which they used for everything, from deep exploration to embalming their dead. As with the Native Americans, and Australian Aborigines, they believed that everything had a Spirit. As Joseph Campbell would say, every thing was a "Thou". Ka and Ba, Spirit and Soul. Spirit and Matter. These were called the Neteru, from which our word Nature comes. The Egyptians are said to have been able to talk to the "spirits" associated with matter so that it would divulge its secrets.

If we look at some of the things that the ancients and native cultures have done, it seems that we should not be so quick to dismiss them. Yet we have. Progress scoffs at the believer, the Indian or Aborigine who is opposed to a development in a seemingly dull piece of landscape. As many flock to a "new age" of widening consciousness, others laugh at their "pseudo-spirituality".

Modern snake oil salesmen

Chemistry has made remarkable gains since it shed mysticism and metaphysical rigmarole. All of the sciences have done this, since the coming of the Age of Reason. Understanding has uncovered the minutiae with which modern agriculture, medicine, industry, and communications have been built. As many have lamented, it is often times bereft of morality and "soul".

Many public and private schools do not consider it their place to provide moral education. There is of course the debate about whose morals and beliefs would be "followed" should this policy change. In the case of schools backed by various religions, the situation is not necessarily any better with regard to a truly broad and developing education. Both concede to the "System" for leadership in terms of curriculum requirements and procedures which today push science and math more than literature and art. Is this in the interest of Youth, or of business: using the time to train future employees who lose out on their own human development?

We spend our time in the typical math or science classroom with text books and standardized tests that winnow out non-mathematicians from the sciences. This merely perpetuates the techno-excess of our times. Youth should be helped to see that the wondrous world of the Modern that they are being hyper-marketed has very dark sides to it. What price progress? Let's look at some of the sides of chemistry that youth often don't consider.

In agriculture, our land is being inundated with chemical agents that now foul our drinking supplies, kill insects and wildlife, and enter our food supply. Industry has emphasized yield over quality, appearance over content, and shelf life over freshness and its inherent nutrition. This does not even consider "Franken-foods". We support this with how and what we purchase. We support it with our ignorance, apathy, and smallness.

In medicine, industry has taken us from simple inexpensive plant and nutritional supplements and remedies (that support the entire body and *prevent* illness) and gone to expensive treatments that perhaps only suppress the symptoms, burying them until even greater illness surfaces – requiring greater expense, chemical assault, or even surgery. We have turned aside from concepts of "wholeness" within the individual, in favor of master-slave mega-business methods where organizations we trust, like the AMA (American Medical Association), the FDA (Food and Drug Administration), and the United States Congress are lobbied, manipulated, and controlled by extremely wealthy special interests. Students should be informed of alternatives in medicine, and perhaps be guided in researching whom these public institutions follow, where the money comes from for election campaigns, and where the elected officials put their emphasis.

With regard to the petro-chemical and energy industry, we continue to decry it, and yet we buy it! We want convenience. But alternative energies have long been available, suffering only from a lack of subsidies that "traditional" energy industries have long enjoyed. A detailed study of the history of these industries, back to their founders, will show in whose interests and how disappointingly they have always acted. Our lands, water, and sky are littered with their products, which break down very slowly: legacy to this industrial bump in our long history. We support this every time we buy, and vote.

There are intelligent and brave people who are trying to stand against this tide. We should help our students to read between the lines in these wars against communism, drugs. and terrorism, particularly who has the most to gain, and how we lose our fundamental rights because of them. Labeling human beings as eco-terrorists harkens back to the Cold War when people like Catholic priests and nuns working for the poor of the third world were labeled communists for standing against the crimes perpetuated for cheap bananas and coffee.

Figure 4 The face of a human, who fought, without weapons, and died in the cause against greed.

We see this still today as the Amazon forest continues to shrink, transformed into a new bread-basket and bio-fuel source. Sister Dorothy Stang was assassinated there in 2005, standing up to these powerful interests after 40 years of work with the poor and displaced (accused of being a communist because of her stance for human rights).

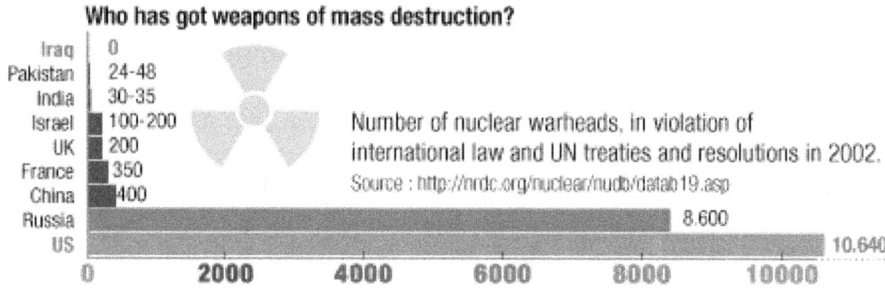

Figure 5 Mathematics we should understand (NRDC)?

Finally, regarding the high-tech and telecommunications industry, we are its supporters, buying ever-increasing quantities of today's electronic gadgetry which will be in tomorrow's landfill, contaminating our water with heavy metals. Others (including child soldiers) are annihilating gorilla and elephant populations in the Congo for food, while fighting for and mining the one special ingredient that these toys need best for operating (coltan). This is another master-slave industry where we must upgrade fairly often just to be able to communicate, download, and function. Most harrowing is that we are enthusiastically buying the components for an Orwellian future, convincing ourselves that life is so much simpler with these things.

These serious issues should be talked about in our schools. Youth want to know, for deep inside they sense there's no leadership on this. Many will say, "But what can we do about it? We can't change anything." Every great journey begins with one small step.

Health

We can begin by educating our children about nutrition for themselves and for the planet. Schools have allowed soft drink and junk food into their facilities in exchange for the money the manufacturers are willing to "donate" to programs. Such "philanthropy" is doing nothing for the health of our children and the continual presence of brand names and advertisement is counter productive to education. Parents who bring artificially colored and sweetened goodies to the classroom are not helping.

Instead, we can get these things out of our schools, putting nutritious alternatives in their place, a new trend which has already begun. We can help students learn about vitamins and minerals and their role in our bodies. Help them see what foods contain the nutrients they need, which do not, and the hazards of artificial ingredients. Is this part of the math we should be teaching? It is part of the entire program we should be teaching. In terms of math, they can count grams and percentages. They can learn how many nutrients are in a carrot and calculate how many carrots they need to eat in a day. They can learn to read information regarding rising health care costs. With health, particularly rooted in nutrition, they can learn, comes certain freedoms.

It is an interesting feature of information-disinformation that our food labels provide virtually no nutritional information. They once did, with the Recommended Daily Allowance label, shown in Figure 6. This clearly showed the percentages of nutrients in the food packaged within. This very informative material was craftily replaced at the end of the 20th century by the "Nutritional facts'" label now affixed to our food. Now there is no clear nutritional difference between a bag of potato chips and a bottle of milk.

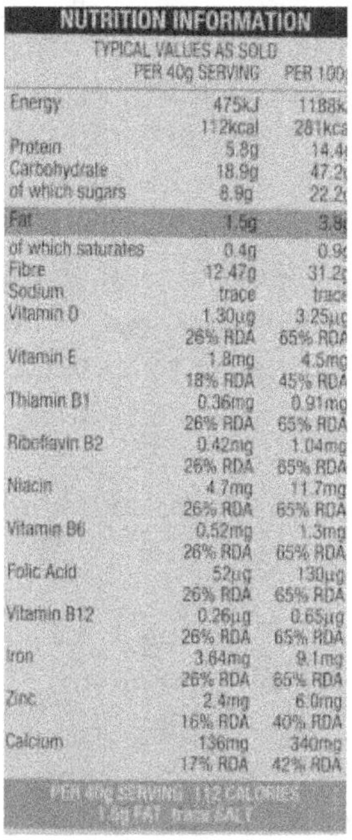

Figure 6 Information – Disinformation. Which would you rather buy? – (FDA).

In the absence of such information, we owe it to ourselves and our children to help them realize how natural foods are vital to them. They should see the divide between the alchemical "thou" and modern chemistry. In the absence of leadership from the top, it is up to parents, teachers, philosophers, and theologians – in *partnership* with science.

Realization

How did we come to this, where our food and lifestyle so threaten us? We can find, read and then provide material to our youth so that they become aware of how we simply cannot be naïve with regard to the dealings of industry and business. They will obviously find this to be unexpected, at times unwanted, but the more aware will ask for more information.

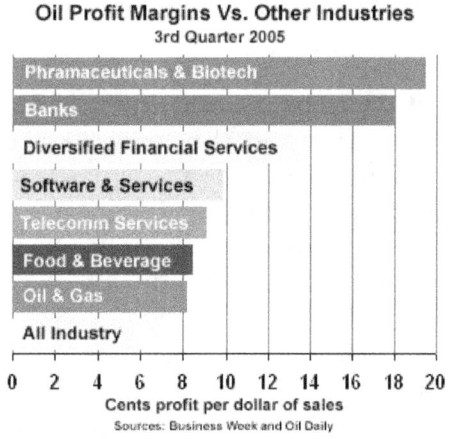

Figure 7 Profit margins of the biggest industries (Business Week and Oil Daily).

Figure 7 shows where the big money is made in our modern world. We can acknowledge that the business world is shrewd, cunning, and at times, ruthless. And yet, as our culture accelerates, it is exhausting itself as it exhausts our resources. We are each helping all of this in our own perception of what is a "necessity".

We teach our children history, and the dark side of cultures of the past, of kings and tyrants. Yet somehow, we have accepted the notion that at present we are living with benevolent industrial and political leadership. This message has probably always been given to the people. We can instead show children the news and someone else's facts that are harder to come by, and must be dug for.

We can let our youth enter the debate about whether mobile phones cause cancer (or worse) or if food colorings and artificial sweeteners lead to ADD, headaches, asthma, etc. We can face reality: biological systems are affected by chemical ingestion and electromagnetic stimulation. In the absence of real scientific investigation, we must use common sense. But we accept that each item in itself is a small dosage and hence harmless, with absolutely no reason to assume this, or to exclude the question of what are long-term effects of the entire mix. We must admit, accept, and do something about the fact that industrialization, modernization, and consumption in their evolving forms are increasingly detrimental to our world. Our health and health of the planet are linked.

Why do we perpetuate this cycle, in the face of more and more evidence to the contrary? We can educate our youth on the concepts of Reduce, Reuse, Recycle, *and* Refuse. Refuse to buy. We can still encourage them to enter into technical careers, but where technology is kept as slave to us and our systems enhance world health.

Chief is not to encourage or push too early. We should allow children their childhood. Making children more competitive early is robbing from them of a valuable treasure, which most of us were allowed to have.

History: a new look at power and control

As we ourselves widen the education that we choose to give our youth, we should consider a second look at how we teach history and some of the numbers involved. Not the near uselessness of today's memorized data, but the real numbers behind history: numbers of peoples murdered, raped and enslaved for profit; effects of whole cultures eradicated and enslaved; financial gain made by conquest; and the whole idea of empire. The German language is most interesting on this point. Their word for war – Krieg – is related to the word "kriegen" (to get).

Where to begin? With Alexander the Great and his campaigns? Earlier? Later? Greed and lust for power and domination is of course not new to the human psyche. Nor is it all "the other guy". We should be aware of these needs that we each have within ourselves. Is it the place of schools to teach restraint in place of materialism? Of course, for where else does our youth have a chance to learn any of this today? They are bombarded with media, to buy a look that they just have to fit into to, or a product that they cannot live without. We need to educate ourselves on the numbers and share this with our students: bourgeoning populations, deforestation, pollution, over-fishing, over-farming, and rise in consumption among the developing world, coupled with on-going consumption among those cultures which have known plenty for so long.

The beginnings of modern banking

The final idea of what we could be teaching about "the numbers" is that we should help ourselves and our students understand the finances of government, so that we perhaps know what we should really concern ourselves with when we vote. To do this, we could begin by looking at how governments do their banking, and how it relates to us.

A great deal of mystery surrounds the Knights Templar, who became very wealthy being among the first international bankers, during the 13th century. Their demise came about when the king of France, Phillip the Fair (a name accorded him by history, but who writes those books anyway?), obtained the blessing of the Pope to disband this religious order and seize their property. Thus ended the first European attempt at international banking (and began the Avignon papacy when there were two popes – one in France under the king's thumb).

Financial intrigue would continue in Europe. Our study could include the Medici family of Florence, and further, where from ancient Rome to the present are many dark sides to Italian banking and finance, woven with papal intrigue (as recent as the death of John Paul I, just as he was opening an investigation of the Vatican bank). Our study could include other families like the Fuggers of Augsburg or the House of Orange.

We could look at Spain and the inquisition, at treasure stolen from the cultures of the Aztecs and Incas, which were obliterated in the process. With the money that empire and colonization brought into Europe, banking as a whole expanded. Key families financed kings and their wars, often supporting and profiting from both sides (probably prolonging each conflict and resultant profit). Can we not expect, too, the instigation of conflicts, to serve financial purposes? How would one get an entire population to go along with it?

Further reading and research is warranted for our students to study the rise of powerful families and the creation of central banking toward the end of the 17th century, transfers of power into England, its central bank, and British hegemony and colonialism on every continent.

Much as we idolize the British Empire in our history classes, we could also show the very dark side of empire; such as the Indian mutiny, the Great Game with Russia (like the Cold War but held a century earlier) the Highland clearances, Irish Famine, and opium wars in China. Let's look too at the role opium, and other drugs, have played during the Vietnam war, and modern events in Afghanistan and central America. Let's look at the history of the "School of the Americas", banana republics, and how the South and Central American countries have historically tried to survive their larger neighbor. We still perpetuate atrocities on indigenous cultures like the American Indian, for natural resources found on the desolate lands to which we shoved them.

We teach in school that the American Revolution was against "taxation without representation". Buried in the rhetoric is the tale that the Bank of England wanted control of colonial finances. In the end, the colonies were able to gain their "freedom". Coincident to these events was begun the First Bank of the United States, which was chartered by the Bank of England. Among the founding fathers were supporters and detractors of the concept of a national bank. What were, and are, the arguments for and against a private institution managing a nation's finances?

The bank was chartered for twenty years, and its time expired without a new charter. Coincidentally came the war of 1812, which the United States also "won". But then began the Second Bank of the United States, again chartered by the Bank of England. It was President Andrew Jackson who finally closed the central bank, which led to great efforts to remove him from office. From his tenure to the American Civil war, and again after, the country had no central bank, and apparently survived handily, printing its own money and drawing no income taxes.

As industrial might grew throughout the 19th century, financial empires rose with it. After the American Civil war arose the "robber barons" who exerted great control in the United States. Immensely wealthy families came to financial power (Rockefellers and Morgans), aided by families and bankers of old Europe (Rothschilds).

A financial panic, perhaps artificially created (as many seem to be), occurred in 1909. It hurt the "common man" enough that he accepted and was convinced by the need for strong governmental action. Soon after, a number of major changes occurred in the United States. One was the 16th amendment, whereby the government began to tax income. Another was the creation of a central bank known as the Federal Reserve. As with all central banks, this institution cheaply prints money that it then lends to the government and the people at face value (with interest) and manages the gold reserves of that country. Overnight, the gold reserves of the United States were given over to a bank created and run by private individuals. Why is it that political parties favorable to business and industry prefer high budgetary deficits (and associated interest)?

As these laws were passed, it could be imagined that the powerful families of America, with their vast finances would be expected, like the common person, to pay income taxes. Yet they created the new system of banking and laws. These financial empires evaporated overnight, "donated" before they could be taxed and given to the common good.

The irony is that these families are portrayed (in the print that their associates control) as great philanthropists, though their "donations" went (and still go) to institutions which continue to make policy in industry, education, medicine, and politics worldwide. Behind the scenes intrigue did not end with Richelieu and Metternich.

Wars of the 18th, 19th and 20th century have intensified, supported by populaces convinced that they had some right, need or fear, to "Krieg" upon another people. Millions have died, as billions have gone into the coffers of those who financed both sides in these conflicts and the industrialists who supplied the belligerents. Between the wars there has been ongoing massive financing of arms and arms races, speculation with national gold reserves and oil. Countries are supporting much of this with massive borrowing from the central and world banks capable of loaning these sums. How does each individual support it?

Our students can be invited to investigate this. They are enamored of (perhaps brainwashed by?) pop culture, yet they can be given a wider view of how that culture thrives on the backs of the world's poor and the decimation of natural resources.

Our youth are the most vulnerable and the most at risk. They, and all of us, are naïve in the realms of power, and particularly the tremendous impact of media and advertisement. We all are guilty of buying what we do not need, and believing what we want to hear. People wish to trust what they see, read, and hear. What is significant about our time is that the media are concentrated more and more on those with the least experience and most easily manipulated by the imagery.

Our children are buying into all of this, and we are allowing it to happen. We are all of us guilty of buying it. It's overwhelming really, the power from without, drawing and pulling at our children, and our own senses.

It is hoped that readers and teachers will include research along these topics in their classes. Can we, as Pythagoras hoped, reform society? The trick is, in whose image would we do this?

This is no call to revolution. That always begins in violence; the original drive gets subverted from within and without, and ends with people being lined up against a wall, assassinated, having "heart attacks", or just disappearing. It is suggesting that our youth not become mindless consumers and employees, that we see honestly what our consumption of resources, and drive to techno mean. We should all come to understand what national debt represents and why people claim that we are borrowing from our children's future. What is a candidate saying when promising things which certainly will increase national debt? Who is behind central banking and who profits from all of this?

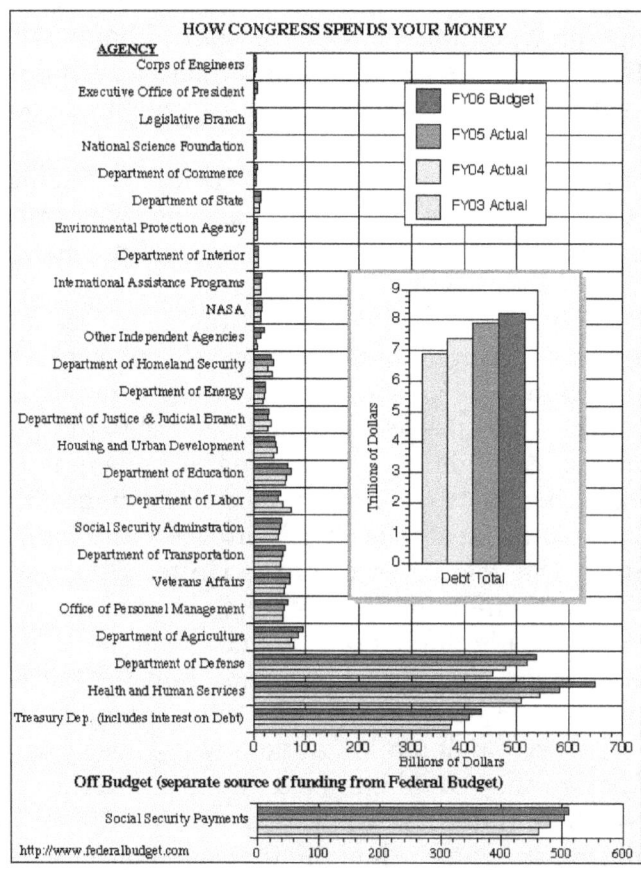

Figure 8 US expenditures (Courtesy National Debt Awareness Campaign).

We thank those who manage a matrix within which we can all live, and "Render unto to Caesar that which is Caesar's", admitting our indebtedness to them. However, the nature of the indebtedness has created an unfortunate situation where our governments are so indebted that we *must* consume to prop the whole thing up. International agreements: NAFTA, CAFTA, and EU entry came with a caveat from politicians. "People should go out and buy." How does devaluing one's currency get foreign countries (their people) to buy the debt? What instead is "sustainable growth"?

We see in Figure 8 the budget for the United States at the start of the 21st century, and that the three biggest expenditures are essentially for military, medicine, and interest (not payment) of debt. Interest alone is most of the annual deficit. What household could survive if it had to borrow more money each year in order to just pay the interest on the money borrowed from previous years?

Note: Social Security is its own separate entity, collecting revenues separately. But it is important to know that the current surplus here has regularly been "lent" back into a system which will not be able to pay off the "IOU's" when the expected shortfall arrives in the not-so-distant future.

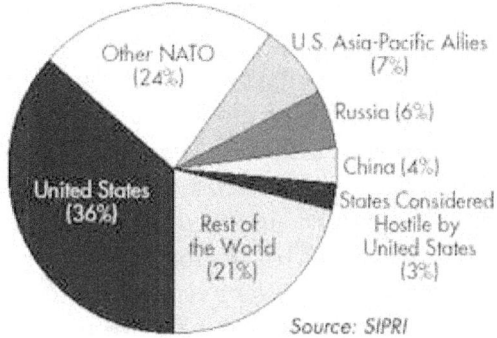

Share of World Military Expenditures, by Country or Group, 2001

Figure 9 Chart of military budgets from the world. – (courtesy SIPRI).

Figure 9 shows where some of the money is going, displaying the share of the military market owned by the United States in 2001, reportedly risen to 48% in 2005 (spending about 10 times as much as each of the next four leading countries of UK, France Japan and China – according to SIPRI). It has been horrific to watch the continued downward economic spiral of the first decade of the 21st century, fueled by a Hegellian war; all feeding what is termed "disaster capitalism".

Techno classrooms

At times, this book may appear against technology, modern, wealth, and politics. It calls for change. It *is* trying to push for a different form of education. The modern world is full of wonder, and amazing possibilities for fun, profit and venture. How best to use the new technologies as a tool for us, and as an educational assistant?

Therein lies the key, for right now it appears that the people making the decisions regarding technology in children's hands seem mostly to be of a top-down mentality; for whom political entities and education departments are making the decisions, probably after having been lobbied by technology firms wanting to "donate" their equipment and software. Then there are the parents who are afraid that their children might be left behind. Fear is unfortunately one of the biggest sales tools being used right now to push a lot of modern tech, and that fact should make us all become more aware.

Studies are beginning to show that childhood computer usage is actually counter-productive and unhealthful.

As a former engineer, I question the fear that a child will be unable to function as an adult in the modern world without these "head starts". Personally I have learned, used, and given instruction in dozens of software languages, programs, and computer types. The youth can and will learn it, but better when the time is appropriate.

As a teacher, I have given specific computer instruction to adults, including CAD design, word processing, data entry, manufacturing applications, spread-sheet, and software languages. Clearly, the tool is most usable by adults. Their minds are ready for instruction *and* they are able to use and expand upon what they have learned.

We can use the computer with upper primary students, for example, to demonstrate eclipses using NASA web pages. It is extraordinary to be able to give real-time, specific information in this manner. But the key is that the teacher is in charge. Most material on the net is written by adults, for adults, who hopefully have some powers of discernment.

For children, it is just too much information, advertisement, and porn. Pages specifically for "kids"? They should be outside playing and breathing.

I have been required by national curriculum to provide two years of instruction at the eighth and ninth grades. It is excessive and too early. It is appropriate that in one of these two years, the students be given instruction on typing, the inner workings of the computer, safety precautions as far as posture of the spine and hands, information about EMF (particularly from laptops), and common sense ideas about use of background lighting and eyestrain. We should then give detailed instruction on topic research across the internet, including proper methods of referencing and using the material, rather than cut and paste.

In this one year, a specific creative software program is also appropriate, so that they learn to think of the machine as a tool, not just something for shopping, play, or telecommunications.

No matter the fear that parents have, that "their child will be left behind"; the fact is that children and teenagers are usually most interested in using computers for things we might prefer they didn't. They want to play their games, with hours lost from more physical and productive activities. What do we teach them especially when we buy for them, or allow them to buy, the really violent games?

I pity the human willingly enslaving themselves to more gadgetry. More, I pity the children who are being manipulated, pushed and forced into it early. Children will get access as they want it, and they will want it. So, we need to be prepared to give it in steps, if at all. We don't need to push them to it, and we can even hold them back just a little. Our relationships and health will improve as a result.

Yes, wait until Grade 8 for real computer work and online research. Let the traditions of books, pens, and pencils remain in the primary school. In their latter years of high school, push finally the computer, when their minds are truly ready to use it as a tool, and are curious what they want to do the rest of their life and how is this box going to be a part of that. Now provide exposure to technical drawing, spreadsheets, presentation software, and publishing and graphics programs. Let them see how to take photographs and get creative with them, which is what they want to do at this age anyway.

Media

When we sit a child at a TV we reduce creativity to mimicry, and fill childhood with quality-questionable and violent programming, vigorously sprinkled with manipulative advertisement. Sure, there are amazing programs we could be watching, though seldom choose to. We give the TV as babysitter.

This book is trying to encourage better forms of education. So it will suggest that for age three, we can introduce TV with occasional stories and fairytales. We often turn to Disney material, but we must caution that it often contains violence, excessive unrealistic colors, marketing ploys, and surprisingly sexual innuendo.

Truly though, we often sit the child in front of a TV even earlier, alone, or let them watch what we are watching, most of which is seriously inappropriate for young people. Why would we want to show murder, fear, talkshows, sitcoms and such to our child?

One of the most important things to be gained from managing the TV is that we choose the external impact on our dearest loved ones. We guide them and protect their childhood.

What then, of the TV and other forms of media, like radio and print? As the industry of media goes into the hands of a very few, our eyes need to become more open to the result. Some have begun. In the United States, many are calling for reform of media. In January 2007 there was a conference held to that aim, hosted from outside of the "loop". In Europe, curriculum reform is stressing that youth be shown how to interpret between media and *reality*, recognize the media's source, methods, and its influence on our children and society.

Communications

When someone gives their child a mobile phone, they feel a greater sense of connection. Does it have a place, as a *tool*? Yes, but mostly for adults. For children however, it is mostly a toy, one to which they are devoting incredible amounts of time, *emotion*, and finances. Manufacturers are keenly aware of who their greatest customer is, as evidenced by the ever increasing range of functions, beyond photography, music playing and such. What however, are its coincident impacts to their development?

As with so much of the modern, there really is little knowledge of what impacts these technologies are going to have. But there is steadily growing concern about use of the phones. There are doctors now seeing that people living near cellular towers are having sleep and psychological disorders and health problems previously not known. The W.H.O. (World Health Organization) is recommending that children *not* have mobile phones. In some communities and countries, tower placement is being controlled until more is known. Rather than let themselves be exposed to unknown risks, many communities are organizing against the towers.

We need to understand how the technology works. Microwaves cook by agitating the water in food. Naturally polarized, water molecules rotate once for each wavelet of energy that strikes them. They rub against adjacent particles and the friction provides heat. This same thing happens inside the brain during a phone call.

More disturbing is that the transmissions are pulsed, in the same frequencies as certain key brain waves which regulate sleep and other psychological functions. Even when not using the phone, if not shut off, it is transmitting and receiving. There is becoming evidence that this technology is capable of changing and damaging DNA, and that this was all known to the industry *in advance*.

We are not helpless in the face of all of this. We can get informed, and then act; turn them off at night, and ask others to do so, don't wear them on our heads or waists (beside reproductive organs). We can try to get the towers off of our schools, though right next door is probably even more dangerous. We should definitely get the phones out of the schools. The distraction and disruption is unbelievable. Parents are often the offender, or said to be. What's wrong with calling the office and leaving a message? Parents should sit in a classroom, or walk the halls, and see how the children are using every chance to check it, when they could instead be doing all of the wonderful things they used to do. We adults had that ability, and right.

This is very important. We are taking away that right from our children. Go to the schools and see how different it was from your experience. See how many children are closed off with their music devices, using the phones to take photographs of each other or look at photographs of someone else, send/receive messages, while-away at vacant conversations with someone who is elsewhere (while others are right in front of them), or toting around their bookbag *and* an even heavier laptop that is more status symbol than learning tool. Is this not somehow a shame?

Pitifully, all of this gadgetry is often the source of socialization today. Our youth often have financial stresses as they devote their money to this, emotional stress over unreturned phone calls and messages, and an inward focus on the device (phone, headset or laptop), rather than the world around them. They are walking now in a fog.

Where do we go from here? Our modern wonder-world is heavily tied to its electronics, (author included). This means more power usage – increasing the greenhouse effect, hotter summers – more air conditioning (more greenhouse effect). Then, more suggestion that we return to nuclear energy and thus more childhood leukemia, environmental effects from ionized radioactive gas, not to mention the risk of nuclear proliferation.

We have to get informed and make decisions for ourselves, before we buy, before we agree, and before we let others decide for us, and our children.

Our children are becoming less healthy, just as our world. They suffer more asthma, attention problems, obesity, diabetes, and general health deficits. We cannot single out only one thing as the cause. As a colleague once said, "It's as though the trap has opened and all the mice are running around. Which should we catch?" That is a fair assessment. Do we focus on one, or all of them? I see no choice, personally.

Physics

Many are the achievements of modern Alchemy, but unfortunately, for every development which is meant to help humankind, there come serious health concerns and the inevitable horrific military application and experimentation.

We are developing tomorrow's scientists in our classrooms. Youth are immured by technology. There may not be one item, however, which does not come without a price of long-term effects; which are uncharted.   We can show them the information which is available, and track past industry attempts at disinformation on other issues.

Let us take them on a journey to discover what the leading edge of technology is up to now. Though it continues material in this chapter, it will be better found in Chapter 11.

Service

How do we make a difference? We not only bring this material out in the classroom, but we live it by example. We go further, getting our students involved with their world.

A number of useful organizations exist with which we can engage students after school. We can take them caroling in December to nursing homes. We can take them to day care facilities and read to children, or shovel snow at such places. They can deliver food to shut-ins. We can get them to donate time and money to service organizations.

We can get them involved in demonstrations. We can get them organized at school, with recycling programs, not just of paper, but of cans, plastic, and batteries.

Concluding Dialogue

How could we teach math and the sciences from a "Thou" perspective? What could it do for our students to see the history of chemistry, and its division between metaphysics, and 'science'?

How does our economy operate? What does the Fed do? What do central banks, the IMF, WTO and World Bank do? What does it mean, the expression, "We are bankrupting our children's future?" Why are Latin American countries trying to free themselves from indebtedness to the IMF?

Do we have the right, or even the responsibility, to balance the advertisement, and at least in some form disillusion our youth to mindless consumerism?

We have come full circle now. For millennia, we traded goods and received gold, in a way creating gold from baser materials. Now, we trade our "goldenness" for base metals and paper money.

This is math we should answer for ourselves and our students. In our sciences, as we teach more and more how to pass standardized tests, gain college admittance, and get a high paying job within the Machine, we are killing our own future as we enable students to jump happily into the world known as modern greed, where we do not try to live simply so that others might simply live.

Figure 10 Modern, or still primitive? Great in our technology, as we deplete the Earth (Miroslav Huptych).

I am the Lorax, I speak for the trees... Sir! You are crazy with greed... Your machinery chugs on.. making gluppity glupp and schloppity schlopp... – I yelled at the Lorax, "Now listen here Dad! All you do is yap yap and say Bad, Bad, Bad!". – Dr. Suess, The Lorax.

We need to re-appropriate a kind and tender relationship with Mother-Earth. Then we will know how to act. –
Sister Dorothy Stang.

Without a global revolution in the sphere of human consciousness a more humane society will not emerge.
Vaclav Havel

Further reading/research and Websites:

Education
http://www.allianceforchildhood.net/ Great information regarding excess and abuse of technology in the classroom.

http://www.suepalmer.co.uk/toxic.php Former school head, trying to pull education away from tech, junk food and competition.

http://www.commondreams.org/ Great alternative news site, guaranteed to ruin your day. See what mainstream media is *not* reporting.

Technology
http://www.emf.dk/Hylandarticleonbasestations.htm Must read site on mobile-phone transmitter exposure risks, by bio-physicist.

http://www.microwavenews.com/ News source providing snippets about tech industries, products and safety concerns.

http://www.osti.gov/energycitations/product.biblio.jsp?osti_id=7076284 Government site showing krypton 85 released by nuclear energy facilities affects natural ionization and weather

http://cnic.jp/english/newsletter/nit111/nit111articles/nit111radtest.html Citizen's nuclear information center, for a nuclear free world. Info on Krypton 85 and Iodine 129.

http://www.cellular-news.com/tower_watch/feb2005.php What others are doing to stop installation of phone masts.

http://en.wikipedia.org/wiki/Mobile_phone_radiation_and_health Discusses mobile phones and tower concerns.

http://www.sixwise.com/newsletters/05/09/28/what_are_the_dangers_of_living_near_cell_phone_towers.htm Title kind of says it all. Do a search under Mobile phone transmitter dangers and see how many hits there are.

Read "In the absence of the Sacred, the failure of Technology & the survival of the Indian Nations" and "Four arguments for the elimination of Television" by Jerry Mander

Positive steps
See the films: "An Inconvenient Truth" and "Blood Diamonds". For the latter, imagine that materials for electronic gadgetry come from a similar reality.

Do internet searches on alternative energy. Find out what grants are available in your area. See if you can sell back excess energy to the power company as some states allow and push for the same in your area. Install alternative energy systems in your home, like micro turbines, solar water heating and solar electricity.

Get off techno and into relationships. Walk. Own fewer cars, TVs, and things.

http://www.buynothingchristmas.org/index.html Enjoy Christmas differently, without being Scrooge or Grinch.

It is difficult for the common good to prevail against the intense concentration of those who have a special interest, especially if the decisions are made behind locked doors. Jimmy Carter

Food and health

http://www.wellnesswallcharts.com/vitamin.html Wallchart showing nutrients in the food.

http://www.alkalizeforhealth.net/about.htm Site offering a variety of book titles such as, "The Medical Mafia : How to Get Out of It Alive and Take Back Our Health and Wealth", "The Buying of Congress; How Special Interests Have Stolen Your Right to Life, Liberty, and the Pursuit of Happiness", " The Truth About Drug Companies, How They Deceive Us and What To Do About It", "The Safe Shopper's Bible: A Consumer's Guide to Nontoxic Household Products, Cosmetics, and Food".

http://www.medicalnewstoday.com/medicalnews.php?newsid=9620 Must read site on food nutrient and quality degradation created by irradiation.

http://www.geneticfoodalert.supanet.com/index1.htm   Informative site about GM foods.

Power and Politics

http://www.chomsky.info/ Dr. Noam Chomsky's Website. Leading intellectual, whose books include: Profit over People; Secrets, Lies and Democracy; Keeping the Rabble in Line; The Prosperous Few and the Restless Many; What Uncle Sam Really Wants; Deterring Democracy; Necessary Illusions. "Human Rights" and American Foreign Policy.

http://www.globalissues.org/ Site discussing geopolitics, environment, trade and health.

http://www.uow.edu.au/arts/sts/bmartin/dissent/documents/health/pharmfraud.html
Fraud within the pharmaceutical industry. Price fixing on vitamins

http://en.wikipedia.org/wiki/Rockefeller_   Info about the Rockefeller family, an exemplary "world leader" and their "philanthropism" to key organizations.

http://en.wikipedia.org/wiki/Rothschilds - Similar, interesting, family history. There are many more, offering the opportunity for further research.

http://en.wikipedia.org/wiki/Bank_of_Credit_and_Commerce_International
Information about a key central bank scandal of our time.

http://ciadrugs.homestead.com/files/index.html   Reports on the CIA and drug trade.

http://www.nrdc.org/nuclear/ Natural resources defense council

http://www.sipri.org/ Stockholm international peace research institute

This is only a start. Read and research for self and for youth. Find information and see through the disinformation.

"From the West we have learned to live in a soulless world of stupid advertisements and even more stupid sitcoms and we are allowing them to drain our lives and our spirits," Vaclav Havel

We must not fail to comprehend the grave implications of and must guard against influence by the military industrial complex. The potential for the disastrous rise of misplaced power exists and will persist. Akin to the sweeping changes in our industrial-military posture has been the technological revolution. Research has become central; the solitary inventor, tinkering in his shop, has been overshadowed; the free university, free ideas and scientific discovery has experienced a substitute for intellectual curiosity. Domination of scholars by the power of money is ever present and is gravely to be regarded. Dwight D. Eisenhower

Class Exercise 1 **Neolithic Chemistry**

Objective:
Learn chemistry through "earthy", artistic, techniques and study.

Materials:
Bricks, firewood, charcoal, potter's clay, buckets, fireplace tongs.

Procedure:
a) Take dry clay and break and crush pieces with a hammer. (SAFETY GLASSES) Describe the fractured pieces and "feel" the material. Put the bits into a container and pour water over them. Observe, noting the bubbles. Soon, the water will be warmer. Let stand and after 30-60 minutes, begin to work the material. Or, let it stand for longer and come back to it when ready. Each student should make some pottery pieces. Weigh the wet products and measure 2-3 dimensions and record. See table 1. Let pieces dry for 1-2 weeks.
b) Go for a walk to the forest, or park, and gather sticks and downed wood and leave to dry. Fifteen or so students should each come back with a couple long pieces or a handful of short ones.
c) Construct a kiln. Lay bricks in a circle 2-3 feet in diameter. Leave an opening of 8-10 inches for feeding the fire, and observation. Build a second and third layer. On the fourth layer, turn some bricks inward, creating shelves for the pottery. Do the same thing on the fifth, staggering the platforms. Build up a few more layers, allowing for placement of the pieces. Figure 1. Weigh and measure the dry pieces and record info, to see changes.
d) Put paper on the floor of the kiln, in the middle, and build a tipi of sticks around it. Have lots of wood and one bag of charcoal ready, plus a bucket of water – just in case. Put the pottery pieces on the shelves, carefully. Then, build up more layers on the kiln, tapering them inward slightly. Everyone needs lab SAFETY GLASSES now as the pieces contain 'water' which will burn off if the heat rises slowly, and will explode if done too quickly. We must also be careful of long hair!
e) Reach in through the bottom and light the fire. At first, the flames might get quite high. When they burn down, carefully feed the fire, dropping short lengths of sticks down through the top, in the middle of the fire. Be careful of the pieces. Feel around the outside of the kiln and use mud and grass to plug any major holes. We need to keep the heat inside. After 20 minutes or so, start adding some charcoal.
f) After about 45 minutes, the outside of the bricks should be getting warm and the danger zone is probably past. Build up the fire and get in more charcoal. After an hour, really feed the charcoal to the fire. Now, build the kiln higher, tapering more and nearly close it off at the top. Leave it to burn down, allowing the heat to really circulate inside. Come back several hours later, or better the next day.
g) Carefully open the kiln and take down the layers. Inspect the pieces and observe how the material has changed. Weigh measure and record one last time.

Homework:
Prepare a lab report, describing this activity and what was learned.

What has caused the pieces to shrink and lose weight at each step? What has caused the change in colors and hardness at each step?

Find a description of the chemical processes which are occurring, and of the chemical processes which occur when copper and iron are smelted. In each case, hydroxide compounds, OH, must be broken off, under intense heat. Interestingly, this is lost as water, H_2O. We don't normally think of metal containing water. What happens when forged steel is quenched; being thrust back into water while hot? The surface is hardened, but more the OH is reattached. What is the smith doing when hammering the metal in his "dirty" smithy? The presence of charcoal and air is imparting CO to the material, tempering it and further strengthening.

Evaluation:
Grade reports, participation and effort, particularly with further research on the homework portion, usually needing to be done over the internet or by consultation with the chemistry teacher.

Bridges:
This class seems to work best when done by the arts teacher, though great involvement with the chemistry teacher should occur.

Class Exercise 2 **Modern "Alchemy" Awareness**

Objective:
Open the eyes of youth to the world that they are readily buying, so that they are informed of the other side behind the smiling faces and bright colors. Teach them that alternatives exist for those who desire them, and why they might want to. Guide them in learning about business, media and politics.

Procedure:
a) Ask the question, "Why do children like eating certain products which are marketed to them?" (Often because of the bright colors, and the taste) Find information on the risks and dangers of food colorings, artificial sweeteners, and excessive sugar consumption. Research healthier foods; containing vitamin and mineral nutrients.
b) Find out about modern farming methods. Research the effects of fertilizer and herbicide use on river and sea ecology, drinking water, food contamination, and air quality. Research fears and risks of genetic engineering on food, pros and cons of food irradiation, hormones and antibiotics in meat and dairy products. What connection is there between global rain forest depletion, global warming, and food and bio-fuel?
c) Research the business interests behind the FDA and the AMA.
d) Research the latest information about the suspected dangers of mobile telephone masts, EMF from laptop computers, and excessive ultrasound observations of developing fetuses.
e) Research about who has the weapons of mass destruction and who is spending the most on their militaries. Compare budget expenditures on bombs verses people and environment.
f) Develop significant study of vitamin and mineral content in foods. Study the role each nutrient plays in the body and which foods contain them.
g) Research organic farming, sustainable agriculture.
h) Study herbal, oriental, and traditional healing methods.
i) Develop a school/community garden. See if the school can provide a piece of ground, or sometimes, the parks department might be willing. Get the students and community involved with some kind of flower, tree or vegetable garden which the students can launch in the spring, the community can nurture during the summer and the students can return to each autumn.
j) Watch the films, "An Inconvenient Truth" and "Blood Diamonds". Research coltan and its use in today's PEDs. "Blood MP3?"

Homework:
Students should be given one of the tasks from 'a' to 'e' for their homework and class assignment to last 1 to 2 weeks, finishing with a report, informative poster and class presentation, so that they have an opportunity to speak to an audience. The posters should be displayed in the school.
Students should then be given one of the tasks from 'f' to 'h' for homework and class time to also do this, interacting with teacher and colleagues. Again, a report, poster and presentation should be delivered and again publicized.
In the end, have the students summarize what they have learned.

Evaluation:
This is a month long effort and should present several opportunities for evaluating effort, quality of work, and meeting of key criterion.

Bridges:
This is a significant investment in time and effort. It can face enormous resistance from students and perhaps parents, who might feel threatened by this. The immediate results may not be so readily seen. But, as with a garden, we are planting seeds. The Bridges here are many, between interdisciplinary instructions, social awareness, career ideas and our very future. The school could focus efforts and make a "project week" on these topics, where each subject area tackles a theme.

Class Exercise 3 Alternative energies installation in the School

Objective:
Positive student initiative to install energy systems on the school.

Procedure:
a) Various work needs to be accomplished: obtaining permits. Research into grants (many are available), Research if excess power can be "sold" back to the grid (a real possibility), Research solar electric, water heating, and wind micro turbines. Research and test best possible locations, Design electrical systems, find materials, coordinate with school maintenance personnel. List these tasks on the board and let students sign up for one.
b) Groups gather. Facilitate discussions. Some preliminary research should already be accomplished so that the teacher can provide pictures of solar panels, wind turbines, and information on some of the pros and cons (like how it looks and if there could be a noise problem from the turbine in high winds).
c) Coordinate this effort with the physics and science classes that are currently learning about electricity, current, voltages and such.

Homework:
Students need to work as teams and get the job done inside/outside of class. Teams need a leader, who will evaluate each member's effort.

Evaluation:
Grade work seen in class and based on a thorough interview of the team leaders, to see what the specific contributions of each team member were.

Bridges:
We often talk about environmental issues in the school. Here, we act, while linking physics, finance, team work and design.

Samrey

Zomeworks

9 – Rocketry and other applications

Opening Dialogue

How could we use rocketry and model aircraft to provide students a fun, exciting, and creative mathematics and physics experience? What other "hands-on" activities can we develop?

How tall are the trees and buildings (mountains) around us? How are they measured, when we cannot get a measuring tape or yardstick from their base to their top? What techniques do surveyors use, and could we do the same thing in the classroom? Yes. And its fun!

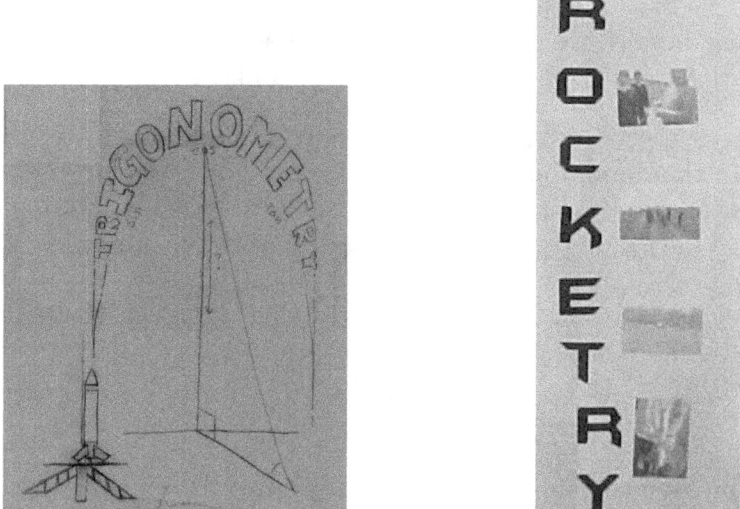

Figure 1 Student-created artwork submitted with rocketry results.

Getting started

In this section, we will see how to make our own trigonometric measuring devices and then put them to use in measuring the heights or distances of things. This is a very practical use of trigonometry and is intended for a cognizant, mature teacher and a class of mature and reasonable high school students.

Figure 2 A basic altitude-angle measuring tube.

First, make the measuring devices. Obtain a tube of some sorts. Be sure to put strings on the ends to make "crosshairs". Tape a protractor exactly along the axis of the tube and with a weighted string that is free to move.

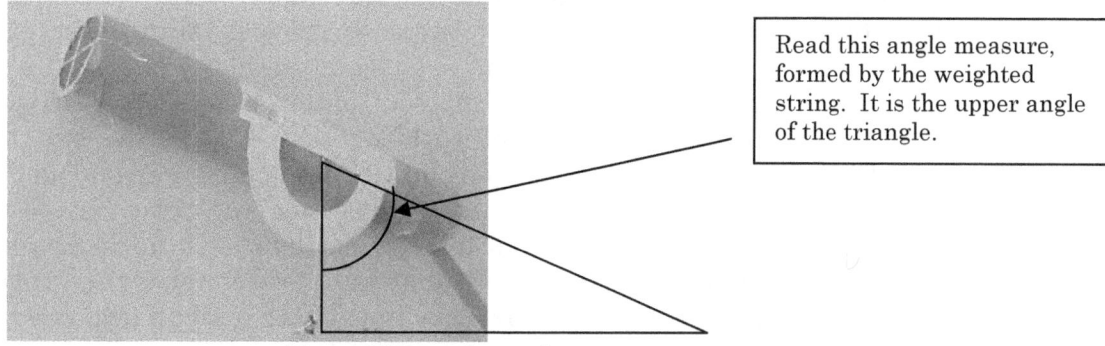

Figure 3 Using the angle measurer.

When the students begin to practice, they will see that they have to keep themselves still. It is a two person operation: one to look through the "spyglass", and the other to steady the string and get a reading. Convince them that accuracy is important, reading angles to the nearest degree, not the nearest five or ten degrees. For angles nearer 0 or 90 degrees, this can represent a big error with the tangent function.

Notice that the angle of the protractor is the top angle of the triangles that we will eventually use in our calculations.

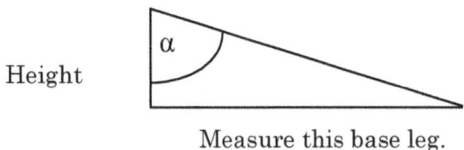

Height

Measure this base leg.

To calculate the height, we can use: $\tan \alpha = \dfrac{\text{base}}{\text{height}}$

This can present a problem for even advanced students because the unknown quantity is height, found in the denominator. So, they must multiply through by height and divide by the tangent α. No matter how many times they practice this technique, with "x" and numbers, it still is surprisingly difficult for many of them in application. Which validates its use.

A second, very useful technique is to have them get the complementary base angle, which we will call ß.

Therefore, we can write: $\tan ß = \dfrac{\text{height}}{\text{base}}$

This makes for an easier operation of multiplying through by the known quantity (the measured base). Either route the teacher takes, he should try both at one time or another, this is a great piece of outdoor math work, so long as it's dry and the wind isn't blowing. Sure, we want to keep our papers dry and the string steady, but more, we have to keep our students healthy, and happy. When it rains, give them the really hard stuff indoors.

Figure 4 shows a "typical" East European tower. We can stand in front of it and take an angle reading. Then, measure the distance (base leg) to the tower.

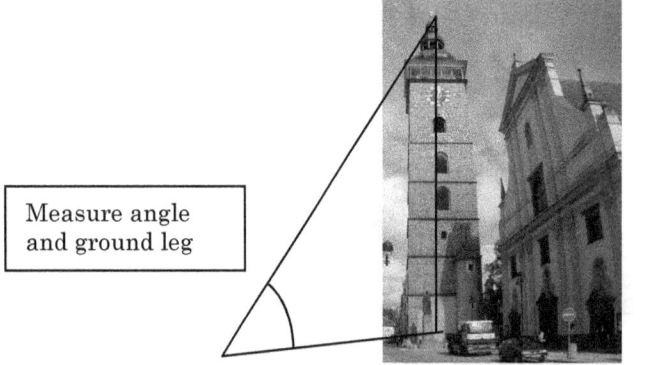

Figure 4 Tower in Europe, in Ceske Budejovice.

Have them take a field trip sometime to see and measure a good piece of architecture. In Denver, this means the cathedral, state capitol, and even an example of Moorish architecture. In each students can see the geometric shapes, stain glass mandalas, and other unique architectural forms. They can see use of marble, metal, and sculpture. We are teaching in our classes tomorrow's architects, interior designers, artists, and more technical types. We can create the kind of world we would like to live out the rest of our lives in if we show the way that others have gone, are going, and can envision.

Another fun thing to do is take students to a lakeside park or river. We can do this when also studying waves in physics. It's fun having them pick up rocks along the way, wondering what they will do with them. Not only is it good for studying waves, but when the rock hits the water, it makes a circular wave in the lake, and an oval one in the river.

Now, at the shore, let them line up on an object on the other side of the water. Ask them how they can use trig to measure its width. Did they guess that they need to make a right angle to it; using a protractor (did anyone bring one? Did you?). They must walk some distance in line with that right angle (did anyone bring a measuring tape?) measure the new angle, and finally draw it and calculate.

These are pretty simple practical examples which we can have students do at school. Having honed our technique, we will proceed either to purchase or build our own rockets and launch them. This seems to be the most popular of all the activities in this book.

Background

While the teacher is doing the above preliminary work of getting the students outside, measuring, and calculating, we must admit that taking students to the great outdoors can be a great test of nerves and patience. Don't take the abuse. Set your ground rules right up front. List the expectations of behavior and effort desired and then the consequences if they are not met. The most serious and effective consequence is that they won't be first in line on rocketry day and may even get to stay in school. The simple fact of the matter is that rocketry DOES have inherent risks. We cannot afford to have an ape on the missile range. Be clear, rigid, and punitive. Everyone will enjoy it and give good care, particularly when they see the teacher is most serious.

This is a lot of fun, but we must be very aware of safety and today's restrictions. We must learn to expect the unexpected from our creative students. The following true stories bring home the serious side to this.

Once, a student decided to put firecrackers in the nose of his store-bought rocket via an ingenious fuse system. The thing actually self-destructed at the top of its flight; making the reading more accurate than normal. But this was a college student and generally it's not a good idea to allow. Whether using an electric starter or match and fuse, there is never a guarantee that the rocket will fly straight, or that this payload will detonate at the desired time. Many is the time that a home-built rocket has launched up about a dozen feet, tumbled and come back to earth, with a scramble by the launch team.

Another time, some girls put confetti in their rocket. Sadly, it was lost to the forest before we could see the confetti shoot out the top. Still, this could be an acceptable payload in any but a dry climate, where the fire risk would be too great.

The first home built rocket I observed was done by a college student. It was a large rocket, with a large motor and fins that seemed overly large but we had no experience with such a thing. We weren't sure how it was going to fly, but we sure found out. It was a breezy day and right after liftoff the wind caught those large fins and put it into a horizontal flight (they are supposed to go mostly vertically) at about 30 feet off the ground. Beautiful, it looked like a guided missile, like in action movies. It went past the third floor windows of the main building and as it cleared the building, the shifting airflow of the wind carried it around the structure, at the same height. I felt then, as many times since, that this was the end of my teaching career. To top it off, we soon saw police officers coming from the direction the rocket was last seen. Thankfully, they turned and went into the building to a special law enforcement conference being held that day...

We must be careful with these things. These stories are not simply reminiscences at the reader's expense. They are included so the teacher will be prepared for as many freaks of nature, politics, and student *creativity* as possible.

Imagine trying to ship rocket engines across international borders or by mail, in the post-9-11 environment. Be careful to confer with the local fire department, especially where there are normally bans on fireworks. They usually know the appropriate laws. We've had to go through some hoops, but in the end, everyone is really happy to see this used in school.

It doesn't work to launch on cloudy days, because the students need to see a little puff of smoke at the end of the travel, which will blend in too much with a grey background. If there is wind the launch stand can be tilted, but this gets tricky. Too much, and the rocket will dive into the wind and can travel for quite some distance. Once, we launched from a hilltop into the wind and the rocket flew with the curvature of the hill for almost a kilometer, when it should have gone up only 150 meters. Luckily it flew over (not into) homes, and landed in a field.

This is an unpredictable science, so we must be careful and find a good remote place. In many areas, there are rocketry clubs which can be contacted for suggestions and help; also try the hobby stores that sell these materials.

Then there was the time that we launched a space shuttle, which curved in flight and happened to find the nearest lights over the parking lot we were using; an incredible shot, to the rear of our launch pad. It bounced off the glass face of the light, and deflected downward, right into a group of students lounging about. Its timed charge went off right at impact, in a glorious crash, among the fleeing bodies. The reader must form a mental picture of these events and see the risk involved. It does have risk and if the teacher or school doesn't want to take the chance, fair enough.

But don't shy away. Simply limit the number of people at the launch site, keeping even these back with open escape routes and at full attention.

When ready to launch, only allow two or three students to be present to light the rocket or keep time, but the others have got to stay well back (minimum 50 feet), preferably with a task: rocket retrieval or angle measure.

For all of the horrors (even on a good day, there are still the times when a rocket may somersault twenty feet above the launch pad and come shooting back to earth), basic common sense and care will result in zero injuries or property damage. The students enjoy learning from successful flights, surely enjoy the failures, and are nonplussed when they lose one to the wind and/or trees, as often happens.

The key thing is that we all respect what we are doing here. With experience comes skill and a great majority of students' launches can land within 20-30 feet of the pad and that is pretty good.

Building the rocket

Let's begin with the rocket. There is nothing wrong with store- bought or internet-purchased rockets. They're easy and generally fly correctly. Eastern Europe is a part of the world where it is difficult to obtain rockets through these options, so we hit upon the idea of making our own.

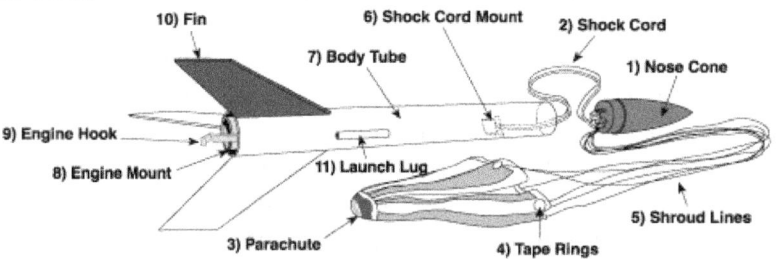

Figure 5 Basic construction of a model rocket – (Estes).

Making rockets is a better activity because the students enjoy personalizing them, learning what makes one actually function and seeing what they did to make for a successful or unsuccessful flight. We have often times cut off parts of wings, or stapled on extensions and launched again, successfully. That kind of range correction is really interesting for all. Basically, if the rocket tumbles in flight, give it bigger fins, or maybe add weight in the nose cone. Rocket balance is a science unto itself. Students should learn about center of gravity and center of pressure.

Making rockets requires fun participation, like having students scour their hometown after New Year's Eve for the nose cones from fireworks, or making them go shopping for engines and be a liaison between the store, the range director (teacher) and the rest of the students. Finally, don't let the school pay for much on this one. A good rocketry program can be run for less than $100, shared among the students, who never have a problem contributing to it, except for teenage procrastination in paying. Don't pay, don't launch. (Tell students to see the teacher privately if there is a financial problem.)

Other than nose cones, we need tubes. Save those rolls from Christmas wrapping paper, paper towel tubes or other specialized source. Or, get good card stock and a broom handle and "roll your own." Be careful about not using too much tape or too many layers as this really can add weight. But, it lets you pick your diameter.

If nosecones are unobtainable, make cardboard cones, or get balsa and sand it into shape. They need cardstock for the wings. Here, we usually fold it over, to give a sharp and stiff leading edge and a stronger wing than one layer provides.

Nosecone should be free to pop open. Attach with string.

Attach guide tube along the lower half of the rocket

Insert wire here (paper-clip), to keep engine from shooting forward

Figure 6a Home built rocket.

On the rocket, one of the most important parts is actually the metal wire that is used to hold the rocket engine in place. If not installed properly above the engine, the motor will shoot unopposed up the tube and out the nosecone, effectively turning your rocket into a shotgun. If not installed properly below the engine, the motor will blast out the rear when the last charge detonates at the top of the flight. This means that the spent engine will come to earth on its own. It has a small potential to be a fire hazard but more, let's not leave debris lying around. Get the students to take pride; being neat and orderly.

Another important part is that a little tube needs to be on the side of the rocket. The launch pad consists of a metal rod sticking out of a metal disk (blast shield). The guide tube can be made from a plastic straw, which keeps the rocket to this rod during the first few feet of flight, helping the rocket get a good straight lift-off. This little tube can be a bit of a nuisance. An appropriate adhesive is needed. A good backup is to tape around the tube and rocket body. The tube needs to be very much in parallel with the axis of the rocket. Too, it shouldn't be too small, or it will retard the launch. NOTE; Always WARN students about leaning over the rod as there is the risk of eye injury!

Figure 6b Homebuilts and happy creators. Skies are clear; go for launch.

We have our rocket, now what? At the start, a really good size engine is the "C" size. These will propel a 12-inch (30 cm) rocket as high as 500 feet (150 meters), depending on how great an impulse the engine has. An engine is a thick cardboard tube with solid fuel inside. Buy one which has the tube about ¾ full. Half full is fine for shorter flights, and completely full is good when your field size is large, or you wish to use a taller rocket. Of course, an even bigger rocket requires "D" and higher-rated motors. Don't even go there at the start. The "C" size is adequate.

One final note: rocket kits usually come with a parachute. This can be experimented with. In the presence of any wind, the rocket will carry a very long distance, increasing the chance of it getting lost. Generally, the rocket is light enough to not need one, though at least some type of streamer paper is required by law. As with most things, check local regulations before launch.

Go for launch?

It is strongly recommended that any teacher or group wishing to do this activity become familiar with the Estes website. This company has a lot of great rocket kits and materials available, plus rocket engines and a good dependable launch stand. These latter two must be store-bought. Let's not risk fire or explosion by trying to make a stand, or engines ourselves.

Once we have the stand, engines and rockets, we need agreeable weather. The sky should be mostly clear, with minimal wind. In the presence of a light wind, we could tilt the stand, maybe 5 to 10 degrees into the wind.

The teacher should stay present at the launch site, along with the few students who built the particular rocket to be launched. They are going to be the ones wanting to push the button or light the match. Within a few yards should be someone with a stop-watch. They need to be close enough to be able to see the precise moment the rocket ignites, to start the clock, but far enough back so that nobody runs into them in haste to escape. Usually, the BMOC is good in this role. Every teacher has "him": the student who can often be a particular pain in the neck. The class "leader". The Big Man on Campus can often help keep the other students in line (safe), is useful in keeping time, and isn't so helpful at any of the other stations. Rockets can be unpredictable and each person on the launch crew needs to be prepared with an escape route. Excess materials should be to the side, out of the way.

Figure 7a RTG - Ready to Go.

Other classes from the school may want to come and watch. This can be allowed and encouraged, but as flight director (and ultimately the person who is responsible), the teacher should insist that these groups come under clear supervision of another teacher, stay well away and that they do not interfere at all with the students participating with this activity. We don't want a circus, nor do we want to detract from the school work aspect of this activity.

There need to be students spread out about 50 to 100 yards away, down range. They are on the recovery team. It is not recommended that they try to catch the rocket, but let it hit the ground. Sometimes the craft float nicely down to earth, sometimes not.

Finally, have two or three teams of observers. Each team consists of two people. One holds the telescope and the other takes the reading. An assistant records the data. They should be reminded that they are essentially measuring the upper angle of the triangle, so should take the compliment and record.

At about the top of its arc the rocket will show a little puff of smoke, as a delayed charge pops open the nose, (Don't glue the nose on or it will blow a hole in the side). The range director (teacher) should yell, "Time!" The student with the stop watch should call out the time of the flight. The people with the telescopes need to freeze on the point in space where they saw the smoke, and not move. Their partner should steady the weighted string and take the reading. They should record what they have. They can concur with the other pair but we will later take an average of the two readings, or throw out any that seem in error.

After each flight, let the next group come in and launch their rocket. Try to keep the observing teams in position for a few launches and then have them switch with another group. The readings will be more consistent the longer observers stay on position. It is important to have the most serious students at this station.

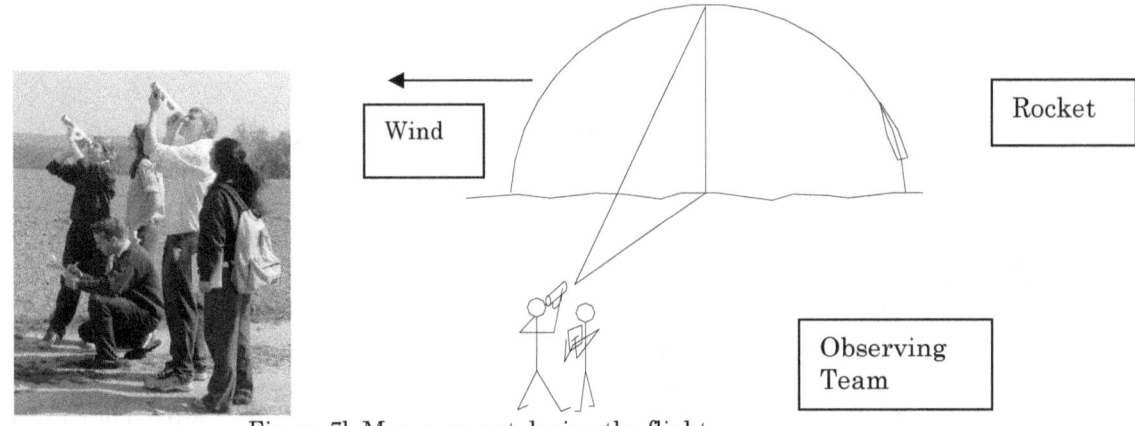

Figure 7b Measurement during the flight

The difficulty of this process for performing our trigonometry is that we can't accurately measure our base leg. But, if we launched without a parachute, we can pretty well estimate a line from launch to landing site, take the midpoint of this, and walk off or measure the distance back to the observers. It might take a couple of launches to get the observers in the right position. In general, they should be perpendicular to the wind direction and about 50 yards distant from the launch site. The people with the telescope need to be ready to get their reading. Their partners must be alert for both of them should the rocket become errant.

The observers should begin to fill in a table, which the rest of the class can later copy down. For now, they need to note name, angles, base leg approximation and the time. We should record each flight, even the failures, and note what happened for those. Later the students will calculate the altitude of the flight.

Rocket name	Angle readings	Base leg	Trig height	Time	Physics height

Table 1 Tabulation of readings and calculations.

The teacher should take card stock, scissors, stapler, string, glue, and a straw to the launch site. A rocket that tumbled in flight could have wing extensions stapled on and launched again. Sometimes, the straws that we glue on as a guide tube break off. We should be ready to glue or tape another in its place. Sometimes, we lose the nose cone, or they break at landing. It's really exciting to do repairs in-situ and go again. In the absence of straws, roll a strip of tape into the shape of a tube and tape it onto the rocket. After the first few launches, the students will care less about how their works of art look and more about how they fly.

Back in class

Once the smell of cordite has passed, the stories have been shared about the good flights and the bad, and with luck no injuries have occurred, we can RTB (return to base).

Now, students need to record all of the data taken.

Rocket name	Angle readings	Base leg	Trig height	Time	Physics height
Shark tooth	57/62°	50 yards		5.3 sec	
Speedy Gonz.	65/70°	40 yards		4.9 sec	
Pink Lady	Flipped in flight	---	---	---	---
TNT	68/65°	60 yards		5.7 sec	
Swifty	Lost wing, shot	sideways	---	---	---

Table 2 Flight information recorded.

Next, they need to do two sets of calculation. Using the tangent function, we have the base leg and base angle of a right triangle. They should now be able to calculate an approximate height of the flight. We need to acknowledge that there are a lot of inaccuracies here but at least it gets us close, the students have fun and see a direct application.

For example, from Table 2, we see that "Shark Tooth" had an average "upper" angle of 30.5°. We use the complimentary angle of 59.5° with the base leg and calculate, finding the rocket went 85 yards. Remember to add the height of the observer, to make 87 yards and record this number.

Then comes the harder work. We need the physics formula: $y = v_i t - \frac{1}{2} g t^2$

For this, we need to calculate a hypothetical initial velocity, though we would need calculus and more effort to be exact. Still, the formula works fairly well. We begin by seeing that the time we recorded is half of the time needed to make the entire parabolic flight (were the rocket aerodynamically sound throughout), though the return trajectory does in fact take longer.

If we set y = 0 (at landing) and double the recorded time, we can derive the physics formula in this form: $v_i = \frac{1}{2} g T$.

With v_i, we use the recorded time, and calculate a height. Since T = 2t (twice measured time), we simplify to v_i = gt . The initial velocity is essentially our time of flight multiplied by the gravitational constant. We will actually see great disparity here. Different rockets fly differently. Some are more heavy, more aerodynamic, or have more vertical flight – all with the same burn time. Still, the calculations are great exercises and many times not so discrepant.

For example, "Shark tooth", flew for 5.3 seconds. Multiply this by 32 to get 170 fps. Put this into the full equation as follows:

$$y = 170(5.3) - \tfrac{1}{2}(32)(5.3)^2 \quad \text{(Doing the algebra, } y = \tfrac{1}{2}gt^2\text{)}.$$

Rocket name	Angle readings	Base leg	Trig height	Time	Physics height
Shark tooth	57/62°	50 yards	87 yards	5.3 sec	150 yards
Speedy Gonz.	65/70°	40 yards	103.5 yards	4.9 sec	128 yards
Pink Lady	Flipped in flight	---	---	---	---
TNT	68/65°	60 yards	138 yards	5.4 sec	155.5 yards
Swifty	Lost wing, shot	sideways	---	---	---

Table 3 Our work completed.

We get in this case 450 feet (150 yards). This is quite a disparity with our angular reading. Usually, the first flight is pretty far off, as the students aren't completely sure what they're doing. Sometimes, they forget to watch the puff of smoke and lower the scope as the rocket falls. Record what they have. Hopefully, it will be seen that at least some launches agree.

The reporting process

The students are expected to turn in a significant piece of documentation summarizing this day. They should have the tabulated data, describe how it was recorded, and show how the calculations were done. They should include extra documentation, in the form of photographs taken during the day, rocket pictures pulled from the internet or other material they decide to use. They should have introductory statements, detailing the process of construction and launch, and final summaries of things that they learned.

If a rocket group wishes to work together on a report, this usually means not every person works equally hard on the project, but it is up to the teacher's discretion. They could have greater requirements placed upon them, though still the output is seldom equal to those who work individually.

Our rockets go fairly high. NASA's go higher, to space, the moon, and further. What does it take to do this? Develop the idea of payload, how much fuel is needed to propel it, how big of a can, with motors to lift it, how much fuel to propel that, and how much bigger of a can to hold this fuel. Calculus!

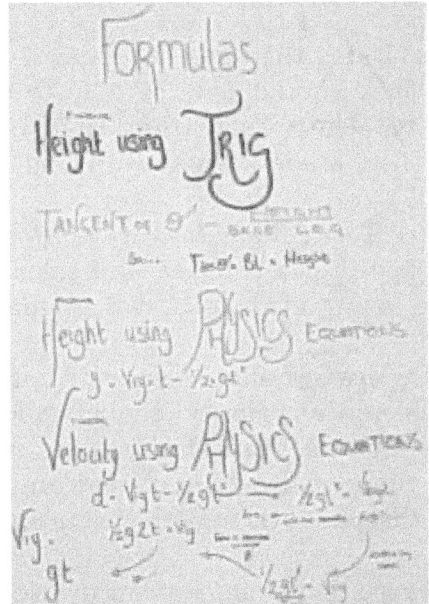

Figure 8 Quality student work – (J. Kucerova, N. Krishnan and M. Sveinsdottir).

In the end, the teacher can expect posters and nicely prepared portfolios. Some students may want to do a techno computer presentation. Experience shows that this diverts effort into being the next "superstar" than in just doing their work.

Have fun. STAY SAFE.

Model Airplanes

When we're not shooting things straight up, we can be launching them sideways. In trigonometry, we can carry out the usual textbook problems. But it is a lot more interesting to show real application, and an airplane in flight matches this well.

If the students can build a rocket, why not an airplane? Talk about building and flying RC airplanes. It's a great hobby, where the student gets a lot of hands-on experience and learns about three flight control surfaces and throttle, and how each affect flight.

Teenagers are interested in fast cars and motorcycles. We can ask them why they are limiting themselves and their thinking to two dimensions. Ask your students, boys *and* girls, if they'd ever like to fly a plane, and encourage all of them to consider it someday.

Figure 9 Airplane club and their creation.

Granted, most of us have no idea how to fly a model airplane. But it should be possible to find an old hand who might be willing to volunteer time on helping show how to build and fly a plane. We can look up clubs in the phone book or at hobby stores.

There are a lot of interesting applications to bring into the math and physics class. We will look at three of them.

Forces in a climb

Flying a plane straight is not difficult. Maneuvering *is*. To turn, climb or dive, a pilot, or radio controller, must change three control surfaces on the aircraft (aileron, elevator and rudder) in tandem with throttle – thrust.

An airplane in constant-speed flight has four basic forces affecting it. Pointing upward is lift, equal and opposite to the weight; acting straight downward. Pointing to the front is the thrust, equal and opposite to the drag; pointing rearward.

The thrust and weight of an aircraft are pretty clear. It has mass and weight, and the engine develops so much power. But lift is a combination of shape of the wing and fuselage, and how fast the air is going over them. Drag is affected by the shape of the wing and fuselage and airspeed (all of which an engineer needs to take into consideration).

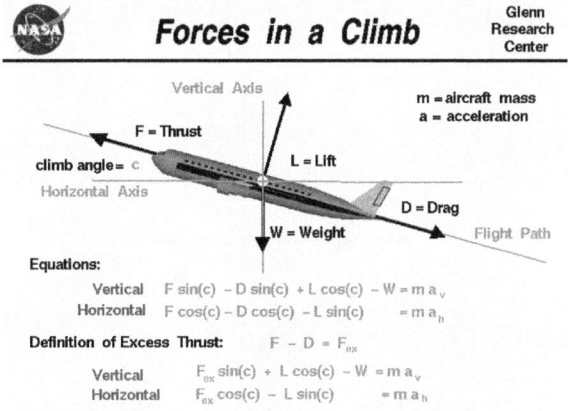

Figure 10 Aircraft in climb-configuration (Courtesy NASA).

The key for trigonometry is to look at what happens when the aircraft climbs. Now, the only force vector which hasn't changed is weight. It still has the same value and direction. Thrust will obviously need to increase, and must be broken into "x" and "y" components. We see that its y-component actually helps counteract weight, and the same is true of lift, but also the x-component of lift tends now to pull the airplane backward, like drag. Finally, the drag component is also affected by partially increasing the downward forces.

Figure 10 shows how the "x" components of force can be combined, depending on the climb angle and excess acceleration. In a constant speed climb, the acceleration is zero. We will write the equations slightly differently than shown in the figure, with zero acceleration:

$$T \cos α = D \cos α + L \sin α$$

We can do a similar thing for the "y" components and obtain:

$$T \sin α + L \cos α = D \sin α + W$$

It should be noted that determining which vectors relate to Sin and Cos require a bit of work and challenge to the students. Have them attempt it. If they can't, just getting them to work the equation is still a challenge. Given that thrust and weight are known, let's rewrite the equations in this form:

$$T \cos α = D \cos α + L \sin α$$

$$T \sin α - W = D \sin α - L \cos α$$

We see that we have two equations and two unknowns: a great opportunity to show how to apply substitution techniques. We can put our numbers in for T, W, and α. Then choose D or L as the variable to isolate, and substitute into the other equation. For example:

$$T \sin α - W = D \sin α - (T \cos α - D \cos α) \cos α / \sin α$$

Eventually, we can find that drag is a negative value, indicating that it points to the rear. We can also obtain our lift and what is called the lift-to-drag ratio. This is *real* application and students in pilot programs at university struggle with it – as well as in high school. There's no guarantee students will get it. But they *will* find it interesting.

Forces in a turn

In a turn, forces can be a bit complicated. There are side forces consisting of centripetal, centrifugal and a component of lift involved in the "x" axis. In "y", it should be seen that the lift must increase, so that its "y" component can still keep the airplane at constant altitude, counterbalancing the weight. How do we increase lift? The airplane must increase thrust and hence speed. As thrust and drag will be equal but opposite, at constant speed, we only really concern ourselves with the y-axis forces.

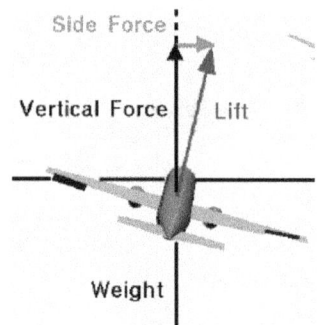

Figure 11 Forces in a banking turn (NASA).

This is a much easier problem than that above, particularly now that the students understand the vectors better. We hope. Here, our equation looks like this: L cos β = W

Knowing the weight and angle of bank, we can easily obtain the necessary Lift being generated. For engineers, there would also be the need to calculate for each given aircraft design the amount of thrust then needed.

Navigation

One of the interesting things about teaching math and science together is that we learn that in mathematics and architecture, the x-axis is considered as 0° and counter-clockwise is positive rotation. In Science and Navigation, North is 0° and *clockwise* for positive rotation. We need to teach both, and students must be able to go back and forth between the two systems. It's a good exercise in frame of reference.

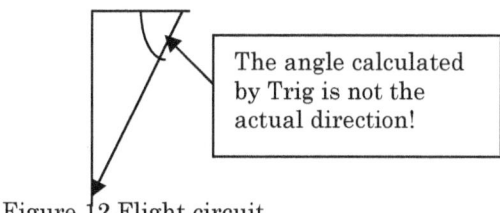

Figure 12 Flight circuit

Let's consider a basic problem. An airplane flies north for 150 km, and then due east for 50 km (Figure 12). What direction and distance must it fly to get home? Typically, the students can easily set up the problem and see the right angle. They can use the Pythagorean Theorem to get the hypotenuse and also the "angle". But they almost never get the true direction from north.

Now, the great part of the problem is that it becomes one of logic and deduction. If west is 270°, then the calculated angle must be subtracted from this value.

A similar application is an airplane (struck by a wind from the side) flying at a given direction and speed. We can set this up to find the true airspeed (the hypotenuse), and direction, again having to deduce from the calculated angle what our direction actually is.

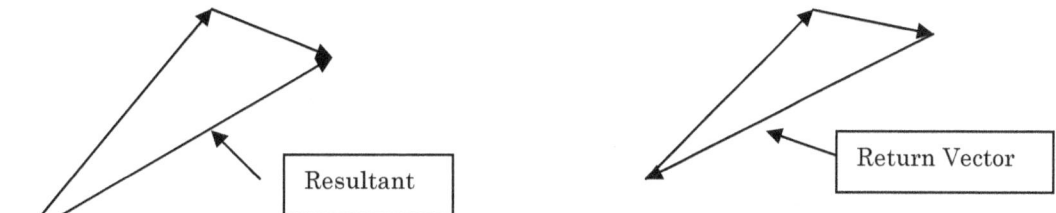

Figure 13a Flight–wind vectors, with resultant.   Figure 13b Flight Circuit.

Finally, having mastered these techniques, we can show a situation where the vectors do not make a right triangle. Here, to do vector addition, each vector must be broken into their "x" and "y" components, which in turn are added, to obtain a right triangle, from which the final 'answer' can be obtained – from trigonometry or use of the Pythagorean Theorem. The *real* final answer must then be determined from North. Getting the students to do that last bit of logic is where we really see who's thinking.

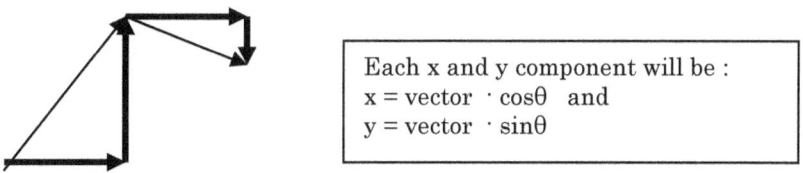

Figure 13c Flight and wind vectors, made into x and y components.

We can do these problems also for those people who might like sailing. It's the same principal.

Building arches

Included in this chapter on fun hands-on activities are two smaller projects. The first process of building arches requires some care, as injuries could result. Materials required are some basic construction bricks, thin blocks of wood, and some "keystones" (see Figure 15).

On a day that is just too hot, or nice, to be inside, take the students outdoors and let them put their muscles (mental and physical) to work on the project of building arches. Here, let them go to work with some rectangular bricks and give them minimal instruction, such as the arch should be circular, and the bricks tilted on equal angles. Give them thin blocks of wood to act as spacers, to help lean each successive brick.

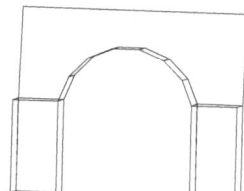

Figure 14 Basic Arch.

NOTE: the arch gets heavy! Hands and feet need to be out of the way and strong students should support the columns as they curve inward, until placement of the keystone.

Figure 15 Students and their arch.

Mostly, they will just want to power through this without calculating. Do the math. Measure the height of each brick, and the angle between bricks as one is laid on the next, with the spacer causing it to tilt. Say this is 10°. If the arch must span 180°, what does this mean? (they need 18 bricks) What does *that* mean? They must now measure the edge of a brick and multiply by 18 to get the arc length. As this represents $\pi \cdot r$ (circumference of the semicircle), they can calculate for the radius, double to get diameter and hence, know how far apart to place the columns.

Have students read about arches and their construction and use. What math is involved in building an arch? What types of arch are there? (the round and the pointed gothic arch) Compare structures made with and without them (like domes). What are they good for? Beauty? Strength? What is the tool most necessary to construct one? (2π times radius) math and geometry are what our world is built upon. Let's use this in the classroom.

Figure 16a Roman arch - Parthenon – Athens   Figure 16b Gothic arch - Chartres cathedral

While on the subject of outdoor activities, why not let students discover π? Get two sticks and tie a string to each. Make one end sharp on each stick. Find a level area of sand or dirt. If you only have pavement, tie a weight to one end and a piece of chalk to the other. However you choose, secure one end, pull the rope taught and then proceed to make a circle. Next, have the students lay the rope out along and according to the curve. Mark this segment and then repeat. Done correctly, they should have six sections and some amount left over. If they fold the rope so the ends meet, and do this again, they should roughly approximate the last, short segment. More precisely, they should have 6.28 or 2π times the radius (the rope). Primary kiddies really like this one.

Concluding dialogue

How do we make Math fun, interesting, and unexpected? What applications could we present so that students learn with their hands? How could we help them develop career interests?

By showing how things work (and how they can come crashing to Earth when the mathematics aren't quite right), they see how the "big boys" do it. In this chapter, we have again seen techniques that work in obtaining more effort from students. That is what we want. One of the great things about this material is that it can get them thinking about being a pilot, or rocket engineer. We should never underestimate our ability to help students form ideas of what to do in their lives. So many teenagers really don't have it that sure for themselves. Ask them, "What do you want to be when you grow up?"

They can easily be inspired by the work they do in high school. Let's put one idea after another in front of them. In earlier chapters, we could have inspired architectural and interior design ideas. Now, we are looking at aerospace. We always assume that students who are good at math will tend to gravitate to technical fields. What if we show the artists, historians and musicians all of the interesting things to do in these fields too?

Further reading/research and Websites:

http://www.estesrockets.com/   Estes Model rockets - Home page for rocketry equipment and such.

http://www.estesrockets.com/Instruction_Manuals1112.html
Page for instruction manuals and procedures for safe rocketry and construction.

http://www.grc.nasa.gov/WWW/K-12/airplane/guided.htm
Nasa's page with the beginner's guide to aeronautics and other great materials for grades 9-12

Class Exercise 1 **Getting started**

Objective:
Through direct application, students will see why so many math operations must be learned.

Procedure:
a) Have the class begin by making some height-altitude measuring devices. They need to obtain some kind of cardboard or plastic tubing. Make a cross-hairs at either end by taping on some string. Tape a weighted string to the center of a protractor and tape this on the tube along its axis. Figure 2.
b) Measure the angle from an observer to the top of the school or tree tops. See that a base leg should be measured, creating a right triangle. Calculate the height, and remember to add the observer's height.
c) Go to a river or some body of water and observe some opposite point. Walk perpendicularly along the shore and observe again, noting the angle to that point. Calculate the width of the water.
d) Go over techniques for measuring a rocket launch, imagining the parabolic flight, where the observers must be, relative to launch and wind, and how to "measure" an approximate ground leg. They are "Go for Launch."

Homework:
Use textbook trigonometric application problems in math and physics so that they get a variety of practice.

Evaluation:
Check participation and interest levels. Early work here is formative, with affective assessment. Observe which students are "goofy" outdoors and put clear boundaries around them. Their safety and that of others will soon be at stake.

Bridges:
Application, coupled with outdoor math and science, is always a plus.

Class Exercise 2 **Rocket launch**.

Objective:
Have a fun, thrilling and educational mathematics experience.

Materials:
Launch pad, rocket engines, rockets, angle measurers, measuring tape, and good weather. (2 hour class required on launch day)

Procedure:
a) Make teams of 2-4 students. Buy or build rockets. A lot of info can be gotten from Estes rockets: http://www.estesrockets.com/
b) Make a launch safety procedure: The only launch personnel should be the team that built the particular rocket, teacher, and time keeper. More active students are recovery and at least two pairs of observers. Invite other classes to come watch, where practicable. Be clear to teachers that supervision, and distance, be maintained.
c) Launch in good weather (mostly blue skies and winds under 10 mph). Record angle and time from launch to the chute popping out. Depending on where it went, estimate the distance from below zenith to the observers. Make sure a few students are recording this. Watch out for bad flights. RTB (return-to-base)
d) Share data. Each student needs to record all information.

Rocket name	Angle readings	Base leg	Trig height	Time	Physics height

Homework:
Prepare multi-page summary, calculating the height by Trig calculation. Also, calculate the height using the formula $y = gt^2/2$. There will be disparities. Why would this be? (aerodynamics, and bad readings)

Evaluation:
Results are usually quite good, but for a few. Grade them on report originality, quality, and inclusion of outside material like pictures.

Bridges:
Enjoy this premiere event in the Mathematics and Physics program.

Class Exercise 3 **Flight**

Objective:
Apply trigonometry to problems of flight. Inspire future pilots.

Procedure:
a) Draw a diagram of an airplane. Show the four forces in constant speed flight: lift = weight, thrust = drag. Draw a plane in a climb, of say 30°. How do the forces change? (it should be seen that weight is still completely downward, but now the other three are vectors which must be broken into x and y components) Do this, using sine and cosine. Obviously, thrust must increase, but with aircraft design comes the reality that there will lift and drag changes with more velocity. For simplicity, assume these numbers don't change. Find the thrust needed to balance the forces.
b) Look at the plane in a turn, now with 30° of bank. Here, we must consider that inward and outward centripetal forces balance with lift and weight. Calculate the lift which now must be generated so the aircraft does not lose attitude. What side forces are there?
c) Finally, assume that the pilot wants to go say due north, at 200 mph but a cross wind from west to east is blowing at 40 mph. What speed and direction does he/she need to make their destination?

Homework:
Assign example problems, like an F-16 whose engine is capable of delivering 30,000 lbs of maximum thrust while the aircraft weighs 30,000 lbs. Assume standard drag is 10,000 lbs and lift is 30,000. Also popular is the 747, with 4 engines, each delivering 55,000 lbs of thrust. If this is reduced by half after takeoff, what is drag, on the aircraft that weighs 400,000 lbs? Lift?

Evaluation:
Check homework for completion. Include questions like these on the next test, along with rocketry and other real applications.

Bridges:
These kind of problems are typical in any flight education program. If we don't show real applications, or more importantly, engender interest in these fields, we are doing our youth a disservice.

Class Exercise 4 **Building arches**

Objective:
Apply geometry to a real life construction of the arch.

Materials:
Bricks, wooden spacers, keystones, yardstick, muscles, and calculator.

Procedure:
a) Obtain basic bricks of about 4" x 6" x 12". Cut some wooden blocks about 6" long and 3/4" x 3/2". On a level piece of ground, have teams of students attempt to build arches, standing at least 18" tall. They need to be careful of fingers and toes.
b) Let them try for a few minutes and then encourage them to make gracefully curved arches. Have available something to act as a keystone, say a wedge-shaped rock, piece of wood or some soft concrete block. Guide them in placing spacers between the outer ends of the blocks, to get them to curve inward. Figure 15.
c) Finally, require that they measure and use the formula $C = 2\pi r$ to associate half the circumference with the radius or diameter. They need to figure out the amount of arc taken up by each brick and then how many bricks will be needed.

Homework:
They should summarize this work, including photos if they have them.

Evaluation:
Grade the quality of their work, effort, and interest.

Bridges:
We are trying to apply and apply mathematics, to see where and how these things are really used, as many students want to know today.

Class Exercise 5 **Dramatic presentation of mathematics**

Objective:
Use drama as a means of communicating math concepts from students to students.

Procedure:
a) Create an educational play, or use "The Calendar" found next in this book. "Wrap" the play around careful character selection. This can be a specific art class or "volunteers" from among the student populace. This can be again a means of pulling in the non-mathematically inclined. Offer extra credit points for those who regularly attend practice and work well. The effort can be entirely after school or during a specific class, should the arts teachers agree.
b) Get the students to help create props and costumes.
c) Perform in front of the entire school. This is valuable to build confidence among the youth, but also allows them to convey a mathematical message to others. The material can later be referred to in mathematics and science classes, during applicable work, for example: "Hey Tom, what can you tell me about Mars?" (Tom was Mars in the play)

Homework:
Students should memorize their lines. The quality of their performance should be part of their grade.

Evaluation:
This can either be extra points awarded in math class, should it be an extracurricular activity, or some arrangement could be made with the arts teacher.

Bridges:
Drama can be used with a historical perspective to show how mathematics underlies much of our world. This engages a variety of intelligences, even sports enthusiasts.

The Calendar a dramatic presentation.
Cast

Donkey	Wife	Teacher	Sun	Moon	Mercury	7,8,9,10	Narrator
Mars	Earth	Neptune	Juno	Uranus/Odin	Maia	Februs	
Julius	Pluto	Saturn	Janus	Augustus	Farmer/man	Venus/Aphrodite	

Interlude
Start with Pink Floyd "Time" lead-in clock tik tik tik...

Scene 1 Act 1
Set: On stage is an easel with "MYTH", "MATH", "THE CALENDAR". Acoustic guitar, begin to play the first song from "Jesus Christ Superstar") TEACHER walks in and 16 Actors come running in, circling, and as directed, sit, as Teacher stands at the "blackboard".

TEACHER (sings with appropriate rhythm from JCSuperstar)
My mind is clearer now
At last all too well I can see how we've all come to be
If you strip away, the myth from the math you will see that it's all easy
The calendar! (As he sings, the cards "MYTH" and "MATH" are removed) - (Moves through, students turn. One hands cell phone to Teacher)

You've started to believe that in this techno age
You've really found tomorrow but its only yesterday(tosses phone)
It started with Stonehenge and the pyramids
The Sumerians saw tomorrow and Egyptians today(goes off stage center)

Listen all you to the words that we give
Just remember this is how we all live
When you see the date, its nothing random oh no-o
It's 6000 years old, written on your very soul
It's in the way the sun and moon seem to move

Optional: I remember how this whole thing began,
here I am back in body again.
We priests were once like Gods, now our memory has gone very cold
We had the power in our hands, holding sway across the land
But it's all given to you now.

La-di da....(4 students dance and then make pyramid joining hands and leaning inward. 12 dance and make Stonehenge crossing arms and putting hands on each others' shoulders, Teacher steps to side) ....dum short pause

ONE of the students steps forward (sings- This part of the music needs to be worked..)
What is this thing, I just don't understand,
how it is written whose was the hand?

TEACHER
All you need to do is hear this history. Then you will see, its really no mystery.
Ee- ah –ee ah ...(students break up and come to the front, forming rows)

STUDENTS (sing, substituting for the word superstar)
The calendar, the calendar! (drums)

TEACHER
Who did it, what is it?
Oh wah he ah.... (everyone looks around for the answer Teacher turns and begins to walk)
ELECTRIC guitar amplifies the rythm.(everyone runs round and exits)

Scene 2 act 1
Set: A barn. Donkey lying. Sun, at rear left, will slowly go to the right
NARRATOR
We begin this story of the calendar, in the dawn of recorded time, with the people who may have created recorded time. On a farm in the ancient land of Sumer, a conversation is taking place between a farmer and his donkey. (Farmer walks in. Kicks donkey)

DONKEY
Hey! Don't kick me.

FARMER (tugging at its rope)
Get up you lazy donkey! Time to plow the field.

DONKEY (sits up and shivers)
It's cold today! It's too early to plough. Don't you know what date it is?

FARMER
How am I supposed to know what date it is? Nobody invented it yet! Get up!

DONKEY (kneels and gestures)
Well, don't you realize that every year it's warm sometimes and cold at others? Why don't you just count up the days, and figure out a way of keeping track of it?

FARMER (thinks for a moment, and then speaks)
Math is too much work! Why should I want to? Hurry up, its getting late! (tugs on rope)

DONKEY (tugs back)
And that is another thing. Don't you know how late it is? Its almost dark. Look at the time! (looks at watch)

FARMER

Time? What's that?
DONKEY (stands up)
Hee Haw. You ignorant human! Don't you know how the two are related? Ok. I'll make you a deal. You pull the plow, and I'll do some counting. (puts rope on farmer and they leave, Sun leaves lights go out.)   (FARMER – optional – I didn't realize what a *smart* ass I have.)

Scene 3 act 1
Set:House. Man sits at table, crying. Wife walks in.
WIFE
Why are you crying dear?

MAN
The frost came late this year. I thought it was warm enough to plant and now, our crops are ruined. I don't know how to feed us! I should have listened to my donkey! (cries)

WIFE
Third year in a row! Why didn't I marry the cave painter? Well, more work for us! Let's ask the village elder if he knows how we can become farmers and not hunter gatherers. Then, we can have leisure time and invent other things such as microwave ovens! (they leave, as does table)

Scene 3 act 2
Set:Tent. Old man sits there.
MAN
Hello village Elder!

VE/TEACHER
Hello simple farmer. How goes it?

MAN
I have failed again. I just don't know when to plant my crops.
VE/TEACHER (stands gestures as he talks)
You know, I have been working on that problem. I see everyday that the sun rises in a different place, over that-a-way. When it rises *there*, the days are short and cold, as the sun doesn't get very high. But, when the sun rises *there*, the days are long and warm. I counted how long it takes to go each way and every time, it is about 180 eighty days. And, on the 123rd day after it is *there*, it is *here*! (stands proudly)

MAN
So?

VE/TEACHER (gesturing as he talks)
So? Hmm well, if we could put some rocks down in a line, pointing this way, each time we see the sun, we'd know when to plant our crops. I will gather the men and we will start this day!

MAN
That will take time! Who will hunt, and bring us food? It is too much!

VE/TEACHER
And that is why it has never been done. Yes, now we will do it!

MAN
Hmmm. What would you call such a thing?

WIFE
Calendar?

VE/TEACHER
No, that's much too complicated of a term. I will call it "tool to measure the movement of the sun!"
    (man and wife smile at each other and nod)
MAN
Oh, I like that.

WIFE

Me too. See dear, I told you he could help. (exit all)

Scene 4 Act 1

Set:Sun behind a curtain, held by two people, also behind the curtain. Enter VE, Man, Wife and others, some carrying "poles" (These are students)

VE/TEACHER (sings as others gather) (Doors: "Waiting for the Sun")
    A bare splash of morning, comes to touch our fields
    And here we stand, to greet its day

ALL(sing)
    Waiting for the sun, waiting for the sun, wai-ting for the sun!

VE/TEACHER (sings)
    We start to build, in the darkness
    But when she comes, we'll need not ever say

ALL   (erecting "poles". Pound them in, poles bend at knees with each strike, Students then form 'stone' rows to audience) (sing)
    Waiting for the sun, waiting for the sun, wai-ting for the sun!
    Waiting, waiting, waiting, waiting
    Waiting, waiting, waiting, waiting ("haka"dance)
    Waiting for you to come along
    Waiting for you to tell us if we're wrong
    Waiting for you to hear our song.
    Waiting for you to hear our song.

VE/TEACHER (sings)
    This is the strangest night I have ever known...
(hush. Curtain lowers SLOWLY and sun "rises" between "posts")

VE/TEACHER (says)
Behold, the Sun!

ALL(sing) Man and VE/Teacher shake hands (all but poles start dancing)
    Let the sunshine, let the sunshine in
    The sun shine in ...   END of Part 1

PART 2

The lights are off. Drums roll and in march the outer planets Jupiter, Saturn, Uranus, Neptune and Pluto. They sit among the audience

Sene 5 Act 1

NARRATOR
A dark place, somewhere in the night. There resides a Star, and those objects called planets, a word meaning "those who wander". They are the members of the solar system. Enter into this dark a brilliant object (turn on lights)

SUN
Solar system indeed! I am called The Sun! Some Latins call me Sol, and name this circle of servants my system. They name long and short days after Me! Solstices. The first day of your week is named after me!

Your days are because of me. Your age is because of me. How many years old are you? You should better ask, how many times you have traveled around ME, for they are the same.

Call me Apollo, call me Amen Ra, as the Greeks and Egyptians once did! Now shall you see a story, and do not forget my part in all of it!

Enter Mercury and make quick journey around the sun (run!)

MERCURY
I am called Mercury. It takes me 88 days to go around the sun. I am the swiftest!

Mercury makes two quick trips around the sun, and then fades into the shadows, nearby.
In come male and female, Venus and Mars, dancing together. They separate and begin orbits, Venus closer/quicker.

VENUS
I am called Venus. I have had many beautiful names, like Ishtar and Aphrodite. I represent the power of Love and Woman! I go around the sun in 240 days.

MARS (yells)
I am called Mars! Others know me as Ares, the God of War! I am the Male! I am called the Red planet. It takes me 680 days to orbit. But, my day is as long as yours!
(Venus and Mars fade out to the sides. Enter Earth, the goddess. She too goes around the Sun.)

EARTH
I am Earth. You know me. I am your home. Each day I turn about myself, making day into night and night to day. Each year I go around the sun, and give you winter and summer.

All begin to rotate around Sun, keeping their order. Enter Juno, and the asteroids. (get children for this part)

ALL
We are called the inner planets!

CHILDREN/JUNO
And asteroids!

Scene 5 Act 2
Jupiter, Saturn, Uranus, Neptune and Pluto stand now.
JUPITER
I am Jupiter, the great one, largest of all these. I was once called Zeus. I go around the Sun in twelve years. The Chinese calendar uses my count to represent each of twelve different years. Many people count in twelves, known as a dozen. Before simpler minds came to accept metric, *my* counting system was known to the empires of Britain, Rome and Sumer!

SATURN
I am Saturn, the ringed one. Some have called me Cronos, father time, and father to this young Jupiter. You may have heard my name used to represent your timepieces, named *chrono*meters. I take almost 30 years to orbit Sun. It is when I return that you come of age.

BOTH
We align with your earth every 60 years. The Chinese calendar calls this the Great Cycle. What else do you count in sixty?

URANUS
I am Ouranus. Be careful how you pronounce my name in your usage of the English language! The stories say that I was father to Saturn, father to Jupiter, father all those closer to Sun. I take 84 years to go around.

NEPTUNE
My name is Neptune. I am named for your god of the oceans. My period is 147 years. I am blue, just as your world.

PLUTO (holding a large ball)
We are the double planetoid called Pluto and Charon. Pluto was the lord of the place of the dead, and Charon drove his ship across the waters that separated you from us. Our orbit lasts 248 years. We are unique, so far away, as we each spin around each other. (hold the ball and twirl)

URANUS, NEPTUNE, PLUTO
We are so far away, that you cannot see us!
(Lights go out, and all depart except Earth.)

Scene 5 Act 3
The lights go back on Earth.

EARTH
I am Earth, and as you know, I am not alone. I would ask some friends to join me so we can explain a few things

Enter Sun and Moon. Sun comes to the center of the stage, and Earth and Moon dance around the sun. They stop and face the audience.

MOON bows and (sings from "Superstar")
I don't know how to tell you
It's in the math and it's easy
Count thirty days count nineteen years
For these cycles of my journey with Earth
Are really what affects you most

You might have noticed
Each night I am different
Sometimes full, sometimes thin
It all depends on my place in space
And Earth with the sun

It's all well known
And crops are sown

It takes thirty days
To make trip round earth
And in 12 times
I'm a few days short
But in 19 years it's straight
That's what Persia says.

It's just a count

EARTH
Well, I did not know we were going to go into all of THAT. Very well then. (sings)
I AM the Earth (Sun and Moon sing "She is the Earth")
I turn in 24 hours (Sun and Moon sing "just like a clock")(spin)
You see all of these numbers (Sun and Moon: "Divide in three sixty")
Relate easily (Sun and Moon: "Oh yes indeed!")

ALL twice sing
It's in the way that we measure
Circles, angles and time
It's in the way that we count
Numbers six twelve and nine
(They all smile and nod to each other)

MOON
I am called simply the Moon. The Latins call me Luna. Some use my name in vain when calling others Lunatics! In either language, and in others, I have the first day of your week named after myself! I take almost 29.5 days to orbit your home world.

EARTH
Your mass causes the tides and storms on me! You cause the ground to shake!

MOON
Oh, not me alone, but I do my fair share. But, look at what good I do as well! Why, all these silly humans can only count so far you know. So, my trip around you helps them count thirty days. Their month comes not only from my period, but also my name!

SUN
Hah. As you said, you are only twenty nine and a half days. Why do months as you call them get counted in 30 and 31, and that awful 28?

MOON
Hey you. You are not so perfect yourself. Why must so many people add four or five days to their calendar because their mathematics work easier with 360 or 361?

EARTH
Well you two, the whole thing would work easier if you Ms. Moon were thirty days, and you Mr. Apollo were exactly 360 days. But hey, close enough. The universe isn't perfect. If it was, we wouldn't have to go to school!

Still, you mention calendars. I've known many in my days. I think the best was the Sumerians'. They actually had two. One was based on you Ms. Sun. It counts all 365 and ¼ days. Most people today use that to stay in communication with each other. But, it's how they use it that can be quite different. The second calendar used the moon. They counted months of 29 and 30 days, one after the other. Jewish and Muslim people both count this way still. And they share one thing that the Egyptian, Persian and Bahai people believed. They all started their year when the day and nights were of equal length, on the 21st of March.

All
Happy New Year! (Lights go out and the stage is cleared.)

Scene 6 Act 1
NARATOR
So, how did we get this calendar that so many of us use? For better or worse, we have the ancient Romans to thank for this. We have some of them here to tell their story.

The light shines on the door. Enter Mars.

MARS
I am Mars! I am the God of war! The Romans were correct in beginning their year with me, and using my name for it. I am when Spring occurs and the Earth comes back to life! You call me March, and use my name to describe martial arts, men marching and...

Enter Aphrodite, interrupting.
APRIL
Yes yes, Mr. Great and wonderful. Well, sure, the year used to start with you. But, it once started with me! Aphrodite. I name the month following you, and I am for the blossoms, particularly of the fruit the apricot!

Enter May
MAY
Thank you Miss April. What an airhead, thinking you could start the year. Where do you think they got the idea of April fools anway? But, you both must know that it is my month when real beauty is seen. That is why we have so many flowers then. Many celebrate my first day as May day.

Enter Juno
JUNO
I am Juno, wife of the God Jupiter. It is in my month that the warmth of summer begins. Someone finally remembered me and named an asteroid after me. Not so flattering to be named after a misshapen rock, but after all, many of the others are just big balls of gas.

Enter Julius. The members turn and salute.
ALL
Ave Caesar!
Julius takes up his place next to the others. salutes

JULIUS
What a horrible calendar. Ten months of 304 days. Some months had names, and others mere numbers. I conquered the world! I went to Egypt, and brought a new calendar. They thought I was mad. But, in the end, they properly named the fifth month, Quintillus, after me! To mark my greatness, they reduced February by one and gave it to me!

Enter Augustus.
ALL, except Caesar
Ave Caesar!
Julius yawns

AUGUSTUS
Yes, my uncle was a great man. But, I too led armies of the empire of Rome. It was I, and not Julius who made Rome great. For this, I named the next month, once called simply "six", after my modest self. And, to match my uncle, I too took a day from the luckless month of February.

Enter 7, 8, 9, 10
SEVEN
They called me Septo, which means seven.

EIGHT
They called me Octo, or eight.

NINE
Novo. Nine.

TEN
Deci. Ten. By the way, I also name the counting system that most of you use! Sure glad the French got around to that, so that now I can count on my fingers!

NARRATOR
Yes, the first Roman calendar had only ten months, of about thirty days. They just added so many on at the end of the year as they thought they needed. The people who kept the count, might add more or less, based on how much they liked the person in charge at the time. You see, the year of office ended with the new year. Even still, it was recognized by someone that they needed two more months.

JULIUS
That was Me!
(Enter Janus and February. They nudge the others out of line.)

JANUS
I am Janus, the guardian of doorways. It was I who the Romans finally selected to start their year.

FEBRUARY
I am Februs, from whom you get the word fever. I am the purifier. Look at how bitter, dark and cold my month is. It is good that it is short or you would all be even more depressed during my time!

ALL
We twelve make up your year!

JULIUS
Thanks to me!

ALL
Kill Caesar!

Lights out, all depart chasing Julius.

Scene 7 Act 1
NARRATOR
We owe a lot to the Romans, and before them, the Sumerians, Egyptians, and Greeks. They invented the time keeping that we use. We count measure around our Earth with the same system. We call the planets by their names. Many people name days of the week after their Gods; Martes, Mercoles, Jueves and Viernes.
Did you know that the whole idea of a week comes from the Sumerian and Jewish culture, for they alone counted by seven days, which is about ¼ of a moon cycle. But, we speakers of English get our language from the Angles, and their German brethren, who gave us the days of our week.

(Play the song; Ride of the valkyrie) Enter Sun, Moon, Mars/Tyr, Odin/Uranus, Jupiter/Thor, Juno/Freya, Saturn.

SUN
As I said, I am the first day of the week. Some people call my day Domingo. But, as with Christmas, it is actually me who they celebrate!

LUNA
And then come I. I name Moonday

MARS
Do not forget Me! The Norsemen called me Tyr, and Tyr's day is my day!

URANUS
I govern the week, from the middle. I am called Odin, or Wodin.

JUPITER
To the Northerners I am called Thor. I give you Thorsday.

JUNO
You have me to thank each day your workweek ends and play begins. I am Freyya. Freyaday is mine!

SATURN
I am Saturn. I give you Saturday.

ALL
We name the days of your week.

Enter the rest of the planets.

ALL
We name the months of your year! You keep track of time thanks to our movements!

Curtain call
ALL (individuals come forward speaking their part, echoed by the rest)
I am Sun, I am Earth, we give you the day(they give you the day)
I am Moon I'm the playwrite this is our little play(this is our little play)
We are the other planets hip hip hooray
We're the rest of the cast listen as we say
We make the muse of the spheres, Which you know now to play
We number hours and the years, Seconds minutes and days
It's been our pleasure to bring you This little show
Keep your wits about you As you all now go

We make the muse of the spheres, Which you know now to play
We number hours and the years, Seconds minutes and days

We make the muse of the spheres
Ca-len-dar!

Sun leads the march out of the room. THE END

10 – Astronomy of Algebra and Trigonometry

Opening dialogue

Why is it that in physics, one of the most interesting topics for students is how the planets move? How can we tap that interest?

If we throw a ball perfectly straight up in the air, will it come back down in exactly the same place (even though the Earth is moving below it)? How high will it go? How long will it take to travel this distance? Is it the same amount of time going up as coming down? Is the concrete floor of your room flat?

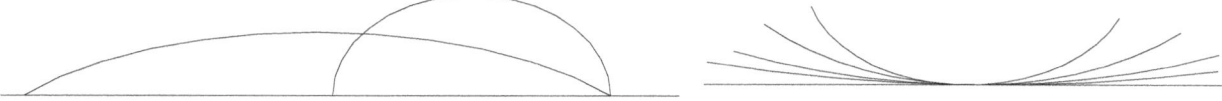

Figure 1a Projectile motions.   Figure 1b "Straight" line.

What path does a rocket take? What about a ball that I throw, or water from a garden hose? How can I write a formula to express these curves, these lines? What is a line? Is a straight line straight......or a curve of infinite radius? Why do we need algebra anyway?

The Parabola

The curved lines shown in Figure 1a/b are called parabolas. As these drawings show, objects travel in parabolic motion, but also circular, elliptical and spirallic; as we will see. We spent quite a bit of time with special applications of linear functions in Chapter 2. We will now work a couple items on curves which can enhance learning of this material.

We can express these shapes mathematically. The first, the parabola, is normally represented by the equation $y = x^2$; a u-shaped curve whose vertex is centered at the origin (0,0). We move this critical point away from (0,0) with more complex equations, like $y = 2x^2 + 4x + 1$ and $y = (x - 3)^2 + 1$. This book is not meant to review things like parabolas but to look for creative mathematics approaches. So, let's look at these two ways of writing a parabolic formula, use an application of $(a + b)^2$, and see what develops.

We want to couple this with graphing, always, to strengthen the learning and help visual learners. Thanks to "p-man" Hai, who first notice...a pattern, we have discovered a relationship between $y = ax^2 + bx + c$ and $y = a(x - h)^2 + k$. Let's see at what point the reader, and student, can find the same pattern when multiplying quantities, working to complete the square, and solving using the quadratic equation.

To begin, let's convert by multiplying $(a + b)^2$ and then obtain our roots:

$y = (x - 2)^2 + 3$ → $x^2 - 4x + 7$ roots: $2 \pm \sqrt{(-3)}$
$y = -(x - 2)^2 + 3$ → $-x^2 - 4x + 7$ roots: $2 \pm \sqrt{3}$
$y = (x - 3)^2 - 2$ → $x^2 - 6x - 7$ roots: $3 \pm \sqrt{2}$

It should be noticed right away that the roots contain 2 and 3 in some form or another, seemingly corresponding to "h" and "k". This is what the advanced student noticed. Given the challenge though, of trying to find the connection they left this for the teacher. Where in our educative process do we get this student to want to dig and make their own finds, experiencing the excitement of discovery?

So far it seems that we only need to consider the terms which determine placement of the vertex. Ask students what, if anything, could affect where the parabola crosses the x-axis. As we understand the parabola, or any function, more and more, we realize that the coefficient in front of the highest order variable determines the steepness of the function.

Let's work with two functions which are more complex:

$y = 2(x - 1)^2 - 3$ → $x^2 - 4x - 1$ roots: $1 \pm \sqrt{6}/2$
$y = -3(x - 1)^2 + 4$ → $-3x^2 + 6x + 1$ roots: $1 \pm 2\sqrt{3}/3$

This work is included here because it is not given in most textbooks, is a great process of discovery for students who are well versed in the quadratic equation, and is a strong application for those who have been weaned from the calculator. What if "b" is odd, or fractional? As my college prof used to say, "That is left as work for the student".

What do we notice about the roots? It looks like "h" still determines the starting point; which should come as no surprise since this is the portion "–b/2a" which locates the axis of symmetry. Ultimately, our work establishes that the roots will be found according to $-h \pm \sqrt{(-ak)}/a$. We can then test this with various formulae to see if it is in fact correct. Try something like $y = 2(3x - 6)^2 + 1$. It will be found that the final result is divided by the coefficient in front of the "x".

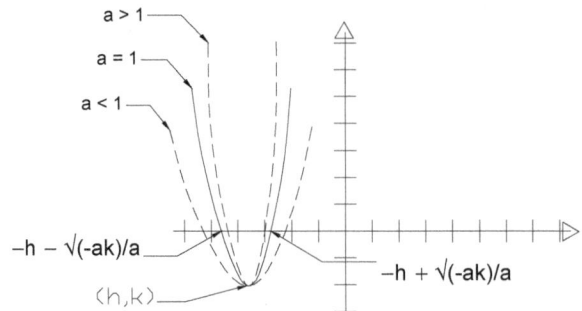

Figure 2a The parabola and x=axis crossings.

We need to understand how $y = (x - h)^2 + k$ works; mainly shifting the key point of the graph (the vertex) by (h,k) units. As we study the conic sections, cubics, and other graphs, we see repeatedly that "h" and "k" are the key to placing the function in coordinate space:

$$\frac{(x-h)^2}{a^2} \pm \frac{(y-k)^2}{b^2} = 1 \qquad y = (x-h)^3 + k \qquad y = \frac{1}{(x-h)} + k$$

Algebra is at its best when we include visual learning and develop the functions that coincide with it. Have a nice day!

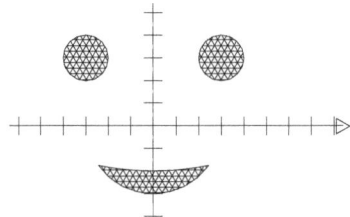

Figure 2b $(x + 3)^2 + (y - 2)^2 \leq 1$ ∪ $(x - 3)^2 + (y - 2)^2 \leq 1$ ∪ $[x^2 + y^2 \leq 9$ ∩ $x^2/25 + y^2/4 \geq 1]$

One final thought on the parabola, and then conic sections, is the process of completing the squares. Experience shows that students struggle with this part, which points to its usefulness in deepening understanding (or confusion when not done properly). It forces the student to work $(a + b)^2$ in reverse. Take a given problem:
$y = x^2 + 4x + 7$ → $(x^2 + 4x + 4) - 4 + 7$ → $(x +2)^2 + 3$

and then do much more complex things:
$2x^2 + 4x + 7$, $\qquad -2x^2 + 3x + 7$, and $\quad 4x^2 + 9y^2 + 16x - 18y = 36$.

As always the students will applaud the chance to improve understanding...

The parabola and its focus

How do the planets, moons, and comets move? We teach young students that planets move in circles around the Sun and that moons travel in circles around their planets. That is all right, as we are also teaching about circles and simpler concepts. In high school the mind is mature enough for more exact detail. According to Kepler, the true paths are elliptical, with the Sun or planet at one of the foci, depending upon whether we are talking then about planetary or satellite motion. (We will see that even *this* is in error.) From the initiate comes the question, "What are foci?"

Figure 3 Parabolas and their foci.

A focal point is just that, a point in space where things focus. When we draw a parabola the focus could be thought of as a point around which the curve, curves. Note from Figure 3 that the tighter the curve, the closer the focus to its vertex.

The focus can be readily identified by our modern students. Ask how many are familiar with the shape of a satellite television dish. They all are. The dish, it can be explained, is shaped to receive low intensity waves that are then reflected by the metal within the curved dish. The focal point is that point through which nearly every reflected wave will pass. We can consider the individual waves as traveling in some direction, and they can be represented by a ray. Further, we can then express their reflection via a ray diagram.

Figure 4 VLA (Image courtesy of NRAO/AUI), satellite TV receiver, and diagram.

On every satellite dish there is some object placed in front. That is the actual receiver, taking in the focused and amplified signal as reflected by the dish.

Optical instruments work the exact same way. Lenses, such as in eyeglasses, are curved to let light waves (again displayed with a ray diagram) pass through a focal point, "focusing" the image. For people with vision problems, glasses move the picture forward or backward within the eye, based on the need of the individual. To do this, the lenses must be specially ground.

This is a whole science in itself called optics, which was particularly developed by Galileo. He was first to report craters on the Moon and the four large moons around Jupiter. This latter item further confirmed the heliocentric theory and helped navigators develop a universal time-keeping method.

It is fun for students to play with magnifying glasses. But, what is the math behind it? In Figure 5, the left (smaller) object can be thought of as emitting light waves (or rays) in all directions (spherical). This is an interesting idea for students, that we see something because it "emits" (reflects) light. We normally think that only the Sun or a light bulb can do this.

We will concern ourselves with only two rays from this infinite quantity: the one parallel to the axis of the lens and the other that passes through the focus nearest the object. They then pass through the lens, and the ray diagram shows where the image will appear, in focus and magnified. This is the same principle behind which microscopes and telescopes function. In this case each focal point is associated to the curve bending inward toward it; in other words, on the opposite side of the lens.

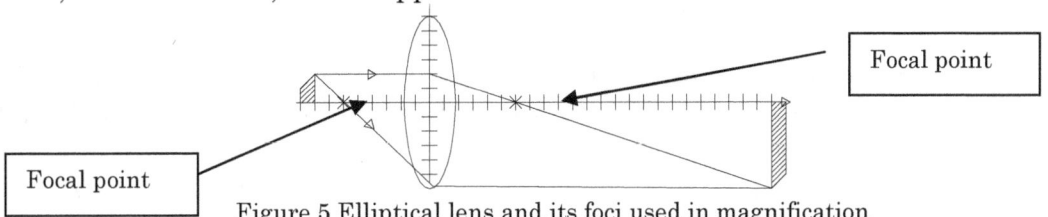

Figure 5 Elliptical lens and its foci used in magnification

Lenses and ray diagrams are great to show applications of parabolas and foci. Once students understand something of what foci are, we can look at the ellipse in more detail.

The Conic Sections

The basics we present on planetary motion are that the Earth goes in a circle around the Sun, and that the Moon goes in a circle around Earth. We will see that nothing could be further from the truth. But it works to get things started. In high school we learn Kepler's laws, particularly that planets move in ellipses; with the Sun being one of the two foci. This is a great time to work with graphs of circles, ellipses, and hyperbolas, for students really see how it all relates to each other.

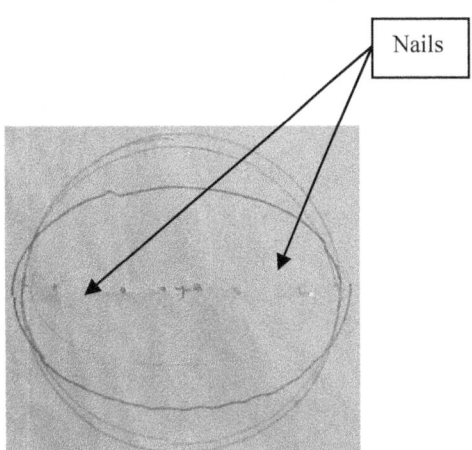

Figure 6a Making the ellipse.   6b Artist's impression "Invitation" (Francine Hart).

Build a model for making ellipses. Simply take a large board (perhaps plywood) and nail into it through plain white paper. Space the nails every inch (2-3 cm), and always use an even number of nails. Then, tie a string to the two central nails, wrapping a pencil inside the string.

Move the pencil around in an elliptical pattern (Figure 6a). Actually, there is no other shape which can be done. The pencil will have to be switched to do above and below the row of nails. Next, use each nail adjacent to those central ones. Repeat the steps again, for the nails further out. It should be noticed that as the nails (our foci) shift outward, the figure becomes obviously elliptical. What happens when the foci become so far apart as to be at or near infinity? A straight line. Or, is it two straight lines?

It should be noted too that as the nails get closer we have nearly a circle. So, is a circle a circle with one central point or an ellipse with two foci at one point? The algebraic equation for an ellipse is as follows:

$$\frac{x^2}{a^2} + \frac{y^2}{b^2} = 1$$

Note when "a" and "b" are equal, we have a circle; a = b = radius:

$$\frac{x^2}{a^2} + \frac{y^2}{a^2} = 1 \qquad \text{or} \qquad x^2 + y^2 = r^2$$

And only another slight change defines the hyperbola: $\frac{x^2}{a^2} - \frac{y^2}{b^2} = 1$

Somewhere along the way, the student should see that every line can be expressed by a formula and every formula can be used to draw a line.

Solar movement

With regard to planetary motion, it is very real to learn about ellipses. From the ellipse equation we can use certain of these values in something very like the Pythagorean theorem to get focal lengths:

$$c = \pm\sqrt{(a^2 - b^2)} \qquad \text{(and } \pm\sqrt{(a^2 + b^2)} \text{ for the hyperbola)}$$

We just have to be careful when using this formula always to use half of the longest length, called the major axis, for our value for "a" (to get a positive result inside the radical), and of course half of the minor axis is "b".

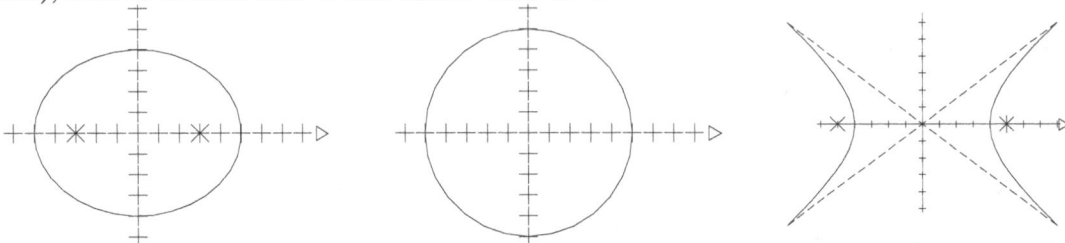

Figure 7 Graphs of the ellipse, circle, and hyperbola.

The ellipse in Figure 7 has a major axis 10 units long, so a = 5, b = 4, and the focal distance is found to be 3. It should be seen that it does not take a great difference between "a" and "b" to move the foci pretty far to the side.

Every ellipse has two foci. This is a good model of planetary motion. The planet, moon or comet, can be thought to follow the path of the ellipse, with the Sun at one of the focal points. What is at the other? Why is it that objects orbit in this way? Generally, planetary paths, such as Earth's, are only slightly elliptical (meaning that the circular model is not so far off), though Pluto's (and other planetoids; newly discovered) are more eccentric. A typical comet has an even "flatter" ellipse. When we teach mathematics, we should always try to relate it to something interesting, like art, music, or astronomy.

In class we use easy numbers to help students get the concept, like 3-4-5 and their squares; 9-16-25. But, the Earth's orbit varies from 90.9 to 94 million miles. Ask students when is the Earth nearest the Sun? The usual answer, standing to reason, is summertime. This is actually true only in the southern hemisphere. For the majority of the world's population, our summer is actually when furthest from the Sun (but with the pole tilted sunwards). Interestingly enough, the nearest point is near the date when Christians celebrate the twelfth day of Christmas, on the feast of the three kings; January 6. The furthest point is at or near July 4th, a date chosen by the Masonic founders of the United States.

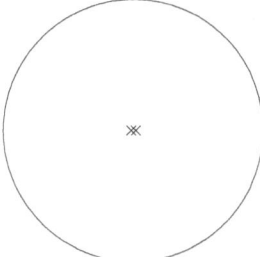

Figure 8 Earth's elliptical orbit. "X's" mark the foci; not one center but "two".

How can students calculate the foci of Earth's orbit? This is a great practical problem. The maximum and minimum distances, at July and January, are 180° apart along the major axis. We must add the two values and divide by 2. This means that the "a" is 92.2 million miles, and that the focal distance from the center of the ellipse is "only" 1.8 million miles. Further, "b" equals 92.18 million miles. We can see from Figure 8, how our "orbit" is very circular, and that the foci have barely any relative distance between them. These numbers show the elongation of Earth's orbit is only around 18,000 miles, meaning 99.986% of a circle. So the circle is not a bad model for younger students.

Having gone through all of this, we can now go about showing that this, and Kepler, were wrong. This work with ellipses would be accurate if the Earth moved about a stationary Sun. But, as they each have a journey of their own, the picture becomes much more complex.

Let us begin with the Moon. And, let us first begin with something a lot more elementary, like high school trigonometry.

Radians

As we saw in Chapter 4, utilizing the hexagon to show the trigonometry of angles of the first quadrant, we saw relationships for sine values as seen in Table 1a.

$$\frac{\sqrt{0}}{2} \quad \frac{\sqrt{1}}{2} \quad \frac{\sqrt{2}}{2} \quad \frac{\sqrt{3}}{2} \quad \frac{\sqrt{4}}{2} \qquad \frac{\sqrt{4}}{2} \quad \frac{\sqrt{3}}{2} \quad \frac{\sqrt{2}}{2} \quad \frac{\sqrt{1}}{2} \quad \frac{\sqrt{0}}{2}$$

Table 1a First quadrant sine values   Table 1b Second quadrant sine values

This set of values corresponds to the sine of 0, 30, 45, 60, and 90 degrees. As we continue rotating, through the second quadrant, we look at specific angles of 120, 135, 150, and finally 180 degrees. The sine values decrease in value: a pattern. A similar pattern follows for greater angles, though now the sine value is negative.

$$\frac{-\sqrt{0}}{2} \quad \frac{-\sqrt{1}}{2} \quad \frac{-\sqrt{2}}{2} \quad \frac{-\sqrt{3}}{2} \quad \frac{-\sqrt{4}}{2} \qquad \frac{-\sqrt{4}}{2} \quad \frac{-\sqrt{3}}{2} \quad \frac{-\sqrt{2}}{2} \quad \frac{-\sqrt{1}}{2} \quad \frac{-\sqrt{0}}{2}$$

Tables 1c and d – Third and fourth quadrant sine values.

How do we use this confusing information? For one, we have to again break out of our primary school "rigidity", and realize that mathematicians and scientists have other ways to measure angles and circles. We do need to teach simplified forms in grade school. But it is interesting how strongly students hold to them in later years.

When we talk about how fast an object is spinning, we talk about its revolutions in a given time interval, like RPM. This was easily recognizable when we had record players. In the absence of such things we should look at power drills and fans to see how fast they turn. We can find how much time it takes to go through one revolution of 360°. The only problem is that we can't use degrees in any form of calculation or in graphing as the scale is not useful (too large). We use for this radian measure.

Radians are difficult for a lot of students to understand. They may not grasp geometry and trig so well and now they must leave degrees and expand into another realm. And, these new values are either fractional values of π, or are decimal numbers. The fraction is always avoided (needn't be) and the decimal is often not understood.

We can use a bicycle to help demonstrate radians. Put a chalk mark on the tire and a mark matching it on the ground. Move the bike forward until the mark on the tire rotates enough to again meet the ground. If we measure this distance we will see that it is 6.28 times the radius of the tire.

Everyone recognizes that the circumference of a circle is written as C = 2πr, where r is the radius. The circumference corresponds to 360°. It should be obvious that the length of half the circle would be πr, corresponding to 180°. The unit of measure for this alternative form of angular measure is called the radian, and the system is set up so that π radians is equivalent to 180°, and 2π radians equals 360°. So, radians are very similar to the idea of circumference and radius. It is critical here, as always, that the math and science student not just write numbers but also record units of measure too.

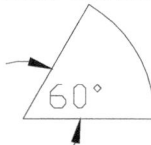

Figure 9 An angle of measure – slightly more than 1 radian.

Using radians, we can measure the lengths of arcs. This is a great project for high school students because they've probably never tried to do this before. The equation for this is S = θr. It is obvious that when we say S is the arc length, the angle cannot possibly be in degrees. Imagine a 60° angle, forming an arc.

If the radius were say, 1 inch, does this mean the arc length could be 60 inch (by multiplication)? Look at Figure 9. The arc looks to be about the same length as the radius. It *is* almost the same.

Unlike degrees, which are a measurement, radians are a proportion: arc length to radius. So,

$$\theta = \frac{S}{r} \quad \rightarrow \quad \text{(answer in radians)}$$

We see that S and r are units of distance. The units of measure cancel. Hence, students must grasp that radian is a label they must "affix" to the calculated value, when discussing rotation.

For 360°, the radian measure is arc length, (which is circumference [2πr] divided by r), and hence: 2π radians. For 180° we have π radians, and 90° is π/2 radians. A great exercise to do is have the students generate the radian measure of all the critical trig angles between 0 and 360 degrees. We could just do it on the calculator, to get decimal answers, but if we don't show real applications and relations of fractions, is it any wonder the students don't want to learn them? In this example, again use 60°, setting up the equation as follows:

$$\frac{\pi \text{ radians}}{180°} = \frac{x}{60°}$$

It should be noted that as π radians is equivalent to 180°, this fraction has a value of '1', though the quantities seem different. Understanding the process of conversion to and from radians is a valuable usage of fractions. Also, it is necessary for use in physics when talking about angular motion and velocity. We should try to teach these subjects together but where that is not possible, the teachers should coordinate their lectures. Teach concepts and apply them.

Now, we cross multiply by 60°, and the reason we use the label and the number is to see that degrees cancel out, leaving us with a fraction of π/3 radians. Make the students do these conversions. By using fractions, they will begin to see patterns and stop needing the conversions, actually saving them time. And π/3? Its value of 1.05 looks appropriate to the image in Figure 9.

For 30°, they will see π/6 radians; for 45°, π/4; and for 90°, they have π/2 radians. Doesn't look like any kind of a pattern yet, but if they tried to get common denominators, they would see 2π/12, 3π/12, 4π/12 and 6π/12. They should see that the two which are missing are 15 and 75 degrees, and they should by now know why we don't use these angles (because they don't fit the pattern seen in the trig table).

Get the students to guess what fraction would be 120°. Have them convert to confirm their results. Did they get 2π/3? One of the fun things with high school students is getting them to realize they can leave π and radical numbers like √2 and √3 in their answers. The value for each of these terms should be memorized; 3.14, 1.414 and 1.732. Again, this can negate the need and dependence on the calculator. This way we can demonstrate the patterns of √2 and √3 that repeat. Don't use the technology more than is needed.

Angle		Sine		Cosine		Tangent	
Degrees	Radians						
	fraction	decimal	fraction	decimal	fraction	decimal	fraction	decimal
0°								
30°								
45°								
60°								
90°								
120°								
..								

Table 2 Format for students to create their own table – by hand.

Instead, to visualize and understand how this works, have the students generate a table, in steps. First, obtain the radian values of the angles, as fractions and also as decimals. Yes, for this, we will use the calculator, and we will laugh at the frequent errors that the students make. It is something to see a student get increasing decimal numbers like 1.047, 1.57, 2.904, 2.356 and 2.618 and then ask if they look right. The students often don't relate to numbers, don't grasp for example that one third of π is about 1; one half of π should be about 1.5 and cannot see that the 2.904 doesn't fit. (Did the reader?)

Put all of these numbers in the table, up to 2π or 6.28 radians. To this point, a student's table should look like Figure 10. Encourage them to make an exemplary table, for this will be allowed as a tool on their tests for the entire school year. The calculator will not necessarily.

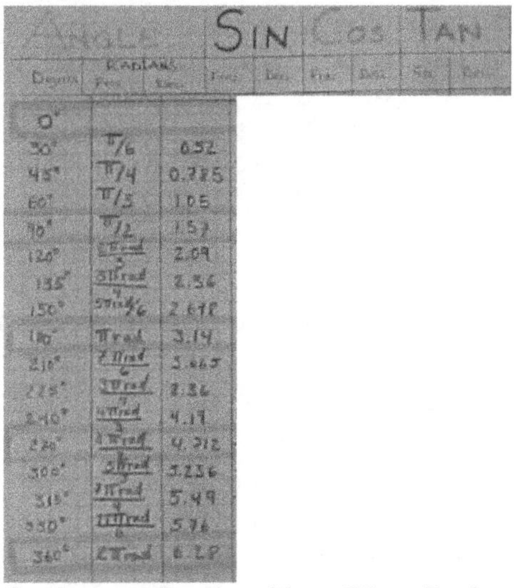

Figure 10 Student-made trig table - (Mona Reyhani).

Next, we will insert the trigonometric ratios. In Chapter 4, we showed the unit circle, which, no matter the size, is said to have a radius of 1. This makes all of our trig calculations much easier. Also, we used x, y, and r to indicate those values of adjacent, opposite and hypotenuse, and the same will be true when putting numbers into the Pythagorean theorem.

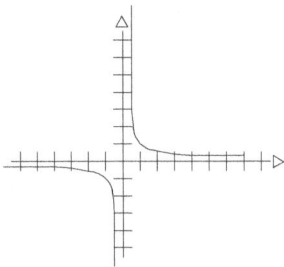

Figure 11 A visual presentation of why 1/0 is undefined, and NOT zero.

As we do this work, we are concerned with angular rotation above the x-axis. The trick is with 0 and 90 degrees. If the students will accept that we are using x and y instead of opposite and adjacent, they understand that at 0°, - y also equals 0, and at 90°, x = 0. This helps define sine, cosine and tangent at these points, though with tangent, getting students to realize that dividing by zero does *not* yield zero is often a chore. For that, we stop and have them work out the graph of 1/x so they see how the graph curves one way for negative values and the other for positive. It helps them realize why 1/0 is undefined. Eventually, graphing the Tangent and Secant functions will also help.

The students like drawing graphs about as much as they like doing fractions. But, as the saying goes, "Practice makes perfect." It is all helpful to their understanding.

Insert into the table the sine values we obtained in Chapter 4 (shown in Figure 12). Revisit the first quadrant, showing what is going on with cosine and tangent. With cosine, we see the same ratios appear. By going into the second quadrant we see patterns develop for the tangent. Ultimately, we are able to use the patterns to complete our table, with fractions and decimal values.

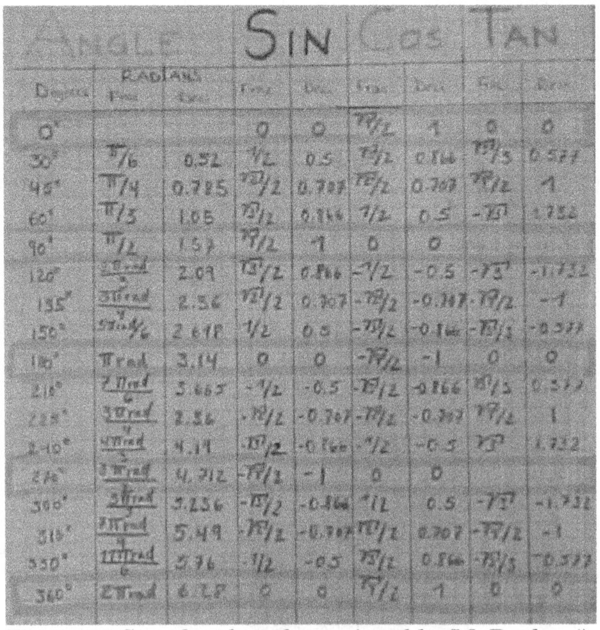

Figure 12 Completed student trig table (M. Reyhani).

Having the table finally complete, we can now use it to generate the graph the sine curve. Why is all of this mathematic calculation and graphing in the middle of a discussion about planetary motion? Because it's all in the math and this book is trying to show how to draw relations between things...

In Chapter 2 we showed that when faced with a new equation, we should make a table of "x" and "y" values. The students see that they need to try some numbers for "x" to achieve a "y". Then, they try to draw the figure, exploring what it might make. With time, they understand how to read each new equation directly and draw it, in its many varied forms (positive/negative, shifted). We go through this process every time we face a new graph. Make a table of x and y values. It's how we work with circles, ellipses, and other shapes too.

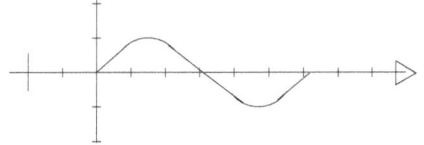

Figure 13 The first graph of the sine function (x scale counting in 1's).

For graphing trigonometric curves, we must decide to use radians (π values or decimals). At the start, we will use decimal-radian values for "x", in y = sin x. We will begin by making a graph that is two units up and down on the y-axis and 7 units out on the x-axis. Graph or grid paper is very useful for this. Have the students count every four blocks as '1'. Take decimal values of radians for x, and the sin x decimal values from the trig table and graph them as pairs. The result should look like Figure 13.

The students have now graphed the sine wave. Note with them where the "zeroes" are located, at or near 0, 3 and 6 (0, π, and 2π) and that the peak and valley are nearly 1.5 and 4.75 ($\pi/2$ and $3\pi/2$). Do the students like music and talking to their friends? The pressure wave of sound going through the air looks basically like this. Do they like talking to their friends on the phone or using a computer or music player? The electrical signal looks like this too, as do the light rays coming off of this page. And, more interesting to our calculations, the orbit of the Moon also resembles this action.

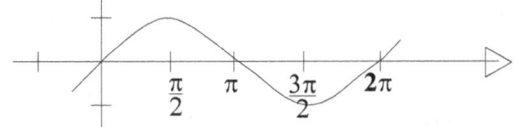

Figure 14 The sine wave on a radian graph (x scale counting in ¼ of 2π).

We will note that the sine wave has peaks and valleys not at whole numbers, but at whole-numbered fractions of π. Have the students continue to do their graphing from here out by changing the x scale and labeling it according to $\pi/2$, π, $3\pi/2$ and 2π radians. It's not hard to do, but it is another step of growth for them as they expand the tools of math, and more, see that they can. They just need to identify the decimal values and graph accordingly. Still using graphing paper, now we use two squares to represent '1'. Therefore, 1.57 is approximately 3 squares. We now mark on the x-axis according to this new scale (Figure 14). This is a really good place to continue then, showing how to phase-shift along the x- or y-axis, changing the frequency and/or the amplitude. That effort will be discussed momentarily.

This is the sine wave. It is like a cross sectional image of how waves move through water, and light and sound through air. Even economic trends are sinusoidal.

Application of the sine wave

Now, the area of primary school instruction that is really in error, due to simplification, is the idea that the Moon goes around the Earth, and that it does so in a circle. Again, we need to give younger minds simpler explanations of things. But, eyes become wide open when we explain to high school students how the Moon *really* moves.

When the Moon is new, that means that it is between the Sun and the Earth, as suggested in Figure 15a, though the scale is of course not accurate.

Figure 15a The new moon.   Figure 15b The first few days.

Now, imagine the Moon going around Earth, but the Earth is also moving. Let's look again after about three or four days (Figure 15b). This is when the Moon appears as a backwards "C" in the hours just after sunset. Note that x marks the starting points for this cycle. Let us continue the Moon's movement to the first quarter (Figure 15c).

Figure 15c The first quarter.

Figure 15c shows the first quarter, when we see the Moon as a white "D". We will continue these motions to the full moon, and the last quarter when the Moon looks like a backwards "D".

In going around the Earth, a new Moon must overtake it, passing finally in front of it. After the last quarter, the Moon slows down but is still moving forward around the Sun, having never actually circled the Earth at all. More, it weaves round the Earth's path. If the diagrams are not clear, then Figure 16a should show in good enough approximation the apparent path of the moon.

Figure 15d The Full Moon.   Figure 15e The last quarter.

We see the Earth's orbit as the fairly circular ellipse and the dance with this path made by the Moon. No moon truly makes circles or ellipses around their planet. They all orbit the Sun, in a path which is modified by the passage of the planet. That orbit has a wavelike motion. Note, too, that the planet's orbit is gravitationally affected and so will also have a sinusoidal nature.

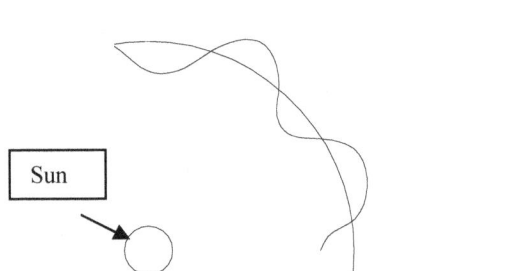

Figure 16a Apparent path of the moon.   16b Serpent mound – (Squier and Davis).

More interesting still is Figure 16b, of a place called Serpent Mound, in southern Ohio, in the U.S. "As above, so below."

There are many things interesting about this mound, as Chapter 7 noted. The construction is ingenious, and if the Native Americans from this time had established that the moon traveled in this sinusoidal course, that is pretty fascinating.

These events have to be witnessed to confirm them. Personally seeing the winter solstice sunset was pretty amazing as the knife of the sun's last rays laid across that spiral.

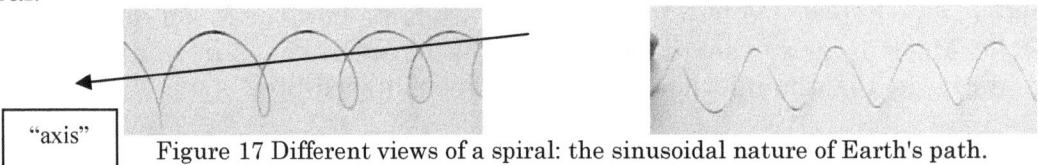

Figure 17 Different views of a spiral: the sinusoidal nature of Earth's path.

And even still, this model of the Moon's "orbit" is in error, for the Sun *moves*. In Figure 15, we must imagine the Sun as though coming out of the page. Each day, the plane that it rides upon, rises with it. That means Earth and its Moon come too. The Earth's path, looking down from above, looks like a circular ellipse. But, in reality it is like a spring. We can imagine Earth moving about on the edge of the spring, shown in Figure 17. The sun would be moving along an axis at its center.

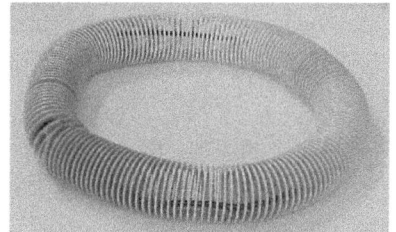

Figure 18 Earth's path through space?

Rotate the image of Earth's motion to see that it is spirallic. In side view, it essentially looks like a sine wave. We say that electromagnetic waves travel like a sine wave. But, is it two dimensional (flat) or three, like a "slinky"? Planets and moons move in this fashion.

And, very slowly for the Earth, that spring curves around the Sun's elliptical orbit, reflecting more some very large torus, which completes its revolution in 25,920 years.

Time and distance

We can note that the time for the precession of the equinoxes to pass through one sign of the zodiac is 2160 years and the total journey is 25,920 years. The Moon's diameter is about 2160 miles and the Earth's circumference is approximately 25,130 miles. The times and distances are close approximations of each other. Were ancient astronomers/geographers choosing to measure time and distance with a 12- and 360-based scale so advanced as to establish these relationships? This is part of why it is sad that many 12-based numbering systems have disappeared.

When we look at our solar system, it is amazingly mathematical. Kepler showed that pairs of planets are in sync with how long it takes to orbit the Sun, and with their average radial distance. Part of this we looked at in the chapter on Φ.

Figure 19 The Cosmographical Glasse (William Cuningham, London, 1559).

Now let's look at the number of days in a moon cycle (from one full moon to the next, *and* one rotation on its own axis) and number of years in Saturn's orbit around the Sun (29.5). If we multiply by 2, we get the rotation of Mercury on its axis: 59 days, and by 3, we have its orbital period: 88 days. Too, it is not so much 9 months for Human gestation, but 9 moons of 29.5 days. (Doctors count nine months from the start of the last menstruation, not the date of impregnation.) Is it possible that within our solar system, 29.5 is a scale of time measure?

Planetary alignments

One thing interesting to astrologers and astronomers is when planets seem to line up in the sky. This occurs, just like when we have new and full moons, and is predictable. Let's begin with the innermost planet and our Earth. Mercury orbits the sun in 88 days, during which time Earth goes almost ¼ of its orbit. Mercury must then "catch up". It takes Earth a bit more than 182 days to complete half of its orbit. During Mercury's second orbit, and still in Earth's first, they align again.

In Figure 20a, the Sun is the central circle, ringed by Mercury's orbit and the outer arc a portion of the Earth's path. It is obvious that Earth will make some amount of angular rotation, which we will call "x". Mercury will make one revolution plus this x. We multiply them by their rates, as follows: $365.25(x) = 88(x + 1)$.

Doing the algebra results in $x = .3174$ rev. This is the fraction of a revolution which Earth has made, which when multiplied by 360, gives the angular rotation of 114.3°. When multiplied by 365.25, it makes almost 116 days (four times 29.5).

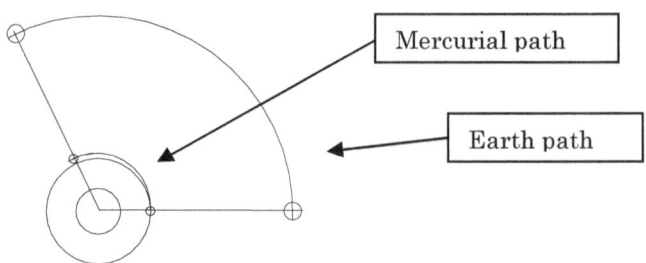

Figure 20a Mercury and Earth's journeys around the Sun.

We can go through similar calculations for Venus, but again we must think first. If Venus takes 224.6 days to go around the Sun, this gets a little complicated to map out. Earth will have completed more than ½ revolution in this time. By the time Earth has made one revolution, Venus will have made: 365.25/224.6 = 1.626 revolutions. In other words, Venus is still trying to catch the Earth. By the time Earth goes around twice (730 days), Venus will have circled more than three times (requiring only 674 days), indicating that they met between one and two Earth revolutions. So now, we use for Earth's path, "x + 1", and for Venus; "x + 2".

Our formula looks like: 365.25(x + 1) = 224.6(x + 2) , and x = .597. So Earth goes around 1.597 times, and Venus 2.597. This means that they meet at 360 degrees, plus 215, or about 583 days.

Earth and Mercury, while aligning each 116 days, align for the fifth time in about the same amount of time for Earth and Venus. Much of this work is calculation, but there is also a lot of logic required.

Students can go through similar processes for other planets, like how Jupiter and Saturn align. Jupiter, orbiting in approximately 11.862 Earth-years, circuits more than once during Saturn's 29.458 years. So, our formula looks like the following: 11.862(x+1) = 29.458x. The result is that the planets meet again after 0.674 Saturn orbits, occurring about 19.86 years, and just over 240° after their last alignment.

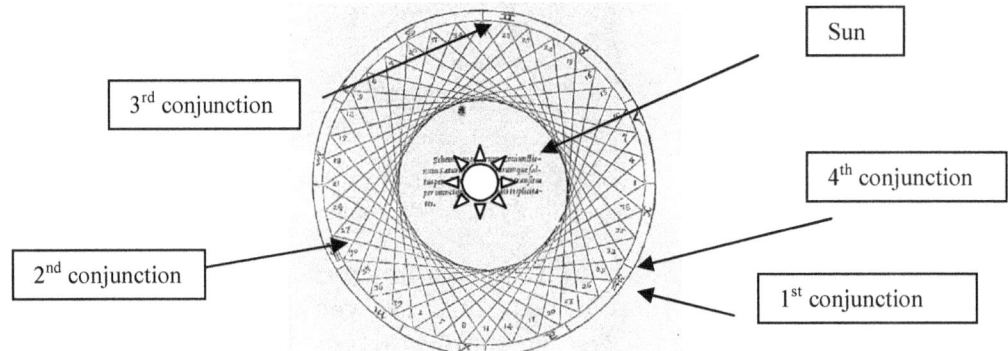

Figure 20b Conjunctions of Saturn - Jupiter (Kepler, Mysterium Cosmographicum).

Note that for the case of Earth and Mercury, and here for Jupiter and Saturn, an equilateral triangle, with the sun in the center, demonstrates approximately where these planets will start and finish, as the angles are very near to this spacing.

What this means for Jupiter and Saturn is that they will realign with the Sun at nearly their "original" starting point in just under 60 years. Actually, they will be about 8° past this point in space. Kepler noted this with the diagram in Figure 20b.

Figure 21 Is there some significance to a great cycle? (National Archive, AP).

When we see that Jupiter's orbit is approximately twelve of ours, that Saturn's is nearly thirty, and their meetings occur after twenty years, we could wonder if this isn't part of what lies behind our number systems, noted in Chapter 6.

A few months shy of 60 years is not only the years when the gas giants realign. It is a Great Cycle in the Chinese calendrical system, which just happens to coincide with the duration of time between the attack on Pearl Harbor, December 7th 1941, and that on New York, September 11, 2001. Now *that* is Algebra.

Geometrical planetary dances

Kepler demonstrated with his nested Platonic solids that planetary spacing seemed to adhere to a model. He took one form, circumscribed a sphere around it, and then put another form about this; so the sphere was inscribed (actually a good approximation). In his laws, he showed that ratios of orbital periods and radii from the Sun, for any two planets, were mathematically related. There is further mathematics involved.

Figure 22a shows (as do all of these to an accuracy of 99.5% and greater) the relative orbits of Mercury and Venus around the Sun. Figure 22b is given from a geocentric perspective. The inner circle represents the Sun's apparent orbital path and the off-centered circle is that of Venus. It is interesting that as Venus and Earth align five times in eight years, their conjunctions will also follow five-point geometry. Figure 22c demonstrates the relative orbits of Jupiter and Earth around the Sun. Here, we see six-point geometry, coincident to the fact that Jupiter's orbit is almost 12 Earth years.

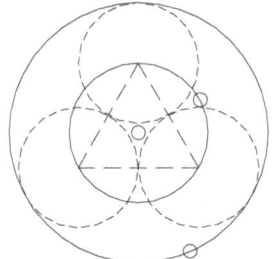 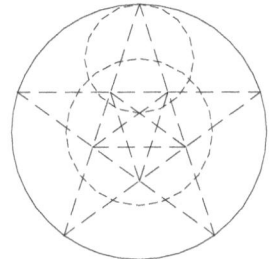 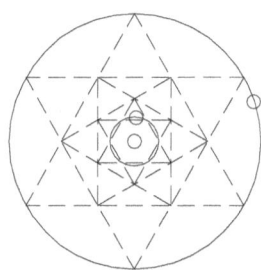

Figure 22a-c Geometries found in certain planetary spacings in the Solar system (courtesy John Martineau).

In Figure 22d we see two ways of expressing the relative orbits of Earth and Mercury around the Sun, noting how the orbit of Mercury meets the intercepts of the 5-pointed star and touches tangentially inside the 8-pointed star. Of further interest is that these diagrams also represent a comparison of the relative sizes of these two planets.

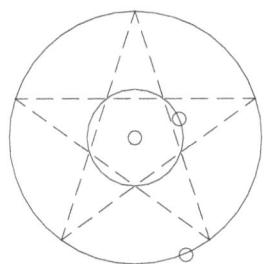 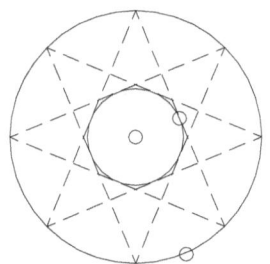 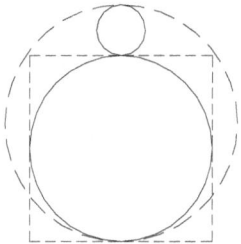

Figure 22d Delineation of orbits of Earth/Mercury (Martineau).   Figure 22e Relative Earth/Lunar sizes.

Figure 22e demonstrates the relative sizes of the Earth and the Moon (an 11:3 ratio). Here, the square and circle are of equal circumference/perimeter. Also, the diagram is strangely reminiscent of da Vinci's Vitruvian Man.

As we do our geometric drawings, trying to pull in student interest and intelligence, we can weave in these interesting arrangements found within our solar system.

Other trigonometric functions

There are six trigonometric functions, and we have worked with one so far. Oh no. Does this mean that we are going to have to *endure* reams and reams of further text? No. As the nurse says, this won't hurt a bit. Let's see what the graph of y = 1/sin x would look like. Why? Why not? This is the equation for the cosecant function. Essentially, all of the values we have on our trig table under sine must be inverted. Let's start this in table 3.

θ	Sin θ	Csc θ	θ	Sin θ	Csc θ
0°	0	Undef.	120°	√3/2	2√3/3
30°	1/2	2	180°	0	Undef.
45°	√2/2	√2	270°	-1	-1
60°	√3/2	2√3/3	360°	0	Undef.
90°	1	1			

Table 3 Cosecant values.

We see that we get into trouble when x, or θ, equals 0°. This is why 1/0 is such a great concept for students to grapple with. Here again will be asymptotes. Graphing the first few points rapidly gives the possibility to concentrate only on key points where the value is ± 1 or undefined. Thus our graph looks like Figure 23a.

We can go through a similar process to obtain the graph of the tangent and cotangent functions. They are reminiscent of the functions x^3 and $-x^3$, contained within asymptotes. Again, the students have the opportunities to see why 1/0 is such an issue.

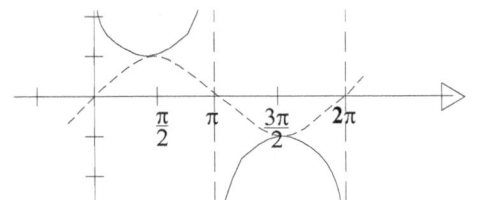
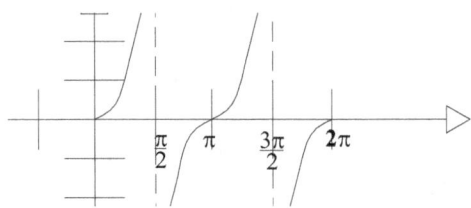

Figure 23a Graph of the cosecant function.   Figure 23b Graph of the tangent function.

The students often ask, "Why do we have to do this stuff?" The answer to that question, time and again, is threefold. Either they are being given the chance to learn something which is a building block for higher concepts, a direct application of a physical application, or a chance to develop higher thinking faculties. The graph of the tangent function might not seem like much, but understanding the numbers and creating a visual representation works those brain synapses. It's what separates us from worms.

AM/FM radio

Remember those days of our own youth where we stayed up late, when our parents were gone, and saw the "Outer Limits" on black and white television? I remember each time I teach this section, the quote; "We can control the vertical and the horizontal." All the producers were doing was to film an oscilloscope, which was being adjusted in real time. Essentially, they were changing the frequency and amplitude of a given signal. Amplitude Modulation and Frequency Modulation are radio terms which our students will recognize and we can show how to create them both mathematically. For the former we should again make a graph of y = sin x. Draw lightly. Next, create a table of values, for the equation y = 2 sin x. This is fairly easy and won't be shown here. The graph in Figure 24a shows that amplitude has doubled.

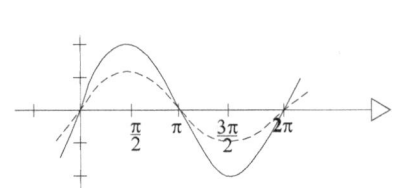
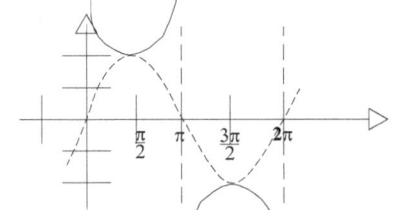

Figure 24a 2 sin x.   Figure 24b 2 csc x.

We can see that as the cosecant graph follows the sine function, to graph 2 csc x we need to either draw the corresponding sine function first (the easier route), or "simply" expand the known cosecant function. How does 2 tan x look? (What does $2x^3$ look like? - steeper)

θ	2θ	Sin2θ	θ	2θ	Sin 2θ
0°	0°	0	120°	240°	- √3/2
30°	60°	√3/2	135°	270°	-1
45°	90°	1	150°	300°	- √3/2
60°	120°	√3/2	180°	360°	0.
90°	180°	0			

Table 4 Sin 2x.

What happens if x doubles? For this, we make again an x-y table (Table 4). We see from the chart that we obtain the usual points, but as we graph them, we see that we have completed one cycle in half the distance, or more appropriately, half the time. So, two waves could occur where one did before. It is two times more frequent, with half the wavelength. In music, we would express that it has twice the pitch or is an octave higher.

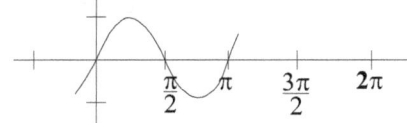
Figure 25 Sin 2x.

We can provide further problems like this, experimenting with tan 2x, csc 3x, or sin x/2 for example. The key is to determine where the max/min points, zeroes, and asymptotes are. Too, odd numbers are fun in that we must change our graphic scale from 1/4 of 2π to 1/3 and 1/6.

Phase shift
We have yet to graph the cosine function. Let us do so now in Figure 26a, again using fractions of π as our reference points along the x-axis.

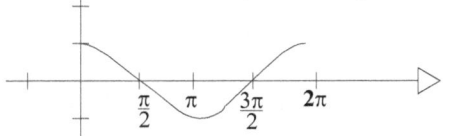 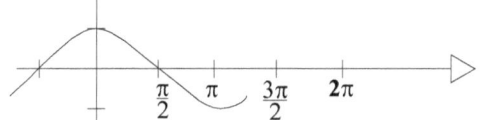
Figure 26a Cosine x.   Figure 26b Cos x = sin (x+90°).

Interesting is not just that this looks like the sine wave. It *is* the sine wave, shifted along the x-axis. How much? (90° or $\pi/2$ radians) We express this, as always, by adding or subtracting within the parenthesis, another application (sin (x + $\pi/2$) = cos x).

Continue with; tan (x-90°), 3 sin (x+45°), 2 sec (x-30°), 2 sin (x-$\pi/2$) and more lovelies from the textbook, while demonstrating with an o-scope in physics class. Then, introduce the monsters, like 3 csc 3(x - π/3). Enjoy. Of course, adding or subtracting a number from the total shifts the entire image up or down along the y-axis (Sin (x – h) +k).

Any textbook will have loads of these problems, but are often short on "text": explanations and diagrams that help or make the material more real.

Graphing trigonometric functions is another rewarding and fulfilling mathematics process. Seriously, again, we see that every line has an equation and every imaginable equation generates some kind of line. Visual mathematics does capture certain students who don't do so well with this subject. Perhaps the genius of Descartes.

Polar graphing
There are exceptional opportunities to further student understanding of trigonometry, and connections to art, which we have been trying to make throughout this text. As we are challenging the students to expand their knowledge, let's further this by getting them out of "masculine" - rectangular, Cartesian coordinate systems and into "feminine" - circular, polar systems.

We return to the equations $x^2 + y^2 = r^2$, cos θ = x/r and sin θ = y/r, also using the latter as: x = r cos θ and y = r sin θ.

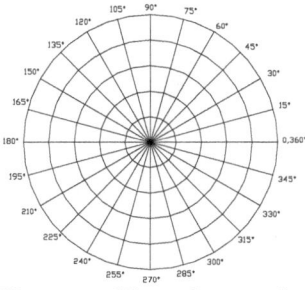
Figure 27 The polar graph.

195

How do we graph something on a circular plot? Let's start by making one. It's fairly easy for the students to do this on their own by drawing concentric circles and dividing the circles to make 12 lines across them. We see a grid like a radar screen, which is an accurate representation (Figure 27).

How does one find a point in this system? They need a distance from the center; radius, and an angle from a reference line. Here, the trick is that in mathematical and architectural applications, the reference line is the +"x" axis, and +rotation is counter-clockwise. To complicate things, physics and navigation use clockwise as +rotation, and north (+"y" axis) is the reference for 0°. Well, we have no choice but to work with them using both. In polar graphing, we depart from (x,y) and go to (r, θ) coordinates, where θ is once again in degrees.

One of the fascinating things about polar graphing is that we readily see that + and − rotation can deposit us in the same place, as can multiple revolutions. Further, radius can equal "0", meaning for example that (0, 30°) will be in the same place as (0, -45°). Also, "r" can be negative, showing finally that when doing the Pythagorean Theorem and taking the square root, we must consider ± r. This means for example that (-5,90°) is found by rotating 90°, following this line across the origin and out 5 units.

To understand polar graphing, let's convert a rectangular point like (4,3). Using the Pythagorean Theorem, we find r is 5. With the inverse tangent, we calculate θ to be 36.9°. Graph this point on the polar graph we made. Graph others, for practice. Convert back to Cartesian. Do negative angles. Do '0' and negative radii.

We will try to make a graph using polar coordinates and equations. For this, we will make our usual "x/y" table, just as always when facing a new situation. But, this time, the table will be different. Given the equation; $y = 5 \cos 3\theta$, let's begin to fill in our table with various angle measures to see what it does for us. Because it is a very unique graph, we will take a lot of points for this first attempt.

We generate Table 5 by using the trig tables we made earlier. Take a given angle, multiply it by 3 and calculate the cosine of the product. (For values greater than 360°, we "merely" repeat.) This answer must be multiplied by the coefficient of 5, which happens to be our radius. This is tabulated, presenting a confusing list of numbers. But let's endeavor to graph them. Take a given θ (not 3θ.) and the final result and plot them as a pair.

θ	3θ	5 cos 3θ	θ	3θ	5 cos 3θ
0°	0°	5	135°	405=45°	3.5
30°	90°	0	150°	450=90°	0
45°	135°	-3.5	180°	540=180°	-5
60°	180°	-5	210°	630=270°	0
90°	270°	0	225°	675=315°	3.5
120°	360°	5	240°	720=0°	5

Table 5 Guide used in our first polar graph.

Begin at zero or the initial axis, and count out five units. Then, the next point is (0, 30°). We need to imagine clocking upward by 30° but then plotting a point at the origin. Next, we take the points (-3.5, 45°) and (-5, 60°) and plot them. Here, we must rotate the first angle; 45° and now trace that line, across the origin and out 3.5 units. *This* is how we use a negative radius.

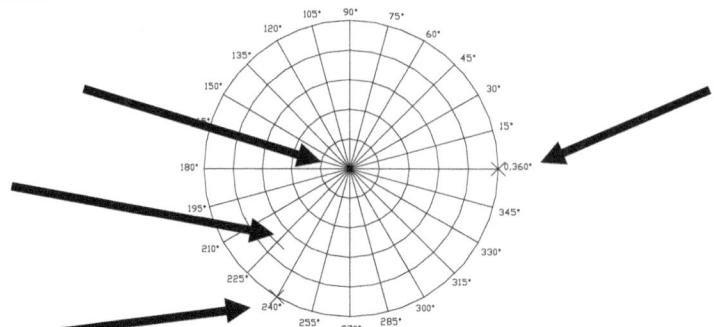

Figure 28a, starting to graph the polar equation.

In Figure 28a, the first few points are graphed. The students should see the need for more information between 0° and 30°. Using 15° helps further define the curve (also 75°

and 105°). From these, a rough idea of the shape should be discernable. The rest of the information can be used to graph the remaining points. Most importantly, have the students draw the shape in the order that it develops, so they see how graceful it actually is. Too, they will see that it repeats, thus overwriting itself. The will have generated the triskellon. If we then draw the negative of this equation, we mirror the form.

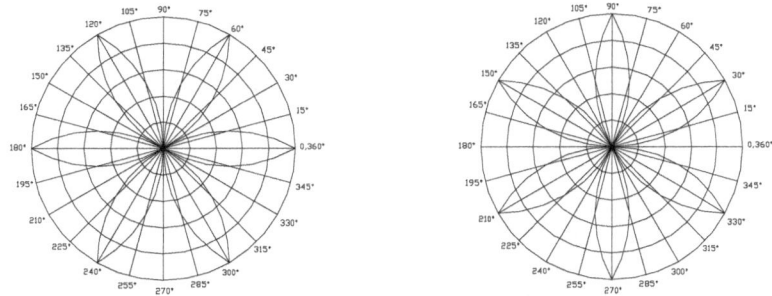

Figure 28b Old "friends": the daisy — $y = \pm r \cos 3\theta$ and $y = \pm r \sin 3\theta$.

Our result is the daisy we drew in Chapter 1. Conversely, graphs $5 \sin 3\theta$ and $-5 \sin 3\theta$ create the same figure, only rotated (Figure 28b).

This is one result. Try something further, such as $y = 3 \cos 2\theta$. For this we should make another table (for now). The result is shown in Figure 28c. Students should be given a variety of graphs to work with. This is work for which our students will appreciate our care.

θ	2θ	3Cos2θ	θ	2θ	3Cos2θ
0°	0°	3	135°	270°	0
30°	60°	1.5	150°	300°	1.5
45°	90°	0	180°	360=0°	3
60°	120°	-1.5	210°	420=60°	1.5
90°	180°	-3	225°	450=90°	0
120°	240°	-1.5	240°	480=120°	-1.5

Table 6 Guide for $y = 3 \cos 2\theta$.

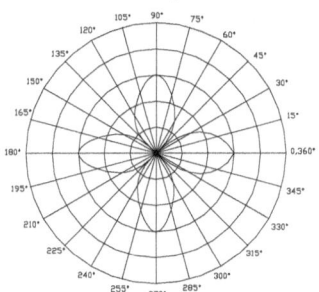

Figure 28c $y = 3 \cos 2\theta$.

At the end of this chapter are photocopy-able sheets with multiple polar graphs.

Cylindrical and spherical graphing

There are even more exceptional opportunities to further student understanding of trigonometry and art, plus geography and technical operations. We do this by introducing "can" and "ball" graphing. Students should have already been exposed to 3D Cartesian space. Bring a tin can and a globe to class. How would one determine a location on these objects?

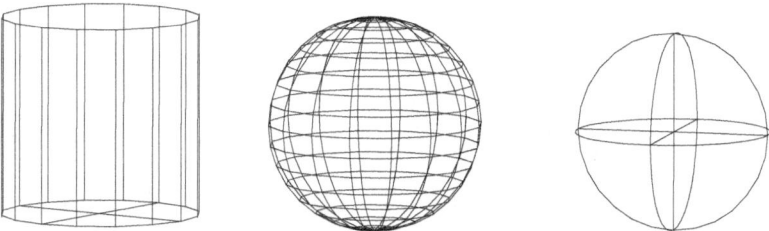

Figure 29 Cylindrical and Spherical systems (2 views).

Cylindrical and spherical systems use both Cartesian and polar graphing. By now we can understand that we need think in terms of a radial distance from a given origin, angular rotation in the plane, and then angular rotation above or below the plane.

For the cylindrical system we think of a radial distance and angular rotation within the plane, and then a height (z) above the plane. Both are shown in Figure 29.

It is possible, with architectural software, to design a cylinder, and then imagine putting a tube into this can, that enters the skin perpendicularly. This is actually a surprisingly difficult maneuver. First, the designer must create the can, specifying the radius of the base and the height of the cylinder. Then, the reference axis must be shifted to the angular location and height desired to find the correct location.

Finally, within the program, which only works in terms of x-y coordinates (the computer is after all only two-dimensional), this new point must be carefully rotated "cylindrically", so that it points in the correct direction for inserting the tube. (Even so, the cylinder will only touch tangentially on the can. So, it must be recessed a calculated distance.) Though this is admittedly a bit much for high school, showing it explains why we do these things. What if the tube enters at an angle (Figure 30)?

Have students attempt to draw a cylinder in 3D. Find points such as (3, 40°, 5) or (r, θ, h) where h is the height, or "z". Convert back and forth.

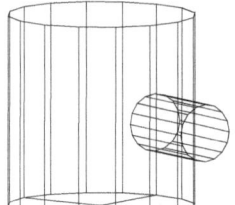 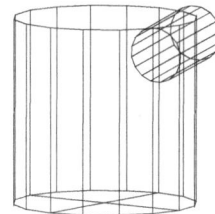

Figure 30 The can with two possible tubes. Real application.

The sphere presents its own challenges. Many students have an interest in astronomy, which is all about spherical trigonometry.

To begin, let's ask the question, how many degrees are in a given triangle? The answer is always 180°, right? Not now. Imagine if the triangle has 2 corners at the equator, separated by a ¼ of the sphere, with the third at the North Pole. The measure of this spherical triangle is 270°.

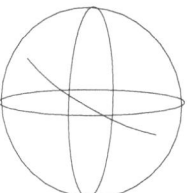 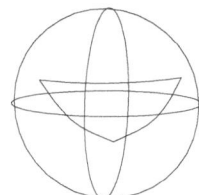

Figure 31 Spherical problems; an arc and a triangle.

Spherical math is a great culmination of trigonometry. At the high school level we will limit ourselves to determining arc length on a globe, say our own, in two cases: one in which the latitude is non-equatorial but constant, and the second being the arc between any two given points.

We begin with Figure 32a, to determine the length of arc CD. Using the equation for arc length $s = \theta r$:

arcs CD = RC•∠CRD   and   AB = OA•∠AOB

Clearly, ∠CRD and ∠AOB are congruent and that lines RC, RD are parallel to OA, OB, respectively.

RC and OR are perpendicular, so RC = OC•Cos ∠RCO.

∠RCO is congruent to ∠AOC due to parallel lines, so: RC = OA•Cos ∠AOC.

What this means is that the radius at a given latitude of a sphere is the spherical equatorial radius times the cosine of the latitude.

Now that we have the radius, we can obtain the arc length, given an angle of rotation. For example, Earth's radius is 4000 miles. What is the circumference of the globe at 38.5°N? Another example: Jupiter's great red spot is located at 21°S on the planet, and covers an arc of 12°. Given Jupiter's radius of 42,000 miles, how long is the spot?

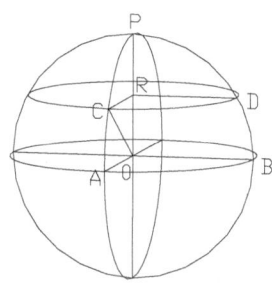 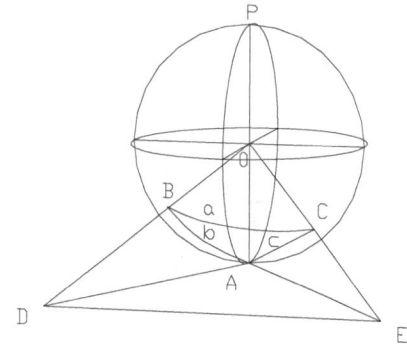

Figure 32a Lateral arc   Figure 32b Spherical arc

This process was actually rather simple, using basic geometric rules of parallel lines and angles, drawn on a spherical diagram. It is a great warm-up to finding the distance between any two points, here labeled B and C in Figure 32b. We will use a great application of trig identities to "simplify" this process.

The trick is not solving a spherical triangle, but to project it onto a plane as a flat triangle. We will use a, b, and c to denote angles for arcs BC, AB and AC, respectively, and A as the planar angle directly beneath "a".

We start with: AD = OA·Tan b   OD = OA·Sec b
                AE = OA·Tan c   OE = OA·Sec c

Let that one sink in for a moment, checking the trigonometric grammar. Let's introduce here and use the Law of Cosines to obtain the following:

$DE^2 = AD^2 + AE^2 - 2AD \cdot AE \cdot \cos A$ and $DE^2 = OD^2 + OE^2 - 2OD \cdot OE \cdot \cos a$

Pause again to verify. Substitute for AD, AE, OD and OE:

$DE^2 = OA^2 \cdot \tan^2 b + OA^2 \cdot \tan^2 c - 2OA \cdot \tan b \cdot OA \cdot \tan c \cdot \cos A$ or
$DE^2 = OA^2 \{\tan^2 b + \tan^2 c - 2\tan b \cdot \tan c \cdot \cos A\}$ and

$DE^2 = OA^2 \cdot \sec^2 b + OA^2 \cdot \sec^2 c - 2OA \cdot \sec b \cdot OA \cdot \sec c \cdot \cos a$ or
$DE^2 = OA^2 \{\sec^2 b + \sec^2 c - 2\sec b \cdot \sec c \cdot \cos a\}$

Set the two equations equal and let the OA^2 terms drop out:

$\tan^2 b + \tan^2 c - 2\tan b \cdot \tan c \cdot \cos A = \sec^2 b + \sec^2 c - 2\sec b \cdot \sec c \cdot \cos a$

Now? Use the identity that $\sec^2 = \tan^2 + 1$, to *simplify*:

$\tan^2 b + \tan^2 c - 2\tan b \cdot \tan c \cdot \cos A = 2 + \tan^2 b + \tan^2 c - 2\sec b \cdot \sec c \cdot \cos a$

Drop out like terms: $-2\tan b \cdot \tan c \cdot \cos A = 2 - 2\sec b \cdot \sec c \cdot \cos a$

Multiply by $\cos b \cdot \cos c / (-2)$: $\sin b \cdot \sin c \cdot \cos A = -\cos b \cdot \cos c + \cos a$

Ultimately, $\cos a = \cos b \cdot \cos c + \sin b \cdot \sin c \cdot \cos A$

This is an incredible amount of work, not always possible for high school students to do. But they can participate with the development and it really opens their eyes as the teacher proceeds, for it shows real application of all of the rules and formulas that must be learned. Students get a kick out of working a problem that takes up an entire page of their notebook.

The final result is that we use this formula and more. Given a latitude and longitude for two locations, we obtain angle c by subtracting the first point's latitude from 90°. We get angle b by also subtracting the second point's latitude from 90° (it is a trick of spherical graphing that we use the complement). Finally, "A" is the angle between the two points' longitude. Once we get these values, we put them into the equation, take the $\cos^{-1}$ of the sum and we have ∠a. This is to be converted into radians, multiplied by the radius of the sphere and the result will be the arc length.

For example, the coordinates of the pyramid is 30N 31.2W, and Stonehenge is 51.3N and 1.85E. Let's find their distances.

Angles ∠c = 60°, ∠b = 38.7°, and ∠A = 33.05°

Thus, cos a = 0.8441 and ∠a = 32.4°, or 0.566 radians and multiplying by the Earth radius gives a result of 2264 miles.

Develop these formulas, as shown. Have the students copy it. There will be some that will want to go home and look more closely at this process. We can't always teach to the best and brightest, but this time we could, while giving a demonstration to the others.

With the formulas worked to their final form a junior or senior class can take latitude and longitude for different places and find the distance between them. Let the students choose the cities, where they need to find the coordinates for each and calculate. Join this effort with something from geography class.

Fun with radians

We come to another activity to show surprising things with radians. Look again at the dodecagon, divided into 12 equal pie sections, where each internal angle measures 30°. This is $\pi/6$ radians ($2\pi/12$). Two segments sum to 60°; $\pi/3$ radians ($4\pi/12$), and three segments make 90°; $\pi/2$ radians ($6\pi/12$). A pattern! Every 30° is a factor of $2\pi/12$.

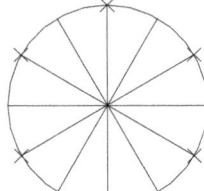

Figure 33 Dodecagon.

Let's now have the students go from any of the side points and draw lines to two vertexes on the other side of the polygon. We see an interesting thing occur. As shown in Figure 34a, the smallest angle is 15° or $\pi/12$ radians. Interestingly, if we use the next higher vertex, we see 30° or $2\pi/12$. If we have a separation of three vertices it gives us $3\pi/12$. The next is $4\pi/12$, and so forth, until we get to 90° and $6\pi/12$.

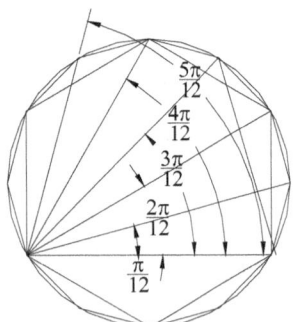 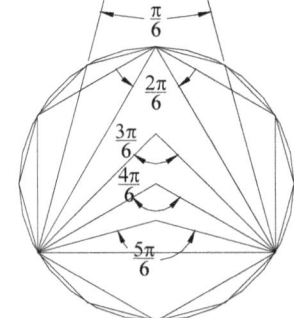

Figure 34a "Fanned" angles from a corner.   34b Corresponding "Vertex" angles.

Look at any given triangle formed by these angles, where they have a congruent angle opposite them (Figure 34b). For the case where two 15° angles are at the bottom of a triangle, the upper angle measures 150° or $5\pi/6$ radians. If both bottom angles increase to 30°, the upper is $4\pi/6$. When the bottom angles are 45°, the upper is $3\pi/6$ and so on.

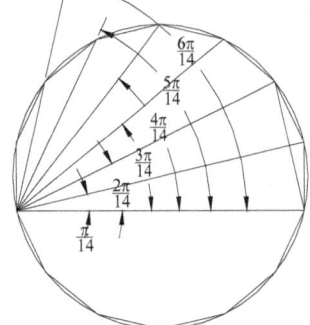 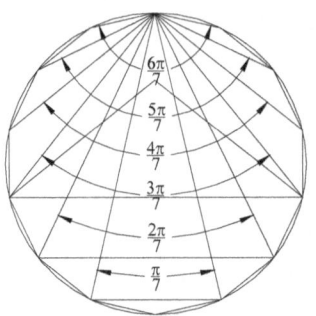

Figure 35 "Fanned" angles from a single point. Corresponding "Vertex" angles.

We can demonstrate this in any given polygon, like the 14-gon (Figure 35). How can we have students *prove* this? The interesting thing is this works for any regular polygon.

Further fun with radicals

The trigonometric identities were developed in a different age, when people sought out solutions to angles by doubling or halving them, and adding and subtracting. Strange rules were developed, like the following sum, difference, and half-angle identities:

$$\cos(\alpha + \beta) = \cos\alpha \cos\beta - \sin\alpha \sin\beta \qquad \cos(\alpha - \beta) = \cos\alpha \cos\beta + \sin\alpha \sin\beta$$

$$\sin(\alpha + \beta) = \sin\alpha \cos\beta + \cos\alpha \sin\beta \qquad \sin(\alpha - \beta) = \sin\alpha \cos\beta - \cos\alpha \sin\beta$$

$$\sin\left(\frac{\alpha}{2}\right) = \pm \frac{\sqrt{1 - \cos\alpha}}{2} \quad \text{and} \quad \cos\left(\frac{\alpha}{2}\right) = \pm \frac{\sqrt{1 + \cos\alpha}}{2}$$

One of the things that is neat about the half-angle identity is that the user has a choice. The answer will be either positive or negative, and they must decide which the case might be.

Let's go through these identities, making another table similar to Table 2. Take half-angles to get a variety of measures relating to 12ths, 16ths, and 24ths of a circle. It's great algebraic practice; these are reasonable divisions to make and they give surprising answers (Table 7). We see that series start to develop, around the ubiquitous $\sqrt{2}$ and $\sqrt{3}$. Start with 30° and calculate 15° and 7.5° (12^{ths}) and then 45°, 22.5° and 11.25° (16^{ths}).

Radians	Revolutions	Angle	SIN	COS	TAN
$\pi/24$	1/48	7.5°	$\frac{\sqrt{2-\sqrt{2+\sqrt{3}}}}{2}$	$\frac{\sqrt{2+\sqrt{2+\sqrt{3}}}}{2}$	
$2\pi/24, \pi/12$	2/48, 1/24	15°	$\frac{\sqrt{2-\sqrt{3}}}{2}$	$\frac{\sqrt{2+\sqrt{3}}}{2}$	$2-\sqrt{3}$
$4\pi/24, \pi/6$	4/48, 1/12	30°	$\frac{\sqrt{1}}{2}$	$\frac{\sqrt{3}}{2}$	$\frac{\sqrt{3}}{3}$
$5\pi/24$	5/48	37.5°	$\frac{\sqrt{2-\sqrt{2-\sqrt{3}}}}{2}$	$\frac{\sqrt{2+\sqrt{2-\sqrt{3}}}}{2}$	
$7\pi/24$	7/48	52.5°	$\frac{\sqrt{2+\sqrt{2-\sqrt{3}}}}{2}$	$\frac{\sqrt{2-\sqrt{2-\sqrt{3}}}}{2}$	
$8\pi/24, \pi/3$	8/48, 1/6	60°	$\frac{\sqrt{3}}{2}$	$\frac{\sqrt{1}}{2}$	$\sqrt{3}$
$10\pi/24, 5\pi/12$	10/48, 5/24	75°	$\frac{\sqrt{2+\sqrt{3}}}{2}$	$\frac{\sqrt{2-\sqrt{3}}}{2}$	$2+\sqrt{3}$
$11\pi/24$	11/48	82.5°	$\frac{\sqrt{2+\sqrt{2+\sqrt{3}}}}{2}$	$\frac{\sqrt{2-\sqrt{2+\sqrt{3}}}}{2}$	
$\pi/16$	1/32	11.25°	$\frac{\sqrt{2-\sqrt{2+\sqrt{2}}}}{2}$	$\frac{\sqrt{2+\sqrt{2+\sqrt{2}}}}{2}$	
$3\pi/24, \pi/8$	2/32, 1/16	22.5°	$\frac{\sqrt{2-\sqrt{2}}}{2}$	$\frac{\sqrt{2+\sqrt{2}}}{2}$	$\sqrt{2}-1$
$6\pi/24, 2\pi/8$	4/32, 1/8	45°	$\frac{\sqrt{2}}{2}$	$\frac{\sqrt{2}}{2}$	1
$9\pi/24, 3\pi/8$	9/48, 6/32	67.5°	$\frac{\sqrt{2+\sqrt{2}}}{2}$	$\frac{\sqrt{2-\sqrt{2}}}{2}$	$\sqrt{2}+1$

Table 7 Another trig table.

A selection of tangential values have been provided in Table 7. Those that are missing are no less interesting but rather ugly combinations such as $2\sqrt{2-\sqrt{3}} - 2 + \sqrt{3}$.

Let us compare the sine and cosine of 15° using not only the half-angle theorem but also the sum and difference. Suddenly, an interesting thing occurs. The answers do not seem the same, and yet...

The Half-angle Theorem works like this: $\sin 30° = \frac{\sqrt{2-\sqrt{3}}}{2}$ and $\cos 30° = \frac{\sqrt{2+\sqrt{3}}}{2}$

The Difference Theorem is as follows: $\sin(45°-30°) = \frac{\sqrt{6}-\sqrt{2}}{4}$ and $\cos(45°-30°) = \frac{\sqrt{6}+\sqrt{2}}{4}$

This means $2\sqrt{2-\sqrt{3}} = \sqrt{2}(\sqrt{3}-1)$ and $2\sqrt{2+\sqrt{3}} = \sqrt{2}(\sqrt{3}+1)$, an interesting prospect.

We can look at further arrangements. In the tenth divisions of the circle, Φ comes in, derived from the five-pointed star; bisecting the tip (36°) to get 18° and 72°. What other discoveries remain?

Radians	Revolutions	Angle	SIN	COS
π/10	1/20	18°	$\frac{\sqrt{5}-1}{4}$, $\frac{Φ-1}{2}$	$\frac{\sqrt{2(5+\sqrt{5})}}{4}$
2π/10, π/5	2/20, 1/10	36°	$\frac{\sqrt{2(5-\sqrt{5})}}{4}$	$\frac{\sqrt{5}+1}{4}$, $\frac{Φ}{2}$
3π/10	3/20	54°	$\frac{\sqrt{5}+1}{4}$, $\frac{Φ}{2}$	$\frac{\sqrt{2(5-\sqrt{5})}}{4}$
4π/10, 2π/5	4/20, 1/5	72°	$\frac{\sqrt{2(5+\sqrt{5})}}{4}$	$\frac{\sqrt{5}-1}{4}$, $\frac{Φ-1}{2}$
5π/10, π/2	12/48, 4/16 5/20, 1/4	90°	$\frac{\sqrt{4}}{2}$	$\frac{\sqrt{0}}{2}$

Table 8 Trig table based on Φ.

There are so many interesting patterns relating to √2, √3, √(2·3), √5, and Φ and numbers in general, some of which we saw while playing with bisectors and slope-tangents in Chapter 2. When we built our trig table for common angles we neglected one tangent.

Angle	Tangent value	pattern
0°	0	√(0/4)
30°	√3/3	√(1/3)
45°	1	√(2/2)
60°	√3	√(3/1)
90°	Undefined	√(4/0)

Table 9 Tangent ratios.

Further Fun with Radicals

Ah the calculator. Give a math problem and watch; as students pick up calculators, and look at them as though the answer is already printed on its face. They'll start working with it, looking for the shortest route to solve the problem. Their thinking is already limited, their hands already engaged. Instead, get them to write the problem, discern it, and come up with a solution. Is the answer the goal, or understanding?

Let's look at another place where *not* using technology gives great process, and interesting results. The reason we learn that $(a + b)^2 = a^2 + 2ab + b^2$ and that $(a+ b)(a - b) = a^2 - b^2$ is so that we apply them. As so often happens on the journey away from technology, we find amazing things if we only push ourselves a little.

It is possible to find the area of any graphed triangle formed by three intersecting lines. We must first determine the length of the sides, using the distance formula (the Pythagorean form we used in Chapter 2), which we will label "a", "b", and "c".

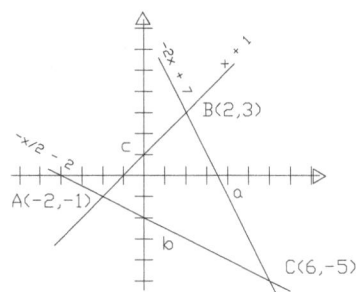

Figure 36 Three intersecting lines and their equations.

A typical problem is shown in Figure 36. The equations for doing this are as follows:

"s": $s = (a + b + c)/2$ and Area = $\sqrt{s(s-a)(s-b)(s-c)}$

Using the distance formula on the lines presented gives the following results:

$a = 4\sqrt{5}$ $b = 4\sqrt{5}$ $c = 4\sqrt{2}$ and $s = 4\sqrt{5} + 2\sqrt{2}$

Before they've obtained "s", most students have the side lengths written as rounded off decimal numbers and so obviously produce "s" as also a decimal number. This process seems very complicated, so why not make it "easier" with the tool? Let's continue without it. We are trying to figure out the area of the triangle. We need for this "s" (half the perimeter). With "s", we then place s – a, s – b, and s – c into the area equation (not hard to do if we know how to work with radicals):

Area = $\sqrt{((4\sqrt{5} + 2\sqrt{2})(2\sqrt{2})(2\sqrt{2})(4\sqrt{5} - 2\sqrt{2}))}$ Note (a + b) (a – b)!

We rewrite: $\sqrt{((4\sqrt{5} + 2\sqrt{2})(4\sqrt{5} - 2\sqrt{2})(2\sqrt{2})^2)}$ = $\sqrt{((80 - 8)(8))}$ = $\sqrt{576}$ = 24

We have obtained a whole number solution! Typical problems of this nature will give whole answers. Why not teach in this manner, stressing process? Not one student will have gotten such an ultimately simple answer using their calculator.

Given a senior project of displaying what they'd learned through the semester, none of my "superior" students took the initiative to solve such a problem without use of the calculator. But one, a brilliant artist, who has struggled throughout life in mathematics, was willing to work this technique. This individual could not pass a typical mathematics test with more than 10% at the beginning of our work together, horribly mixing the jumble of rules and formulas. With time results have improved to 40% on tests, and effort and interest have become exemplary. This represents tremendous progress. Given graphing; a visual form, they tested at over 60%, and better than half of the class.

We can teach mathematics to a broader spectrum, encourage thinking, and derive an incredible feeling when we see someone achieve, push themselves further, and believe that they can do it. This is mathematics we can be teaching; whereas standardized curriculum, to classes of over 30 human beings, takes joy from teaching, and learning.

Final fun

Imaginary numbers is one more avenue in which we can play: $(a + bi)^2$ or $(a + bi)^n$! Again, this is why we learn these steps in algebra. Applying this to for example $(1+3i)^2$ and $(1 + 3i)^3$, we obtain; $-2 + 6i$ and $1 - 27i$, respectively. Enjoy this with your class.

Concluding dialogue

We have seen throughout this book deepening use of $\sqrt{2}$ and $\sqrt{3}$ in key angles, through fractions, drawings, paper, and Zome/Astro-logix constructions – and now sinusoidal graphing. How has this work tapped upon the different intelligence types outlined in chapter 5? What is surprising to the reader about the applications of the sine wave?

In Figure 36, we see armillary spheres. These are devices which we could construct, with our students, to further understand the movement of the heavens, and a whole lot of geometry.

Figure 36 Illustrated Book of Celestial Phenomena (1633)   Coelifer Atlas (Cuningham, London 1559).

Polar graphs are included on the last page as Figure 37

Class Exercise 1 **Introduction to Foci**

Objective:
Develop understanding of the conic sections with hands-on learning and practical applications.

Procedure:
a) Have students choose and research a topic: how do magnifying glasses, eyeglasses, optics, telescopes, microscopes, satellite dishes, curved acoustic chambers or very large array (VLA) function? Give class time to find info. Note the relationship between the curve and point of focus. For homework they should copy or print a good picture or diagram and paste it into their notebooks with a brief description on how it works.
b) Review with students how to graph parabolas and circles, from the respective equations: based at the origin, and shifted away
c) Draw a curve and explain how the focus relates. Explain numerical relationships found in a parabola: e.g. the equivalent expressions $2(x-1)^2 - 1$ and $2x^2 - 4x + 1$. Show how terms 'a', 'h' and 'k', can be used to get the vertex, intercepts, and the focal point of the curve, and remind how 'a', 'b', and 'c' provide information for obtaining x- and y-intercepts. Use textbook equations, noting the relationship between 'a' and the distance between the focus and vertex.
d) Use a board, about 8" x 11", and lay white paper on it. Have students drive a nail into the center. Tie a string to the nail, and a pencil to the other end. Draw a circle in this fashion. Now, drive two nails an inch to either side of the center and then twice again, each an inch further. Use a longer string, tied to pairs of nails, looping the pencil in it. Draw a curve, showing how successive pair of nails, further out tend to elongate the form, making an oval or ellipse. Figure 6.
e) Use equation $x^2 + y^2 = 25$ for graphing. Put it in the equivalent form $x^2/25 + y^2/25 = 1$. Make sure the students are able to understand this step. Change one denominator ($x^2/25 + y^2/16 = 1$) to see how this redefines the curve. Terms 'a' and 'b' now provide lengths along each axis and the Pythagorean theorem reveals for us the location of the focus: two of them ($\sqrt{a^2-b^2} = \pm f$). Repeat for the equation $x^2/25 + y^2/9 = 1$, to show how the numbers change the shape of the graph and location of foci.
f) Do hyperbolic equations, differing only by a negative sign. See how to graph $x^2/25 - y^2/16 = 1$, and how information now provides the slope for the asymptotes, location of vertices, and also foci. ($\sqrt{a^2+b^2} = \pm f$)
g) Do shifted centers: $(x-h)^2/a^2 \pm (y-h)^2/b^2 = 1$ for $a = b$ and $a \neq b$.

Homework:
Assign textbook problems after steps c, e, f, and g. Briefly check in class where students exchange papers and grade/review each other's work. Keep assignments small, so that homework and class review are quick. Those who "get it" don't need additional repetition. Those who don't can be given further problems for extra credit. Be generous on these extra efforts as the students respond to the encouragement and of course their results will improve from extra practice. So will attitude. Tremendous progress can be made.

Evaluation:
Assess completion of each step, involvement in class, and quality of work.

Bridges:
Lines and curves can be presented visually. This pulls in artistic students. Kepler's laws, radio communication, optics, etc. show that receivers, transmitters and planetary (satellite, comet, lunar) motions are mathematically defined by the same equations. Ask students questions: "What kind of ellipse has both foci at the same place?" (circle) "What is a circle with two centers?" (ellipse) "As the focus of a parabola gets further way from the vertex, what is the result?" (a flat line). "What happens as foci in an ellipse go further and further apart?" (also a line - two of them) "Is the floor of the classroom flat or curved?" (curved. The concrete, in liquid and then solid form, is gravitationally attracted to the Earth's center, and hence, curved.)

Class Exercise 2 Radian measure

Objective:
Prepare students for trigonometric graphing and rotational motion.

Procedure:
a) Review equations for circumference and area of a circle. Most won't accurately remember completely how to use the 2, π, and r. Only 'r' is a distance. Circumference is distance; area is distance "squared". So, we arrange the symbols accordingly to get C = 2πr and A = πr².
b) Introduce the equation S = θr; arc length equals the product of angle and radius. Demonstrate by drawing a 60° angle, with its arc, using a radius of 3". Figure 9. Multiply 3 x 60. Ask the students to look at the diagram and notice that the radius and arc length appear to be about the same, and yet, we have the values of 3 and 180. Explain the key idea that we rarely multiply or divide by degrees, particularly because the scale doesn't work. So we need another scale.
c) We have for this the radian. Review that a circle measures 360°, and that we can now think in terms of this being 2π radians, reminiscent of the circumference equation. So 2π radians = 360° and therefore, π radians = 180°. Further, one term 'divided' by the other equals unity. Demonstrate conversion of 60° to π/3 radians. Use this to now find that the above arc length; S, is 3" ▪ π/3 rad., simplified to π inches or 3.14". We have a value that seems realistic (and is), and the difficult idea that the unit of measure, radians, simply drops out.
d) Convert 30°, 45°, 90° and 120° to radians. Have students attempt these in class, showing that it is acceptable to leave π in the answer.

Homework:
Pull out the trig table constructed in chapter 4. Write in the radian values: fractional and decimal. Complete the entire table. Figure 10.

Evaluation:
Check tables. Allow one or more students to make a large poster for classes to come, this year and ongoing. Be generous with extra credit for this effort.

Bridges:
Graphing of trig functions, particularly the sine wave and understanding circular motion is key to advanced math and physical motion.

Class Exercise 3 **Fun constructions with radians**

Objective:
Practice using radians and discover something interesting about them in regular polygonal figures.

Procedure:
a) Draw our friend the dodecagon. Overlay a hexagon (figure 34a). From one corner of the hexagon, draw a horizontal line to another corner. From that first corner, also draw a line to the top. Recall that this angle measures 60°. Draw a line to the vertex between the two (30°). From that center, to the lower right corner, we create a 120° angle below the center, meaning each angle at the corners is now 30°. We have perfectly bisected the first angle. If we draw lines to those in between points, on the dodecagon, they also bisect perfectly. We are able to see that not only would each line fanning out from the center of a dodecagon equal 15°, so too does each line radiating from one corner to all other possible corners. Convert these angles to radians to discover what radian pattern could be contained here.
b) Draw a similar figure, this time with the lines truncating at, above or below the center, meeting a symmetrical line coming from the other side. Go through logic and calculation to get the radian measures for these angles. Another pattern (figure 34b).
c) Have the students try this on their own for an octagonal figure. Confirm their work in class.

Homework:
Assign 14- and 16-sided figures as homework, seeing if the students understand the pattern and can expand on the concept. Figure 35.

Evaluation:
Grade effort and participation in class, quality of work and effort with homework.

Bridges:
This is part of what makes mathematics so much more interesting and alive than can be imagined. Draw comparisons to fan-shaped seashells, for a biology bridge.

Class Exercise 4 **Further fun with radicals**

Objective:
Apply trig identities to discover interesting things about √2, √3 and √5 in half angles, sum and difference, and 24-, 16-, and 10- division of a circle

Procedure:
a) Take the table of Sin, Cos and Tan values for the angles from 0° to 360°. Use half angle identities, and 30° to obtain Sin and Cos for 15° and then 7.5°. Look for interesting relations. Do the same using 45° to get Sin and Cos for 22.5° and 11.25°. Guess what the values would be for 3.75° and 5.625°.
b) Do half angles to obtain the other trig ratios of 75°, 67.5°, 52.5° and 37.5°. Use logic to obtain the values for 82.5°.
c) Create another trig table, with separate sections for 24- and 16- (64) based division of the circle, for angles up to 90° (table 7).
d) Provide the values for 54° and 72° and have them obtain those of 18° and 36°, all of which are fundamental angles in the star, with surprising relations to √5 and Φ.
e) Use difference identities to get values for sine and cosine of 15°. See that they don't agree with the table. Use a calculator to find that the values actually do equate.
f) Finally, use the identity that Tan = Sin/Cos and derive the tangent for angles shown in the table, manipulating the equations so that radicals are not in the denominator. This is a great exercise.

Homework:
See that the table is completed. Have students review it and reflect upon what they find unique about it. Hopefully they will have a lot to say about √2, √3 and √5.

Evaluation:
Assess effort inside and outside of class and quality of the final product and their summaries.

Bridges:
This is part of the magic of mathematics, the way these specific irrational numbers weave in and out of the trigonometric functions, an art that is lost if we just punch out numbers on a calculator.

Class Exercise 5 Angular velocity

Objective:
Apply radians to problems of rotational velocity.

Procedure:
a) Tie a string to a lightweight object and swing it around, demonstrating angular velocity. Hold the string loosely, so that as it is twirling it is possible to pull on it, thus shortening the radius. The object seems to rotate more quickly. At some point release it. Rotational motion becomes linear! During each moment of an object's rotation, it has both angular and linear velocity: $V = \omega r$. Further, $\omega = \theta/t$: angle rotated, in radians, per unit time.
b) How fast are students moving while sitting still? The Earth spins once (2π radians) in 24 hours; ω seems quite small: $\pi/12$ rad/hour. When we multiply by Earth's radius of 4000 miles, we see that they are moving with a speed of $1000\pi/3$ (more than 1000) miles per hour! Earth is also rotating around the Sun, completing 2π radians in 365.25 x 24 hours. This extremely small angular velocity when multiplied by Earth's distance from the Sun (93,000,000 miles) makes a linear velocity essentially 66,660 mph. Do we then add the two speeds? Yes, for a person on the side rotating currently *with* the direction of travel. For someone on the opposite side of the globe, the lesser value subtracts. So, we are all actually moving, at completely different speeds.
c) Another good problem is the relationship between how fast the tire of a bicycle or car is turning and the vehicle speed. The point of the wheel touching the ground has angular and linear velocity, and the vehicle must have equal linear velocity in the other direction. Given a bicycle whose wheel has a radius of say 12", how many RPM must be developed in order to go 15 MPH? To solve with $V = \omega r$ we need to convert and divide:

$$\frac{15 \text{ miles}}{1 \text{ hour}} \times \frac{5280 \text{ feet}}{1 \text{ mile}} \times \frac{1 \text{ hour}}{3600 \text{ sec}} \div 12 \text{ inches} \times \frac{1 \text{ foot}}{12 \text{ inches}}$$

This is a valuable opportunity to show conversions, which we must use at each chance. The wheel must rotate 22 radians a second; about 3.5 revolutions (210 per minute). That's why the spokes are a blur. $C = 2\pi r$ gives the distance around the wheel of 24π inches: the distance traveled by the wheel each time it rotates. The wheel and bicycle will have gone forward (multiply by 3.5) 250 inches, or 21 feet.
d) A great bridge to this material, along with Kepler's laws of motion and problems of ellipses, is to introduce the material by showing the film "Apollo 13". Upon completing the unit show "Red Planet". Both present great technological concepts, science adventure, and real applications of physical laws. Have the students take notes while viewing, and questions on parts they want further explanation for. They will be graded accordingly. The next class, answer the questions during discussion.

Homework:
Assign various problems based on this material from appropriate mathematics and physics books. Popular topics include the Ferris wheel, planetary motion, space shuttle velocities, etc.

Evaluation:
Grade problems in class, having students write the problems on the board as the teacher checks for completion. It is important to see how they are doing with this material. Assess their involvement, interest and participation.

Bridges:
Radians and angular velocity are often not taught simultaneously in math and physics classes. Thus we miss a great chance to strengthen instruction with direct application. Science teachers often lament the poor math skills of students yet miss opportunities to work together to improve the situation. The fact is that planetary motion *is* of interest to a lot of students, as is the practical relationship between a rotating tire and its vehicle.

Class Exercise 6 **Graph of the Sine wave**

Objective:
Apply radians to graphical analysis of the sine function; spread out over a few classes.

Procedure:
a) Draw a graph whose scale on "x" is –1 to +7 and on "y" is –2 to +2. It is great when students have square grid paper in their notebooks. Use four marks to denote each unit '1'. So, the graph will actually be about 16 x 32. Take the decimal values for radians and for sine and graph the points in terms of x and y. The reason for four divisions is the relative ease with which we can thus graph 1.57; π/2, 3.14; π, 4.71; 3π/2 and 6.28; 2π (approximately). A graph like Figure 13 should be the result. This is the basic sine wave, a repetitive form under which all waves travel.
b) Do another graph but now count two squares per unit '1' and use the π fractional scale, marking only π/2, π, 3π/2 and 2π (so π/2 is basically three marks). We get the same image, with the same spacing. From now on this is the scale to be used, and we must think that for each unit 1 that we count on the y-axis, we should consider basically 1.5 units on x for each ¼ of 2π. From now on, the graphs can be smaller, but must be accurate.
c) Use an appropriate graph, and now do the Cosine function. Observe the relation to the sine graph and the idea of phase shift. Basically, the number in the parenthesis denotes a shift along x, just like other graphs we've seen. So, what will –sin x and/or 1 + sin x look like? The graph flips, or shifts just like any other.
d) Demonstrate lunar motion and Serpent Mound (figures 15 and 16). Provide pictures of DNA. Explain the real path of the Earth around a moving Sun (figures 17 and 18). In physics show sound, light, and other wave forms (particularly electricity and radio).
e) Begin to explain the other trig functions, starting with the cosecant, since it can be derived right on the Sine graph. Here, it is first a good idea to study more in depth why 1/0 is undefined. Have students graph the function 1/x, on a normal graph (figure 11). Next, have them graph 1/sinx on top of a sin wave. They should generate a table for this (table 3). Use it to then generate the cosecant graph, with asymptotes. Here, the y-scale should be larger (figure 23a).
f) Play with sin and csc functions, seeing how a coefficient elongates the graph. This is called amplitude modulation. See how the graph can be shifted up and down, or left and right (phase and amplitude shift).
g) On a new graph use the trig table to give values for graphing the tangent function. Again, the y-scale should be larger and also we have more asymptotes (figure 23b). We can further define now the remaining trig functions and their graphs.
h) Lastly, let us see what happens for Sin2x. Again make a table of values and calculations, and graph the result. The students see that all of the numbers and terms generate a variety of graphs, and that again, each symbol means something. Work through various problems from the text. This final act is called frequency modulation. Figure 25.

Homework:
Assign various problems from the text after steps b, d, g and h. Go through the work in class, letting students put problems on the board as you circulate, seeing how they are doing. Again, assign just a few, as there is a lot of drawing involved. Give follow-on assignments as extra credit (simpler and more difficult for the ability levels in the class).

Evaluation:
Assess in-class effort and participation, quality of work, and completion of homework.

Bridges:
Understanding the sine wave shows yet another form of graph, one that is cyclical. For physics, it is valuable to know that all waveforms travel in this fashion. We study y = sin x, but for the speed of sound, this becomes y = sin 400x, and for light perhaps sin 4000000x. Teach this material concurrently to physics, so that one reinforces the other.

Class Exercise 7 **Polar coordinate systems**

Objective:
Expand abilities through a new graphing system.

Procedure:
a) Introduce the polar coordinate system by overlaying concentric circles on an x-y graph. Make circles with radius 1 to 5. On the graph, plot the point (4,3) to see that it falls on the outer circle. Confirm this with the Pythagorean Theorem. Remind students that when taking a square root, we have two possible solutions; + and − . That matters now as we inform them that radius can be negative. Do inverse tangent to get the angle from the x-axis. Show that the polar coordinate for this point is (5, 36.9°). Find polar coordinates for further 3-4-5 triangles.
b) Explain how to work with negative radii, and how to convert from polar back to rectangular. Give them some polar coordinates and have them describe equivalent coordinates which have negative radii, negative revolution, and revolution greater than 360°
c) Take the sheet of polar graphs at the end of the chapter and begin to work through how to graph a polar equation. Create one of the images shown in Figure 28b, and then have the students create the other. Work with them on the graphs of $y = 3\cos 2\theta$ and $y = 3\cos 4\theta$. Figure 28c.

Homework:
Assign various polar problems from the textbook. Have them create cardioids and even lemniscates.

Evaluation:
Grade effort and participation in class. Review homework together to track progress.

Bridges:
Polar graphing relates to navigation and provides a means to graph diagrams which cannot be made on a rectangular graph. Just what artistic intelligence needs to know!

Class Exercise 8 Spherical coordinate systems

Objective:
Expand abilities through further three-dimensional graphing systems.

Procedure:
a) Introduce the cylindrical and spherical coordinate systems by drawing diagrams that represent them, asking students to think about how one would find their position on the surface of such objects. (Through a combination of radius and rotation, by a height above the plane or a second rotation on a different axis – depending on the system)
b) Draw an x-y-z graph, with the z axis denoted by drawing it down and to the left. Get the students to practice graphing a few points 3 dimensionally. The x-y coordinates are the same, but then the third component must be counted in parallel with that Z axis. See that students can draw a cylinder in 3D and that they can find a point on its surface according to (r, θ, h). Give them coordinates of (r, θ, α) and ensure that they can also graph this, now by laying the x-y axis on the plane, with Z pointing straight up. Rotate θ from the x – axis and then α above the "plane". It's tricky.
c) Draw a sphere as shown in Figure 32a and go through the steps to derive the formula; $RC = OA \cdot \cos \angle AOC$. Use this to find the arc lengths of certain factors from our solar system, like the circumference of the arctic and tropical circles, the size of the red spot on Jupiter etc.
d) Draw a diagram; Figure 32b and go through the complex steps to derive the formula; $\cos a = \cos b \cdot \cos c + \sin b \cdot \sin c \cdot \cos A$. Use this to find the arc lengths between a variety of cities on the Earth.

Homework:
Make up a number of problems for the students to work through, as there are not usually any in the textbooks.

Evaluation:
Grade effort, participation, and homework.

Bridges:
Spherical and cylindrical graphing relates to navigation, astronomy and aerospace, pop cans, parts of a car or bicycle, and further applications. Students often have an interest in one or more of these subjects.

Class Exercise 9 Planetary alignment

Objective:
Apply algebra to planetary motion as an interesting application

Procedure:
a) Present to students that planets rotate at various speeds around the Sun. Two planets that align will do so again, elsewhere along their paths after one, or both have made at least one full revolution. Try to calculate after how long this will occur. We begin with Mercury. It rotates once in 88 days, and Earth will have made about a ¼ turn in this time. Now, will Mercury make a full revolution again before Earth completes its first? (no) They will meet sooner. Since the answer is no, we can make an equation that uses their two rates: $365.25(x) = 88(x + 1)$, where x is the portion of a revolution that Earth will make. Mercury goes the same amount, plus one full turn. Have the students go through the process on their own to relate Earth and Venus, providing their orbital periods. See figure 20.
b) Let students discover for themselves further relationships with Mars, Jupiter and Saturn, each time requiring that they research the given periods and determine after how many revolutions of the quicker, and perhaps the other, the twain shall meet.
c) Obtain information about planetary distances from an astronomy book or encyclopedia. Use them to draw the geometries for the planets shown in figures 22a-e.

Homework:
Have them calculate three conjunctions of Jupiter and Saturn, arriving at a start and finishing point in the sky, and the approximate duration of three meetings. Interesting that it is very close to 360° and 60 years.

Evaluation:
Assess effort, participation, and homework quality and effort.

Bridges:
It is interesting to witness an occultation of a planet. This strange term describes the moment that the Moon crosses the path of a planet. Any two planets also align with each other at regular intervals. These astronomical activities are behind a lot of why people first studied math, hence we can bridge here to history, culture, science or other fields.

We can do this material in parallel to physics class (work with Kepler's laws), or just do it *in* physics class.

Class Exercise 10 **Wall map of the solar system**

Objective:
Creative Arts project in cooperation with Physics and Mathematics.

Preliminary:
Find a large blank wall, preferably in the Physics lab or classroom upon which a map of the solar system could be laid out. Obtain colored paints which may be applied to the wall.

Procedure:
a) List the planets of the solar system on a board, including the Sun, asteroids, and Kuiper bodies like Pluto and recently discovered Quaoar, Ersa and the unique 2003NG. Students pick a "planet" (or group of dwarf planets/asteroids) they are interested in and divide the work accordingly, ensuring every planet is covered. Measure the wall where the map will be painted.
b) Have students research their "planet": color photo, size, distance from Sun (for asteroids use Ceres, Juno and Pallas), rings, major moons (like ours, the 4 Jovian, Titan and Charon). They should even prepare a small report. Work in class and as homework. Also, they should prepare an overall design idea on how the solar system should look on the wall.
c) Review the materials the students provided, regarding size and distance of the planets, and their plan for the layout. One obvious choice is to place them in a line, trying to make the chart realistic. In our case, we used 6 meters to represent 6 billion miles to Pluto. Scaling the spacing then amazed the students with how close the inner planets are to Sun. We also scaled the planets by size, again giving interesting information.

Or, put the Sun at the center. Students need to work out elliptical paths. Make it large so as to maximize the number of people who can work at once. A great technique is to draw out the plan and project it onto the wall as a guide.

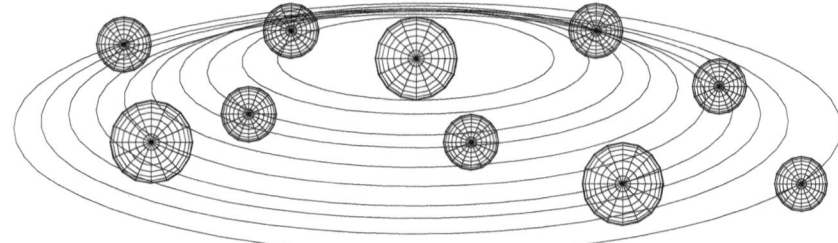

d) Prepare the design(s) from the plans submitted. Help the students measure out the wall and begin to draw their planets. At first, its very labor intensive for the teacher and a lot of students tend to not have enough to do. But, once the project is rolling, it's pretty easy to keep a large group busy.

Homework:
They will need to complete their research as outlined in step b, and also prepare a plan of how they think the solar system should be mapped on the wall.

Evaluation:
Grade effort at obtaining data and its accuracy. Evaluate participation. It is easy for them to dive in, or to sit and say, "There's no room for me to work." Grade them for how they did their "planet". Did they rush and does the result reflect this, or were they serious?

Bridges:
Hands-on creative work, that they will see regularly, knowing it is quality, and knowing that peers and subsequent classes will also admire it, is very meaningful. Combined with the work on Φ will help them see their connection to the cosmic dance. Teamwork, planning, applying arts, and using measurement and proportion, link this work across several disciplines.

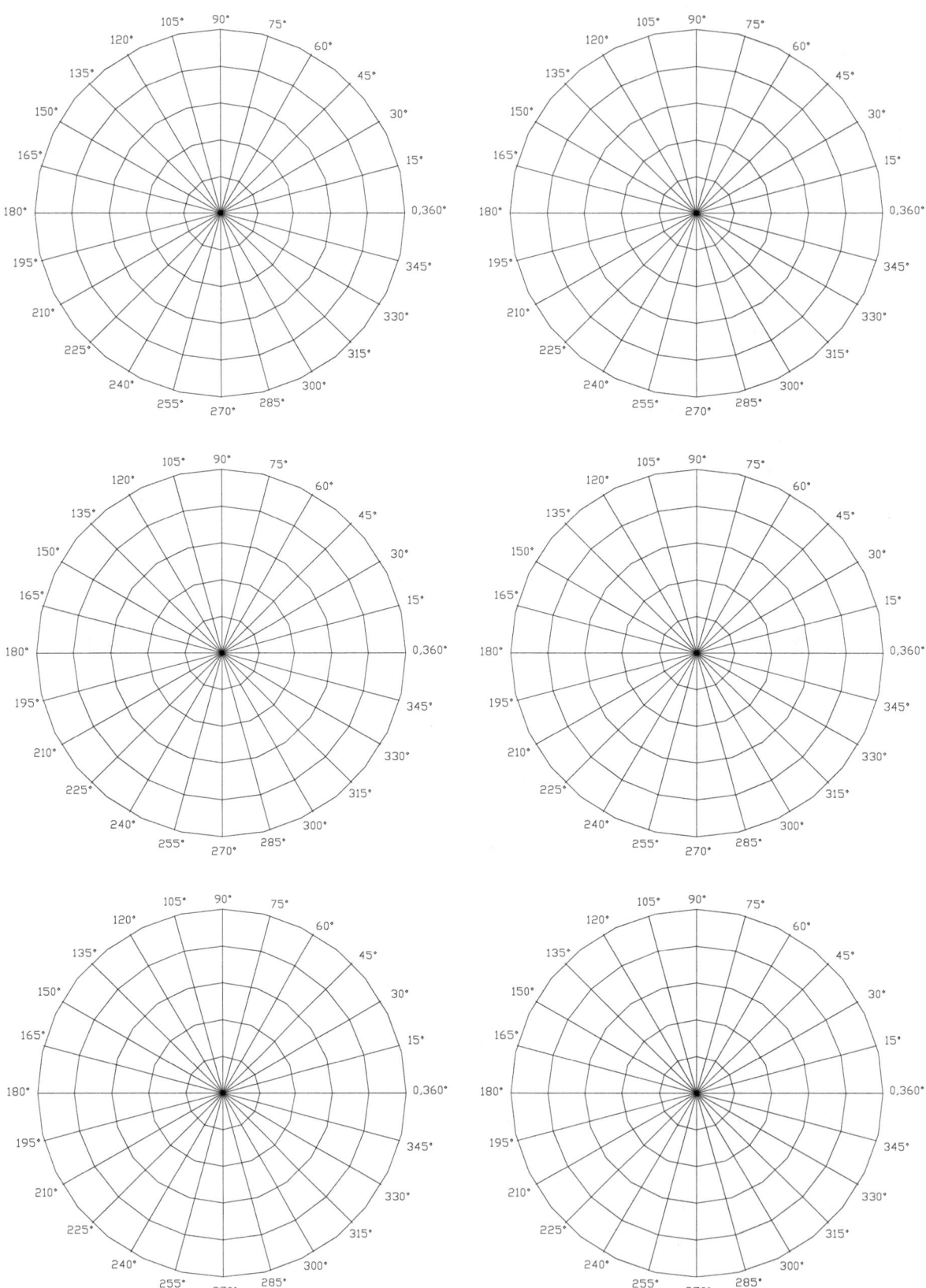

11 – Astro Logos

Opening dialogue

How can we use facets of popular culture, like astrology, for educational means? What is the etymology of this subject? What mathematics does it contain?

The science of astrology

What is your sign? Most people can answer this question. Many share a mundane interest in idly reading their horoscope each day in the newspaper. Our sign, or so-called "Sun sign", denotes one of the 12 signs of the zodiac in which the Sun was present at the time of our birth.

What does this mean actually? In Sumeria and Egypt, maybe even earlier, stargazers divided the sky above Earth's equator into 12 equally spaced segments (the Egyptians had 36, called decans). Today, we know the twelve divisions, or constellations, by such names as Aries, Taurus, Gemini, etc. These are Greek names, while the planets retain Roman names, as do days of the week; in Romance languages (English uses the Norse).

The words astronomy and astrology also come from Greek. The first, today considered to be the actual science, has the rather uninspiring translation of "naming the stars", while the latter reads as "logic of the stars". Today, most people do not consider astrology to be a serious science at all, but we will see that there are those who do.

As we look into space, above Earth's equator and in line with its path around the Sun (these are tilted by 23.5°), constellations of stars form a backdrop to Earth's orbit, at the "celestial equator". (Though Earth orbits the Sun, the opposite appears to be the case – as reflected in astrology). These are called the zodiac. There are many other stars and constellations, some recognizable even to children, such as Orion, and the big and little dippers. Stars that we see at night are on the other side of us from the Sun.

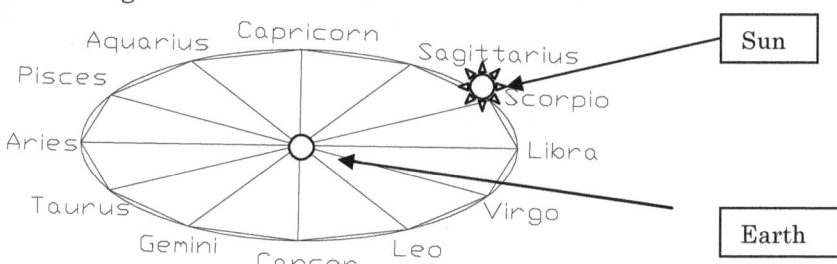

Figure 1 Earth centered perspective of Sun against a backdrop of constellations.

As Earth goes around the Sun, clocking 30° in just a fraction over 30 days, it appears that the Sun has moved into another sign of the zodiac. At night, we will see that the constellations are different from what we saw last month. For a given time, say midnight, they will have "clocked" around by 30°.

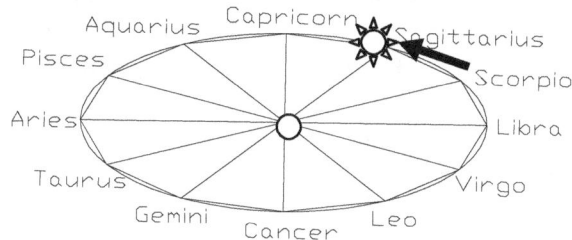

Figure 2 Earth centered perspective of Sun's "movement" against the stars.

As the Sun "enters" a sign, it means that the sunrise begins to occur there and we no longer see that constellation in our nighttime sky. (Actually, we would have stopped seeing that sign a month or more earlier as it would be very low in the horizon as the sky lightens at dawn) It is interesting to track a constellation in winter, with the longer viewing times. A good one is Orion, clearly visible in the south, near the clump of stars known as the Pleiades. In the immediate vicinity are the zodiacal signs of Gemini and Taurus. There's a big difference in Orion's position at 9 p.m. in November, compared with 9 p.m. in February.

215

By hosting an astronomy club at school, we have a great educational tool to use beside the classroom to draw in interest and show practical applications of several themes.

Knowing our "sign" is much more involved to the astrologer. Due to Earth spinning on its axis once every 23 hours and 56 minutes, it appears that the Sun has rotated around us in this amount of time, hence the long held geo-centric theory. Sun has some position in the Earth's sky at any given time of day, or night. It has therefore a specific position for each of us at the time of our birth. Does it happen to be directly overhead? This happens at, or near, 12 noon each day (1 pm in "summer" time). Is it directly underneath us, at about midnight? Is it at sunrise, or sunset, or simply any other position above the horizon or below?

The position of the Sun is not just in which of twelve monthly signs it is in but also in which of twelve two-hour time periods, called a house. Astrologers further define a person and their personality by placement of the houses, and other factors.

Figure 3 is a typical astrological chart. The outer circle or wheel shows the signs of the zodiac. Inside is a circle of numbers. These denote the "house". We see that houses are not necessarily equally divided around the sky at a given time on a particular date. The system of houses, and their calculation, is a complicated process based upon the season and time of day.

The zodiac turns clockwise, once each day, and also in each year, slowly shifting round the circle. The houses stay fixed.

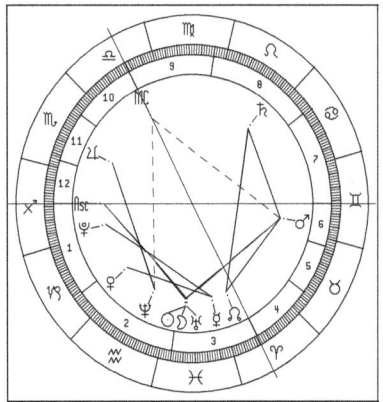 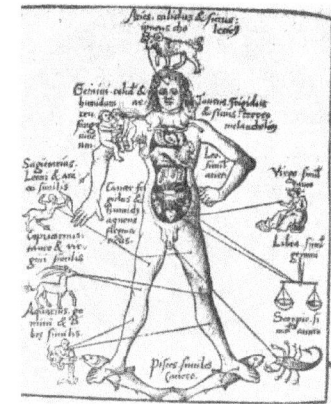

Figure 3 Astrological chart.   Figure 4 Body and zodiac (Gregor Reisch 1525).

Not just Western astrologers do this but interestingly, the Chinese system (used also in Japan and further in Asia), and Vedic system (used in India) also divide the sky similarly, also in their systems of medicine, applying each two-hour period to an organ of the body. This may seem strange to our Western culture but this is actually a 'modern' disparity. Medieval astrologers and doctors in Europe also associated parts of the body with signs of the zodiac, and planets (Figure 4).

It is well known that the Chinese also have a zodiac (the term is Greek – meaning "Animal wheel"), but with a different set of 12 animals: Dog, pig, sheep, dragon, etc. In their system, each month is named after an animal, and those same animals are used to name individual years.

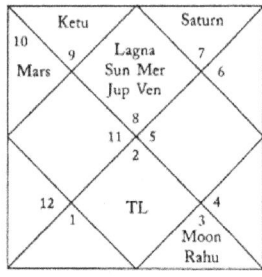 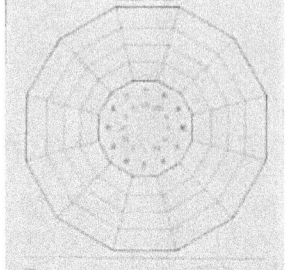 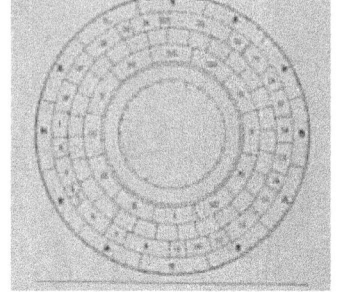

Figure 5 Indian – Vedic and Chinese astrological charts.

The Sun is indeed important, in its sign and house, but so too the Moon and other planets. (Sun and Moon are referred to as planets in astrology) In the Western system, not much is heard about Moon but in the East it is very important (there being 28 "lunar mansions" in the Chinese system and 27 in the Hindu, and their calendars are lunar in orientation – not such a strange system, as the Muslim and Jewish people to this day also use lunar and lunar-solar calendars, with alternating months of 29 and 30 days, corresponding to Moon's approximately 29.5 day period).

The study of houses and mansions is not the purpose of this chapter or this book. But, aspects of astrology are interesting and full of complicated mathematics (as are celestial mechanics). This relates to this book because again they are practical applications of mathematics and we need to understand some of the math involved here if we are going to appreciate the topic (and have a great tool for drawing in student interest).

Now that we understand something of the twelve signs of the zodiac and twelve houses, we can place the Sun, Moon and planets upon that chart. We will use the Western version, as it is more relevant to our study of angles and trigonometry.

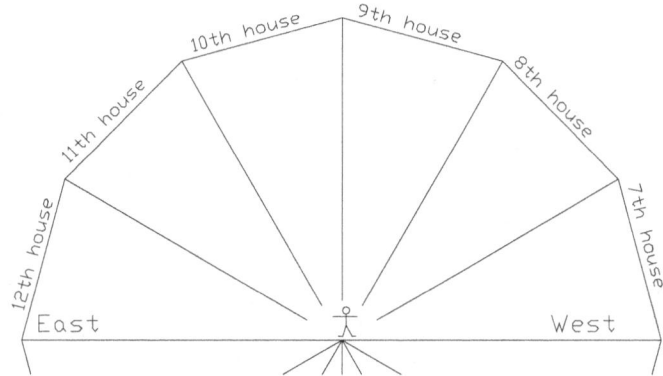

Figure 6 The "houses" overhead at our birth. The others are beneath the horizon.

When a person is born, each planet is in some angular place in the sky, around the point of birth. To astronomers and astrologers of the past (until even the recent past they were one and the same person) it seems as though the planets travel in a circle around us, except for some amount of time when they surprisingly seem to go in reverse with respect to the backdrop of stars. Geocentric astronomers came up with rather tricky means to explain these events, but when we put the Sun in the center and look at the motions of two planets, it is just what happens when the orbit of the inner planet reaches a tangential relationship to the outer. As the inner planet then races around in front of the other, it tends to create for an observer on that inner planet the impression of backward, or retrograde, movement in the other.

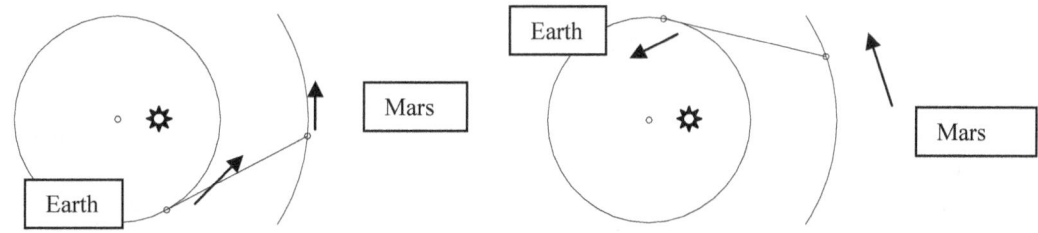

Figure 7a Tangents: Mars "goes retrograde".   Figure 7b Mars "goes direct".

Mars seems to travel from left to right (which it does) from our perspective. But when Earth reaches a point in its orbit, tangential to Mars' position, the red planet *appears* to move backward in the sky. This continues until Earth reaches another part of its orbit, as they both are in motion, where a second tangential relation occurs. Now it appears that Mars is again moving forward. Every planet, inside and outside of our orbit, appears to do this every year or so. Mercury does it several times.

Trivial and the not-so mundane

The planets have some placement on the chart at the time of our birth. Astrologers look at charts all the time. What was going on in the "sky" at the same moment an earthquake hit somewhere on earth? Is a specific date, place, and time favorable for getting married or for starting a war? It is known that many famous people such as Hitler, the Hapsburghs, and the Reagans all had their astrologers.

The planets, within the zodiac, and specific houses, are all thought to have key meanings. Are there any planets in the first house: the point just under the Eastern

217

horizon (note, left is East), where they are about to rise (hence the name ascendant)? Are they directly overhead or below or at the western horizon? Each of these is significant.

Astrologers also look at planets interacting with each other. This portion we will explore. It is of interest to us because it contains the greatest amount of mathematics.

The education of the Middle Ages consisted of two parts. Early university education focused on three subject areas (called the Trivium) consisting of grammar, logic, and rhetoric. This was in preparation to a more detailed education known as the Quadrivium, where a student was expected to study mathematics through understanding numbers (arithmetic), geometry, astronomy and music. An advanced education continued with the study of philosophy or theology.

This represents a great contrast between Then and Now. We value very little of this in modern education, focusing more on computer and information skills than real knowledge and wisdom, or God. To the medievalist, there was not our modern separation between religion and science. Today do we see both at polar extremes?

What was the Quadrivium? Understanding numbers is neither about punching them on a calculator to get solutions nor performing operations of addition or division. Throughout this book, we have shown part of the magic behind numbers. This could be further chapters unto itself. The point is, number and pattern are much more involved than is taught in school. This *is* the math we should be learning, and at times in history have been. There are further great sources of information about this topic.

As for geometry, the ancients needed it to understand stellar and planetary motion. Geometry means basically "Earth measure". With it we could build houses (a 90° wall stands better than others), measure fields, and conduct warfare. Artists need it with number theory to understand proportion. Behind every great painter there is at some point or other a geometer, as we saw with Da Vinci in Chapter 7 and here in Figure 8.

Figure 8 The School of Athens by Raphael (Vatican Museum). Notice lines to the vanishing point.

That music would be considered part of mathematic instruction is an interesting feature of this form of education.

Those who perform music may or may not know that there are tremendous mathematics involved. Who hasn't heard the term octave? The interesting thing about an octave is that in music, the notes are counted from one note to what sounds very much like that same note, but at a higher pitch, or frequency. Actually, it is at exactly twice higher frequency. In between these two notes are six other notes. Hence, "do-re-mi-fa-so-la-ti-do". What is interesting here is that there are really only seven notes, but the first note of the next octave is also counted.

Music is a great item to include in math and physics classes. What makes sound in a drum? The tension of the skin, and the shape and volume of the resonance cavity. In the stringed instruments, the tension of the string and the shape of the resonance chamber over which it is stretched and vibrated work to amplify the sound. What makes the woodwinds and brass function? The shape and volume, and hole placement with respect to the wavelengths of the complex sound waves passing through. There is no musical instrument for which physics and math are not involved in its design and performance.

Is the guitar shaped as that shown in Figure 9 so that it fits well in our lap as we play? Why then are smaller violins and larger bass instruments the same? Actually, as the figure shows, the internal geometry being circular is most beneficial to resonance, to help build the sound, just like in a grand piano, concert hall, or cathedral.

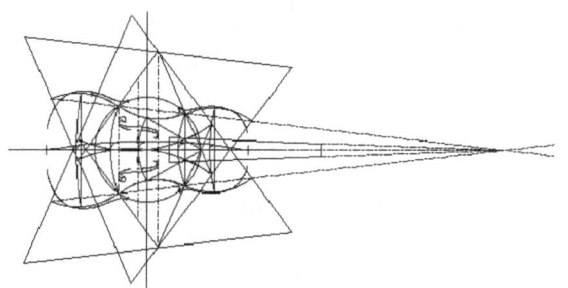

Figure 9 The geometry of a violin (Courtesy of Robert Zuger).

We will remember from earlier in this book, that many have thought the motions of the planets to have their own "music", or harmony.

Angular measure

Regarding astronomy, the fourth member of the Quadrivium, we cannot put a ruler into space, to measure planetary motion. We need to triangulate. Hence, astronomy is measurement through trigonometry: triangle measure. Our familiar, specific angles are very interesting to study.

These same angles are also pertinent to the astrologer, with respect to relationships between planetary positions, particularly angles of 0, 90, 120 and 180 degrees, and even 60 and 45. We will look at some of these in detail. Again, our purpose is not to study astrology fully but to look at how it works with mathematics and perhaps why. It is hoped that this is interesting to those who read this, and that it is therefore mathematics we should be learning.

Let's select an actual birth-chart, where the two "planets", Sun and Moon, are in line with each other. For this we will use the solar eclipse of August 11, 1999, which passed over major European cities of London, Paris, Munich, Vienna, Bucharest and Istanbul. The time shown is for the maxima which occurred over Deva, Romania. This was an exact alignment though astrologers usually consider anything within 8° of 0, 90,120 or 180 to be "close enough".

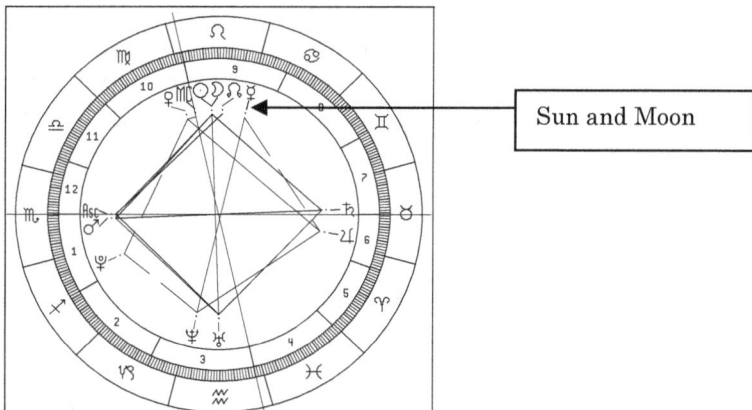

Figure 10 August 11, 1999 – Eclipse of the Sun over Deva, Romania.

When two planets are in line, on the same side of Earth, they are said to be in conjunction. This is considered to be a favorable alignment between the two, and usually mingles what are considered to be the positive natures of the planets involved. What each of the planets represents is very complex and open to wide debate.

We won't get involved with the debate because this is a mathematics book. But, there is an interesting "error" now, which we *will* address. When we refer to signs of the zodiac, we are using Greek names; the Greeks, particularly Ptolemy of Alexandria are the ones who codified for us astronomy and astrology. As we might surmise, Ptolemy garnished his knowledge from the Egyptian schools, and we can thank him, and later the Arabs, for bringing their wisdom to us. The only thing is that in Ptolemy's time, the stars worked with this system. At the spring Equinox, March 21st, the Sun was in Aries.

But this is no longer the case. What does it mean that this is the "dawning of the Age of Aquarius"? It means that soon, the Spring Equinox, March 21st, will see Sun in Aquarius. (It has been occurring not in Aries but in Pisces for 2000 years since Ptolemy)

The interesting thing to present to students is that the Sun is also moving. Its motion is also "circular", about some point in our motive galaxy, in our expanding universe. For us on Earth, it means that our reference to Sun is changing. During Ptolemy's time the zodiac worked as we consider it today: The Sun entered Aries on the 21st of March. But, every 72 years, the position of the Sun against the backdrop of zodiacal stars shifts by 1 degree, meaning the Sun would rise in Aries almost 1 day later than the spring equinox. After 2160 years, it will have shifted by thirty degrees, or almost 30 days.

Most Western astrology books don't talk about the error that they reflect in the sky. If we would choose to teach astronomy to our students, astrological tables (called ephemeredes) can help us determine in which constellation we might find a planet. The only thing is that those ephemeredes are all in accordance with some hypothetical position of the constellations. The fact is, if one expects to find a planet at the horns of Taurus, they need to look more to the tail for we are now nearly 30° out of sync.

The concept that we are entering the Aquarian Age, or so-called "New Age" is very interesting to people. Whether they believe in it or not, most have heard of it. It simply means that the Sun has actually been rising at the spring equinox in Pisces for the last 2000 years and is about to begin to do so in Aquarius. This is why the fish as an early symbol for Christianity, or the concept of "lamb of God" (God at the time was represented by Ares the Ram) are so interesting.

So, when everyone thinks they know their "sign" they are in error, in a way. If a person says, "Hey, I'm Scorpio, and that means...", they might have been born at the time of year traditionally associated with Scorpio, but the Sun was actually in Libra. Does that mean they are or aren't Scorpio? That is a question which seems to challenge the system, and is included here to challenge the "reality" we take for granted.

We could of course change the whole thing, and get it realigned. This is in fact what the Vedic system does. Theirs is probably the oldest documented astrological system (3500 years) and they have continually updated the signs of the zodiac to correspond with this action, whose name is called the Precession of the Equinoxes.

That is not necessarily suggested here, as the "energies" associated with the zodiac may relate more to what is below, on the Earth, rather than what is above, in the sky. We can consider still, if we want, that an Aries person is born in late March or early April, at a time when there's a lot of fresh energy. Perhaps we don't need to be astrologers to observe whether or not this person's behavior reflects this. For at least 5000 years Humans have developed and followed belief structures that there is something behind the planetary motions and these "yardsticks" in the sky. Perhaps we could delve into them scientifically and mathematically.

Alignments of planets: opposites

We will look at how the planets at times align with each other, and whether certain positions have meaning. The word "Planet" comes from Greek: "Planetos" means "the wanderers". Observers of the nighttime sky can see each winter Orion in the south, joined by Taurus and Gemini. Year after year, these will remain the same throughout our lifetime, and are called the fixed stars.

Occasionally, we may notice a new point of light in one of these constellations. Night after night, it slowly (or more rapidly) moves to a new position, relative to those others. It is a planet.

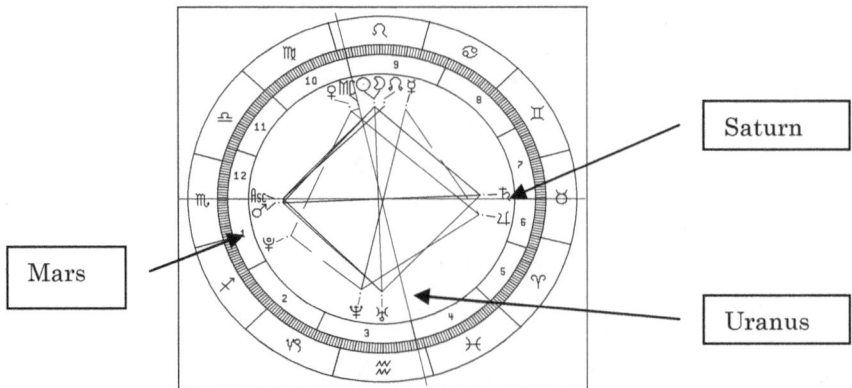

Figure 13 Another look at the eclipse chart.

On August 11, 1999, across from the Sun/Moon eclipse we find the planet Uranus. For some reason, high school students always laugh when hearing the name of this planet. Use it. Use humor every chance you can in math and science. It's harmless enough and happy students tend to be more interactive. Uranus, in this example, is what we call opposite the other two, or in opposition. Astrologers like to say that the energies of the two are in a tug-of-war. Which will it be: spirit or mind, action or inaction? We also see that Uranus and Sun are near exactly under and above us (key positions). Astrologers have explanations for all of these things and we can encourage further reading. Hosting an extra-curricular course on astrology can be very interesting to students (and hence, motivational).

See in the chart that planets Mars and Saturn are *also* in opposition, at right angles to the original "planets" under discussion. This is called a square, and like the opposition, can be considered to be a difficult time, or difficult situation to be born under.

The interesting thing about squares and oppositions are that they can combine into things known as "T-squares" and grand crosses. The chart shown above is just one such case, a grand cross. These are major astrological events, occurring at the sunrise/set and noon/midnight positions.

This eclipse was very educational personally. For one, the shadow that the Moon casts upon the Earth moves opposite to the apparent track of the skies above us. On this date, it began west of England. As the Moon moved in front of the Sun, and Earth rotated, the shadow broadened in coverage and duration at each point on the Earth. As it went East-by-southeast across Europe each place along its path saw darkness for an increasing amount of time, up to almost two-and-a-half minutes. After peaking, over the Transylvanian hills of Romania, it declined until ending around Istanbul.

We were present in Transylvania to witness this event, at a most peculiar place called Deva. What is this site doing in Europe, with the name of Hindu nature spirits? The local lore says that on the hill of Deva, the core of a long eroded volcano, there was once fought a battle between the spirits of sky and earth. It even sounds like a Hindu story. (As it turns out, the name of Deva can be found throughout Europe and Asia.)

We were witness to just such an event. Later, traveling westward by train, we were made aware that everywhere else had seen the eclipse totally, with not a cloud in the sky.

For us, under the peak of this astronomical event, we awoke to the same sunny day. But, as we ascended the mountain, clouds moved in. As the time for eclipse neared, we could see lightning flash in the far distant hills. Winds gathered around us. The fact that we were in the land that seems to still have werewolves and vampires added an eerie feel to the place. It was funny that the Romanian travel brochures were wanting to portray that the country was more than all of that but in prelude to the event, the TV stations were showing Bram Stoker's Dracula the night before.

As the time of eclipse was only minutes away, and the sky darkened, the people, sitting among the ruins of the castle atop this berg, began to wail. It was most unnerving. Lightning began to rend the sky and the wind became worse. And then, a black wall came over us. It was not only the shadow of the Moon, but a wave of lashing rain. We had hid among the walls to avoid getting hit by lightning; now we had to dive for whatever hole we could find in those walls.

It was a torrential downpour, with an electrical discharge and freak winds that lasted little more than those two-and-a-half minutes. As the shadow passed, so did the storm. We shook off and forlornly started our descent. Within fifteen minutes we were almost down and the clouds opened up so that we could see the Sun still more than half blocked. The remainder of the day was hot, dry and very still. Three days later, a massive earthquake hit Turkey, at the terminus of the shadow's path.

These events and others − through years of observation − suggest that there could in fact be something to astrology, astronomy, and planetary alignments. The question is − What?

It is obvious that the Moon and Sun have a gravitational effect upon us by the action of the tides. It should be realized that the moon is massive enough to have an effect upon our very core. Another way to shake the reality of students is to tell them that the center of gravity of the Earth is not near to the center at all. It works pretty much the same way as a lever or seesaw. From the fulcrum, $Mass_1 \times distance_1 = Mass_2 \times distance_2$.

This is a challenging equation to set up for high school students. We don't know the distance from the center of the Earth to the CG. But, we do know the distance to the moon: 3.88×10^8 meters. Knowing Earth's and Moon's mass, we can set up the following equation:

$$6 \times 10^{24} \text{ kg} \cdot d = 7 \times 10^{22} \text{ kg} \cdot (3.88 \times 10^8 - d) \text{ meters}$$

Mathematically, this works out to roughly 4500 kilometers from the center of the Earth or about 2/3 of the distance to the surface. If the Moon can move the ocean mass around the Earth, what is it doing to the molten core? Certainly, the Sun also has some pull. At times, it could balance lunar effects, but only rarely. At other times, like this eclipse (and all eclipses), it stands to reason that it could intensify.

In the year 2005, there was an eclipse on October 3rd. This terminated in the Indian Ocean and due north of this location there was a massive earthquake just days later in Pakistan. Are there relations here or mere coincidences?

Forgetting Earth movements for a moment, let us consider the other events of August 11th. Could there have been something in the planetary positions to have affected the weather? Could the rain and lightning have been not a random event? The fact that the eclipse was seen throughout Europe, except at the point of maximum is interesting.

The weather observed

When we look to the works of Ptolemy we see that the ancients believed each planet, in addition to how it affected events, people, the gods, and our fortune, also affected the weather. The Sun, of course, and Mars were thought to represent heat, and aridity. Saturn: cold. Each planet in turn represented hot/cold, in combination with wet or dry. Each longitude on Earth was also associated to the zodiac, with an associated hot-wet-dry-cold quality. A given planet within a given sign was a harbinger of particular weather.

Today, there are astrologers who try to predict weather based on planetary position "around" the globe. There are those, just as Ptolemy, who believe that certain signs of the zodiac correspond to specific zones of the Earth. So, when Mars is in one sign, the corresponding region of the Earth might experience hot dry weather, for example.

Is this possible? Based on observational data concerning the weather and astronomical events, it seems so. The reader is invited to become a weather observer/astronomer too and verify for themselves whether *weather* relationships exist.

Firstly, when the Moon aligns with the Sun and Earth, at new moon, there is often a change in weather (at any given location). In Europe or the eastern U.S., this can be easily noted. In drier, desert regions, it is more difficult, due to there not being enough water to make a good storm. Still, there can be a change in pressure, winds, and temperature. It is just more of a subtle change and harder to track.

More interestingly, there seems to be roughly a two-month cycle to weather patterns. Not always, but often, when a new weather system comes in, at the new moon, it can signal what the next two months will be like. In 2004, weather in northern Europe was warm and sunny for almost two entire months from mid-March to mid-May. It ended with a snow storm on the 23rd, following the new moon of the 19th. What followed could not really be called the start of summer. The season didn't really come until the new moon in mid July. In between were cool rainy conditions which flooded the fields and stunted crop growth.

Similarly, two-month cycles of weather have been consistently observed, often starting at or near the new moon. An is from the year 2005. The winter seemed delayed through the end of 2004, as the weather seemed like spring one day and autumn the next, but almost never like winter. That winter weather cycle began on January 10th, at the new moon. It was deceptive at first, as the Sun was present with warm temperatures. Next came nearly two months of massive snow, which the plows piled to heights of three meters. Students were horribly sick. Overloaded hospitals were shut to visitors.

March and April followed with pleasant spring weather of rain and shine as the gardens began to grow well. May and June were also pleasant. There started to grow a bumper-crop of vegetables. But, the two months of summer saw consistent rain and cold, with a decided lack of sun. Those root crops rotted as the ground became saturated. Conversely, in the United States temperatures and drought were in the extreme.

Finally, the Sun returned with the new moon of August 19th. There began then an amazing Indian Summer which saw Sun, unusual warmth and brilliant fall colors until the end of October. This was also the time of the hurricane which swamped New Orleans.

With our observations, we will begin to notice other things. Whatever pattern does develop after a new moon, there will often be a change at full moon. And tucked away, in the latter third of each calendar month, is a zodiacal change, as Sun "goes" from one sign to the next. This happens around the 21st. Simply observe the weather at this day and it will be often seen to change. Maybe two weeks of clouds will give way to one, and only one day of Sun. This is a great process to study with students in science. They too can look for weather patterns and attempt to predict the weather. Good luck!

That a relation exists between the Moon and water cycle should come as no surprise. Certainly, many people plant crops by the phases of the Moon. The Farmer's Almanac and astrological calendars are written with this in mind. But, why the two-month weather pattern, and why would the Sun or Moon crossing some point in the sky make a change in weather?

Ask students, "What causes the tides?" They will of course say, "The Moon." What about the Moon? Gravity? Does it pull clouds?

Let's try a calculation, for which we will use Newton's force equation between two bodies:

$$F = \frac{GM_1M_2}{d^2} \quad \text{where } G = 6.67 \times 10^{-11} \text{ Nm}^2/\text{kg}^2$$

We will use for this the Gravitational constant, and the following data:

Object	Mass	Distance to Earth
Sun	2×10^{30} kg	1.5×10^{11} m
Moon	7.3×10^{22} kg	3.9×10^8 m
Earth	6×10^{24} kg	----------

Table 1 Mass and distance for Earth's significant partners.

When we put the numbers into the equation, an interesting thing happens. We find that the force of gravity between Earth and Moon is 1.9×10^{20} N. More importantly, the force between Sun and Earth is 3.6×10^{22} N. This is 185 times greater! What it means is that though the Moon does exert the greater pull on the tides, it is not the result of gravity. Perhaps the tides are more due to centrifugal force.

The point of this exercise is to show that we might find that the water cycle on our planet is worth investigating further.

Alignments of planets: triangulation

There is one other interplanetary relation to be considered and that is when planets appear to be spaced at 120° from each other (relative to us). When we talk about this spacing it is difficult to comprehend accurately because the planets are actually some linear distance from the Sun and have some angular position around it. But, from our perspective, they appear as points of light in the sky, and some angular rotation from each other, again with respect to us.

This triangular relationship is considered favorable by astrologers, and is called a trine. We will look at Figure 14.

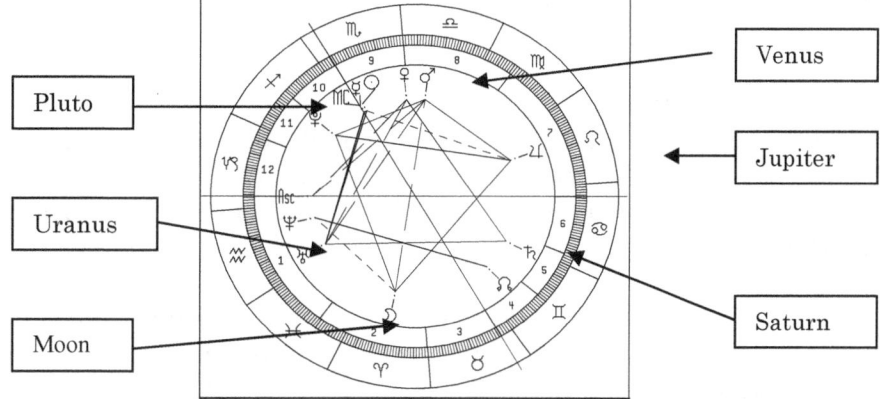

Figure 14 A rare warm and sunny day, squeezed in among the clouds.

This chart dates from November 16th, 2002. We see Pluto, Jupiter and Moon at the corners of a triangle, each nearly 120° from the others. This is called a "grand trine". With the Moon (whose movement is rapid), it can only last for about a day. Interesting to this date, it can be noted that Venus, Saturn and Uranus also form a grand trine, and the two triangles together form almost a Star of David. This is rather rare. In Northern Europe, we enjoyed that the usual cold, grey, and rainy weather of mid-November gave way to one day of unusual warmth and brilliant Sun. We had a picnic!

Could triangulation of these bodies, their electromagnetic fields or something further cause this effect? It seems clear that Moon, Sun and planetary alignments do have some affect on our weather. What is also notable is how and when. A given rain storm will start at *some* time on a given day; severe storms, with lightning as well. Is this starting time random? Ever notice how storms may occur day after day, at about the same time?

In late spring 2002, our observation region had strong lightning storms, which were arriving at nearly the same time every night, 9:30. According to astrological charts, Pluto was at the eastern horizon, and the Sun at the western. As mentioned, though placement of the planets in a zodiacal sign is in question, their location above or below us at a specific time is accurate.

Looking to the eclipse of 1999, we wonder if the Sun *could* have something to do with electric discharge in the sky. Why not? It is, after all, a giant fusion reactor whose electromagnetic energies reach us in 500 seconds from the time they are emitted, or erupted. But, could tiny, distant Pluto have an effect (despite being downgraded from planet status)?

Pluto is a very interesting "planet". In our solar system, all of the other planets with a moon are extremely large compared to their satellite, and there is a great distance between the two. That means the center of gravity is pretty much near the center of the planet. Earth departs from this a little, as the Moon is relatively large in comparison. For us, the CG (center of gravity) is pretty far out from the center but still within the planet.

Pluto, however, is not much bigger that its moon, Charon, and not very far away from it, on a planetary scale. It acts more like a "binary" planet, rotating around some point in space between, but closer to Pluto.

Imagine an example for the Earth and Moon of a strong man swinging a heavy weight around himself, connected by a rope. He will feel the pull of the mass and it will tend to tug him off his feet. But still, he holds on and the center of gravity is somewhere in his extended arms. In the case of Pluto, imagine a set of dumbbells, where two unequal weights are held by a bar and that the whole thing is spinning around freely in space (like a dynamo). But, the question is, "Is there somehow electricity associated with this?" And then, is there a relationship between electricity and rain?

The answer to the latter is yes. When raindrops fall, the friction of the drop falling through air can pull electrons off of the droplet. Therefore, negatively charged particles are left between the cloud and the ground, where there is a constant stream of these now positively charged rain drops. The drops strike the ground, giving it a locally positive charge. When conditions are just right, and the air mass is unstable enough, lightning occurs as electric current reaches from the cloud to the ground. This is interesting that the movement of water can create electricity.

It raises the question whether electricity could create water, and hence; rain. This also appears possible, as science has reported that solar storms and space weather (ion flow) directly affect Earth weather.

The water – ion relationship

We learn in chemistry that water is a polar molecule, meaning that the electrons from the two hydrogens tend to be pulled toward the oxygen, due to differences in what are called electronegativity. This tends to give the oxygen end of the molecule a more negative charge and the hydrogens more positive, though the whole molecule is thought to be balanced.

This explains a lot about how water is able to dissolve things like salt and sugar, as the compounds become ionized in the water and positive and negative ions attract to the oxygen and hydrogens in turn.

In the air, water needs some kind of particles to adhere to in order to form drops. It is obvious that these particles must be ionized, either positively or negatively. It is easy to imagine that Sun, flooding us with electromagnetic energy, could somehow affect the ionization of the air, and thus affect the water cycle. But could the Moon? Could the distant planets?

In a microwave oven, the oscillating waves cause the polar water molecules within food to flip back and forth at extremely high speeds. The resulting friction between molecules creates the heat which cooks the food. What do Sun's rays do to water molecules in the air, and to particles? Are there ionization factors which can then lead to rain? Do those portions of solar energy reflected by a full Moon effect a change in ionization of particles in the sky, again affecting the weather?

Sir Isaac Newton, and others, identified that any two objects affect each other gravitationally. This means that we are attracted to others, whether we like them or not. More, each planet gravitationally affects the next. For us, it means that between Earth and Mars, at their closest approach, there exists a force in the scale of 10^{16} N. This massive force is overshadowed by that of the Moon at 10^{22} N, and the Sun, at 10^{25} N.

If there are gravitational effects from each body to the next, what about electromagnetic? The electric current in a wire can affect the direction a compass needle points, and a magnet in motion can create electric current flow. Are there effects of planetary magnetism on the atmospheres of said planet, or even upon other planets? Each planet having an electro-magnetic field (and most have one) is like them having a giant radio transmitter. The Moon has recently been found to have high voltage static electricity. When Kepler talked of the "music of the spheres", perhaps he was not so wrong.

Primarily the Sun, but also the planets, are electromagnetic wave generators. Could alignments and triangulations create current paths and geometries that affect ionization? From further observation it is seen that rain begins to fall, skies begin to clear, and lightning begins to strike at nearly the precise moment the Sun, Moon, or any planet is either rising, setting, or directly overhead at the 12 o'clock position. In rising or setting, that planetary body's transmission "begins or ends". At the noontime position, it peaks.

A similar, interesting phenomenon is how the daily temperature then seems to peak at about 3 or 4 o'clock in summer. Growing up in the Midwest of the United States, I am reminded of all the thundershowers and rain which began at about 3:30 each day. This represents the Sun at about 40 degrees from its noontime position (which in summer occurs at 1pm). Why did the ancients celebrate May Day as the birth of spring, (when spring began on March 21st, about 40 days – and degrees – prior)? Is here some further mathematical/angular relationship between Earth and Sun regarding the heat and energy exchange between both?

We know that sunspots and flares affect radio communication on Earth. The question for the astrologer is what effect do the gravitational, electrical, and magnetic fields of the Sun, Moon, and planets have on us, on our moods, emotion (perhaps on the water content and electro-chemical balance in the brain) and the planet's water cycle? Is there some triangulation which can occur, one which astrologers have long ascribed to geometrical-"magical" relationships? Can astrology be explained by *real* electromagnetic, gravitational, or other physical relationships between the planets? Can it be used as a tool for weather (or even earthquake) forecasting? Does a human, born under certain alignments, become tuned to the energies at that time in such a way as to be affected when those angular relationships are revisited or massaged by motive planets?

Could we use this understanding somehow? Could we, as Tesla suggested, harness natural energies and then design ways to affect the weather, if we understood properties of atmospheric ionization?

Where some man has gone before

This is in fact possibly, probably being done and has been for some time. When the United States detonated the first nuclear device, many new developments resulted. One was that further testing proceeded which to date has resulted in over 2000 tests, 500 of which have been in the atmosphere. Interesting discoveries were made from these, not just regarding the destructive nature of each new engineering creation. The nature of light and particles has been studied, and properties of the ionosphere have been discovered. It is interesting to see films of mushroom clouds, and to wonder at the energy release and why it should create the unique cloud formations. Is it massive sudden ionization which causes water vapor in the air to gather?

When one watches films of the aftermath of the first atomic tests, it is possible to see sailors cleaning up soon after, walking on ships that were just exposed to a blast, removing test animals, and spraying water to cool the metal. None of these participants was wearing breathing apparatus or protective clothes. This illustrates the naïveté with which Humanity approaches its creations. There was no concern at the time, of fallout from blasts in desert areas affecting downwind communities. The quantity of nuclear testing, particularly atmospheric have raised the background ionic radiation levels of the Earth by 7%. We can only wonder at the health effects of this.

The scientists who developed the first atomic bomb knew they were being naïve in their experiments. They had calculated everything well, and the final results pretty closely matched expectations. But when they were experimenting under the University of Chicago, they weren't sure if they would vaporize the city or not. When they lit the fuse on the Trinity test in New Mexico, they weren't sure if it could destroy our world or not. Yet, they took the risk. This experimentation continues…

There are reports that the Soviet Union worked with electrical transmission to affect brain activity and modify weather for thirty years. For nearly ten, the United States has been developing a project in Alaska called HAARP (High Frequency Active Auroral Research Project). Their website is very informative and clearly states that they are experimenting with "heating" the ionosphere, basically to see what could result from this. (This and other experiments continue surprising discoveries made during atmospheric atomic weapons testing of the fifties and sixties.) They are also attempting to bounce radio waves off the ionosphere as a means of communication. The supposedly peaceful project is run by the Air Force, meaning of course that its mission is *not* benign. Too, in light of global warming, perhaps heating the atmosphere is not such a good idea.

Figure 15a HAARP antenna array (HAARP).

Microwaves are an interesting form of electromagnetic radiation. They come naturally from the Sun and are able to penetrate skin, bone, and stone for some distance. Researchers have found that the plants within crop circles have probably been affected by microwave energy, as they exhibit the same cellular features as food cooked in a microwave oven. Crop circles may have begun occurring coincident to the creation of HAARP. It is interesting to see New-Age people and UFO enthusiasts preaching about the beautiful geometric structures contained within crop circles, and how they must be meant as peaceful transmissions to us.

Is it possible that some engineer or tech sergeant in Alaska is laughing himself silly by such notions, as they program another geometric design into their transmitter and attempt to beam it around the Earth? The potentials of such a device are horrific. With such precision, it could be the "Death ray", which Tesla talked about. If it seems far-fetched, read about the new weapons the US military are creating with microwave technology. They can get "terrorists" to flee a house by transmitting high intensity microwave energy through the walls, causing the skin of those inside to itch and burn. Similar toys are already in use for "non-lethal" crowd control (of even peaceful demonstrations). A car can be stopped by police using another application. An aircraft could be brought down by it.

Microwave technology is seen as a means of heating the air in front of a hurricane to redirect its path. Further, it could be used to blast a tornado and render it harmless, though it is not clear if it would reduce or intensify it. I, as a part-time researcher and former engineer can conceive of such things, and have found reports that they are becoming reality. Would world militaries not want these? Literature is becoming available in the realm of "weather wars". Were it possible to harness, would such technology not be strategically useful for military, political, or economic interests?

Figure 15b "Typical" crop circle – (@ Steve Alexander).

The idea of mass mind control seems admittedly far-fetched. Yet science is only now discovering that within the brain; at the ears and in certain glands, there exist micro-sized crystals. If one presses on or otherwise manipulates a crystal, electric current is produced. Hence, there is a connection between eardrum vibration and brain signal, and fluid flow and brain-wave emission. How could fluids, hormones, and brainwaves be affected by external electronic transmission?

Tesla and others have long seen the potentials of radio for wireless technologies, work within the ionosphere, mass human mind control and weather manipulation, just to name a few of the more fascinating, and alarming! Is the human race at this time gifted or understanding enough to continue such experimentation or should we realize that a change in one location could affect another, possibly disastrously?

Humanity is capable of marvelous invention, which someone, regrettably, inevitably turns into some form of weapon.

Conclusion

What mathematical processes are used in astrology? Can we scientifically observe, to confirm or disprove this "field"? If there are in fact electrical and magnetic effects from planets on weather, how could this be used beneficially? What concern should we have that perhaps our governments are attempting to harness this malevolently?

As we desire progress, and strive for an ever easier, and better, world, have we gotten it? Has industrialization given us cleaner air, food, and water? Does electronic convenience come with no, or acceptable, health risks? Is it not worthwhile as teachers to investigate for ourselves, and have our students investigate too?

We need to know about the great potentials of natural energy. The people who built stone-age circles and alignments to calendrical events, upon ley lines, and using special crystalline stone, may have been experimenting with those energies. Why did they erect thousands of stones in rows at Brittany in France? Why did they put such geometric precision into circles, ellipses and egg-shaped stone structures all over Europe?

We have got to return our engineers to the humanities, so that they consider the ramifications of their research and accept responsibility for what they are creating. What joy is there for us living for generations under the threat of someone unleashing *the* Holocaust? We need artists and humanists in technical fields so that we have people there who would be perhaps less likely to want to conceive of such horrible devices.

This last is a naïve hope, that our own children will inherit a world where they can still be free, healthy and yes, progressing.

The studies preliminary to astronomical prognostication are two: the one, first alike in order and in power leads to the knowledge of the figurations of the Sun, the Moon, and the stars; and of their relative aspects to each other and the Earth: the other takes into consideration the changes which their aspects create, by means of their natural properties, in objects under their influence. – Claudius Ptolemy – Tetrabiblos

Figure 16 "Power" – (Miroslav Huptych)

Further reading/research and websites :
http://www.docweather.com/   Site of Dennis Klocek, author of "Weather and the Cosmos", and weather-astrological researcher.

http://www.astropro.com/homeIE45.html   Richard Nolle. Forecasts of weather, natural disasters, economics and politics.

http://www.weathersage.com/   Includes a list of historical and present forecasters and their astrological weather prediction.

http://www.haarp.alaska.edu/   Home page for HAARP.

http://www.earthpulse.com/src/category.asp?catid=1   Website of the authors of "Angels don't play this HAARP". Knowledgeable sources about the dangers of HAARP for which we should be aware.

http://www.abc.net.au/science/news/space/SpaceRepublish_760839.htm   Shows ocean magnetic fields.

http://en.wikipedia.org/wiki/Electric_fields_ocean
Describes how the oceans are a giant electrolytic conductor.

http://www.astrolog.org/astrolog.htm   Free astrology program.

http://earthquake.usgs.gov/   Geological page on earthquakes. Great info for tracking earthquake location and times.

http://sunearth.gsfc.nasa.gov/eclipse/eclipse.html   Tells of upcoming eclipses, with great global maps describing the paths.

Obtain a copy of the film "Trinity and Beyond". Watch it with your students, with regard to atomic weapons testing.

Class Exercise 1 Astrology 101 + 1

Objective:
Learn the mathematics of astrology, particularly 90°, 120°, and 180° relationships. Seek correlations between planetary alignments and weather changes on Earth.

Procedure:
a) Obtain astrology software and a rudimentary understanding of astrology. Have students find the date, time and place of their birth. (Be sensitive as some mothers don't remember, and in case of adoption.) Date and place are good enough. Use the software to obtain each "birth-chart". The chart can be copied to Word, and enlarged.
b) Instruct students on square, triangular and opposite relationships. Have them try to find such configurations in their own chart. Interest will be high because *everyone* has a curiosity about this. They should list their discoveries.
c) Set up a weather observation program, noting the temperature, pressure, and conditions each day. Some material can be gotten from local weather information. Note changes, such as the exact time that clouds gather, when it rains, when a lightning storm begins, the occurrence of a rainbow, hail, or freak winds.
d) Continue observation. Chart key events to see if specific planets align, are at the "noon", horizon, or "midnight". Observe phases of the moon and eclipses. Find out if earthquakes occurred in the days after an eclipse and paths coincided. Note local weather changes after an eclipse. Use NASA and USGS websites for this information.
e) Study the water-ion relationship where falling drops of rain lose electrons due to friction. This creates a path of free negative ions and positive water droplets. Clouds have negative imbalance and the wet surface of the ground positive, creating a lightning discharge.
f) Calculate the amount of electrons and water needed for an average bolt of lightning if 5 coulombs of energy is discharged. There are 6.25×10^{18} electrons in a coulomb; Avogadro's number is $6,02 \times 10^{23}$. The result is about 1/1000 of a gram (a raindrop).
g) Study the relationship of ionically charged particles in air; that polar water molecules have something upon which to adhere, build up, and create clouds and precipitate.
h) Read the internet article "Earth and Space Weather Connected", http://www.livescience.com/environment/060912_spaceweather_link.html
i) Read the government page on weather effects of nuclear power plants. http://www.osti.gov/energycitations/product.biblio.jsp?osti_id=7076284
j) Read current sites on Weather Control, HAARP; see NASA's site at:
    http://www.niac.usra. edu/studies/study.jsp?id=589&cpnum=00-02&phase=I&last=Hoffman&first=Ross&middle=N&title=ControllingtheGlobalWeather&organization=Atmospheric&EnvironmentalResearch,Inc&begin_date=2001-06-0100:00:00.0&end_date=2001-11-3000:00:00.0
k) Having seen that nuclear power and solar storms might affect weather, and that governments are possibly seeing it as a strategic tool, have students pick planets and research about their electro-magnetic fields and any anomalies. Calculate how long it would take their EM fields to contact Earth after they "rise" above the horizon.

Homework:
Finish birthchart analyses at home. Weather observation can be extra-credit mostly outside of class. Let them try to predict the weather, and host a contest. The physics material requires class sessions and homework effort to read, and then submit findings.

Evaluation:
Assess effort and participation. This can be mostly extra credit awarded to participants in weather observation. Physics findings should be adequately sourced and documented.

Bridges:
We are looking for physical connections between planets and their electromagnetic, gravitational or other effects on the ion relationship and weather, while also seeing pretty fascinating modern physical experiments (depressingly real ones).

Lesson plan 2   Music and Sound lab

Objective
Discover geometries of musical instruments and the sound they generate.

Procedure
a) Rotate around the stations in small groups, create and observe sound. Do the following, in any order, taking notes as you proceed.

b) With the piano top open, play notes. Observe the action within the piano. What is it that creates and amplifies the sound? Play a note, and then another near to it. Why are sounds different? Play a note, and then another, seven white keys higher, or lower. How are the notes different, and similar? Play three white keys together, leaving a key between each. Record anything you note about the sound.

c) Go to the drums. Beat on each one. Record any observations. What is it you think that makes the sound in the drums? Why does each have a different sound? Strike the cymbals. What creates its sound?

d) Play notes on the flute. Why does covering the holes make different sounds? Which has the higher pitch – more or less holes covered?

e) Pluck strings on the guitar. Why does each string make a different sound? What is it about the guitar that amplifies the sound? Pluck a string. Then, put your finger exactly in the middle of that string and hold it down. Pluck the string again. What is different or similar? (one octave higher) Pluck both sides (same note). Put a finger at 1/3 the length and pluck both sides. (One portion of the string is twice the other in length and so they carry the same note, separated by an octave.)

Homework:
Answer the questions given in the procedure. What is it about these instruments that creates different sound? This material should be written up as a formal lab report. Record any further observations

Evaluation:
Assess participation, note-taking and quality of final product. Keep students who are gifted on particular instruments from stealing the show, so all get a chance. Some will just want to play, but not work.

Bridges:
This is one of those places where we can make tremendous connections between physics, geometry and the arts.

12 Light

Opening dialogue

Hopefully the reader has been inspired and intrigued by application, bridges, and routes to further investigate. Have they obtained any sense of wonder; a feeling of mystique perhaps?

What is meant by the term Sacred Geometry? Why do some feel drawn to such a concept, while others feel it necessary to completely refute it? Are there subtle energies beyond which we've discovered, and developed instrumentation to measure?

Sybolism

This idea of the sacredness of geometry is not so difficult to define, especially now at the end of this book. We have seen repeatedly that geometric symbols and forms are all embedded in our holiest edifices, reliquaries, and psyche. Many times these geometries have been used in ceremony, meditation, and magic, as though they imbue the act with *something*; some special essence, or perhaps power. The question is, "*Is* there power?" Or is it just the creation of the human mind and do these numbers, proportions and shapes merely go together mathematically and should we not read too much into it all?

Figure 1 Tibetan Infinity symbol, drawn in a square, rotated 45°.

It is difficult as modern people to believe that geometry, or even science, can relate to God. We have perhaps the followers of God, dogmatic and fundamentalist, to thank for this, for throughout history there have been many attempts to block scientific and metaphysical exploration and practice. Also, since the time of the French Revolution and industrialization, whence science so forcefully removed itself from theology, our world has been unable and unwilling to put God back into things. We once built our shrines as the tallest structure in the towns and cities. Now, our sky monuments are symbols of something else.

And yet, we have seen that *something* underlies all of this Creation around us. We can believe in Darwinian thought, where things just happen and evolve. But the fact is that so many things are concrete and mathematical - systematical.

Phi shows that within a Chaos of seemingly random shapes there is a geometry that unites them and us. Yet, pi, and not phi, is taught in schools. Too often mathematicians vociferously dispel discussion of this number, ascribing it to "math-mythology".

Fractals demonstrate further that within nature exist patterns which repeat. Geometries found in the micro expand themselves in landscapes and elsewhere to generate the macro. But, is it necessary to discover fact about everything, and remove the mystique and Godhead from *every* shadowy item which remains? As humanity reaches for adulthood, is it too childlike to believe that still around us is God? Or can we see that we are all part of God, and co-creating? The idea that we are "created in God's image" sounds like a fractal pattern.

We have seen that growth and movement is often spirallic: for example, that the Moon's path is not around us, but around the Sun, dancing in a sinusoidal pattern as we share this orbit. But as anyone familiar with an oscilloscope knows, the sinusoidal pattern is flat, two-dimensional. Or is it? For the Moon, we must consider one more factor in our exhaustive study of its trajectory. It moves between extreme northern and southern points each moonth. Therefore, the sinusoidal pattern we created was not complete.

More, it is like the double helix of DNA. In a cylindrical wire, would not the electrical current also move in such a wave?

We've seen that waves (sound) carry with them geometries. The very vibrations have a mathematical structure. As light, both visible and other forms (like microwave, radio, and UV), travel as waves, should we not assume that here too, the motion is spirallic and capable of making mathematical structure?

What form of structure? Two-dimensional or three? Or perhaps further dimensions? Holography gives us the chance to create "forms" with light. But can the light, this high-speed vibration, create form, as sound apparently can? "In the Beginning was darkness, without form. In the Beginning was the Word, and the word was God."

What if within the void is not shapeless darkness but instead vibration? Does darkness mean absence of all forms of energy, or only that visible light is missing? What if it was not Word, but sound? The music of the spheres. And then came light.

The physics of the aura

This text has talked about chakras. Associated with them are the 12 meridians of the Chinese – and also the concept of auras. Most people have heard the term, and many believe in their existence, just as they believe in the idea of the soul. When we consider the soul, do we think of it as something which resides within us? Around us? Is it the size of a pea? The shape of a sphere?

The ancient Egyptians had exhaustive rituals associated with these "spirit" bodies, as seen by how they embalmed their Pharaohs. It is interesting to investigate King Tutankhamen's tomb. Here, an elaborately painted room contained a gold-leaf covered rectangular wooden box. When removed, it revealed a framework, covering a further "golden" box, covering two more such structures, each containing fine ornamentation and script. Then came the stone sarcophagus, carved in red granite. Within this was the gold-foil wooden outer anthropomorphic coffin; itself covered by two layers of linen. Inside was another such coffin, though much finer in decoration. Inside this came another linen cloth, covering a layer of liquid resin which hid the solid gold coffin contained within. Finally came the body, wrapped in linen, gold bands, and a golden burial death mask. All of these layers, and their size and spacing from the body, are representative of modern views of the aura!

Figure 1a Tut's sarcophagi (Morrison), Chartres' portal and Aura (M. Brofman).

There are those who study auras and "heal" through them, with the so-called "higher forms of energy". They "see" not just one aura around a person, but several; some say 7, others say 12; each relating to one of the chakras.

These concepts may not seem mathematical, may not seem realistic. But they are both. Researchers are in fact trying to use special techniques to photograph energy fields around life forms. We must remember that the vibration that we see and hear is not the only vibration around or within us. This is why we cannot assume that human-induced increases in vibrational energies, while unseen, are benign.

It is felt that the chakras and auras are energies in non-visible regions of vibration like microwave, infrared, and UV. They and their associated "auric" level can supposedly be affected by color and sound.

The lower chakras, associated with the physical body, its functions and health, and DNA is thought to vibrate at microwave levels. What could this mean to life forms exposed to increasing forms of microwave energy transmission? Even the W.H.O. acknowledges DNA is at risk from microwave technology.

The upper chakras are believed to be associated with Spirit, and higher UV frequencies – something to consider before lying on a tanning bed. While we need sunlight to manufacture certain nutrients in the body, the Sun constantly emits unseen energies of the entire "light" spectrum, including x-ray, gamma ray, radio wave, and those already mentioned here. Apart from food, what are the *energies* that our body and spirit need? What might be in imbalance now from human energy transmission and radioactive pollution from land and atmospheric testing and ongoing nuclear power emission?

Those who study chakras, meridians, auras, and herbal remedies agree that there are subtle forms of energy around us, not just the grander sources we combust to power our world. Earth itself is thought to have a system of energy channels which flow over it. Dowsers are very familiar with it as they search for underground water currents and find also this "current". Some call these ley lines, others say telluric.

We learn so much in history about the Ancient Egyptians and Sumerians, as these cultures left for us immense treasures of text, gold and monuments, concentrated in relatively small geographical locations. But other than Stonehenge, we don't hear about that *other* culture.

Concurrent to the "civilizations" on the Tigris-Euphrates and Nile rivers, there lived a culture which also erected great monuments in stone, shaping rocks even larger than those used in the pyramids, and moving them over larger distances.

Peoples from Ireland to Russia, Scandinavia to Morocco, and Israel to India erected tumuli; which many call tombs (but others describe as ritual enclaves), gigantic circular enclosures and stone circles, rows and rectangles. Many, perhaps all, of these sites have clear astronomical alignments and calendrical features.

More importantly, the stones themselves are usually unique. They generally have some type of quartz running through them. We know that quartz is a great conductor of electricity and energy. That is why early radio sets used quartz, and why all of our electronic watches, phones, laptop computers and other equipment use Liquid Crystal Displays. But, did the primitives somehow know this too?

These stones are often placed next to the sea. Could the people have known of the special energy associated with the ocean, particularly the ionic, and hence energetic, nature of the salty water? Did the two interact, just as our antennas receive signals? There are those who believe this to be the case.

Ultimately, these stone formations are always placed either upon ley lines, or at the junction of multiple leys. What purpose could this serve? Was it meant as a place to gather a community of people for certain festivals? Did the energy flow differently at different times of the year? Were the stones standing to act like antennas? Was there some understanding of natural energies which "mud hut" people had that we do not? Certainly, today's crystal therapists believe that there are specific energies related to specific stones.

What could the effects be of placing rings of crystalline, standing stones on Earth's supposed energy grid? Tesla himself proposed that the Earth could be tapped as a giant electrical transmitter, providing free electricity for the world's population. Sounds like a solution to many of our environmental problems, and sure to be a hit with the industries which profit from current energy markets and speculations.

For the Chinese, the land is alive with energy. Each hilltop and valley has some form of "dragon" energy flowing through it, whether Yang or Yin. This is behind their system of Feng Shui. They would not necessarily put a building, or structure, in the same place as others might.

Figure 2 Image from 9-Dragon wall, Beijing and Yin/Yang.

What could be the effects as we now erect telephone masts on many of these same (primarily Yang) energy points? In the system of acupuncture, the needle is placed at energy points temporarily, to stimulate, remove blockage, and improve energy flow. The same is true of acupressure. Temporary massaging of a point is very painful, but healing, and then the pressure is removed. Could transmitters, placed on such a grid of energy, have an effect?

In Figure 2 we see imagery of the Oriental view of dragons, and of energies which are unseen. Note the sinusoidal nature. The interesting thing about the Chinese is that they still believe that "dragons" fly through the sky, and in the land and water, as energy. This culture never apparently felt the need to "kill" the dragon. Of course, as towers rise in Shanghai and elsewhere, and the modern comes to China, perhaps this too will change.

Today's physicists are looking to space, the Sun, the atom – still trying to understand. We seem to know so much, compared with our past, but what will the Future say about us? Someday, we may have fusion, and faster than light travel. But first, we must learn more about different forms of energy.

Deep within our psyche lie ideas of faeries, demons, and angels. Is it possible that they exist as energy and vibration that we simply cannot see, sense, or measure; awaiting discovery? If so, could their "wavelengths" be shared now by our profusion of electronic transmission? Could this be harmful to them, and to those parts of us which share these vibrational frequencies? For now, all of this is virtually impossible to prove, particularly as there doesn't seem to be a lot of interest in such exploration, at least publicly.

Scattered around so many varied Eastern spiritual systems, each often prejudged in Western minds, it is difficult to collect all of the possibilities and make it understandable. Further, bombarded now with information, our minds are being asked to gather and retain an ocean of input and to store away fragments in a mash of memories.

Science of coming into being

The interesting thing about a lot of modern thought on auras and vibrational energies is that it is no longer only the realm of "traditional" sources like Hindu shamans, Chinese medicinal practitioners, fortune tellers, casters of oracle bones, or tarot readers and astrologers. Today's researchers and believers include doctorates experienced in NASA and military physics. Something to consider before the reader or student might choose to dismiss this discussion.

We saw the geometries of sound in Chapter 1, yet only in two dimensions, on a plate. Sound and light transmit three-dimensionally, spherically. If we imagine that there are nodes, as on the Chladni plate, where the waves cross and build, how do these meet in 3D? Researches are suggesting that the nodes are spaced regularly. Energy vibrates or is transmitted in basic forms: the platonic shapes! Imagine energy coming off a radio tower not spherically but as an icosahedron. What if it could be a stellated dodecahedron? With each frequency, or range of frequencies, perhaps a different geometry or fractal forms in the ethers. Maybe a different color, sound, or smell.

We know that many crystals grow often from a surface of some kind in specific geometric forms. Some, like diamonds, are definitely octahedral. What vibration brings crystals into form? How do they grow in the absence of a surface, and without gravity?

Infinitesimally small units like the basic atom have in their levels 2, 6, 10, and 14 electrons. These fundamental building blocks of binary, 5-, 6-, decimal, and 7-based counting, also build into octahedral forms in the form of specific electron shells.

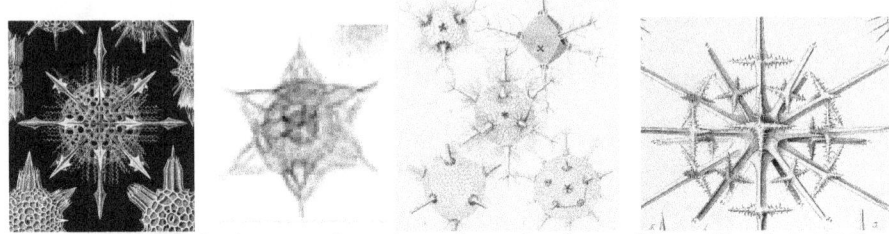

Figure 3a Radiolariens, as platonic and regular forms (Ernst Haeckel 1862).

Increasing many factors in size, we come to radiolarians, single cell organisms, many with regular geometries (Figure 3a).

Snowflakes come next in our evolutionary scale of regular geometric construction. Why, in the presence of so much three-dimensional creation, do these shapes exist in 2D?

Why are salt, calcium, and other minerals crystalline, meaning that they are organized in regular, geometric forms? Why are rose family blossoms in the shape of the phi star, and their fruit in the shape of phi spirals? Does nature have codes which the primitive mind can read?

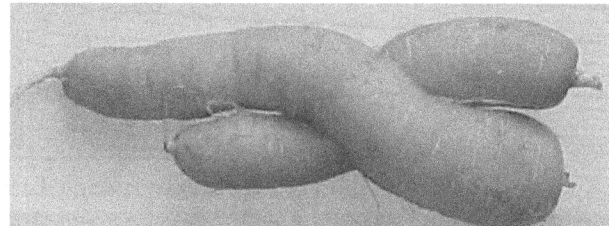

Figure 3b Two carrots that grew next to each other, in a helix.

Scientists have only recently found that contained within the ear and glands central to the brain are tiny crystals. These piezoelectric materials change external sounds and internal fluid mechanics into electrical impulses within the brain.

Why do we like certain colors, sounds, and shapes? Is their "vibration" tuned to our own? Can vibrations be altered, stimulated, helped, or hurt by electronic transmission?

These topics are fanciful. Yet wouldn't it be something if we were to explore this, rather than using our scientific understanding of energy to develop new toys that might be hurting us inadvertently or weapons systems that outright kill?

Magic squares

We will return to more "grounded" mathematics one last time, so that the reader is reminded that the material here-in is not just paranormal, or paranoic. In this final unit, we will make new "mandalas"; squares with beautiful "masculine" geometric forms.

Let's draw a square of 16 dots. Number them 1-4 along the top row, 5-8 for the next and so forth. How could we connect them? Can we arrange the numbers themselves, in a square, so that the sum along each column, row and the two diagonals is the same? Yes, and that is why they are called magic squares.

We will connect certain dots, to create a pattern. Then, we will follow each route, and record the numbers of the dots it includes, putting these into our table.

 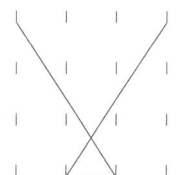

Figure 4a The dot pattern.   Figure 4b Begin to connect specific dots.

If we look at a continuous path; Figure 4b, we see that the dots numbered 1, 15, 14 and 4 are connected. Their sum is 34. The other three geometries have the same sum. How then to arrange them in a square table? With a little calculation and effort, it can be found that the arrangement in Table 1 works.

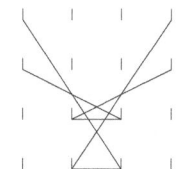 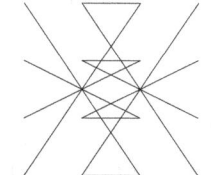

1	15	14	4
8	10	11	5
12	6	7	9
13	3	2	16

Figure 4c Do the "inner" points.   Figure 4d Mirror the image.   Table 1 A square of 4.

There are patterns to how we present the numbers. In the first and last rows, the first and last numbers increase, while they decrease in the middle two rows. This could help us should we wish to continue this process with more difficult squares. So let's do this.

There are many possibilities. Table 2 and Figure 5 come from Albrecht Dürer's piece Melancholia: rich in mystical and geometrical imagery as shown in Chapter 3, where we see the Angel Michael, a geometric form and a magic square table. Sacred geometry? Not only do the rows, columns and diagonals total to make 34, but also notice that any four adjacent squares, the four inner and outer corners also make this total.

16	3	2	13
5	10	11	8
9	6	7	12
4	15	14	1

Table 2 Dürer's square of 4.

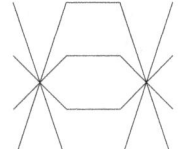

Figure 5 The diagram it creates

Let students be free to create with 6 now. One rather neat image is shown in Figure 6a. The lines will start to be a bit confused as we draw more of them, so let's do half of the figure first, and then finish it.

The image is bold. Here, adding the numbers of the dots connected for the first route around the square, provides a sum of 81. The only problem is that if we perform an arithmetic sum of the 36 numbers, with the sequence being 1 + 2 + 3 + 4 +... we get the interesting number 666 (each of the six pathways around the square must total 111). So, our beautiful image is not a "magic" square, which we notice by the fact that it engages four points in one row, and two in the other. So, this process is a bit more complicated.

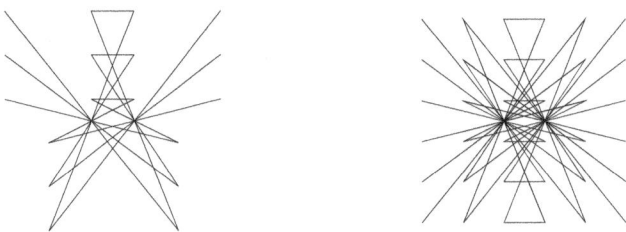

Figure 6a A "square" of 6.

We must arrange our square so that each column, row and cross diagonal equates to this sum. In Figure 6b are steps to create a further image. At first, it does not seem so perfect. As we draw it to completion it works, at least as far as a uniform image.

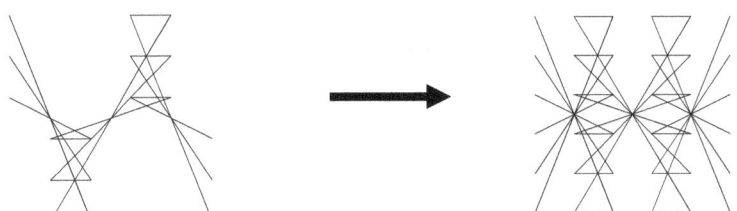

Figure 6b A functional image of the square of 6.

1	33	32	5	4	36

→

1	33	32	5	4	36
30	10	11	26	27	7
13	21	20	17	16	24
18	22	23	14	15	19
25	9	8	29	28	12
6	34	35	2	3	31

Table 3 Creating a table for the "magic" square.

Let's begin to make a table with the information given, initially using the left image from Figure 6b. The first row is easy, using the numbers 1, 33, 32, 5, 4, and 36. We see the sum is 111. Which numbers should go in the next row, and how to arrange them? Let's do as before and experiment with writing each row in an opposite "direction".

Each row makes 111, but columns and diagonals do not; meaning that either the sequence of rows is incorrect, or the image, and hence the sequence within each row is incorrect. One of the things that makes magic squares so interesting is that other number combinations are also present. Note from Table 3 that the central four numbers total to make 74, as do the four corners, the four squares at each corner and also four otherwise corresponding squares. However, it is still not perfect.

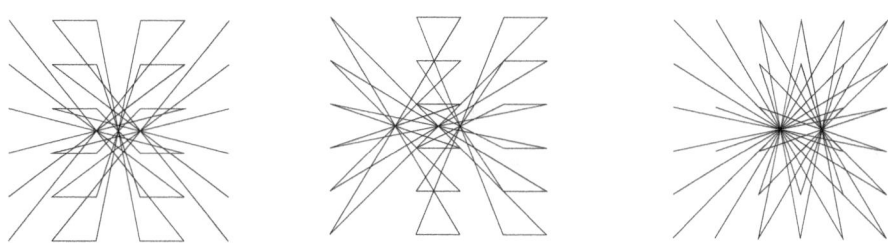

Figure 6c Further drawings on the 6-square.

A number of beautiful forms are possible within the 6-square, and though each will have 111 as a sum of connected points they will be no better at getting columns and diagonals to agree. A challenge!

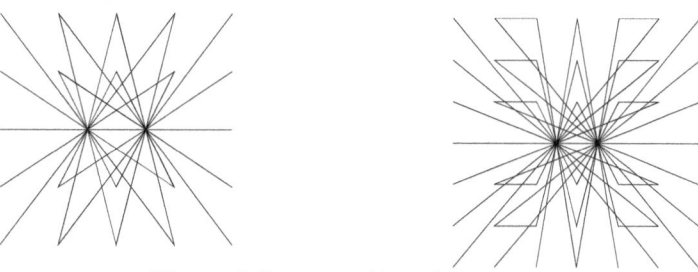

Figure 7 Squares of 5 and 7.

So far, we have only worked with even-numbered squares. There are no possible tabulations due to the odd-numbered nature of the forms but we can nonetheless draw amazing figures based on squares of 5, 7 and 9 as shown in Figures 9 and 12.

We can continue the process with the square of 8, and find here one that works well and easily.

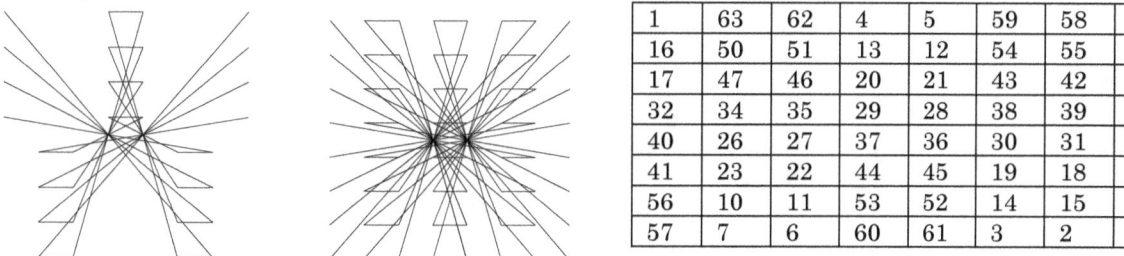

1	63	62	4	5	59	58	8
16	50	51	13	12	54	55	9
17	47	46	20	21	43	42	24
32	34	35	29	28	38	39	25
40	26	27	37	36	30	31	33
41	23	22	44	45	19	18	48
56	10	11	53	52	14	15	49
57	7	6	60	61	3	2	64

Figure 8 Developing the Magic Square of 8.   Table 4 Rows, columns, diagonals total 260.

Write down the numbers of the connected dots in the table, alternating each row; increasing, from 1 to 8, and then decreasing. Eventually, we obtain the material shown in Table 4, and find that it works well, totaling 260 in each column, row, and diagonal. Too, the four numbers in the corners, at the center, and elsewhere add up to make 130. Interesting relationships. See any further patterns?

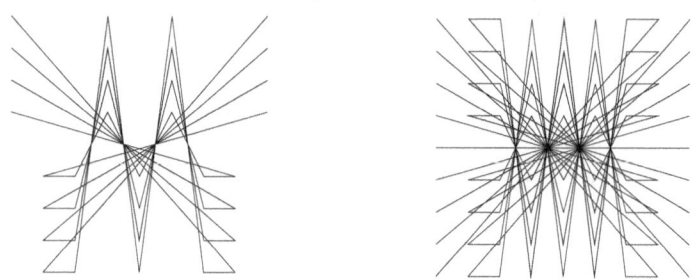

Figure 9 Developing a square of 9.

There is no end to the "joy" of discovery with magic squares. That of 12 is particularly elegant, and a great exercise in seeing how patterns develop with numbers. We will leave that as an exercise for the enthusiast (Figure 10a).

We can of course do many things artistically with these forms, like erasing "busy" lines and eventually coloring the shape. A great deal of effort pays off as always with a beautiful drawing for our classrooms and homes.

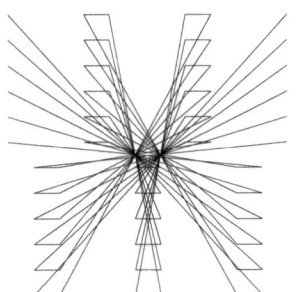 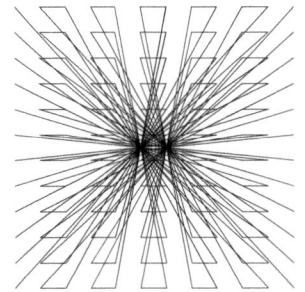 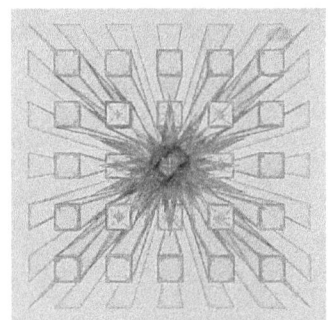

Figure 10a Developing the Magic Square of 12.   10b Image copied on second axis and colored.

The shapes that our students can generate here are exciting and beautiful. If we look at them again, as a progression, it is fascinating to see how a matrix of expansion seems to form.

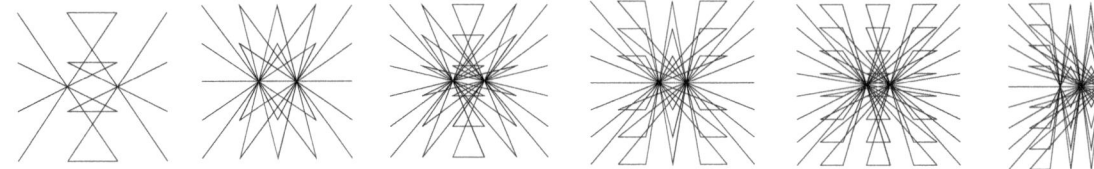

Figure 11 A geometric progression of square stars.

Lattice structures

We go now to one final use of the straight line, to give the illusion of … "curves". This is a rather simple technique of drawing two lines that meet perpendicularly (or at other angles), marking equal spaces along them, and finally drawing lines from the marks on one to marks on the other (working from outside to inside), slowly changing toward inside to outside.

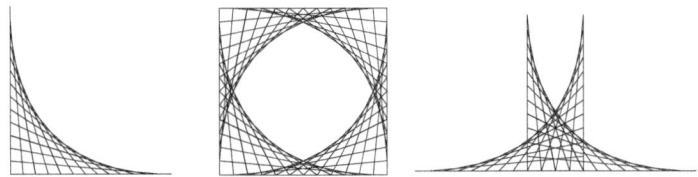

Figure 12a The basic and slightly more "deluxe" versions of the lattice structure.

Let's take the last form of Figure 12a, and rotate it about a central point 12 times. As the location for the center of rotation rises up between the two peaks, the emerging flower takes on beautiful new shapes, surrounded by a twelve-pointed figure.

Figure 12b Some final play.

These pictures were generated with a computer aided design software package. The computer is a useful tool for trying new ideas and for saving so much erasure on a potential artistic piece. But the initial experiments and final product should always be done by hand.

Figure 13 Some examples.

Young artists need to hold a pencil, or a brush, and go through the steps, making mistakes, taking hours trying to create and being frustrated by the outcomes, experimenting with color and light, and breathing while they are doing so. Let's let our mathematician artists do so as well. Use the technology when appropriate, but otherwise... use skill and intelligence.

Last but not least; 9

We have found a multitude of ways to divide a circle. Here at the end, we will examine one final factor: 9-fold division.

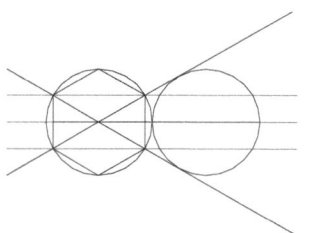
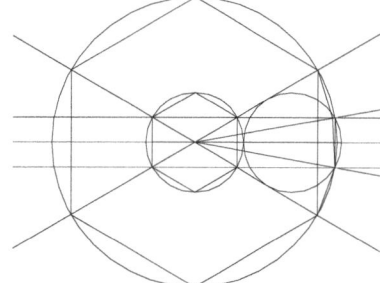

Figure 14a Circles, hexagon, lines,   b) trisectors, larger circle/hexagon (99%).

Draw a horizontal line and upon this place two circles of radius '1' (touching tangentially). Draw a hexagon and then diagonal and horizontal lines as shown in Figure 14a. Draw diagonal lines from the center of the left circle to the far crossing points, *trisecting* the 60° angle of the hexagon (99% accuracy). Draw a large diameter circle (centered again at that left circle) set to these "trisector" intercepts. A larger hexagon, based upon the diagonal intercepts of the large circle, nearly defines three points of an 18-sided figure. This is accurate enough in the classroom.

The problem is that 9-fold division depends on angles which seem easy enough, like 20° and 40°, but to generate them we need something we've not done yet; divide an angle by three.

Trisection

We can bisect a line and an angle, and trisect a line. But as yet, no one in the history of mathematics has apparently found a consistent means of trisecting an angle. While the author is forced for the time being to agree, after fighting this to exhaustion, there are amazing numerical discoveries which are deemed interesting enough to include.

We begin with an old friend; the vesica piscis. Drawing the first regular polygons shows how they relate within this geometry. (Figure 15)

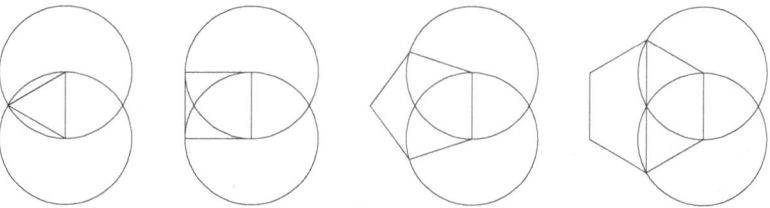

Figure 15 Vesica Piscis used to define four regular polygons.

Using the same techniques as at the beginning of this book we generate a hexagon, and easily trisect the straight line (180°).

Proceeding with the octagon, we will generate a vesica piscis whose circles each have radius of '1'. The edge length (distance between the two centers) is thus defined. We can use our well-tried methods to get the points of intersect to determine further sides.

In Figure 16, the octagon has been placed upon the vesica piscis and a straight line drawn between two vertexes. It's interesting that the lengths of that line, where it meets the inner curve measure the same '1'. We will find this is not unique. Further, note the "coincidence" of 0.5 and √2 − 1 (0.4142). And while 0.7654 and 1.3066 may not be recognizable, a little examination reveals that they are reciprocals, and we can eventually obtain them using regular geometric practices like?... The half angle theorem on 45°!

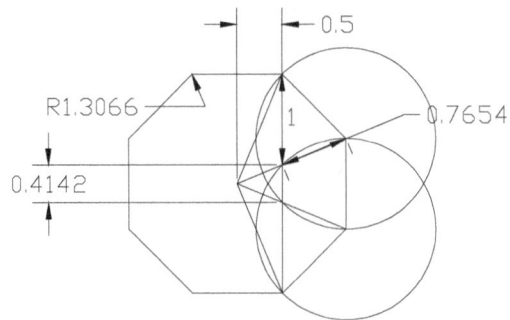

Figure 16 The octagon and key geometries found in the vesica piscis.

Let's look at the pentagon which can be contained within our vesica piscis. If we trace inside it, note how the star is defined. Outside we overlay a decagon on the drawing (Figure 17) and see that the geometries are most interesting.

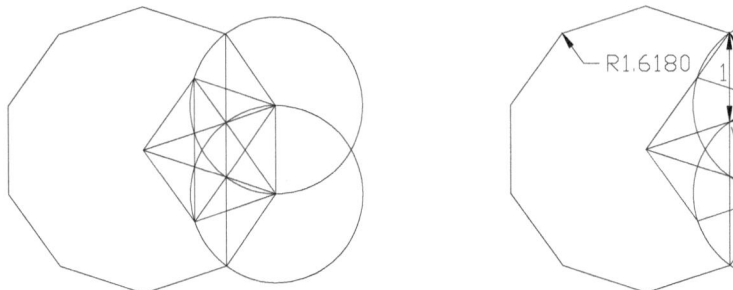

Figure 17 Pentagonal and decagonal geometries on the vesica piscis.

We continue this work, on the dodecagon. The final results are shown in Figure 18. We readily note √2 and √3 − 1. If we look to our table for half angles (15°) we find that 1.9319 is √(2 + √3). We'll come back to this.

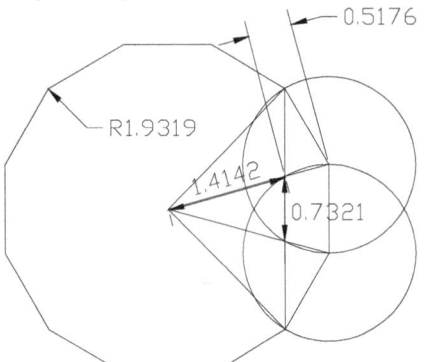   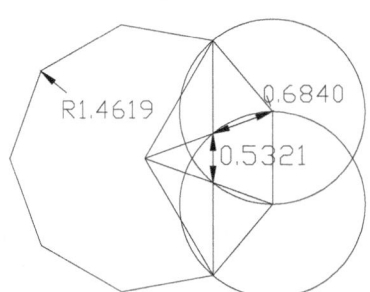

Figure 18 The Dodecagon overlay.   Figure 19 The nonagon overlay

The vesica piscis is a great assistant in developing an understanding of polygons, and helps in "trisecting" several of them. We learned in earlier chapters how to divide the circle to get 8, 12, and 5 (and thus 10) sided figures. This does not enable us to divide by 9. Unfortunately, for the nonagon (the 9 sided figure we are eventually aiming for) this will come down to just another attempt at trisecting, by using a "floating" point. Still, if one looks on the internet to find other possibilities, it is seen that this technique is more user friendly.

Figure 19 shows a nonagon on the vesica piscis, with two key decimal values denoted. Work with the "sister" 18-gon will help us further define the geometries there-in. Portions of the process, on 18-gonal format are demonstrated in Figure 20. Notice the 20° angle. Interestingly, the angle in this position always corresponds to the angle from the center of the polygon. The key here is that the vesica piscis generates for us a radius of 2.8794 on the 18-gon. The value determined is the irrational number 2.87938…

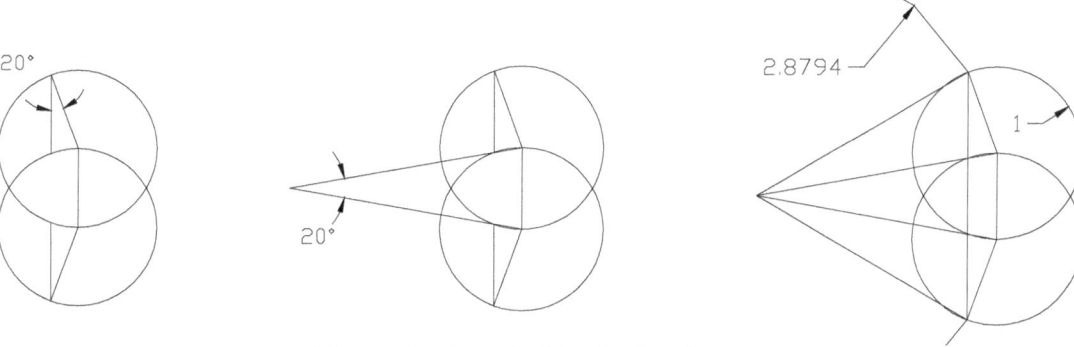

Figure 20a, b, and c Developing the 18-gon

The drawing so far incorporates an equilateral triangle included with the vesica piscis and portions of the 18-gon. If we play with this a little by drawing some lines at 30° we generate intersecting points upon which we can overlay two more lines at 20° (this leads to figure 28). All of this creates a spider web of lines and each of these segments could be measured to reveal the "secrets" of 9-fold geometry.

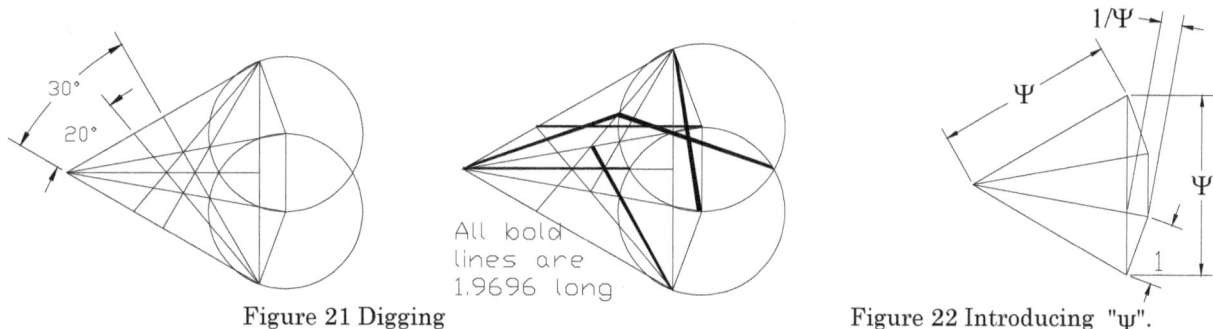

Figure 21 Digging   Figure 22 Introducing "ψ".

Ψ – another proportion

One value in particular repeats itself and is shown in Figure 21. This number; 1.9696 relates mathematically to 2.8794. If we add '1' to the larger and take the root of the sum, we obtain the smaller. 2.8794 behaves very much like our much-studied phi. For this reason, and in keeping with tradition I will identify this proportion by the letter "psi" – ψ; having an exact value of 1/(2 cos 80°).

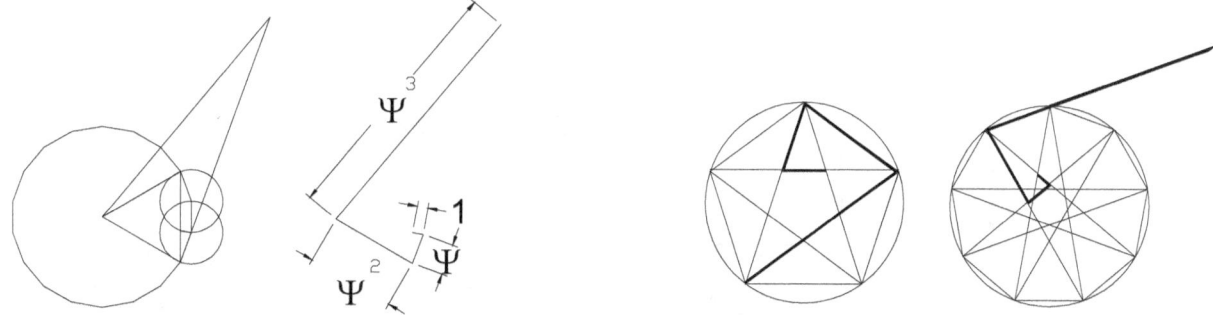

Figure 23a Psi proportions build the 9-pointed star.   23b Phi and Psi spirals found in 5 and 9-pointed stars.

Figure 23 shows one such similarity. Notice the spirallic nature by which a nine pointed star can be created and how each leg increases in length by the factor ψ, just as we did with phi. Figures 24a and b show interesting proportional relationships within 9-pointed stars; and how they also relate to ψ.

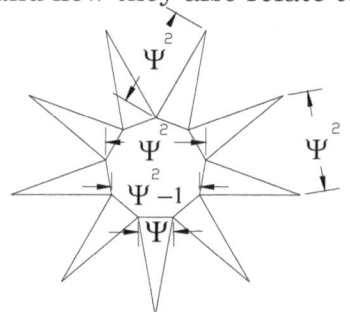   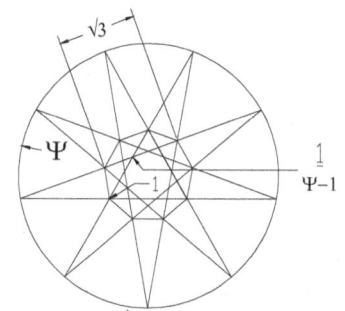

Figure 24a Ψ proportions found in the 9-pointed star.   24b Ψ, 1, and √3 relations.

241

By generating a table of cosine values for key angles, and then working and *working* with Ψ, we find that it functions in many ways like its more attractive relative.

	2 x Trig value	Function of Ψ
2Cos 10°	1.9696	$\sqrt{(Ψ + 1)}$
2Cos 20°	1.8794	$Ψ - 1$
2Cos 40°	1.5321	$\sqrt{((2Ψ + 1)/Ψ)}$
2Cos 50°	1.2586	$\sqrt{((2Ψ - 1)/Ψ)}$
2Cos 70°	0.6840	$\sqrt{(Ψ + 1)}/Ψ$
2Cos 80°	0.3473	$1/Ψ$

Table 5 Nonagon cosine values in decimal and Ψ

Remember that 2cos 36° makes 1.618, and 2cos 30° makes 1.732, both of which are key proportions. Similarly 2cos 40° makes 1.532 and it is not yet clear whether this or 2.8794 is the more relevant. Notice in Figure 25 how 1.9696 is found in the 9-pointed star, and being part of an equilateral triangle means that the adjacent legs are of equal measure. See here how Ψ, ½, 1 and √3 are contained. Look at the last line of Table 6. Not only does Ψ behave like phi, but there seems some relation between them. Can we find it?

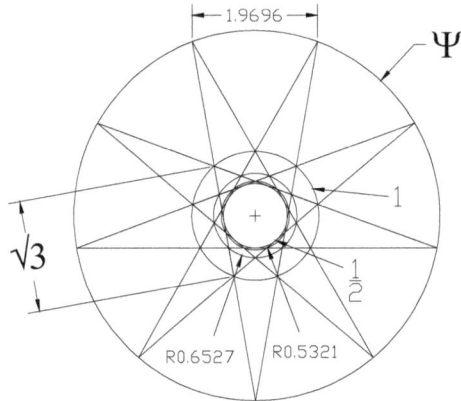

Figure 25 Values in the 9-pointed star radius Ψ

0.5321	$1/(Ψ - 1)$		
0.6527	$(Ψ - 1)/Ψ$		
0.6840	$\sqrt{(Ψ + 1)}/Ψ$	$\sqrt{((Ψ - 2)/(Ψ - 1))}$	
1.2586	$\sqrt{3}Ψ/\sqrt{(Ψ + 1)}$	$\sqrt{((2Ψ - 1)/Ψ)}$	
1.5321	$Ψ/(Ψ - 1)$	$\sqrt{((2Ψ + 1)/Ψ)}$	
1.8794	$Ψ - 1$		
1.9696	$\sqrt{(Ψ + 1)}$	$(\sqrt{(4Ψ^2 - 1)})/Ψ$	$\sqrt{3}Ψ^2/(Ψ^2 - 1)$
2.5321	$Ψ^2 - 2Ψ$	$(Ψ^2 - 1)/Ψ$	$(2Ψ - 1)/(Ψ - 1)$
2.8794	$Ψ$		
3	$(Ψ^3 + 1)/Ψ^2$	$(Φ^4 + 1)/Φ^2$	

Table 6 Critical values associated with understanding Ψ, and interesting equivalent terms

Research into these diagrams and patterns has repeatedly resulted in a cubic equation: $x^3 - 3x^2 + 1 = 0$. The reader is welcome to expend hours and reams of paper to the cause and they will return to this.

The interesting thing is that phi has a similar equation: $x^3 - 2x^2 + 1 = 0$. We will look at their graphs, along with $x^3 - 4x^2 + 1 = 0$, to seek any clues (and provide further areas of unique mathematics studies for our students!

Figure 26 provides the graphs for our analysis. With x-y tables, we can find whole numbered solutions for x = − 1, 0, 1, 2, 3 etc. Interestingly, see the straight lines we can draw over some these points. Notice that for our psi graph it looks like the drawing is symmetrical above and below this line. How could we confirm this? By using the integral in calculus. Application!

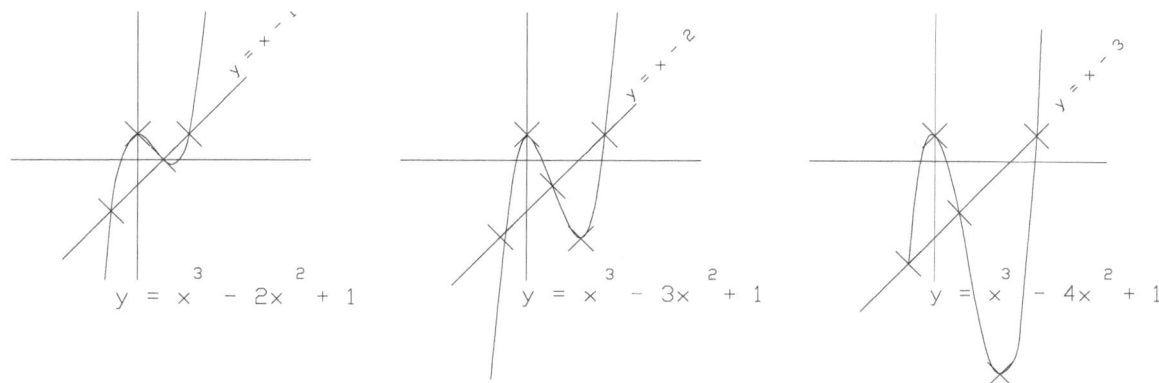

Figure 26 Cubic equations

Where does the phi graph cross the x-axis? Guesses? At Φ, 1 and -1/Φ (or − (Φ − 1)). And the psi graph? At Ψ, −1/(Ψ − 1), and (Ψ − 1)/Ψ; numbers which readily appear in Figure 25, and elsewhere.

The thing about Ψ is that unlike phi, some form of "whole"-number answer remains elusive. We find clues in phi, and √3; tantalizing ones. We see that cos 30° = √3/2, and that cos 36° = (1 + √5)/4. As certain terms contained therein relate to the quantity of sides in the regular trigon and pentagon, does this mean that cos 40° will have √9 as part of its numerator and 8 in its denominator? Should there be three terms, of some complex nature in that numerator? These ideas would fit with the 17-gon, where Gauss discovered the following (and we should wonder how!):

$$\text{Cos } \frac{2\pi}{17} = \frac{-1 + \sqrt{17} + \sqrt{(34 - 2\sqrt{17})} + 2\sqrt{(17 + 3\sqrt{17} - \sqrt{(34 - 2\sqrt{17})} - 2\sqrt{(34 + 2\sqrt{17}))}}}{16}$$

Patterns; one of the themes of this book, and found all over this new proportion, but still of no help in conclusively defining what Ψ's value is, other than 1/(2cos 80°). Unfortunately for the author, and maybe reader, we're left with that. Through use of the diagrams we find that a common solution occurs in; Ψsin 20° = sin 80°, (Ψ − 1)sin 20° = sin 40°, etc. and that sin 20° + sin 40° = sin 80°. Further, cos 20°·cos 40°·cos 80° = 1/8, equal to cos 1π /7·cos 2π /7·cos 3π /7, thus suggesting a connection between 9- and 7-fold division... Were the builders of Stonehenge mathematically advanced enough to realize any of this in their apparent use of seven and nine?

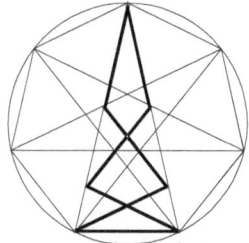 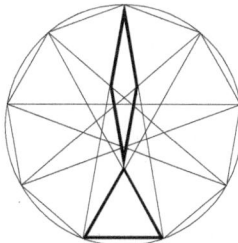

Figure 27 Seven sticks of equal length can build the basic geometry of the 7 and 9-pointed stars.

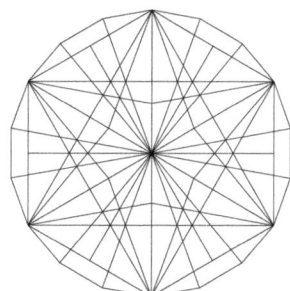

Figure 28 Beauty within 18-fold geometry.

Figure 29 shows further fascinating numerical patterns found in regular polygons. Note that the radius of the inner circle is unity in each form.

Psi you later!

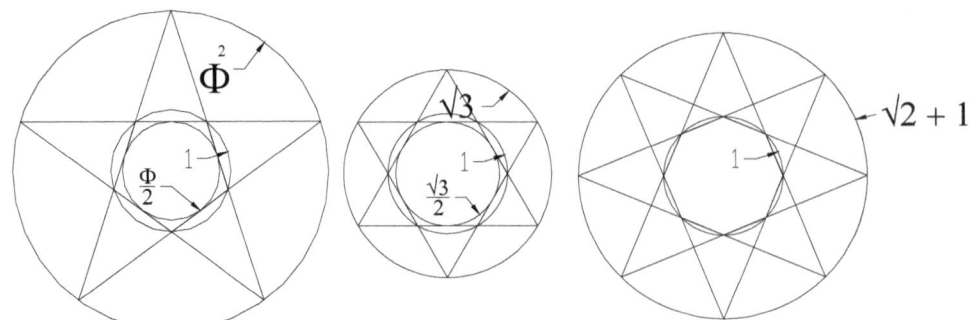

Figure 29a Easily recognized proportions in our favorite polygons.

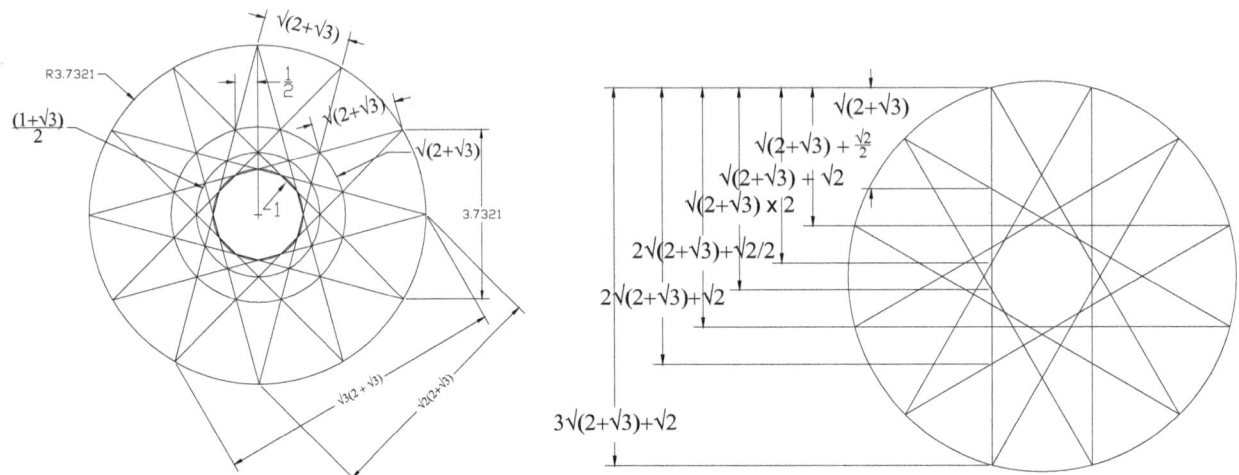

Figure 29b The complexity of the dodecagon, built around $\sqrt{2 + \sqrt{3}}$.

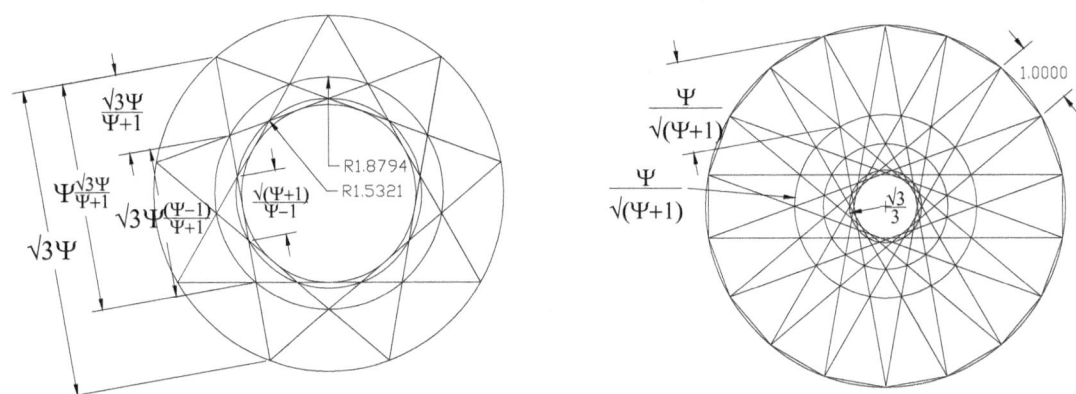

Figure 30 The complexity of 9 and 18 point stars, both with radius Ψ

Concluding dialogue

How can we open ourselves to the mathematical/philosophical concepts included within this book, alongside usable mathematics? If we can, as Joseph Campbell suggested, consider our world as Thou, our entire perspective *will* change. That has been the goal of this book and the result that the author has obtained at least for himself.

These are things about which we must educate ourselves and our students. Information. There are many more deeply valuable concepts we *should* impart. Actualization.

"The release of atom power has changed everything except our way of thinking ... The solution to this problem lies in the heart of mankind. If only I had known, I should have become a watchmaker." - Albert Einstein

Appendix on Alternatives in Assessment

Opening dialogue

How do we attempt alternative teaching methods, as outlined in this book, and then grade our students with analytical measure? How do we get results we wish to see of quality notes and effort?

Assessing our students

The last section of this book concerns evaluation of our beloved students. Love them we do; for certainly, most people who prefer money and *things*, instead of people, end up being something that pays better than a teacher's salary.

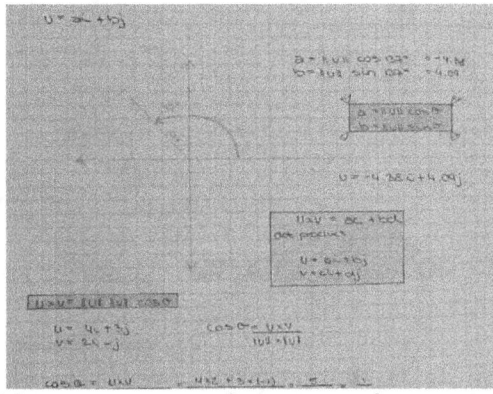

Figure 31 A student with average test results, yet superb presentation of work (L. Scholz).

What are the signs of a student who does poorly in math? Would we say low test scores, incomplete homework, low attention and effort, sloppy work and disruptive behaviors? (These are not always the entire picture.) What are negative signs of a good mathematics student? Rushed, sloppy work and tendency to disrupt when finished

Many times we assess our students based on test scores. Do tests reflect whether the student generally understands the material? Yes. Do they help students develop? There's the question. The techniques in this book, coupled with care, have enabled students to show marked improvement, and have also helped students with career choices. Testing occasionally, is necessary, to push students to finally study and attempt things completely on their own, and be assessed for it. But, there is so much more that we can do to develop each individual.

Do students with low test scores have other strengths? We would be amazed by their abilities if we only investigate them further. Often they have really well-structured notes – **best in the class**, precise drawings of graphs, with key areas and ideas highlighted, exceptional memorization of facts and key information. Their notebooks are often usable by the teacher in later years as notes.

The same will not be true of those who *seem* to be the best and brightest. Do students with high scores have weaknesses we overlook? Many times yes. Their notes are often a mess of disorganized paper, with sloppy handwriting throughout and are boring and dull to attempt to read. It won't be if we hold them to a higher expectation. They often have an inability to communicate in verbal or written form the things that they know, are very reluctant to do work at the chalkboard and often show a decided lack of creativity. They don't mix well with classmates. This is the type of person we want inventing our world and future?

This is not a textbook. But, it can be a curriculum, or at least a basis for a math program (and art and science too). It is a supplement, an alternative approach. So is the method of grading.

Testing

We can still give tests. But, how much should we weight them? Should they be 90% of the total grade? 80%? We think this is normal. We see that students fall in the bell curve and accept it, along with the thought that some students just don't do well in mathematics. Or, we think that eventually, the student who cares will pull themselves out of the dregs and take an interest.

Repetitive testing is basically useless because we see after the first or second test who the "bright" ones are. Many students don't do well with how mathematics is taught and tested and perceive as youth that they are a "failure" and accept it, instead of taking all the "helpful" advice to improve themselves. When we perpetuate this, we guarantee that a portion of the class will not do well, because a lot of people don't perform well on tests. But, if we work with them we find the facts are in their heads. They just can't always put them all together. The greatest surprise is that their memorization of key ideas may be best in the class.

How often should we test? Some teachers think they are holding their students accountable if they test or quiz fairly frequently. For students who have anxiety over testing, this is supposed to encourage them? More, testing by item, rather that more fully developed themes takes away too much instruction time and can interrupt the process.

Let's instead weight the tests at only 30% of the total, and only give three or four through the semester. Now *that* is a change. Those "A" students aren't going to sail through now. Not unless they get off of their cozy couch and learn the new things that are required of them. Don't we want to give them new challenges and chances to develop anyway? Let's even the playing field, and give a lot more people a chance.

Finally, we will change the way we test too. Instead of writing problems that begin "Mark and Sally were counting pennies...", let's personalize the tests and put the students themselves in the word problems. Also, let's put fun stories and pictures in those problems. "Cathy was pulling Mike's little sister in a wagon to the store. If the angle of the handle was..."

The student and teacher will really like this part. Sometimes someone will laugh, or draw a comic on the test. Isn't it better when students are in good humor during a math or science test? Often, they will be curious who the "star" of the next test will be.

One thing to do at the time that students begin to apply trigonometry in-depth is to teach the Greek alphabet. This doesn't have to be much. For homework go to the library and copy down all the letters, their name and pronunciation. On the next few tests, have them translate a few Greek words, like Γεομετρει, ΦιλοσωΦια and Πυραμιδοσ. Have them learn to write their first and last name in Greek, by how each letter or syllable sounds. The spelling doesn't have to be 100% accurate. The point is, can they begin to recognize, and be comfortable with those Greek symbols, so many of which we use in math and science?

Maths Level 2 Test five

1) Jarda is 1.7 meters tall. Using the telescope, he sees the top of the tower at an angle of 33 degrees. He then measures his distance to the center of the tower as 74 meters. How tall is the tower? 10 %

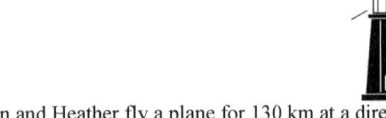

2) Maarten and Heather fly a plane for 130 km at a direction of 180 degrees. Then, they turn and fly for 200 km at a direction of 300 degrees. What distance and course must they fly to get home? 15 %

3) Looking out her window, Magda sees that the top of the tree is at an angle of 28° above the horizontal. Looking again, the bottom is at an angle of 18° from the horizontal. Outside, Krystina measures the ground distance to the tree, from the window as 13 meters. How tall is the tree? 15 %

4) A plane's engine develops 5 kN of thrust. Mass is 1,300 kg. In straight and level flight, calculate and show all the forces acting on the plane.

Figure 32 Typical creative test with student names in the situations

Award one or two extra points to students for the rest of their career each time they write their name in Greek on a test. In our point system, it means almost nothing. But they will surely remember what these symbols mean, and its fun, so why not? Any time we can make learning formulas fun, an easier time of it will be had by math, physics and chemistry teachers. Too, we never know when that student might someday go to Greece or Russia, Bulgaria, Albania, Serbia, or further a field and be helped by this.

Demonstration of Learning

We have testing alternatives that are formative assessments, intended to help the student develop, and motivate them to manage their own learning. They give excellent results.

What we want as teachers is that the students learn. Parents, college admissions and future employers look at grades and perhaps assume that learning is what the student has done. This is not always the case. Today, real emphasis is placed on grades – a final tally, rather than actual learning. How can we teachers satisfy both ourselves and this system?

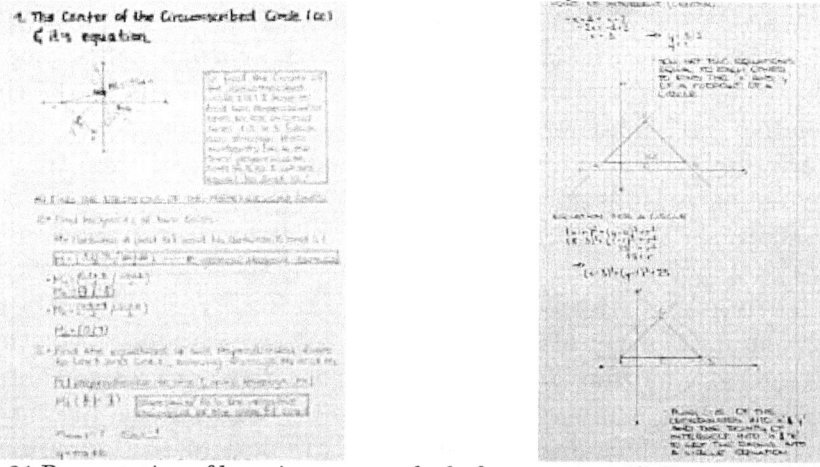
Figure 21 Presentation of learning as a method of assessment (C. Preston and N. Statecnà).

Typically, we work through a lot of material during the semester, testing as we go and then reviewing the entire semester at its end before giving a cumulative test. Wow, this really forces the students to learn. They can't get off the hook. We pushed them to study it, and study it again and we can show the grade that they got from being tested in it – twice. Next year, we start with a whole new bunch of students. But, if we had those same students in the next year, we might be really amazed, and depressed, by how poorly they retain this material, when a math or science teacher is trying to get them to build off of it.

Instead of going through this second, final exam testing routine, let's have them prepare a "demonstration of learning". The teacher can select the key items they would normally review from the semester and have the students study them more independently. Rather than test them, (essentially useless anyway as the results of testing are usually fairly predictable by the end of the term) have them work through example problems that they must individually create. The criteria would be that they must work through the given problem, detailing the steps as though they were teaching it. Allow them to work together, but insist that they change partners for each problem. In this way the weaker students not only are guided by the teacher but will actually seek out the stronger ones

This is a significant effort, resulting in anywhere from 8 to 12 pages of documentation. The students show much more effort and enthusiasm for this than they do for a test and the teacher who attempts this will be amazed by the atmosphere in the classroom as students prepare their materials, work together to solve problems, put extra time in at home and take pride in what they eventually turn in, plus the volume and quality of the work created. It can be worth 20% of the grade. Students can be assessed on how well they followed instructions, how well they worked with others and how neat the presentation is, in addition to the evidence of learning. We can justify assessing by all of these subjective criteria because the steps the student takes to improve notes, seek collegial help, and work as though he is the teacher, can only help him in math, other subjects; and in life.

An alternative to this written "test" would be to have the students pick a topic from a list of those items covered through the year and have them give a presentation on just that. This is another way to help them develop. They must ensure that their materials are accurate. They can be creative as they like with visual aides and they will have the *joy* of giving an oral presentation before their peers. Again, this can be graded for 20 points (meaning 20% of their final grade), based on collection of materials, strength of visuals, accuracy, individual work, quality of the presentation, and successfully meeting their time limit.

Participation

Look for **presence** and **participation** and reward these traits. A student who is present, aware, and following stands a better chance of understanding things. Reward them if they are, and take away points if they are absent. Reward them if they participate and take away points if they don't. Take away more if they disrupt.

At semester end, invite each student to actually assess their own participation and effort. It is surprising how they may grade themselves more harshly than the teacher would. It gives them an appreciation too for how their grade is developed and how their choices each day affect their results. This is very effective at the end of the first semester.

What is positive participation? Did they come to each class prepared with the proper materials? Were they punctual and ready at the start of class? Did they assist in creating a positive learning atmosphere, offer answers to questions posited in class and assist struggling classmates? Did they ask questions to better their understanding, showing an interest? Were they polite, courteous and professional? Did they work independently, or at least try to when asked? If the answer to all of this is "yes", or pretty much so, they can again expect 20 points. Lesser efforts are rewarded accordingly. The student who chooses to do his work quietly, neither disrupting the class nor generally "taking hold of it" can expect a score of 14 or perhaps 16, which probably will not be taking advantage of the chance of easily improving his grade. Those who are detrimental to a productive space can have the satisfaction of achieving worse results. Negative participation can include head on the table, looking out the window and chatting too much with friends.

Included in assessing their participation grade is not the number of times they are absent, but whether they act responsibly in this regard. Sickness happens. Family emergencies and crises also. In cases where student and staff are in agreement about any serious nature, certain exceptions might be workable. However, many times sickness can be used as an attempted excuse for not having gotten notice of a homework assignment or test. This can not be accepted. It is expected that students select appropriate colleagues with whom to share assignment information. Tests will be expected to be completed the very next time the student can return to the classroom, though it is recommended that study hall time be used so the student is not missing even more helpful information.

The reason so much emphasis is placed upon participation is because we know that the student who is present is going to learn more. The student who tries and is rewarded for that is going to try again. And, these people, when they see that they are being rewarded for things other than testing, will start over, will try harder and lo-and-behold *will* test **better**. Participation, effort and responsibility can twice reward the student.

One way to easily assess and reward participation is at the start of class each day. Have the students put up the previous homework assignment as the teacher circulates, checking that the students have their homework. When we check, we have no way to rapidly determine if the student did it or copied it. We can trust that it all comes out in the end when they are tested. But, did they at least take it serious enough to come to class with something on their paper? This review takes a few minutes for the teacher, allowing them to easily see if the students grasped the assignment, find any trouble spots and is a relaxing entry into the class. By this time, those students who volunteered to put a problem on the board have also been checked, and credited for participation.

Try this. Build a routine with it. At the start of class ask, "Who wants to put a problem on the board?" Somewhere along the way, the teacher will be satisfied to see more raised hands than problems which were assigned. Fine, let two students do each problem, and encourage others to come up. Students who normally can sit the entire class, or semester, without doing anything, will suddenly be vying with each other to do the problems. They might already be at the board before the bell, and the arrival of the teacher. That is enthusiasm that is contagious.

What a change this makes in the creative classroom.

Portfolio

What type of notes do students take? Teachers should take the time to look at them. Often a student may do poorly on tests, but are present, work productively, and have incredible order and quality in their notes. Reward and encourage it. Better structure in notes will always improve understanding for students. When they see reward for these types of things, they work harder and get better results.

The portfolio is a professional-artistic word for the compilation of notes, exercises, and other work. This is meant as a reward for students who have often been found not to do well in testing, but can present their highly detailed material professionally, neatly, and proudly. While not necessarily a direct math skill, good notes are a tremendous tool to the user and vital for a mathematician or scientist in being able to communicate with others.

It is easy for a math teacher to rush through the material. We see the "A" students write down a problem or step, solve it and we think we should proceed. After all, we don't want to be accused of teaching to the slowest student in the class, while holding up the rest. Often times this is where and why we lose the "weaker" students. If we circulate, we will see why. The "A" student has scribbled down information, calculated in his head (which we want), thrown down or shouted out the answer and is hungry for the next step. But, the teacher, and even the student-author himself cannot read what has been recorded. Perhaps not all of the information is even present.

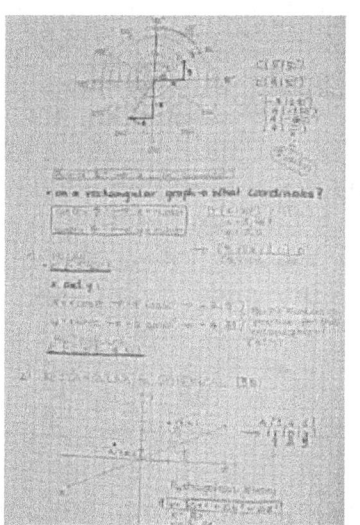 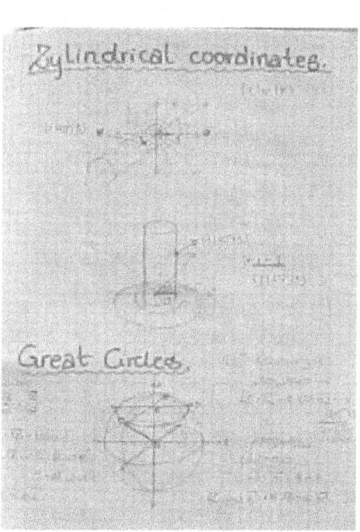

Figure 34 Encourage students to take time to make quality notes (E. Vacková).

On the other hand, the "weak" student may have used a ruler, to draw crisp lines and exact graphs. Maybe they have taken a marker to highlight some point that they or the teacher deemed important. *This* is what we should want. We will be surprised by the penmanship and creativity. When we show this to the class and use it as an example of what we want and expect, this student will beam with pride after feeling, or even hearing, his whole life that he was a failure. Maybe he won't ever get an "A" on a test. But, it is proven that with recognition, he will begin to work harder and in fact have better test results. A "B" is better than a "C" or "D". Then, we will see our bell curve shift towards better grades and we will wonder if we are too easy or lax.

The portfolio can be awarded up to 10 points for excellence. There will be a few cases of this, particularly with time. But it takes time to build up in students an awareness of how they should be taking their notes, and for the teacher to see and develop an idea of the type of notes they wish to see.

What we should look for initially is simply, did they put their name on their notebook? Did they date each item of work? Is it sequential? Did they number the homework assignments? Hopefully the teacher asked them to, for ready reference. Did they highlight key points, and each new section, for easier review prior to tests? Did they record in their notes what the teacher put on the board each day? Did they make corrections to homework problems after the daily class review?

It takes time to discern whether a notebook is an "A", or a "B". If it's not quite, give it 8.9 points. If it's barely a "B", give it 8 or 8.1 Generally, reasonable effort should be seen as a "C" or higher. If they turn in a glop of loose papers, without dates, or any idea of order, we have to decide then what kind of grade to give. If this mess seems to at least have most or all of the work present, we can give a 6 and a lot of clear instruction as to what we expect. If the mess has less, reduce. If the student at least provides something, the minimum is usually a 4 or 5. There are students who will choose to turn in nothing, throwing away a letter grade from their final score. Note that 10% or 10 points are the same thing – of a total of 100 points they will have for determining the letter grade.

The portfolio grade, as with many things is meant to round out skills, be a free chance to improve student grades, and hold accountable those sloppy geniuses.

Homework

Homework is vital. It helps the student remain in contact with material and how ideas build on top of each other. Give daily assignments, but rather than take 20 problems from a book, try a handful that get the point across, and which can easily be reviewed in about fifteen minutes, so that more class time remains for the next material. True, practice makes perfect, but repetition breeds boredom.

There will be approximately 20-30 assignments through the semester. The student who consistently attempts and mostly completes his homework will understand more, perform better when testing, has greater satisfaction in class and recognition from peers and teacher. He can expect to receive a full 10 points toward his "grade" point total.

When checking this at the start of each class simply mark "H" if the student has the whole thing completed, regardless of it being correct or original work. (Those students who copy will meet their "karma" at test time, which is still weighted enough to matter.) If one problem out of five is missing, mark it "H-". This basically means 8 out of ten for that day. An "H" can have any number of minus signs next to it to indicate completeness or quality. Don't accept any excuses. Just tell the students up front to say, "Sorry, I don't have it today." Mark them with something like "Δ". Give them the chance to still turn in the assignment later and mark it "HL", for being late and only give them half credit. Don't let them off the hook for being absent. They need to get the notes from classmates. Again, holding them responsible will get the "slackers" to *be* more responsible.

So, at the end of the semester, total up all the little minuses as 0.1 each, lates as 0.5 and those missing assignments (even if they were sick – to be fair to the rest) as '1'. Take the total and subtract it from the whole that was attainable. Divide by the whole to get a percentage, say 93%. This means their homework grade is 9.3 points.

It's pretty hard, but not so impossible to get a final "10", for homework. But, by encouraging the students to do their work, they will be more involved, in and outside of class, which will of course help them understand more and do better on tests. Again, there are students who don't test well, but come to class after class with completed homework. Maybe someone 'helped' them too much with it, but there it is. Rewarding the effort will lead to improved understanding and results. They get twice the benefit from having done it and are encouraged to try more. Sooner or later, experience will show positive results.

Special project

Finally, we can give non-math math projects, like rocketry and reports about rocketry, mathematicians, astronomers, and scientists who are related to the work at hand. For example, who was Pythagoras and what else was so significant about him? Who was Euclid and why is the geometry we study called Euclidean? Who was al-Kwarizmi and how is it that an Arab, a culture for which we in the West have such stigma, gave us algebra? Who were the Greek, Arab, Indian, Egyptian, and Sumerian mathematicians and astronomers? What did *they* give us?

Instead of written reports have the students draw mandalas, and create Platonic and Archimedian solids, with techniques shown in this book. To grade it, see if they followed color usage recommendations on a mandala, or tried to fill in every piece with a different color, as Gaudi might have done. Did they make good crisp intersections or is it sloppy?

Did they show "scientific drawing", or do lines and arcs just appear and end with no relation to other pieces? Did they use the techniques developed in class, drawing a six sided piece, per instructions, and not four or eight sided? Did they try to give some free-hand or Picasso-esque drawing when symmetry was assigned? There are many ways to assess an artistic presentation.

The 10 points that are attainable here are meant as a free giveaway. The student will have to do adequate work, and they usually do. It is rare to give less than a "B", or 8 points.

Let them have this project. It gives variety and interest into the classroom, and allows a wider range of achievement. It is very satisfying to see smiles on the faces of students who have always failed, and to see their grades slowly climb from "F" and disenfranchised, to "D", and the next year "C". It's great to see and reward a "C" student with an "A", in some category.

Tallying the score

At the end of the semester, we now have a complicated job ahead of us. We first go through our grade sheets, take the test scores, average, multiply by 0.30, and record (maximum 30 points). This is the easiest and least subjective part of the process.

We add up all the "P's" that we gave for participation, and deduct when they were naughty (P-), or didn't have a book or other needed item (B-). There will be one or two students who will have many more "P's" than the rest. Maybe we could even give 21 points for participation. Figure the median number that are hoped for and call that say 15 points. For the student who just sits there and never does anything, but at least is not disruptive, give him an average mark, and remind him that hi is walking away from a free chance to improve his grade. We aren't expecting everyone to be an extrovert. We're looking for them to be involved.

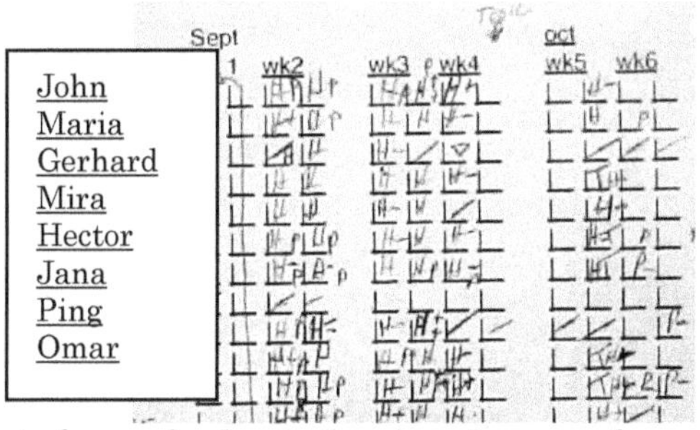

Figure 35 Extract of a grade sheet, showing absences, homework, and participation.

Take the presentation of learning score, which should have already been rated on a scale of 0 (not turned in) to 20 for excellence. Rarely will a grade here be lower than 15 or 16 points. It doesn't mean, however, that it is an easy "A". Hold the work accountable to a high standard. But the students will generally excel on this assignment, particularly if we give enough class time for it (though the project should require home effort as well). There would have been this amount of time devoted anyway to a review for the final exam that this is meant to replace.

Count up all the homework assignments. Count up all the missing and partially incompletes, and deduct from the total. Divide the result by the total and multiply by ten to get some score. Perfection is hard to obtain, as is a score of less than 6.

Look too for any extra work the students have done, and invite them through the semester to try and improve their score. If they are willing, why not? Did they perform in the subject-oriented play? Did they make more artwork, instead of going out on Saturday night? Maybe they wrote another report about astronomy. We don't have to be exceedingly generous. But we can be creative in how we assess, always trying to use it to encourage learning and human development.

In the end, we will be happy to see students rise above their test scores. We will be in a quandary about one or two students who test as "A" students and yet do not now achieve an "A". We have to then decide whether our alternatives, meant to help weaker students find paths to success, are inappropriate for these people, or if we should hold them to this new standard. So often, it is not the "weak" student who is lazy. It is the brighter one.

Concluding dialogue

How can we make math more fun and rewarding, for the best and the rest? Can our goal as math teachers be to emphasize growth and learning, in place of testing and grades?

Why should we make such a major change in the classroom? Is it fair to make the math expert correct and improve his work, help the class, make art, learn about humanities, and have less time for rote math? Is it worthwhile to expand the opportunities for others to perform well with the material? Is it reasonable to think we can give them math credit for these other activities?

We live in times of major change; what a senior Waldorf teacher describes as "going into the dark ages". Despite all of the free information, the general process is one of "dumbing-down" the population, and succoring them with shopping and technology.

Today a growing movement of home schooling is occurring, where individuals are taking charge and providing the leadership, at least in their own lives. We must think of what lies ahead for our children; a dearth of natural resources counter to what we have enjoyed, the effects of environmental degradation, massive climate change, and rapid technological development, all racing towards ...? At every opportunity, let's do whatever we can to help our own children, and any with whom we come into contact, that their eyes are open and that they be prepared for as many possibilities as are foreseeable.

We must think of the generations which will follow us.

Further reading/research and websites:

http://home.clara.net/lovely/homepg.html   Interesting site about crop circles and the energies that might have made them

http://www.kheper.net/topics/subtlebody/ethericbodies.html The Three Planes and the Seven Energy Field Bodies

http://www.vesica.org/sacredgeometry.html   Great site on the approach taken by a doctorate in Physics.

http://ngm.nationalgeographic.com/ngm/tut/mysteries/wrappings.html   Great site showing the layered boxes and devices which covered King tut's mummified remains.

Class Exercise 1 **Compiling better mathematics notes**

Objective:
Many times in this book, we have gone back to basics in order to strengthen critical skills that are vital to higher education. We do so again, conducting basic writing exercises to improve quality, readability, and presentation of notes.

Procedure:
a) Use plain white paper throughout. Have students write (print – not cursive) a few sentences on an easy topic; what they did on over the weekend that was fun. This will be our writing example.
b) Make a series of straight vertical lines, about 1" – 1½" long. Give examples and then circulate, pointing out the ones that each has done best. Repeat now, with horizontal lines, and again with diagonal lines going one way, and then again another. Give examples and circulate each time. Students should now have 30 – 40 lines on their paper. Stress always quality over quantity.
c) Next, draw a straight vertical line and then cross it with a central horizontal line. Make these +'s about ¾" – 1" tall and wide. Do examples and circulate, making sure that they are drawing good perpendicular lines. Repeat – making X's.

d) Move on to equilateral triangles, where each side is about 1" long. As before, do examples. If the teacher is anything like the author, these exercises are good for the self as well. Make sure the Δ is equilateral and not isosceles or something else. Flip the triangle up-side-down and repeat. Then do 45-45-90 triangles, facing left, right and again up-side-down. Do squares, that are perfectly □. Do letters then; H, I, L, F, E, N, M, V, W, Z

Quality over quantity. Students who have the sloppiest handwriting, usually due to haste, will be rushing sloppily through this as well. Slow them down. Encourage them also to hold the pencil or apply pressure differently. The main thing is to not strain in the attempt.

e) Next we will do round exercises. It is a totally different movement, and for this we must loosen up the wrists. Now, draw spirals on the board, as shown below. Spin left, doing continuous loops. Then, repeat to the right. Stay in one place, looping about one center for one series, then let the pen wander, making a "tube". Finally, make a spiral that closes as the pen swirls, and then one that opens. Always do pairs – clockwise and counter.

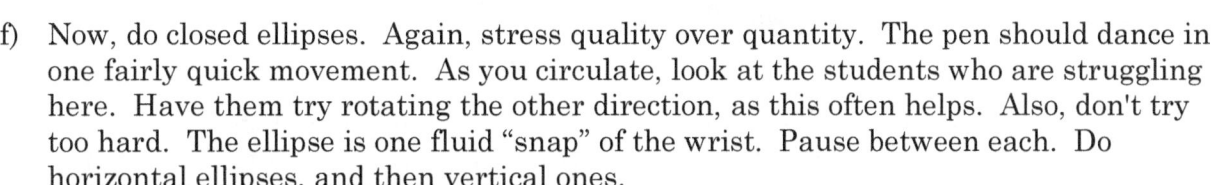

f) Now, do closed ellipses. Again, stress quality over quantity. The pen should dance in one fairly quick movement. As you circulate, look at the students who are struggling here. Have them try rotating the other direction, as this often helps. Also, don't try too hard. The ellipse is one fluid "snap" of the wrist. Pause between each. Do horizontal ellipses, and then vertical ones.

g) Finally comes the trick. Have the students sit upright. Stress that if they wish to improve their work, this is actually the proper posture to be in. Put both hands on the table and both feet firmly on the floor and be still. No talking or moving. When the class has the stillness you want, take a deep breath, turn to the board and draw a large circle. All will be amazed at how near-perfect it is. Tell them now that when they feel ready, they should also attempt this, radius of about 1". They can do larger, and smaller, but not too small, because that is too easy.

h) Now, let them put circles and lines together, going through these shapes: Φ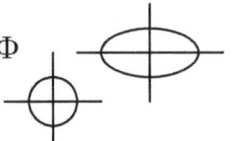
Already, graphs will improve.

i) Do the following letters, one example each, but they should repeat any that they are not satisfied with: d, Q, P, 6, 9, C, S, R, B.

j) Speed drills: mixing lines, letters, circles, triangles, squares etc.

k) Have them write out the alphabet, in block letters, and then repeat, playing with the letters, being creative and artistic, as shown here:

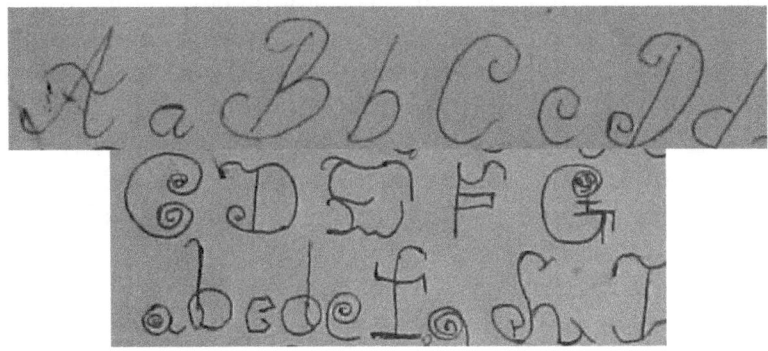

l) Finish by letting them again write about a topic, perhaps about their friends, a pet, or some other positive theme. They can print how they like. Always encourage this to be happy work.

m) This procedure fills 1½ hours. Repeat, a week later. Get the lines in step b to be parallel and uniform in length. In fact, have all shapes and symbols be equal in dimension, so that the symbols will look like an ordered form of writing. In steps 'i' and 'j', provide a sheet of paper (with bold, dark lines, spaced about ¾" apart) that they can put behind their papers. Let them use this as a guide. Emphasize that they need to print large in accordance. Finally, let them again write about something they like, say, a letter to Santa.

Homework:
We wish to encourage writing. Mandatory homework will probably not do this. Nor will extra credit necessarily, because the students who need the practice most (usually the boys) will be least inclined to do it.

Evaluation:
Attitude (affective) is a big part of this process. Is the student curious, trying seriously to improve, or is their head on the table as they slouch through yet another "dull" routine? Do they see the improvement that they are quickly able to make and try harder, or are they just rushing through as always?

Bridges:
Stress better notes in every class. Most subject teachers will support this, but its mostly up to the art teacher to initiate. It's a great introduction to calligraphy. The mathematics teacher should do occasional straight line and curve work, say 10 minutes practice here and there. Graphing will improve, as will structure, if we insist upon it. In other subjects, lettering work can be done.

Class Exercise 2 **The Outer Limits**

Objective:
Further the possibilities in our physics studies.

Procedure:
a) If, as this book suggests, the math and physics teachers have attempted to bridge their instruction on waves to include the entire electromagnetic spectrum, music, color, planetary effects on the weather and mobile communication effects on the brain, they will find fertile ground to pursue the concept of auras, chakra wavelength, earth energy fields and even the "spirit realm". The teacher should prepare a brief summary (2-4 pages) of those topics they feel comfortable with, pulling information perhaps from the websites suggested for further reading.
b) Have students read this summary. People are aware of these ideas and yet do and simultaneously don't believe. For now, we can not scientifically be so sure.
c) Introduce the subject of kirlian photography, a process whereby the aura can supposedly be captured as an image. The key is that if these "things" exist, as many people insist, and can perceive, could it be as a vibration for which we have not yet created detection equipment? If natural energy fields are in a radio wave, UV, or other wavelength, we would need a receiver capable of detecting them, tuned to their frequency and able to display whatever they consist of. It may seem far-fetched, but x-ray photography and Magneto Resonance were too.
d) Get students to individually research a topic in these areas.

Homework:
Individual research papers, two pages long.

Evaluation:
Grade the quality of their effort.

Bridges:
This topic is aptly named. Not every teacher will want to touch it. Physics and science are trying to push back the shadows, and have to a great extent. Could we map the human energy fields, and use that to heal illness, understand natural energies and harness them in less destructive ways than current energy generation, or see angels and faeries?

Class Exercise 3 **Magic squares and Lattices**

Objective:
Create mathematical-artistic imagery, using measurement, deduction, and calculation to find patterns and have fun.

Procedure:
a) Draw a square of dots: 4 x 4, Figure 4a. Draw over them, the lines shown in Figures 4b-d. Make a 4 x 4 table, and in each row put the four numbers from each 'route' that was drawn. Table 1. Add up each row. Add up each column and diagonal. Add the four numbers in each corner, and the four in the center (34.). Magic? No, Magic Square!
b) Repeat for Dürer's square. Table 2, Figure 5.
c) Try now a 6 x 6 pattern. Let the students try their own sketches here. The key is to start at the top row of dots, and connect with the bottom, using 6 dots. The second route should use the second row, connected with the next-to-the-last row, and the third route uses the middle two rows. Students should strive for symmetry, for they sill start to notice that in each diagram, there seem to be foci. They should try to make a table then of numbers and see what the sum in each row, column and diagonal should be. If the numbers are not equal, and probably won't be, what could they do differently? Could they change the sequence of how the rows were written or flip some from left to right? Or, would they need a different image? Figures 6a-c.
d) Create the square of 8 as shown in Figure 8, and build a table whose columns, rows and diagonals will all be equal. Table 4 is a workable final form.
e) Create squares of 5, 7, and 9, comparing with the even numbers, seeing how the odds seem to create a branch, through which the evens seem to spread.

f) Draw two equidistant lines, perpendicular to each other and 4-6" long. Note, they don't need to be perpendicular, nor equidistant for this to work. Make marks along the lines each ¼" or ½". Draw a line from the top dot on the vertical line to the inner dot on the horizontal. Do a second line from the second vertical point to the second horizontal point and so on. Eventually, the web is formed. Figure 12a. A variety of forms can be made, as shown in this figure. Further shapes, regular and otherwise, can be used to create beautiful images. Figure 13.
g) Have the students attempt a complex shape, such as that shown in Figure 12b. Here, the style of dodecagon must be selected, and location of the overlapping webs.

Homework:
Have students draw a magic square, web, or both together, and color their creation. More beauty for the walls of the classroom.

For extra credit and challenge, let students draw the square of 12 (Figure 10), and develop the table. It's actually not so hard, once the pattern is seen.

Evaluation:
Assess how they challenge themselves mathematically and artistically. Teenagers like to find something to complain about, nearly always, and will do so now, saying that it's too geometrical. Let them eat cake. There are worse things they could be tasked with doing in a math or art class.

Bridges:
These figures again make connections between art and math. The magic squares have also long had metaphysical use, as some have been related by alchemists to various planets, associations of specific numbers with each.

Another good approach with this work is to pound nails in a board and use different colored string to create the forms, interweaving the strands.

About the Author

Paul "Sky" Stang is a teacher, student, and artist of Sacred Geometry, Mathematics, Astrology, Archaeo-Astronomy, Leylines and Sciences. His initial education and career was in Aviation Engineering, where he saw first-hand application of mathematics. He then traveled the world, studying cultures, art and architecture, doing odd-jobs along the way; managing a medicinal herbal company, assisting the engineer on an environmental boat and building houses.

Coincidental to obtaining an advanced degree in Arts he began a new career in teaching. Each summer travel season continued to imbue new inspirations into his efforts, both artistic and practical. He has taught an ever-growing range of materials at high school, university, and adult workshops in the US, and at an international high school, further workshops, and teacher training seminars throughout Europe.

Specific themes presented, taught, or published to date include "Wisdom in Mathematics", "Using Mandalas in Mathematics Instruction", "2 and 3 Dimensional Constructions in Mathematics Instruction", "Zometools in the Creative Classroom", "Phi - The Golden Section", "In the Footsteps of the Masters – Stonehenge, Pyramids and da Vinci", "I as Symbol in the Circle of Life", "Rocketry for Physics and Mathematics Lessons", "The Historical Development of Alchemy as a Means of Teaching Chemistry", "The Geometry of the Goddess", and "Theatrical Presentation of Educational Materials".

Bibliography

Books

Michael Schneider, A beginner's guide to constructing the Universe, 1994, HarperCollins, New York

Bruce Rawles, Sacred Geometry Design Sourcebook., 1997 Elysian Publishing

Robert Lawlor, Sacred Geometry, Philosophy and Practise, 1982

W. M. Smart, Spherical Astronomy, 1962, Cambridge Universtiy Press.

Euclid, The Thirteen books of the Elements. Translated by Sir Thomas Heath, 1956

Irving Adler, Mathematics exploring the world of numbers and space, 1960, Golden Press

Hugh Kenner, Geodesic Math and how to use it, 1976, University of California Press

Bettye Hall, Algebra 2 with Trigonometry, 1993, Prentice Hall

Paul Zitzewitz, Physics, Principles and Problems, 2002, Mcgraw-Hill

Antony Wilbraham, Chemistry, 2000, Prentice-Hall

Linda Verlle Williams, Teaching for the Two-sided Mind, 1983, Touchstone, New York

Gerald S. Hawkins, Stonehenge Decoded, 1965, Doubleday and Company, New York

Plato, The dialogues of Timaeus and Critias translated by Benjamin Jowett, 1871, Scribner and Sons, NY

John Martineau, A little book of Coincidences in the Solar System, 2001, Wooden Books

Sir Norman Lockyer, Dawn of Astronomy, 1894, Macmillan, New York

Sir Norman Lockyer, Stonehenge and other British stone Monuments, astronomically considered, 1906, Macmillan

Alexander Thom, Megalithic Sites in Britain, 1967, Oxford University Press, London

W. M. Flinders Petrie, The Pyramids and Temples of Gizeh, 1883

Aubrey Burl, A guide to Stone Circles of Britain, Ireland and Brittany, 1995, Yale University

John Michell, The view over Atlantis, 1969

John Michell, City of Revelation, 1972

Zecharia Sitchin, When Time Began, 1993, Avon Books

Nikola Tesla, The Tesla Papers, Edited by David Hatcher Childress, 2000, Adventures unlimited press

Claudius Ptolemy, Tetrabiblos, Translated by J.M. Ashmand
Salvador Dali, 50 Secrets of Magic Craftsmanship, 1948 Dover

Shalila Sharamon and Bodo Baginski, Zakladni Kniha o Čakrach, 1988

Der Himmel über dem Menschen der Steinzeit, Rolf Müller, 1970

Alchemy & Mysticism, the Hermetic Museum, Alexander Roob, 2001

Derek Walters, The Chinese Astrology Workbook, 1988

Dennis Klocek, Weather and the Cosmos, 1991, Rudolf Steiner College

Christopher Knight and Robert Lomas, The Hiram Key, 1997

James Lewis, Astrology Encyclopedia, 1994

John Anthony West, Serpent in the Sky 1993, Quest Books

Manly Hall, The Secret Teachings of all Ages. 1928

Thor Heyerdal, Man and the Ocean 1979, Doubleday

Jan Amos Comenius, Orbis Sensualium Pictus, Reprinted 1991

Alfred Watkins, Early British Trackways, 1922, London

Articles:

Watching TV too young is found damaging, Lindsey Tanner, AP

The lists of Antediluvian Kings Dr. Patrice Guinard, translated by Matyas Becvarov
http://cura.free.fr/11kings.html

Gulf of Cambay Cradle of Ancient Civilization By Badrinaryan Badrinaryan, 2006

Rujm el Hiri The Geometry and Astronomy of Rujm el-Hiri, a Megalithic Site in the Southern Levant Anthony Aveni, Yonatha Mizrachi 1997

De Divina Proportione oder Über di fünf Platonischen Körper, Peter Werth

Pythagoras and the Music of the Spheres. Geometry in Art & Architecture Unit 3. Paul Calter, 1998. Dartmouth College

History of Mathematics – al'khwarizmi & al Jabr
http://members.aol.com/bbyars1/algebra.html

Megaliths and Neolithic astronomy in southern Egypt, J. McKim Malville, Fred Wendorf, Ali A Mazar, Romauld Schild, 1998, Nature

Applications in Ancient Egyptian Mathematics, James Lowdermilk, 2005

The Complex and Dynamic codes of the Station Stones, Martin Doutre, 2000

Introduction to Yantra http://sivasakti.com/articles/intro-yantra.html

ALCHEMY: The Science of BEING   http://www.spirit-alembic.com/alchemy.html

Cymatics: A Study of Wave Phenomena and Vibration. ©2001 MACROmedia Publishing, Newmarket NH, USA. www.cymaticsource.com

Websites (not already referenced in the text)

http://www.cahokiamounds.com/ahokia.html

http://www.ohiohistory.org/places/serpent/

http://www.crystalinks.com/merkaba.html

http://www.ancient-egypt.org/glossary/religion/ka.html

http://www-geology.ucdavis.edu/~cowen/~GEL115/index.html   Preliminary course notes being prepared for publishing under the title - Exploiting the Earth, by Richard Cowen

http://web.genie.it/utenti/m/malta_mega_temples/xaghrasc/xscani.html

http://www.isourcecom.com/maya/cities/chichenitza/shadowof.htm

http://www.jazclass.aust.com/basicth/bt1.htm   Michael Forstner

http://www.mlahanas.de/Greeks/PythagorasStar.htm

http://music.washcoll.edu/

http://www.cyberspaceorbit.com/phikent/japan/japan2.html

http://www.karahundj.com/

http://www.bretagne-celtic.com/an/accueil_an.htm

http://www.single-serving.com/Hungarian/TB/numbers.php

Wikipedia

Other books by Paul

Explore the Sacred is a great companion to We as Architects. Not only is the question " What is Sacred Geometry?" covered in detail but the reader is invited to participate with discovering the meaning through the drawing of mandalas, creation of 3D forms and specific meditation.

No art or math background? No problem, as the exercises are quite easy. But, there is also great challenge for those gifted in mathematics.

More can be found out about Paul's books, art, creative math, and workshops at
http://mysterymath.wordpress.com

The Forest of Dlahomila is a wonderful children's fairytale about Faeries and Gnomes and the world they inhabit.

At first the two have a great distrust for each other but come to find that they are really not so different and even become friends.

Full of beautiful artwork, mischief, and morals. Great for bedtime stories.

This and all books can be found on Paul's storefront on Lulu.com

Meditation to Activate your Chakras and Cleanse your Auric Layers is a booklet which came out as a result of Exploring the Sacred and is meant as a companion. Within are great color paintings, some inspired by Barbara Brennan's much more extensive work.

This small work is a guide to you creating your own healing and energizing mandalas and then how to use them.

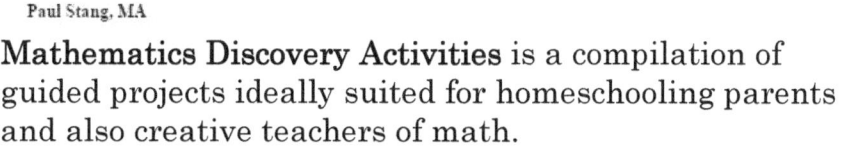

Mathematics Discovery Activities is a compilation of guided projects ideally suited for homeschooling parents and also creative teachers of math.

www.ingramcontent.com/pod-product-compliance
Lightning Source LLC
Chambersburg PA
CBHW080845230426
43662CB00013B/2029